Different Germans, Many Germanies

DIFFERENT GERMANS, MANY GERMANIES

New Transantlantic Perspectives

Edited by
Konrad H Jarausch, Harald Wenzel, and Karin Goihl

berghahn
NEW YORK · OXFORD
www.berghahnbooks.com

Published in 2017 by
Berghahn Books
www.berghahnbooks.com

Library of Congress Cataloging-in-Publication Data

Names: Jarausch, Konrad Hugo, editor of compilation. | Wenzel, Harald, editor of
compilation. | Goihl, Karin, editor of compilation.
Title: Different Germans, many Germanies : new transatlantic perspectives /
edited by Konrad Jarausch, Harald Wenzel, and Karin Goihl.
Description: First edition. | New York : Berghahn Books, [2017] | Includes
bibliographical references and index.
Identifiers: LCCN 2016026099 | ISBN 9781785334306 (hardback : alk. paper)
Subjects: LCSH: Germany–Civilization. | Germany–History, 19th and 20th
centuries. | National characteristics, German. | Germany–Social conditions. |
Germany–Politics and government.
Classification: LCC DD67 .D55 2017 | DDC 943.08–dc23
LC record available at hmps://lccn.loc.gov/2016026099

British Library Cataloguing in Publication Data

A catalogue record for this book is available from the British Library

ISBN 978-1-78533-430-6 (hardback)
ISBN 978-1-78533-431-3 (ebook)

Contents

Figures and Tables

Figures

Tables

Preface

More than seventy years after the end of World War II and over twenty-five years after German unification, German-American political relations are in flux. After a bumpy period of fierce debates in Germany about large-scale spying by the United States on both the German public and Angela Merkel and the secretive negotiations on the Transatlantic Trade and Investment Partnership (TTIP), the German public is busy with multiple crises. The influx of more than a million migrants and refugees presents significant social and political challenges. Britain's decision to leave the European Union (EU) has raised the specter of a weak and divided Europe. Adding to the feeling of uncertainty are increasing domestic security concerns in the wake of several deadly attacks in the summer of 2016, some of which have had jihadist motives. Across the Atlantic, Republican presidential candidate Donald Trump has lambasted Germany's refugee policy as "a tragic mistake", complained about its insufficient military burden sharing and announced that Germans (and French) could face "extreme vetting" before entering the United States because both countries have been "compromised by terrorism." Yet, more than half of Americans consider Germany the third most important partner according to the survey "Perceptions of Germany among the U.S. Population," commissioned by the German Embassy in Washington, D.C. and published in April 2016.

Although some would describe these conflicts as passing tensions in current affairs, other experts have identified a much deeper and more consequential development. In his 2014 publication "Transatlantic Ambivalences: Germany and the United States since the 1980s," historian Paul Nolte argues that the United States and Germany have been on different trajectories in significant ways. Both countries, he explains, have seen major changes in their political cultures, economies, and societies that challenge the assumption of a common Western pattern of modernity. The resulting growing transatlantic ambivalences are here to stay and need to be properly understood and addressed on both sides of the pond.

Across the English Channel, the British Museum opened its exhibition "Germany: Memories of a Nation" in October 2014 to mark the twenty-fifth anniversary of the fall of the Berlin Wall. Shortly before the show's opening, Neil MacGregor—at the time director of the British Museum and presently artistic director of Berlin's new Humboldt Forum—delivered a lecture titled "Looking Backward into the Future: Germany's Many Pasts." In his opening remarks he explained the exhibition's objective to make available Germany's long and complex history by arguing "that most people in Britain learn German history almost limited to the First World War and 1933 to 1945—years that are absolutely central to our history of the twentieth century, to the world and which are of course a critical part of Germany's story." Acclaimed as "long-overdue and truly important" by the leading daily *The Guardian,* the show was flanked with a companion book and a 30-part series on BBC 4 featuring objects, art, literature, and landmarks from the past 600 years.

MacGregor's companion book is one of several publications in Britain that point to a new curiosity and shifting attitudes toward Germany. Both Simon Winder's *Germania. A Personal History of Germans Ancient and Modern* and Peter Watson's *The German Genius: Europe's Third Renaissance, the Second Scientific Revolution and the Twentieth Century* provide ample food for thought for more nuanced understandings of Germany. These *Deutschlandversteher* may not offer new insights to scholars in the field, but these publications set out to provide fresh probes into a difficult subject in order to help shape more timely perceptions. In a similar vein, the present volume seeks to complicate frames of understanding and demonstrate the critical potential of tracing the multifaceted realities of different Germanies and many Germans.

But first things first. Neil MacGregor in his talk remarked that "nothing is simple about German history." Being German I might add that Germany is a difficult father/mother/land. Two world wars and the Holocaust's murderous crimes stand as Germany's lowest points in history, and the grave responsibility of their legacy is still being felt. Today, there is much concern about the numerous racist attacks, the success of the populist right-wing party Alternative für Deutschland (AfD, Alternative for Germany), and the far-right PEGIDA group (Patriotische Europäer gegen die Islamisierung des Abendlandes, Patriotic Europeans against the Islamization of the Occident). Admittedly, the ambivalence with which Germany is sometimes seen is not astonishing. Neither is the fact that German history of the twentieth century has led to some homogenizing clichés.

Sergeant Schultz in the TV series *Hogan's Heroes* has caricatured a dumb and unquestioning German mentality to older American audiences. Students use the phrase "grammar Nazis" to refer to the strict and aggressive application of rules. Even in the twenty-first century, the symbols of German Nazi dictatorship are still powerful. The right-wing Greek daily *Dimokratia* has repeatedly used Nazi references to criticize the German government's policy insistence on reforms and austerity during Greece's sovereign debt crisis and so have others. Clearly, these allusions were meant as the ultimate provocation, but they show us something about the raw emotions evoked by Germany's new role as—in the words of the *Economist*—"Europe's reluctant hegemon."

Germany has gone through many transformations and has been self-consciously contemplating its new place as Europe's central power in both its geographical and economic sense. No doubt, the peaceful unification of the two Germanies was admired the world over. So has the economic turn-around from "the sick man of Europe" to a booming global economy. Some observers have even described Germany's development since unification as a "rebirth." Henry Kissinger perhaps would know today whom to call when he wants to call Europe, but leadership has come with formidable challenges—balancing Europe's increasingly divergent interests and centrifugal forces among others.

Since we started to work on this volume, global events have again put different Germans and many Germanies in the limelight. Chancellor Merkel's humanistic and welcoming response to the refugee and migrant influx into Europe in 2015 and her optimistic *Wir schaffen das* (we can do it!) have shaken the political landscape. The search for policy responses has laid bare bitter divisions in Europe and on German streets. The battle over Germany's self-understanding is raging in the *Feuilleton* and at ballot boxes. Yet, the generous outpouring of support for refugees by tens of thousands of German volunteers has surprised and impressed many commentators. In the meantime, the open door policy has given way to restrictive and controversial measures, e.g. the deal between the European Union and Turkey struck in March 2016 to limit the numbers of asylum seekers coming to Europe. But for the *Washington Post* in December 2015, Germany's "defiant decency" was to be admired as this "was the way the United States once imagined itself, which seems like long ago."

So what does this complicated web of past and present entanglements mean for scholars working on Germany? Why is it important to understand where we stand and where we come from when studying what postcolonial theory calls "the other?" The short vignettes above highlight some potent current entanglements. In their introduction to this volume, Konrad H

Jarausch and Harald Wenzel sketch out the contours of German-American encounters of immigration, wars, cooperation, and mutual impact on each other in the last two centuries. But they also ask us to take a step back and reflect on the powerful narratives that shape academic work. If scholarship is seen as a series of interventions in a dialogue of mirrors, it is crucial to be aware of one's own positionality in the transatlantic construction of the other.

In the case of German-American and German-British exchanges, being enemies in two horrific world wars as well as being political and economic competitors, has left a powerful legacy of rather ambivalent if not outright skeptical perceptions of Germany in the United States and Britain, they explain. Thus, many important developments in Germany have received insufficient attention due to the understandable, but overshadowing weight of history. The renewed interest in Germany and its changing global role creates a space to help shape more nuanced insights, and the Berlin Program is in a unique position to do so.

In "Different Germans, Many Germanies: New Transatlantic Perspectives," a younger generation of scholars traces some of these complex and multifaceted realities through their case studies. The contributors of this volume's chapters are—with one exception—alumni of the Berlin Program for Advanced German and European Studies, which has supported more than 300 scholars with research fellowships at the Freie Universität Berlin since 1986. The program, located at one of the most renowned German universities, has helped educate some of the most eminent scholars who now teach these subjects at major research universities and colleges in North America and beyond. Designed to immerse fellows "in the field," the program's multidisciplinary research colloquium is the central site for academic engagement where fellows share their research and learn about studies in other areas. To advance understanding for developments in Germany and Europe, the program casts the net wide to invite distinguished scholars, writers, and public intellectuals. Joint events with our North American partner, the German Studies Association (GSA), allow us to feature and support exceptional scholarship. By many accounts, the Berlin Program Fellowship is a formative experience that has helped shape academic careers.

The present volume grew out of research and encounters facilitated by this intellectually vibrant program and attests to its thriving alumni network. We hope that the fascinating work on overlooked and underinterpreted aspects of German history, its culture, and its socioeconomic makeup will make a timely intervention on the sometimes crooked road of transatlantic exchanges.

This book would not be in your hands were it not for the dedication of Konrad H Jarausch (University of North Carolina, Chapel Hill) and Harald Wenzel (Freie Universität Berlin, John F Kennedy Institute) to the Berlin Program as long-time members of the program's academic advisory committee. Their conceptualization of the volume lies at the heart of this project. Their numerous distinguished publications and decades-long teaching demonstrate their resolute commitment to foster deeper transatlantic understanding. Finally, I wish to thank the Freie Universität Berlin, the Deutscher Akademischer Austauschdienst (DAAD, German Academic Exchange Service), and the German Foreign Office for their generous support.

Karin Goihl
Academic Coordinator, Berlin Program for
Advanced German and European Studies

Karin Goihl is Academic Coordinator of the Berlin Program for Advanced German and European Studies at the Freie Universität Berlin. She holds an MA in North American Studies and Linguistics from the Freie Universität Berlin and has served the Berlin Program since 1998.

Introduction

Konrad H Jarausch and Harald Wenzel

In recent years, politicians as well as pundits in Washington and London have become frustrated with the Germans as partners because they are increasingly unwilling to follow their lead. After unification, Anglo-American leaders expected that the Federal Republic would become a normal Western country. But rejecting its militarist past, Germany turned pacifist, relying on soft power, and proved reluctant to engage in preventive wars like the second invasion of Iraq. In the recent financial meltdown, often mislabeled as the Euro crisis, Berlin has been critical of Anglo-American casino capitalism and insisted upon austerity as a condition of aid instead of adopting soft monetary policies. In the Edward Snowden scandal, Germans have objected to the tapping of Chancellor Merkel's telephone as well as other US efforts to spy on their NATO ally. Finally, in the Ukraine conflict, they have sought to keep communication lines with Vladimir Putin open in spite of Russian violations of international law. From across the American political spectrum, commentators are asking, "What is the matter with these Germans?"[1]

Because of the impact of World Wars I and II, Anglo-American public intellectuals have been little help in answering this question because many of them are trapped in a negative perception of the past, failing to appreciate the degree to which Germany changed after 1945. As exemplified by battlefield tourism in Flanders fields and on the coast of Normandy, memory culture views the Germans as enemies who twice in the first half of the twentieth century had to be stopped by military force at the cost of countless Anglo-American lives. While the Kaiser inspires ridicule rather than fear, Hitler and the Nazis have been a subject of endless fascination in the popular media, inspiring scores of movies and paperbacks. Going beyond the special concerns of the Jewish community, the Holocaust in particular has developed into a universalized exemplar of human evil that inspires the current dedication to human rights, therefore playing a central role in fashioning liberal identities.[2] Compared with these widespread constructions of Germany as a perpetrator nation, other voices emphasizing German contributions to Western culture are few and far between.[3]

In contrast to such elite skepticism, popular attitudes, based on personal contacts, military duty, tourist travel, and economic dealings have become increasingly positive, as public opinion surveys reveal. When Americans and Germans meet, they are often surprised how much they have in common and how well they get along. Most tourists experience Germany as a hospitable place that functions predictably and that makes them feel welcome. Many of the millions of veterans who served in Central Europe recall having a good time in contrast to more dangerous billings, preferring to be "back home in Germany" rather than in Vietnam. Businesspeople like to deal with German companies, since they produce excellent products, provide reliable service, and can be depended upon to fulfill their contracts, even if they charge higher prices.[4] Recent sports events such as the men's and women's World Cups have shown the country's friendly and cosmopolitan face, since German fans were ready to cheer for the players of other nations as much as for their own team.

Though highly competent, Anglo-American scholars are having a difficult time in dealing with "the German problem" too, since their studies have also been affected by the crosscurrents of public sentiment after 1989 and September 11. Fortunately, the United States-based German Studies Association is a flourishing professional society with several thousand members and interesting annual conferences that bring together researchers from both sides of the Atlantic. But in high schools, the teaching of the German language is shrinking due to the popular shift toward Spanish, and even in colleges and universities, German studies departments are struggling to maintain their independence.[5] In the field of twentieth-century history, German topics still play a considerable role, but the number of positions is barely larger than that of Russia, remaining behind France and Britain as a specialty.[6] In the social sciences, investigations of the Federal Republic are often being subsumed by research in European studies or even wider transnational frameworks, thereby reducing their visibility. Ironically, interest in Germany is dependent upon crises, rising when there is a problem such as the tidal wave of refugees and subsiding when things are going well.[7]

Solving the German puzzle therefore requires a self-reflexive approach that is more conscious of its own agenda and better informed about recent developments. The traditional investigation of perceptions, such as the American picture of Germany and vice versa, can provide interesting quotations, but lacks analytical rigor. Instead, postcolonial thought suggests that the process of "othering" is to a considerable degree a projection of one's own preoccupations upon a foreign subject, much like the invention of "Orientalism" by the West to describe the inscrutable East.[8] The starting point for Americans to evaluate their familiar yet different German cousins must therefore be an examination of how internal American interests have conditioned perceptions of events in Germany. Another precondition for overcoming historical stereotyping is a closer scrutiny of recent developments, which are continually outpacing judgments based on past performance. Fortunately a younger generation of scholars, less weighted down by traditional baggage, is ready to step in. This volume presents some of their work.

AMERICAN PERCEPTIONS

Even a cursory glance reveals that American perceptions of Germany have drastically changed over the past two centuries as a result of a contentious relationship that has fluctuated between cooperation and conflict. As immigrant societies interested in new settlers, the original seaboard colonies generally welcomed newcomers from Central Europe. The first, mostly positive impressions of Germans were formed by several waves of immigration, beginning in 1683 with the Moravians from Krefeld, intensifying in 1848 with the liberals exiled after the failed revolution, and peaking in the 1890s with farmers and industrial workers arriving by the hundreds of thousands. As a result, former German speakers are still one of the top ancestry groups in the United States due to their actual number and rate of reproduction during the initial generations. But as suggested by a carmaker's name change from Kreisler to Chrysler, or the forebears of a president altering their surname from Eisenhauer to Eisenhower, many of these connections have in the meantime been forgotten by the public due to the successful assimilation of German immigrants.[9]

While developing its own higher education system, the United States sent thousands of students to the renowned German universities in order to learn at what were considered to be the leading institutions in the world in the nineteenth century. The country was seen as an attractive place due to its romantic movement, its literature and music, and—last but not least—its outstanding achievements in science. It was in Germany that the neohumanist spirit inspired the modern research imperative and the tradition of academic freedom, which were both eagerly copied by Americans. The import of the research seminar, the footnoted monograph, and the PhD degree fundamentally transformed undergraduate colleges into graduate universities that were soon able to compete with the original.[10] Moreover, Bismarck's revolutionary conservatism pioneered the development of the welfare state—a process of reforms that caught the attention of some Americans because they were lacking at home. The progressive movement in the United States found other aspects such as urban reform and infrastructure worth emulating as well.[11]

Owing to their imperial rivalry, American perceptions of Germany deteriorated at the turn of the twentieth century, reaching a first low point during World War I. Increasingly, commentators pointed to evidence of German authoritarianism and decried the vagaries of the unpredictable emperor William II. The conflict over unrestricted submarine warfare that led to the US entry into the war strained previously positive relations. Moreover, the venomous propaganda of the British media during World War I as well as the anti-German hysteria in the United States, fed by the Committee for Public Information, suppressed the German language and ruptured the hybrid German-American culture.[12] As a result, the American public gradually reversed its opinion and came to see Germans as enemies that needed to be defeated in order "to make the world safe for democracy." Thereafter, reactions to Germany alternated between an earlier appreciation that continued to see positive cultural elements and a suspicion that construed the Germans as an authoritarian danger to what came to be called "Western Civilization."[13]

Gratified by their reputation as the world's leading democracy, US observers greeted the progressive ferment of the Weimar Republic with hope, as it seemed to reflect Wilsonian ideals. Germans once again became acceptable, because they followed the American example when building upon their own liberal traditions. Resuming their earlier connections, US visitors like Gordon Craig were fascinated by Berlin's experimental culture including the expressionist movies, the epic theater, or the architectural innovations of the Bauhaus. Moreover, the massive loans from New York kept the first German democracy solvent, while American mediation eventually helped settle the noxious reparation issue. These connections also helped open doors for some Jewish academic or artistic refugees like Hans Rosenberg when they had to flee anti-Semitic persecution. The descent of the Weimar democracy into an authoritarian regime was therefore a profound disappointment that created deep doubts about whether the Germans might not, indeed, be incorrigible.[14]

Understanding themselves to be the chief defenders of Western values, liberal American politicians and intellectuals loathed the rise of the Nazi dictatorship, whose crimes permanently stained the German name. When

Germany succumbed to the longing for a charismatic *Führer* who would lead it out of defeat and depression, intellectual émigrés like Franz Neumann and Ernst Fraenkel provided critical analyses of the Nazi system. A close-knit group of German immigrants and Americans with experience in Germany called for US involvement in the fight against fascism in order to defend a democratic, rational Western culture. During the war, this intellectual network, centered in leading universities and the Office of Strategic Services, was instrumental in planning for reconstruction. Commentators argued essentially over whether the Germans were inherently dictatorial and therefore beyond help or merely temporarily misled, making it possible to reclaim them.[15] Though Allied propaganda was less vicious than during World War I, the liberation of the living skeletons and discovery of piles of corpses in the concentration camps confirmed the worst fears of crimes against humanity that would darken the German image forever.

Convinced of the superiority of their own capitalist democracy, American occupiers set out to reconstruct the Western zones in their own image after 1945. As joint preconditions of the victorious Grand Alliance, the Potsdam agreement insisted on a comprehensive demilitarization in order to prevent World War III, a thorough denazification so as to remove the party's control of public life and a broad-ranging decartelization for the sake of breaking up the military industrial complex. Despite the nonfraternization order, the practice of the occupation gradually revived the older pattern of German-American kinship as many close personal contacts developed. In spite of punitive pressure from home, the US occupation government combined reorientation with economic revival, extending the hand of the Marshall Plan to the western zones and supporting their transformation into the Federal Republic.[16] The success of physical and psychological rebuilding fed into a self-congratulatory pro-consul view that assigned most of the credit to Allied policy.

Initially American observers were rather pleased with the "star-pupil syndrome" of the Federal Republic of Germany, because it showed that the Germans tried to Westernize themselves. They took satisfaction in the stability offered by Konrad Adenauer's "chancellor democracy"; they were encouraged by Ludwig Erhard's economic miracle; and they were able to point to the civic reliability of the new military, called Bundeswehr, providing much of the land force in the NATO alliance. Nonetheless, American social scientists like Gabriel Almond and Sidney Verba continued to be skeptical about how deeply rooted democracy was in Germany.[17] One source of doubt was the reluctance to admit the atrocities that Nazis had perpetrated and to address the horror of the Holocaust. A second problem was the refugees' refusal to recognize the Oder-Neisse-border with Poland by claiming "a right to a homeland" within the frontiers of 1937. But the common effort against communism in the Cold War, cemented by the Berlin airlift in defense of this "outpost of freedom," created a renewed sense of transatlantic harmony, with Germans now in a subordinate learning role.[18]

Eventually Washington grew frustrated when Bonn showed signs of emancipating itself from Anglo-American tutelage. While Adenauer's flirtation with Gaullism annoyed American leaders, the TV pictures of brutality in Vietnam shocked German viewers. Though the student rebels drew upon nonviolent methods, pioneered in the American civil rights movement, and admired US popular culture, they embraced the critiques of organizations like the Students for a Democratic Society in rejecting Washington's policies as capitalist imperialism. Moreover, the social-liberal coalition under Willy Brandt began to pursue an independent *Ostpolitik,* seeking reconciliation with the Soviet Union, its satellites, and the German Democratic Republic (GDR). The dramatic gesture of his kneeling at the Warsaw Ghetto Memorial was not understood by American leaders as a symbol of contrition and the independent course created much anxiety for German-born Secretary of State Henry Kissinger. These developments led to public criticism of US policies that in turn angered American observers, who inferred that the Germans were beginning to show too much political independence.[19] Washington was quick to resent any critique as anti-Americanism.

Once the United States began to have its own difficulties, the German reluctance to follow its lead became even more annoying to commentators. The Vietnam-caused deficit forced the Deutsche mark to be revalued upward, making it a harder currency than the dollar—a sacrilege for Wall Street. The oil shocks of the 1970s elicited divergent responses, because Germany began to turn toward conservation rather than military intervention in order to reduce its carbon footprint. Though the environmental movement had started in the United States, in the context of antinuclear *Angst,* it grew more radical in the Federal Republic of Germany (FRG). Helmut Schmidt's perceived arrogance offended Jimmy Carter, when he dared lecture the US president on how to get the economy out of stagflation. The American government viewed the signing of the Helsinki Accords in 1975 with some suspicion, because it feared that Bonn might drift into the Soviet orbit. While the second Cold War caused by the Afghanistan invasion and the NATO dual track decision once again increased cooperation, the massive peace movement in the FRG as well as the "community of responsibility" between Bonn and East Berlin raised eyebrows on the Potomac.[20]

With Washington's endorsement of neoliberalism, the transatlantic tensions between the United States and Europe grew even stronger. While Margaret Thatcher and Ronald Reagan embarked on a neoliberal economic path, advocating deregulation, privatization, and tax cuts, German trade unions and many intellectuals rebelled in order to preserve the core of the welfare state. As a result of the rise of neoconservatism and the Christian Right, a substantial segment of the US public began to wage a culture war against the liberal-progressive currents and the mainstream media. Though Helmut Kohl also proclaimed a "moral-political turn" toward conservative values, the Federal Republic essentially remained a welfare state with a peaceful, multilateral foreign policy. Social Democratic majorities in the federal states permitted only a moderate neoliberal policy to be implemented, preventing more radical measures. The result was a growing divergence between American and German opinion regarding issues like the legitimacy of war, the need for gun control, the abolition of the death penalty, public funding of culture, and the maintenance of the welfare state.[21]

During the peaceful revolution of 1989–90, President George Bush's support for unification temporarily bridged this gap in the common effort to promote the overthrow of communism. Made possible by Mikhail Gorbachev's surprising liberalization, Bush's careful advocacy of change in the Eastern Bloc facilitated the uprising against dictatorship and the national rejection of Soviet hegemony. Moreover, his resolute support of unification overcame British and French reluctance and eventually allowed united Germany to remain in the NATO alliance. Though the cooperation between Secretary of State James Baker, Chancellor Kohl, and Foreign Minister Hans-Dietrich Genscher was exemplary, paths diverged thereafter again: Washington crowed about winning the Cold War while Bonn set about reintegrating the divided country.[22] Tempers flared over the German refusal to participate in the Iraq wars and the recognition of Slovenia and Croatia. Aggravated by September 11 and international terrorism, Washington and Bonn chose alternate ways of responding to subsequent crises.

American media representations of Germany therefore reflect changing internal US dynamics that create selective perceptions of actual developments in Germany.[23] On the one hand, conservative outlets like Fox News, talk radio, and Christian networks praise the traditional "secondary virtues" of German culture like hard work and discipline. But, particularly in the aftermath of September 11, journalists like Charles Krauthammer attacked German policies as dangerously pacifist, state-oriented, secular, and socialist due to Berlin's reluctance to get involved in preventive wars. Left-leaning American media like the *New York Times,* the *Washington Post,* and National Public Radio find German self-criticism generally sympathetic. But columnists like Paul Krugman have nonetheless criticized the Federal Republic's fiscally conservative austerity policy during the Euro crisis. Moreover, they are worried about bouts of anti-immigrant xenophobia. In their reporting, journalists draw on a whole range of historical images that are available as sediments of prior encounters, both positive and negative. These have created ambivalent stereotypes, laden with associations that call up a welter of contradictory feelings.[24]

A key problem for American commentators in explaining recurrent differences between Germans and Americans is the unconscious conditioning of their work by the reverberation of this repertoire of contradictory images. The continual changes in perception suggest that US scholars are not just disinterested observers, but rather participants in a transatlantic debate that constructs the other in the context of divergent interests. Their interpretative moves are interventions in a dialogue of mirrors in which each side seeks to discover something about the other, while at the same time interrogating itself. If used self-consciously, this dual perspective can be liberating, because it broadens the point of view from which observations are made. But as the all too brief allusions above suggest, such interpretations will only be productive, if they recognize their dialogic quality and do not just judge the other by the standards of their own identity, but are also willing to question themselves. In drawing conclusions, Anglo-American observers therefore need to keep this complicated record of German-American conflict and cooperation in mind in order to see those ambivalences as fertile ground for mutual dialogue.[25]

POSTWAR TRANSFORMATIONS

The understandable dominance of past images in public perceptions is as problematic for policy decisions as for academic interpretations, because it obscures the extent to which Germans have transformed during the last half century. Of course war veterans and Holocaust victims have every right to emphasize their suffering, but their efforts have created a negative frame that has somewhat taken on a life of its own. Much of the problem is simply an information gap—reporting on Germany in leading US media is sporadic, and articles often use historic references in order to dramatize their messages. Among some scholars such as Daniel Goldhagen, there tends to be a curious disconnect between their research emphasis on past atrocities and a lack of reference to more recent positive signs of peacefulness and democracy that results in telling only half of the story.[26] While social scientists usually engage the current changes more openly, many cultural specialists or historians are still exploring the catastrophic aspects of the German record, thereby reinforcing older stereotypes in the public mind. A second challenge for scholars is therefore the exploration of German trans-formations after Hitler.[27]

The joint American and German effort to establish a postwar democracy has, for instance, been an impressive success story that has silenced most internal and external critics. Of course, it was necessary to defeat national socialism militarily and to discredit its following in order to give the exiled and incarcerated democrats a second chance. Unlike the Soviet effort to impose a "dictatorship of the proletariat," the policies of the Western allies were just the right mix of forceful intervention and liberal rehabilitation to effect regime change and to allow new institutions to take root. In contrast to other failed nation-building attempts, the eager collaboration of the minority of liberal Germans provided a necessary internal legitimacy for efforts at reorientation. No doubt, it took a combination of unusual circumstances such as the strong personalities of Adenauer or Heuss, the Cold War threat from the outside, the integration into the West as well as the rise in prosperity in order to convince skeptical Germans that democracy was superior. But in the end all right-wing efforts were beaten back and the Federal Republic became so stable as to be boring.[28]

Largely spared the cycles of hyperinflation and depression, the economic development of the Federal Republic has also been successful enough to become the envy of most of its neighbors. Though Nazi war production laid some of the groundwork, it was Allied intervention that broke up the cartels and American pressure that revived market competition by stopping the nationalization of enterprises. Even if Ludwig Erhard's ordo-liberal gamble of the currency reform triggered the Berlin blockade, this risky policy ignited such rapid growth as to sweep all critics before it. Of course, American credit, notably in the Marshall Plan, as well as West European economic integration also helped the revival of the German economy. Moreover, the neocorporate consensus culture of Rhenish capitalism in which management and labor bargained in good faith also aided the continuation of the postwar boom into sustained growth. While most profits were initially reinvested in business, eventually the increase of exports also led to a rise in wages that generated an unprecedented prosperity, impressing even the citizens of the GDR.[29]

Although Allied decisions also helped somewhat, the establishment of an elaborate welfare state was more of an indigenous German achievement, because it could draw on Bismarckian traditions. First Hitler's "socialism of the fools" had to be discredited and the Nazi propaganda of the *Volks-gemeinschaft* proven fallacious. Then the more radical communist alternative to construct Stalinist socialism had to be rejected as well in order to allow more moderate reforms, modeled somewhat on the New Deal and Labour

Party legislation. But initiatives like the famous "Equalization of Burdens Law" that taxed those who had survived the war without damage in order to help the suffering veterans, widows, orphans, refugees, and prisoners of war (POWs) were exemplary German measures. While neighboring countries also developed a comprehensive system of pensions, unemployment insurance, and health benefits, the Federal Republic's provisions, like the indexing of retirement pay in 1957, tended to be more generous.[30] By reducing class cleavages, this social safety net solidified both democracy and prosperity.

In the fundamental liberalization of West Germany, associated with the generational revolt of 1968, the United States played a dual role as positive and negative exemplar. Protesters borrowed the trappings of long hair, blue jeans, and rock music from Hollywood and also adopted the nonviolent methods of the civil rights movement. At the same time, they resolutely opposed Washington's war in Vietnam, denounced the GIs' atrocities, and polemicized against American imperialism, thereby signaling a growing emancipation from transatlantic tutelage.[31] In the German context, the youth rebellion gained a special edge, because its criticism of the older generation focused on their presumed complicity with Nazi crimes. In their rejection of the West, many of the protesters went overboard, embracing a vulgar Marxism, with some intellectuals supporting and others even becoming terrorists in the Red Army Faction. But the majority followed Willy Brandt's call to "dare more democracy" and reintegrated itself in the system through the new social movements of environmentalism, feminism, and pacifism.[32]

When the Soviet Union reluctantly relinquished control with the help of American prodding, Germany was able to spread its Western achievements to the disadvantaged East through unification. The peaceful revolution of 1989 was an unexpected grassroots movement that first wanted to reform and then to overthrow the dictatorship of the Socialist Unity Party (SED) altogether. The transformation from a planned economy to market competition and global capitalism has been painful, causing much deindustrialization, but the massive financial transfers have improved living standards noticeably. Moreover, the elaborate welfare system of the FRG has cushioned some of the social disruptions that dissolved communist institutions in favor of new civil society initiatives. In some ways, the cultural adjustment from collectivism to individualism has been most difficult because the unification shock had not been foreseen in the joy over the fall of the wall. Though many Western intellectuals had already become postnational, the accession of the five new states to the Federal Republic revived a chastened and democratized nation-state.[33]

United Germany is still struggling somewhat to find an appropriate role in Europe and the world. Initial fears of the rise of a Fourth Reich were proven wrong, because the Berlin Republic refused to join the Iraq wars and clung to its tradition of a pacifist foreign policy, developed under the US nuclear umbrella. Much to Washington's frustration, Helmut Kohl was only willing to provide funds for the first Gulf War, while Gerhard Schröder joined France, Russia, and China in opposing the second US intervention to overthrow Saddam Hussein. Nonetheless, the pressure of foreign expectations and the gradual redefinition of internal interests has led to a foreign area deployment of German military forces first in peace missions and then even in actual military combat. In the mid 1990s, the German Constitutional Court ratified this reinterpretation of the constitutional prohibition against war by insisting on UN or NATO sponsorship as well as parliamentary approval. The key change was Joschka Fischer's reinterpretation of the Auschwitz lesson from "never again war" to "never again dictatorship" in the face of the violence in Bosnia in 1995—which created the precedent for Germany's participation in NATO's Kosovo campaign some years later. Though clinging to its civilian tradition of multilateralism, united Germany has gradually assumed more international responsibility especially in the Euro crisis where it has acted, in the *Economist*'s words, as "reluctant hegemon."[34]

Today, many Germans, especially the younger generation, are beginning to show a new pride in their country, stepping out of the shadows of the problematic past. In international comparisons, Germans have been consistently among those who showed the weakest identification with their state and the least amount of nationalism. Ironically, it took athletic competitions like the men's and women's World Cups in soccer to make a new civic pride public by both applauding the play of other nations' teams and rooting for their own. Having absorbed the painful lessons of the Holocaust and the wars in school and in visits to memorials, the young are less troubled by the burden of their past than their elders. No longer feeling personally responsible for Nazi atrocities, they compare the criminal actions during the first half with the successful rehabilitation of their country during the second half of the century. Even if they also criticize problems like overcrowded universities or rising resentment against immigrants, their wide-ranging travel and European outlook make them appreciate the ease and importance of the country they live in.[35]

If outside observers want to understand German reactions to international crises better, they ought to acknowledge these important changes more openly, especially since many are the result of beneficial American interventions. There is little danger of retrospective whitewashing of German guilt, because the memory tourism of the World War sites as well as the establishment of a broad-based Holocaust memorialization will prevent any such amnesia. The interpretative challenge therefore consists of also recognizing the fundamental transformation of the Germans, which has forced them to learn bitter lessons from their catastrophic past in order to create a better future. Both sides of this Janus-faced coin are intimately related to each other, because it was the horrific impact of the Third Reich not only on its many victims but on the Germans themselves that made them pause and change directions.[36] In this effort, the United States played a crucial and constructive role—a reason for considerable satisfaction. But while grateful for such help, the Germans have in the meantime sought their own, somewhat different path.

Mediating between the past memories and the present images requires staying abreast of recent developments by using recent technological developments in an intelligent fashion. Transatlantic travel has become much easier with airplanes, overcoming long distances in a few hours rather than taking days like ships, even if it leaves a nasty jet lag that inhibits clear thinking. Moreover, the Internet and other real-time media may have made it easier to access all types of information—whether these be newspaper articles, TV debates, video documentations, or movies. Electronic connectivity functions instantaneously and with less effort than the printing of a North American edition of *Die Zeit* or *Der Spiegel* that once took days to arrive by mail.[37] But in substituting for personal communication and firsthand experience, the growing selectivity and partiality of electronic media have made the acquisition of a thoroughly grounded knowledge of contemporary affairs more precarious for citizens, journalists, and academics alike. Therefore staying abreast of current developments such as the effort to cope with the refugee crisis and the exit of Great Britain from the EU still requires a considerable commitment of time.

NEW SCHOLARLY CONTRIBUTIONS

In navigating between traditional American perspectives and recent German developments, the essays in this volume intend to illustrate the transatlantic difference as well as the diversity of Central European experiences. They have been written by a younger generation of North American scholars who are exploring new areas beyond the established political master narrative of catastrophe and redemption that tends to focus on Prussia and the Reich to the detriment of southwestern or Catholic history.[38] Moreover, their research projects were conceived after the collapse of communism, presupposing the revival of a German national state, and after the September 11 attack on the World Trade Center, hastening an American turn away from Europe.[39] The historical essays begin with the nineteenth century, extend to Weimar, explore the immediate postwar period, and then follow the Federal Republic and the GDR after 1945. Because the murderous policies of Hitler's Third Reich are already well-known to Anglo-American readers through a burgeoning Holocaust literature, the editors decided not to include any chapters on the Nazi dictatorship. Meanwhile, the contributions from social scientists deal with the postwar development of a new German model and its response to various crises closer to the present. The volume concludes with a series of cultural retrospectives that raise painful issues of collective memory.

These essays address some of the key questions of Germany's recent historical trajectory in fresh ways by pointing to aspects that foreigners have found interesting. Yet unaware of the disasters that were to come, American visitors considered Imperial Germany quite modern, full of potential solutions to common problems. In his exploration of a dozen accounts ranging from Mark Twain to Theodore Dreiser, Scott Krause establishes what struck such travelers as positive and which points they subjected to criticism.[40] Outside commentators were also drawn by the romantic allure of the German woods celebrated in poems and songs. Presenting some arguments from his recent book on the German forest, Jeffrey Wilson contrasts volkish initiatives with progressive efforts to preserve green space in rapidly growing Berlin as recreation resource.[41] Many visitors have also commented on the dual training system of apprenticeship that provided not only higher education but also trained skilled craftsmen. Hal Hansen investigates the manner in which trade school instruction transformed artisans into machine operators, laying the basis for later engineering excellence.[42] Finally, German medicine also enjoyed a high reputation around the turn of the century, inspiring the reform of medical education in the United States. Spelling out some ideas from her recent monograph, Annette Timm demonstrates that the Weimar Republic led the field in providing public health benefits, seeking to improve longevity through preventative medicine.[43] Even if visitors also commented on some of the Reich's authoritarian features, Imperial Germany and then the Weimar Republic set the international standard in numerous other areas such as higher education or urban reform.

After horrors of the Third Reich and World War II, many foreign observers marveled at the surprisingly rapid recovery of democracy in the Federal Republic of Germany. The Swiss journalist Fritz René Allemann therefore concluded already by the mid 1950s that "Bonn is not Weimar."[44]

One important contributor to the repudiation of the authoritarian legacy was the ideology of antifascism, before it hardened into an apology for communist rule. Drawing on her dissertation, Clara Oberle presents case studies of youth appeals and housing redistribution in postwar Berlin to show how a victimization narrative reinforced the repudiation of the Nazi legacy.[45] Another factor was the adoption of democratic reforms within the Western schools which acquainted pupils with self-government and press freedom. Exploring some issues raised in his book, Brian Puaca suggests that beyond the retention of the tripartite school structure, important reforms occurred in teacher training, lesson content, and pupil self-government.[46] During the Cold War competition, the SED-regime claimed to represent the "better Germany" that had broken completely with fascism. However, Sarah Pugach argues in her chapter that in the GDR's socialist development policy toward Africa, considerable traces of racism survived unchanged.[47] Yet another element was the gradual turn to human rights for legitimizing protests that led to the peaceful revolution. Comparing the instrumentalization of the concept during East-West conflict, Ned Richardson-Little asserts that in the end, the communists proved less responsive and therefore lost the competition.[48] This external pressure and internal rethinking produced a collective learning process that eventually led to rehabilitation after prior transgression.

Yet another dimension that has drawn international interest is the success of the West German model in achieving political stability, economic prosperity, and social solidarity. Belying critics of its neocorporatism, the Federal Republic of Germany weathered not only the student revolt, but also coped with the challenge of reunification while providing a high standard of living and an extensive social safety net. Supported by a vocal antinuclear protest movement, Germany has become a leader in renewable energy development by shutting down its reactors. In a suggestive case study, Carol Hager demonstrates that grassroots pressure broadened the neocorporative governance of the Federal Republic to include a participatory dimension that successfully pushed for alternate energy sources.[49] Based on a quantitative content analysis of responses to the financial crisis of 2008, Mark Cassell argues that the difference in political culture between inflation fears and market speculation made the Federal Republic seek to restore public trust in banking rather than focus on tighter regulation like the United States.[50] Because Germany had increased its global competitiveness through outsourcing and wage restraint, the solidarity of the social market economy became a counter model to Anglo-American speculative excesses. In a sensitive exploration of one postmigrant play staged in Berlin, Jeffrey Jurgens demonstrates the pluralization of German memories as a result of Turkish immigration. By his close reading of a key text, he addresses the cultural challenge of including migrants in the dominant conceptions of the German past that requires breaking the ethnic mold of identity narratives. While coping with Islam remains a work in progress, the presence of multicultural migrants has forced the Federal Republic to broaden its definitions of what it means to be German.[51]

Finally, some peculiarities of German culture have also achieved global renown by inspiring debate elsewhere. No doubt, the presence of the German language and of cultural products from Germany is now smaller than during the "flight of the muses" that brought Weimar innovations like the Bauhaus architecture or the cultural criticism of the Frankfurt School to British and American shores.[52] But there has been something of a revival of interest in German cinema, leading even to some movie scripts to be refashioned and rereleased as Hollywood films. In her transnational essay, Sara F Hall shows how the propaganda uses of film during World War I led to the establishment of the German Ufa movie conglomerate whose products rivaled Hollywood's in the 1920s.[53] What makes contemporary German culture so interesting is also its confrontation with the dark past from a perspective that seeks to derive constructive lessons from its calamities. Drawing on the critical theory of the Frankfurt School, Matthew Miller addresses the literary intervention of Alexander Kluge's short stories as well as Jürgen Habermas's memorandum in order to spell out European criticism of the invasion in Iraq.[54] After the Holocaust came into public eye, the key challenge has therefore been to come to terms with the implications of genocide for postwar culture. In line with his prize-winning book on the German and Polish confrontation with Jewish spaces, Michael Meng argues that even well-intentioned contrition can become a hollow ritual, if it serves to prevent genuine admission of guilt.[55] In contrast to Wilhelmian arrogance, it is now the self-critical exploration of Germany's own failings that has become exemplary.

These examples of current academic work show a more differentiated appreciation of the German experience than the stereotypical references that often dominate the media. The increasing temporal distance from the horrors of the Holocaust is making it possible to explore the multiple continuities of the German past—some of which led to heinous crimes, while others also inspired fascinating creativity. Not intending to replace the accepted political narrative, the historical essays explore neglected older traditions and contribute to a fuller understanding of the contradictions in postwar German development that continue to fascinate new generations of scholars. Without glossing over some of the unresolved problems, the social science chapters also reveal some aspects of the German model that might provide clues to the comparative success of the Berlin Republic in coping with current challenges. Precisely by addressing the tension between initial catastrophe and ensuing recovery of civility, the cultural reflections open a window into a rich realm of artistic creativity and moral reflection. Escaping some of the wartime baggage, which has constrained an older generation, these fresh looks reveal the degree to which Germany once was and has again become part of the West, albeit with a distinctive voice, both exchanging with but also competing against the Anglo-American world.[56]

IMPLICATIONS FOR GERMAN STUDIES

Transatlantic German Studies therefore face the challenge of coming to terms with the fundamental ambivalence of the German record that contains the extremes of both genocide and humanity. To begin with, such an effort needs to address the horrible atrocities of the Third Reich as well as the pervasive repression of the GDR. But focusing on the negative dimensions of the two dictatorships alone merely reinforces prevailing transatlantic stereotypes, doing injustice both to the complexity of the German past and ignoring the problematic nature of the Anglo-American present. Much of the actual research already addresses constructive aspects of the German experience before 1933 and after 1945—but the framework within which it is placed remains generally condemnatory. No doubt, the critical approach captures the descent from the hothouse of the Weimar Republic into the racist repression of the Third Reich and the communist dictatorship of the GDR. But such a perspective fails to account for the learning processes that established democracy in the West after 1945 and made the peaceful revolution of 1989 possible in the East.[57] It is therefore time that these latter developments also receive their interpretative due.

Such a rethinking also requires a greater awareness of the factors at play in the Anglo-American interest in the German case. It is important to recall that the United Kingdom and the United States were not merely uninvolved spectators, able to pass disinterested judgment, but key combatants in both World Wars who developed elaborate justifications for fighting the Germans. Elements of this moralistic Western civilization rhetoric continue to linger in college survey courses and public attitudes. Exploring the German case just to prove the superiority of the West is problematic, because it misses an opportunity for interrogating some of the shortcomings of the Anglo-American record. Undoubtedly the Holocaust must remain the universal standard of absolute evil that will always be associated with German crimes. But reflection on Nazi atrocities should rather inspire one to reject racism, imperialism, economic exploitation, and male chauvinism not just in Central Europe but everywhere in the world.[58] As Paul Nolte points out in a recent volume, it would therefore be more productive to talk about "transatlantic ambivalences" in which both sides have criticized and learned from each other with different degrees of success.[59]

At the same time, a more equitable reconsideration would involve greater attention to the postwar rehabilitation of Germany which set the country on a more constructive course with American help. As mentioned earlier, after World War II, the occupying US forces used just the right mixture of compulsion and leniency to reorient a dispirited and defeated Germany. Moreover, many Germans were eager to Americanize themselves in style and content in order to be accepted into the Western community. But since then, the welfare state of the Federal Republic has become more elaborate, the health insurance provision more equitable, public funding of culture more extensive, and attitudes toward violence more humane, while the willingness to go to war has declined considerably. Moreover, the halting process of European integration appears to be a more constructive response than the American neoconservative unilateralism in trying to make the world peaceful and livable.[60] In these and other areas, the Germans have recovered so much as to provide some positive counterexamples that should be considered when seeking to assess current Anglo-American policies.

A more self-reflexive approach to the hidden subtexts of interpretative frameworks will yield a more complex understanding of the contradictions of the German past and present. Already in his famous 1945 lecture on "Germany and the Germans" in which he reflected in American exile on what had gone wrong in his home country, Thomas Mann concluded that the tendency toward "inwardness" showed that "there are not two Germanys, a good one and a bad one, but only one, whose best turned evil through the devil's cunning. The bad Germany is the good one gone astray."[61] If this assessment is correct, the intellectual challenge of dealing with the German case consists of exploring the deep entanglement of its positive and negative aspects with each other. Revealing divergent trajectories, such a perspective stresses the paradoxical commonality in basic values but considerable variance in implementation between the United States and Germany. Moreover, the recognition of such a plurality creates space for appreciating the enormous diversity of regional, religious, class, and gender identities within Germany itself. Acknowledgement of this double difference is therefore crucial for reconstructing the full range of German experiences during the past two centuries.

In many ways, the interaction between Germans and Americans can be interpreted as the encounter of two related but competing modernities.

While the imperial Germans sought to combine a strong state, bureaucracy and military with scientific advancement, urban reform, and social welfare, the dynamic Americans were more liberal, market-driven, individualistic, and therefore also democratic. When facing similar problems such as technological changes, rapid urbanization, and claims for political participation, both sides found different solutions that often influenced each other. The German version of modernization failed during World War I, and after the breathtaking innovation of Weimar politics and culture, it led into a racist dictatorship, another World War, and the Holocaust.[62] Moreover, the communist utopia, installed by the Soviet Union in the GDR, also proved repressive and unsuccessful. After the defeat in World War II, the United States helped pave the way to a modern democracy for the Western sectors, and after the failure of communism, it advocated a reunification of both Germanies. Despite this helpful influence, Germany has not simply joined America's path of modernization, but sought to claim a certain independence by maintaining its own traditions such as the welfare state.[63] That this transatlantic difference was not just a deviance from the correct path but rather a fascinating story of mutual encounter is the central message of this volume.

Konrad H Jarausch is Lurcy Professor for European civilization at the University of North Carolina at Chapel Hill. He has written or edited some forty books on modern German and European history. His research interests include World War I, the history of students and the professions, German unification, postwar democratization as well as methodological questions. He has codirected the Zentrum für Zeithistorische Forschung in Potsdam and cofounded the UNC Center for European Studies. His most recent book is *Out of Ashes: A New History of Europe in the Twentieth Century* (Princeton, NJ, 2015).

Harald Wenzel is Professor of Sociology at the John F Kennedy Institute for North American Studies of the Freie Universität Berlin. His research focuses on sociological theory, the sociology of mass media, religion, and catastrophes. Publications include *Die Abenteuer der Kommunikation: Echtzeitmassenmedien und der Handlungsraum der Hochmoderne, Die Ordnung des Handelns: Talcott Parsons' allgemeines Handlungssystem,* and *George Herbert Mead zur Einführung.*

NOTES

1. Rebecca Leber, "Thomas Friedman Is Tired of German Pacifism," *New Republic,* 6 May 2015; and Paul Krugman, "Germany Turned Europe's Problems into a Morality Play," *Business Insider,* 25 February 2016. For a classic introduction see Gordon A Craig, *The Germans* (New York, 1982).
2. Peter Novick, *The Holocaust and Collective Memory: The American Experience* (London, 2001).
3. Peter Watson, *The German Genius: Europe's Third Renaissance, the Second Scientific Revolution, and the Twentieth Century* (New York, 2010).
4. FORSA survey, *Das Image Deutschlands in Rußland und den USA* (Berlin, 2004).
5. Frank Trommler, "Post-Unification German Studies: Momentum Gained or Lost?," http://aicgs.org/2014/10.
6. Catherine Epstein, "Central European Historians at the Back of the Pack: Hiring Patterns in Modern European History, 1945–2010," *Central European History* 46, no. 3 (2013): 599–639.
7. Roger Cohen, "Germany: Refugee Nation," *New York Times,* 21 December 2015.
8. Edward W Said, *Orientalism* (Harmondsworth, 1995); and Konrad H Jarausch and Michael Geyer, *Shattered Past: Reconstructing German Histories* (Princeton, NJ, 2003).
9. Wolfgang Helbich and Walter Kamphoefner, eds, *German-American Immigration and Ethnicity in Comparative Perspective* (Madison, WI, 2004).
10. Thomas Adam and Gisela Mettele, eds, *Two Boston Brahmins in Goethe's Germany: The Travel Journals of Anna and George Ticknor* (Lanham, MD, 2009).
11. Daniel Rodgers, *Atlantic Crossings: Social Politics in a Progressive Age* (Cambridge, MA, 1998).
12. Hans W Gatzke, *Germany and the United States: A Special Relationship?* (Cambridge, MA, 1980).
13. See the forthcoming study of the concept of "Western Civilization" by Michael Kimmage.
14. Hartmut Lehmann and James J Sheehan, eds, *An Interrupted Past: German-Speaking Refugee Historians in the United States after 1933* (Washington, DC, 1991). See also Andreas Daum, Hartmut Lehmann, and James J Sheehan, eds, *The Second Generation: Emigres from Nazi Germany as Historians* (New York, 2015).
15. Christof Mauch, *The Shadow War against Hitler: The Covert Operations of America's Wartime Secret Intelligence Service* (New York, 2003) and Michaela Hönicke-Moore, *'Know Your Enemy': The American Debate on Nazism, 1933–1945* (New York, 2010).
16. Klaus-Dietmar Henke, *Die Amerikanische Besetzung Deutschlands* (Munich, 1995). Cf. Maria Höhn, *GIs and Fräuleins: The German-American Encounter in 1950s West Germany* (Chapel Hill, NC, 2002).
17. Gabriel A Almond and Sidney Verba, *The Civic Culture: Political Attitudes and Democracy in Five Nations* (Princeton, NJ, 1963).

18. See the German Studies Association seminar on "Cold War Berlin," organized by Steffi Eisenhut, Hanno Hochmuth, Konrad H Jarausch, and Scott Krause (Kansas City, MO, 2014).

19. Alexander Stephan, ed., *Americanization and Anti-Americanism: The German Encounter with American Culture after 1945* (New York, 2005).

20. One effort at reassurance was Walter Laqueur's essay on *Germany Today: A Personal Report* (Boston, 1985).

21. Konrad H Jarausch, "Drifting Apart: Cultural Dimensions of the Transatlantic Estrangement," in *Safeguarding Transatlantic Relations in the New Century: Understanding and Accepting Mutual Differences,* ed. Hermann Kurthen, Antonio V Menéndez Alarcón, and Stefan Immerfall (Lanham, MD, 2006), 17–32.

22. Mary Sarotte, *1989: The Struggle to Create Post–Cold War Europe* (Princeton, NJ, 2009).

23. Jim Willis, ed., *Images of Germany in the American Media* (Westport, CT, 1999).

24. Wolfgang-Uwe Friedrich, ed., *Germany and America: Essays in Honor of Gerald R Kleinfeld* (New York, 2001).

25. Frank Trommler and Elliot Shore, eds, *The German-American Encounter: Conflict and Cooperation between Two Cultures, 1800–2000* (New York, 2001).

26. Daniel Jonah Goldhagen, *Hitler's Willing Executioners: Ordinary Germans and the Holocaust* (New York, 1996).

27. Konrad H Jarausch, *After Hitler: Recivilizing Germans, 1945–1995* (New York, 2005).

28. Arnd Bauerkämper, Konrad H Jarausch, and Markus Payk, eds, *Demokratiewunder: Transatlantische Mittler und die kulturelle Öffnung Westdeutschlands* (Göttingen, 2005).

29. Anthony J Nicholls, *Freedom with Responsibility: The Social Market Economy in Germany, 1918–1963* (Oxford, 1994).

30. Michael L Hughes, *Shouldering the Burdens of Defeat: West Germany and the Reconstruction of Social Justice* (Chapel Hill, NC, 1999); and Gabriele Metzler, *Der deutsche Sozialstaat. Vom bismarckschen Erfolgsmodell zum Pflegefall* (Stuttgart, 2003).

31. Martin Klimke, *The Other Alliance: Student Protest in West Germany and the United States in the Global Sixties* (Princeton, NJ, 2010); and Timothy Brown, *West Germany in the Global Sixties: The Anti-Authoritarian Revolt, 1962–1978* (New York, 2013).

32. See the special issue of *German Politics and Society* 33 (2015), no. 4 on the Greens, edited by Konrad H Jarausch and Steven Milder.

33. Konrad H Jarausch, ed., *United Germany: Debating Processes and Prospects* (New York, 2013).

34. Helga Haftendorn, *Coming of Age: German Foreign Policy since 1945* (Lanham, MD, 2006).

35. "Die entkrampfte Nation," *Der Spiegel,* 14 July 2014.

36. Ulrich Herbert, *Geschichte Deutschlands im 20. Jahrhundert* (Munich, 2014).

37. Jürgen Danyel, "Zeitgeschichte der Informationsgesellschaft," *Zeithistorische Forschungen* 9, no. 2 (2012).

38. James J Sheehan, "What Is German History? Reflections on the Role of the Nation in German History and Historiography," *Journal of Modern History* 53, no. 1 (1981): 1–23.

39. Konrad H Jarausch, "Beyond the National Narrative: Implications of Reunification for Recent German History," *German History* 28, no. 4 (2010): 498–514.

40. Scott Krause, "Outpost of Freedom: A German-American Network's Campaign to bring Cold War Democracy to West Berlin, 1933-72" (PhD dissertation, University of North Carolina, 2016).

41. Jeffrey Wilson, *The German Forest: Nature, Identity, and the Contestation of a National Symbol, 1871–1914* (Toronto, 2012).

42. Hal E Hansen, "Caps and Gowns: Historical Reflections on the Institutions that Shaped Learning for and at Work in Germany and the United States, 1800–1945" (PhD dissertation, University of Wisconsin–Madison, 1997).

43. Annette Timm, *The Politics of Fertility in Twentieth Century Berlin* (New York, 2010).

44. Fritz René Allemann, *Bonn ist nicht Weimar* (Cologne, 1956).

45. Clara Oberle has written her dissertation on "City in Transit: Ruins, Railways, and the Search for Order in Berlin, 1945–1947" at Princeton University in 2006.

46. Brian Puaca, *Learning Democracy: Education Reform in West Germany, 1945–1965* (New York, 2009).

47. Sara Pugach has embarked upon a new project. Her first book is on *Africa in Translation: A History of Colonial Linguistics in Germany and Beyond, 1814–1945* (Ann Arbor, MI, 2012).

48. Ned Richardson-Little, "Between Dictatorship and Dissent: Ideology, Legitimacy, and Human Rights in East Germany, 1945–1990" (PhD dissertation, University of North Carolina, 2013).

49. Carol J Hager "From NIMBY to Networks: Protest and Innovation in German Energy Politics," in *NIMBY Is Beautiful: Cases of Local Activism and Environmental Innovation around the World,* ed. Carol J Hager and Mary Alice Haddad (New York, 2015), 33–59.

50. Mark Cassell, *How Governments Privatize: The Politics of Divestment in Germany and the United States* (Washington, DC, 2002).

51. Jeffrey Jurgens, "The Legacies of Labor Recruitment: The Guest Worker and Green Card Programs in the Federal Republic of Germany," *Policy and Society* 29, no. 4 (2010): 345–55.

52. Jarrell C Jackman and Carla M Borden, eds, *The Muses Flee Hitler: Cultural Transfer and Adaptation, 1930–1945* (Washington, DC, 1983).

53. Lilian Friedberg and Sara Hall, "Drums along the Amazon: The Rhythm of the Iron System of Werner Herzog's Fitzcaraldo," in *The Cosmopolitan Screen: German Cinema and the Global Imaginary, 1945 to the Present,* ed. Stephan K Schindler and Lutz Koepnick (Ann Arbor, MI, 2007).

54. Liel Leibovitz and Matthew Miller, *Lili Marlene: The Soldiers' Song of World War II* (New York, 2009).

55. Michael Meng, *Shattered Spaces: Encountering Jewish Ruins in Postwar Germany and Poland* (Cambridge, MA, 2011).

56. Konrad H Jarausch, "Rivalen der Moderne: Amerika und Deutschland im 20. Jahrhundert," in *Feinde, Freunde, Fremde: Die Deutsch-Amerikanischen Beziehungen im Wandel*, ed. Volker Benkert (Tutzing, 2017).

57. Jarausch, *After Hitler*, passim.

58. Konrad H Jarausch, "Towards a Critical Memory: Some German Reflections" (keynote paper at comparative conference on mass dictatorships, Osaka, 29 November 2015).

59. Paul Nolte, *Transatlantische Ambivalenzen: Studien zur Sozial- und Ideengeschichte des 18. bis 20. Jahrhunderts* (Munich, 2014).

60. Konrad H Jarausch, "Friends and Enemies: As Europe Redefines Itself, It Is Moving Away from the United States," *Chronicle of Higher Education,* 1 June 2015.

61. Thomas Mann, *Rede über Deutschland und die Deutschen* (Berlin, 1947).

62. Christof Mauch and Kiran Klaus Patel, eds, *The United States and Germany during the Twentieth Century: Competition and Convergence* (New York, 2010).

63. For a fuller exposition of these themes, see Konrad H Jarausch, *Out of Ashes: A New History of Europe in the Twentieth Century* (Princeton, NJ, 2015).

Part I

Responses to Modernity

Chapter 1

A Modern Reich?

American Perceptions of Wilhelmine Germany, 1890–1914

Scott H Krause

> I cannot say that I admired the personnel of the German Empire ... half
> so much as I admired some of the things they had achieved.
> —Theodore Dreiser, *A Traveler at Forty*, p. 428

Wilhelmine Berlin dazzled thousands of newly arrived with its rapid growth
and distinctively urban lifestyle. Even seasoned travelers like American
visitor Samuel L Clemens confided in 1890: "I feel lost in Berlin. ... It is a
new city; the newest I have ever seen." Even Chicago, a contemporary American eponym for rapid urban growth, "would seem venerable beside Berlin."
Heaping praise on the Wilhelmine Empire's capital, Clemens exclaimed that
"all of Berlin is stately, substantial, and ... uniformly beautiful." Clemens
credited Berlin's interventionist city government: "It seems to be the most
governed city in the world, but one must admit that it also seems to be the
best governed."[1] Clemens's Berlin impressions confound common wisdom
in two regards and raise a larger question.

In contrast to the perception of the Wilhelmine Empire as Europe's
authoritarian behemoth that the American government would foster during
World War I, Clemens found contemporary Germany comparable with the
United States in its dynamic of social change and economic growth. Moreover, Clemens considered particular policies worth emulating, even though
he was one of imperialism's best known critics under his pen name Mark

Twain. Hence Clemens's example extends an invitation to reassess contemporary American observers' perception of the German Empire.

Far from being viewed as incompatible, American observers curiously studied the Wilhelmine Empire as a fellow—statist—pioneer of modernity. German society came to exemplify state intervention in meeting shared challenges wrought by industrialization, urbanization, and mass culture. Hence the German example could include both positive and negative connotations, but the identity of the challenges reinforced its relevance to American observers. Hence the observers' perspectives could accommodate ambivalent perceptions. For example, high esteem for vigorous municipal government stood in stark contrast to the skepticism for Wilhelm II and his political regime.

This ambivalence of American contemporaries conflicts with an established historiographical interpretation of the Kaiserreich. Hans-Ulrich Wehler has continuously portrayed the Wilhelmine era as the watershed moment for German divergence onto its ultimately destructive *Sonderweg*.[2] Multiple historians have resisted such sweeping judgments, maintaining that study of the Kaiserreich should not limit itself to the "sum of its flaws."[3] Recent literature has supported this view by pointing to the Kaiserreich's economic dynamism, social volatility, and close global links.[4] More broadly, the rise of an entire field of subaltern studies within the last twenty-five years has questioned the existence of a single benign modernity in the Anglo-American vein upon which the Sonderweg thesis rests. Instead, scholars such as Arjun Appadurai and Dipesh Chakrabarty have opened up fruitful new research questions by insisting that multiple modernities could interact with each other—although far too often uneasily.[5]

But since the late 1980s, other scholars have reevaluated the years from 1890 to 1914–17 as a pivotal, if contradictory era of its own, rather than merely the prehistory of the Great War. Detlev JK Peukert led the way in describing these years as the era of *classical modernity*, highlighting the vast implications of societal changes wrought by industrialization across North America and Western Europe since the 1890s.[6] Since Peukert's untimely death, his concept has been expanded by Ulrich Herbert, who has characterized the era as the "breakthrough of modernity" that entailed a feverish search for solutions to "the challenges posed by modernity" that prefigured "ideological confrontations of the following decades."[7] Most recently, two monographs have surveyed Europe's cultural and political diversity, contradictions, and dynamism in this era for a broader audience on occasion of World War I's centennial.[8] Conversely, new research on the war's origins has characterized its outbreak as one of many possible outcomes of the 1914 July Crisis,[9] thus heightening interest in contemporaries' perception of volatility.

Interpreting the years between 1890 and 1914 as a contradictory era of its own provides the opportunity to get beyond purely antagonistic American perceptions of Germany and to grasp its nuances.[10] For example, Clemens mocked Berlin firemen as bureaucratic despite his enthusiasm for the city administration's sweeping authority.[11] This implies a more expansive, but paradoxical American perception of the Wilhelmine Empire than has previously been acknowledged. Clemens's example suggests that Germany served simultaneously as mirror and projection screen in contemporary American writing. The gaze across the Atlantic at the ostensive Old World limited itself not only to a "yardstick for measuring the success of any homegrown success," as Christof Mauch and Kiran Klaus Patel have suggested.[12]

The German Empire rather served as preeminent example for a society in which state intervention had been commonplace to a degree hitherto unknown for Americans. Challenging the dogma of laissez-faire individualism in US federal policies, the heterogeneous progressive movement frequently cited European examples as successes of governmental regulations.[13] In effect, turn of the century travel writings on Germany became political interventions in contemporary American debates. The combination of intellectual curiosity and a considerable audience encouraged American travel writing from the Kaiserreich. The European activities of American businessmen fostered the naturalist author Theodore Dreiser's interest in the ostensibly Old World.[14] Eminent publishing house Charles Scribner's Sons solicited a manuscript from the journalist Elmer Roberts, convinced that it "would have many interested readers."[15]

Between Wilhelm II's coronation in 1888 and the outbreak of World War I in 1914, no less than ten American journalists, writers, scholars, and activists published their experiences in Germany in book-length monographs. These form the sources for this essay.[16] Among the authors ranked contemporarily prominent figures such as Dreiser, William Jennings Bryan, erstwhile Democratic presidential nominee and future secretary of state in the Wilson administration, and Booker T Washington. The writings of these contemporary celebrities are complemented with those of Roberts, Ray Stannard Baker, Frederic C Howe, and Price Collier who have written the most extensive monographs. Save Collier, these three authors could be linked to the progressive movement.[17] Without exception, all authors were men and all except one of them white.

These observers interviewed German politicians, businessmen, and professors in search of their responses to the challenges wrought by industrialization, urbanization, and mass culture. Regardless of their different social origins and political convictions, they analyzed the organization of German bureaucracy, higher education, and infrastructure in astonishing detail.

In their studies of contemporary Germany, they projected contemporary American debates and issues onto the empire. Hence, an interest in
alternative solutions to American contemporary problems motivated study
of the German Empire. This essay seeks to recreate contemporary American debates on Imperial Germany through qualitative content analysis and
juxtaposition of different, individual pieces of travel writing.[18] Exemplary
quotes have been selected to illustrate the most prominent tropes.[19] This
essay outlines the relevance of the German case for contemporaries first, to
then address American perceptions of the Wilhelmine Empire's political
system and American esteem of individual policies.

RAPID INDUSTRIALIZATION

Three historical processes invite comparisons between the United States
and Germany around 1900 and made the German example particularly
relevant to American contemporaries.[20] First, both societies witnessed "a
new birth" of the nation-state (Lincoln) through "blood and iron" (Bismarck)
between the 1860s and 1870s. Second, both societies underwent sweeping
and rapid industrialization in the following decades, establishing themselves as two of the largest economies in the world of the era. Third, the
speed and intensity of industrialization and urbanization created a sense of
volatile growth that dazzled German and American contemporaries alike.
These parallel developments made the Wilhelmine Reich particularly fascinating for American intellectuals. Ray Stannard Baker, billed as "America's
Reporter Number One," for example, explicitly highlighted the common
experience of industrialization: "I sometimes think that we Americans are
becoming a race of mechanics. ... And Germany seems to be following in
the same direction."[21]

German strategies for confronting industrialization's consequences fascinated representatives of the American political left in particular. Bryan,
who first brought the social question to the center stage of American politics,
explained to his readers the relevance of the German example:

> Those who believe that the right is sure of ultimate triumph will watch the
> struggle in Germany and profit by the lessons taught. ... The Germans are a
> studious and a thoughtful people and just now they are absorbed in the con-
> sideration of the aims and methods of the socialist movement (mingled with
> a greater or less amount of governmental reform), and the world awaits their
> verdict with deep interest.[22]

Bryan's statement characteristically reflected American perceptions of the Wilhelmine Reich. He assigned tremendous—potentially positive—importance to developments in Germany. But he viewed them cautiously, choosing to "await the verdict," and placed great priority on the benefits of governmental regulation of the economy and everyday life.

The author's position within the American political spectrum determined his judgment of Wilhelmine Germany, as Bryan's example demonstrated. He identified positive traits of Imperial German policies as a left-wing stalwart, but Price Collier as representative of laissez-faire liberalism disagreed vigorously. Although Price was convinced as well "that we all have much to learn from Germany," its example had demonstrated instead the dangers of governmental regulation for him: "She [Germany] has shown us that the short-cut to the governing of a people by suppression and strangulation results in a dreary development of mediocrity."[23]

The rapid pace of change within the German Empire attracted most interest by American observers. In their eyes, German socioeconomic developments could—as one of few—keep pace with those in the United States. The speed and breadth of change in Germany must have impressed American travelers, as all authors in unison wrote of great changes that industrialization engendered. American observers oscillated between enthusiasm and horror in their attempts to evaluate the transformations sweeping German society. This ambivalence became palpable in the assessment of Collier. Compared with the German states he had known during his school years, the German Empire must have indeed undergone a "fairy-like change" by 1913. Collier confessed to have never imagined "that Auerbach's Black Forest Stories would be less known than Albert Ballin's fleet of mercantile ships" as German international icons.[24]

Germany astonished American visitors not only through the intensity, but also the extent of its transformation. For these observers, only German politics dominated by conservatives seemed insulated from these seismic shifts.[25] American intellectuals consistently identified the rapid industrialization of the Wilhelmine Reich as motor for these changes. Theodore Dreiser went so far as describing Germany in its entirety through the imagery of heavy industry, noting that the empire "is very much like the heat and glow of a furnace. Germany is a great forge or workshop. It resounds with the industry of a busy nation."[26] In addition, American observers were keenly aware of the diversifying industrial basis of the German economy. New sectors such as the chemical or electrical industries grew at an astonishing rate making Badische Annalin- und Soda-Fabrik (BASF), Bayer, Siemens & Halske, or Allgemeine Elektricitäts-Gesellschaft (AEG) global leaders in their respective industries. Already in 1902, Baker concluded that "no country in the world, not even the United States, is advancing more rapidly in electrical development than Germany." In the same breath, Baker chided his compatriots that "We in America have been content to take our progress more slowly." By contending that American competitors were lagging behind in an industry of the future, Baker tried to prod his contemporaries into action. Moreover, Baker exclaimed "the Kaiser has taken the greatest interest in spreading industrial and technical education."[27] In effect, Baker constructed the image of German society that reconciled fantastic economic growth rates with astonishing social stability through close state regulation.

This image proved enduring and attractive for other American intellectuals to essentialize. Germany's first economic miracle had such an impression on American observers that some ascribed it to particularly German national traits. Dreiser characterized the German economy as "blazing force and defiance," which seemingly knew no boundaries.[28] Industrial expansion not only overcame centuries of economic backwardness, but had started to change nature itself. Collier cited the construction of new waterways as a vivid example:

> [The Rhine] has been made a great commercial highway. Cologne, one hundred and fifty miles from the sea, is now a seaport; Strasburg, three hundred miles inland, can receive boats of six hundred tons; ... Now the Dortmund Ems canal, which is one hundred and sixty-eight miles long, and can be used by ships of a thousand tons, gives an outlet, via the Rhine, at Emden. All this is the work of a patient, persistent, and economical people working under great natural disadvantages.[29]

Obviously impressed, Collier described the expansion of the waterway network in Western Germany in detailed fashion, as it underpinned German economic growth. He interpreted the 1899 opening of the Dortmund-Ems-Canal, which bypassed the Netherlands in connecting the Ruhr area with the North Sea, as capstone of a gigantic reshaping of nature.

American observers could simultaneously admire and criticize these grand designs of state supported economic development. While Collier admired the results of the state-controlled expansion of infrastructure, he detested the logic of controllability of economic growth it stemmed from. Claiming that Americans were "at peace with ourselves and with others" with personal responsibility, Collier pitied the subjects of the Kaiserreich: "No people of modern times has been so harried and harrowed as these Germans." In his view, governmental policies had only succeeded in postponing larger societal problems: "[German leadership] has suppressed them, strangled them, suffocated them." Collier went on to dismiss the notion of Germany as an example to emulate: "To point out Germany as a model of successful achievement ... in order to bolster up political cure-alls at home, is a betrayal of crass ignorance of the general internal situation of the country." Collier's assessment is striking in two regards: first, it was highly skeptical of the German political system. Second, its harsh tone was a deliberate intervention in a domestic American debate, where left-leaning intellectuals touted the German example to implement governmental measures to improve social security. Collier acknowledged the mechanism explicitly, denouncing his opponents' goal to promote "political cure-alls" in the United States.[30]

THE PERPLEXING POLITICAL SYSTEM

Emperor Wilhelm II personified the differences in political systems for these American observers of Germany. His cultivation of an image of strength in the public sphere succeeded in bringing him to the center of American perception of the German political system—at the expense of other political actors.[31] While they agreed on Wilhelm II's dominant position, erratic decisions, and mercurial temperament, American observers differed starkly in their judgments. Collier saw Wilhelm II's reign as a result of a general lack of virile leaders among Germans, noting that "they are coddled in every direction; but they have no stuff for colonizers, and ... lacking in stalwart statesmen, and leaders."[32] On the other hand, Frederic C Howe, pioneer of urban planning in the United States, described Wilhelm II as national leader who was deeply concerned with the challenges his subjects faced: "Far-sighted statesman that he is, the Kaiser sees that his regiments and his battle-ships ... must be manned by strong and well-educated men. These the city is imperiling. It is sapping the Life of the people. And the Kaiser and his ministers are studying the city as they do their engines of warfare."[33] Even in this flattering assessment of Wilhelm II's reign, military considerations appeared at the center of his agenda. Associated Press Berlin correspondent Elmer Roberts exemplified American uncertainty of Wilhem II by labeling him a simultaneous "democrat and monarchist," noting "as democrat the Emperor lives intellectually in all the progressive thought of the time ... As monarchist he is tenacious of prerogative, ... determined to pass on the splendid estate unimpaired to his children."[34] Notably, Roberts distinguished between Wilhelm II's policies, which deserved close study, and his adherence to dynastic rule, which Roberts deemed a German peculiarity.

　　The American observers paid passing attention to the bourgeoning parliamentarianism and workers' movement at best. Howe was the only observer who commented on the Reich's constitution. Two sentences sufficed: "The constitution crystallized feudalism into legal form. Privilege, which was previously subject to protest or revolution, as in 1830 and 1848, is now authoritative."[35] Given the particular importance of the constitution for American readers, this assessment had to be understood as particularly dismissive. In spite of growing powers of the Reichstag, Collier citied the three-tiered suffrage in Prussia, making it "impregnable against any assault from the democratically inclined."[36] Hence American intellectuals saw in the German Empire's democratic traits little more than fig leafs that Wilhelm II's autocracy could discard easily in an opportune moment.

Consequently, the contrast between the political system they indicted as autocratic and the domestic policies it enacted baffled American intellectuals. Howe summarized succinctly:

> There are many other anomalies that the ... American mind, cannot explain. Governed by an almost feudal aristocracy with a detachment and disdain for all other classes, Germany has worked out the most elaborate programme [!] of social legislation and state socialism of any country in the world.[37]

Collier concurred with Howe, characterizing the German Empire as "a strange state of affairs."[38] The inexplicable German paradox of a self-proclaimed reactionary monarchy that deliberately tackled challenges of modernity fascinated American contemporaries. Howe commented respectfully: "Germany has given a new conception of the state to the world. It may not be a beautiful conception. It certainly violates our ideas of personal and political freedom. But at least the idea is a successful one."[39] Torn between objection to the political system and close study of its policies as potential blueprints, Howe's perception epitomized American ambivalence toward the German political system and its elites.

This skepticism is closely linked to the persona of Wilhelm II. American observers took Wilhelm II's reactionary rhetoric at face value while omitting its context of increasing domestic competition. The rise of mass media and the advent of mass politics refigured political communication within Germany.[40] Wilhelm II had to subscribe to a code of conduct to reach his subjects through a press proudly independent of the monarchy. Deliberately or unwittingly, his string of incendiary statements filled headlines.[41] In a remarkable consensus, American observers attentively listened to Wilhelm II's loud voice in the cacophonic chatter of the Reich's numerous political factions. This offered them the convenience of easily projecting differences onto a single person. Yet by privileging Wilhelm II as personification of the empire, this interpretation necessarily obfuscated the empire's complex federal structure and fragile power balance, and marginalized the opposition.

The Social Democratic Party (SPD), as political arm of the workers' movement, appeared as the only noteworthy opposition to Wilhelm II's regime. In spite of the Hohenzollern's rhetoric, American observers sensed the sharp ideological antagonisms within German society. Roberts chose drastic words to explain them:

> An extraordinary mental and political civil war is in full movement, in which monarchical socialism keeps the mastery of material development against republican revolutionary socialism.[42]

Roberts saw control over the German economic engine at stake in the domestic politics he deemed a "civil war." Already Marxist socialism, paraphrased as "republican revolutionary socialism," had succeeded in extracting direct state intervention in the economy as a concession from the conservative monarchy.

The observers' concentration on Social Democrats derived from the context of contemporary American society. The bourgeoning class of white collar workers—of which the American observers originated—feared the specter of socialism since Chicago's 1886 Haymarket Bombing. The violence between workers on strike and policemen signified the arrival of a diffuse, but potent urban political force that endangered public order for the nascent American middle class. Through these impressions, American observers primarily perceived the SPD as a phenomenon of social crisis. The party's success and future policies became an indicator for the Reich's domestic stability and potential for reform in light of the pressing social question. Roberts, for example, marveled at the German Empire's flexibility in its social policies, noting "that which is still considered destructive socialism in some countries is appropriated by the Crown and called monarchy in Germany."[43] Contrary to Roberts, who touted German conciliatory social policies' pacifying effect as a model to emulate, Baker compared the social question in the German Empire to a powder keg. For Baker, industrialization's rapid breakthrough had triggered developments of unforeseeable consequences:

> One who realizes the mighty industrial progress of Germany is struck with the vital question as to whether the workman will be able to keep pace. Surely the limit of his wages has nearly been reached ... When will the danger line be reached? Will the German toiler plod always onward, working always for continually diminishing profits, drinking his Sunday beer, forever the model of patience and simple enjoyment of life?[44]

Hence, the observers characterized the SPD as a social movement, rather than political actor in its own right, citing the perceived political impotence

of the Reichstag, the Imperial diet. Collier asked rhetorically: "What journalist or what patriot indeed can take seriously a majority that has no
power? ... the taxes are fixtures, a constitution is a dream." Thus, the 1912
Social Democratic landslide would have little effect: "Not since 1874 has
there been a Reichstag so strongly radical, but nothing will come of it."[45]
This dismissive judgment implied an inability of the Reich's political structure to reform and shaped the American view of the Social Democrats as a
social movement of the German workers.

The rise of the SPD invited competing explanations. Roberts, for
example, underscored the relative political cohesion of German workers.[46]
The SPD won the sympathies of some American observers as the perceived
representative of the German working class. These sympathies did not
derive from shared Marxist convictions, but from German authorities'
attempts to curtail workers' civil rights. Baker accused German imperial
elites of ignoring workers' worth as individuals: "The individual is nothing,
the workman everything."[47] Strikingly, Baker's dichotomy between American individualism and German collectivism anticipated the main trope for
the future construction of enemy stereotypes—although with one important qualification: Baker viewed German collectivism as a preoccupation
of German elites and thus supported the German working class in their
struggle for political participation:

> If he [the German worker] does begin to consider his condition, he does one of
> two things,—he either becomes a socialist or he commits suicide. So socialism,
> though held down by bands of steel, is rampant everywhere in Germany.[48]

In drastic words, Baker explained the German working-class enthusiasm for
socialism not as consequence of its living condition, but through its yearning
for dignity. From the other side of the political spectrum, Collier contended
that the SPD was best understood as an ineffectual product of frustration.[49]
Collier's rabid rejection of socialism in all stripes colored his assessment of
the SPD. Obsessive idealization of individual strength as ordained by God
shaped his worldview:

> Neither God nor Nature gives anything to those who do not struggle, and
> both ... appoint the stern task-master, Necessity, to see to it that we do struggle.
> Now come the ignorant and the socialists, demanding that the state step in
> and roll back the very laws of creation ... Who cannot see anarchy looming
> ahead of this programme, for it is surely a lunatic negation of all the laws of
> God and Nature? ... Legislation was never intended to be the father of a people,
> but their policeman.[50]

Hence any state intervention to improve the living condition of its citizens would negate the divine law of the strongest. Subsequently, the German example provided Americans with a cautionary tale. In this context, Collier's positive assessment of the SPD's policies appeared rather surprising.

> Their demands at this present time are far from the radical theory that all sources of production should be in the hands of the people. Only a small number of very red radicals demand that. Their successes have been, and they are real successes, along the lines of greater protection and more political liberty for the workingman.[51]

The discrepancy between radical theory and pragmatic policy of German Social Democrats was visible even for ardent anti-socialists like Collier. Bryan questioned the accuracy of the attribute "socialist" to describe the SPD's revisionist course: "It is certain that the socialists of Germany are securing reforms, but so far they are reforms which have either already been secured in other countries or are advocated elsewhere by other parties as well as by the socialist party."[52]

INNOVATIVE STATE INTERVENTION

American observers ascribed to the German bureaucracy a particular efficiency in moving goods as well as urban dwellers. Their observations did not limit themselves to the contemporary icon of progress, the railroad, but also included the concurrent expansion of German waterways.[53] Dreiser described Berlin's mass transit system as a landmark: "One panegyric I should like to write on Berlin concerns ... specifically its traffic and travel arrangements," especially as it put American mass transit systems to shame:

> I wish all Americans who at present suffer the indignities of the American street-railway and steam-railway suburban service could go to Berlin and see what that city has to teach them in this respect. Berlin is much larger than Chicago. It is certain soon to be a city of five or six millions of people—very soon. The plans for handling this mass of people comfortably and courteously are already in operation.[54]

The contrast between Berlin and Chicago could not be starker for Dreiser. While the Germans might have been "underlings to an imperial Kaiser, subject to conscription and eternal inspection," their government spared them of American railroad magnates, "'Christian gentlemen' who want to 'pack 'em in.'" Moreover, experiencing Berlin's mass transit system prompted Dreiser to criticize contemporary American culture:

> Strange, isn't it? Queer, how Imperialism apparently teaches people to be civil, while Democracy does the reverse. We ought to get a little "Imperialism" into our government, I should say.[55]

For Dreiser, daily life in the German Empire's capital highlighted the greed that American captains of industries inflicted. Dreiser's furor could not be construed of an endorsement of the German political system, but should rather be understood as a critique of classical Liberalism. Dreiser called instead for a stronger federal government to protect the rights of consumers.

The German infrastructure outclassed its American counterparts in the verdict of all transatlantic visitors, even if individual opinions varied. Roberts did not use the German example to fundamentally criticize corporate America, but to cite it as a role model for selective reforms. Shunning outright socialization of railroads, Roberts advocated centralized coordination and fare-setting by a federal agency modeled after the German Bundesratskommision.[56] Roberts contended that such a German inspired policy in the United States would help consumers without changing ownership.[57] The trope of state-coordinated economic growth fascinated many American observers repeatedly.

American observers stressed governmental agendas for increasing exports, rationalization, and workplace safety as examples of a comprehensive German economic policy.[58] Ray Stannard Baker explained the empire's "extraordinary strides in commercial affairs" through the example of Carl Zeiss optical systems in Jena: "Out of Science, assisted by the state, has sprung a new and profitable industry." Anticipating present-day venture capital, the state invested into Zeiss to commercially exploit scientific advances. Thus Zeiss symbolized to Baker industrial finance of the future: "Such an enterprise as this is certainly typically modern, and it may be significant as indicating how the great new industries of the future are to have their origin."[59]

The volume of German exports seemingly resulted from a national priority. According to Baker, "no monarch in Europe takes such a keen interest ... in the extension of the export business of his domain as William [II]." His particularly capable bureaucracy and corporate Germany coordinated "trade conquest told quarterly in the thin brochures of the imperial statistical office."[60] Both Baker and Roberts identified a formidable threat to the American share in global trade in this pairing.[61]

State subsidies for high-tech industries fitted into a larger narrative of economic rationalization. The widespread application of the scientific method in German industries impressed the American observers. For Baker, German enterprises aggressively strove beyond the limits of accumulated experience in manufacturing. Designated Research and Development divisions who had found their "most perfect development in Germany," served as crucial sources of innovation.[62] This application of new research derived from the hard as well as social sciences. Roberts reported approvingly of the Prussian government's efforts to better allocate employment opportunities through centrally tabulated statistics: "The central labor bureau for Prussia draws up a sheet at the end of each month which shows exactly the number out of employment in all trades. Taken over a period of years, it is thus easy, of course, to determine relatively the chances of employment."[63] In spite of its still rudimentary method, the Prussian goal of improved employment rates through social scientific research impressed Roberts. The volatile industrial growth of the era carried boom and bust cycles that caused frequent spells of unemployment for workers. To shorten unemployment phases, select cities and trade associations within the Reich had started to open *Arbeitsnachweise,* literally work certificates, since the late nineteenth century. Roberts hailed these corporatist job centers as a preeminent tool of social policy: "No individual runs the hazard of not finding work for months." Roberts explained their success through a consensus within German society that Americans lacked. Germans of all political stripes agreed that unemployment was a social rather than solely an individual problem: "the kind of thinking that is still called radical in Great Britain or in America, but in Germany is conservative."[64]

These political considerations also determined perceptions of the already introduced Bismarckian social insurance program. Even though the general pension, disability, and occupational accident insurance omitted health care and unemployment, American observers differed strongly in their judgments on the pioneer of modern welfare policy—according to their own political leanings. Roberts likened its relevance to the creation of Bismarck's Empire itself. "Compulsory provisions against social maladies" contributed directly to the domestic stability of a hierarchically stratified society. Moreover, individuals benefited immensely as well: unemployment "does not shade off so quickly into pauperism next-door to starvation" as in American cities. Collier came to diametrically opposed conclusions. Through compulsory insurances, the state had "gained an appalling control over the minute details of human intercourse." The German workers lost their personal freedom through the loss of personal responsibility: "Every vote the workingman gives to a policy of wider state control is another link for the chains that are meant for his ankles, his wrists, and his neck."[65] Collier saw individuals' freedom of contract endangered, while Roberts directly rebutted this anticipated objection: "Labor has become standardized, as it were, and the personal side of the free contract between the master and man has disappeared."[66]

Contemporaries viewed explosive urban growth as a particularly evident feature of the modern era. While this seismic process affected lives and cityscapes across the globe, American observers developed a unique appreciation for German cities in general and Berlin in particular. According to Howe, a pioneer of urban planning in the United States, the best solutions to problems engendered by rapid growth could be found in the Wilhelmine Reich.[67] The nearly unanimous agreement of other observers with Howe's thesis underscored the German example's relevance compared with its European peers. In Berlin, Dreiser believed to have visited nothing less than the city of the future:

> If I laugh at it forever and ever as a blunder-headed, vainglorious, self-appreciative city I shall always love it too. Paris has had its day, and will no doubt have others; London is content with an endless, conservative day; Berlin's is still to come and come brilliantly. The blood is there, and the hope, and the moody, lustful, Wagnerian temperament.[68]

While Berlin's mercurial atmosphere amused Dreiser, its dynamism impressed him deeply. Other observers shared his admiration for German cities' capable bureaucracy, rather than their aesthetics. Howe, for example, dismissed the pompous displays of imperial splendor in Mitte, only to praise Berlin's rapidly erected residential neighborhoods as results of an "administration [that] is a model of efficiency and farsightedness."[69]

In spite of Berlin's great importance, American admiration also extended to other German cities. Howe claimed enthusiastically that "Germany is treating the new behemoth of civilization, the modern industrial city, as a creature to be controlled, and made to serve" and not to loathe as American contemporaries.[70] Howe insisted that even Essen, the "Pittsburgh of Germany," looked admirable compared with its American equivalent and "reflects the German idea of what a city should be." Booker T Washington shared the impression that German municipal bureaucracies had succeeded in taming modern metropolises where contemporary America failed:

> In that part of Germany which I visited I noticed that nothing was allowed to grow up naturally, in the comfortable and haphazard disorder that one finds

in some parts of America. This is particularly true of the cities. Everything is tagged and labelled [!], and ordered with military precision. Even the rose-bushes in the gardens seem to show the effect of military discipline. Trimmed and pruned, they stand up straight, in long and regular rows, as if they were continually presenting arms.[71]

This quote illustrated again how American experiences colored perceptions abroad. Washington's background as an educator at the Tuskegee Normal and Industrial Institute determined his choice of examples. His allusion to prevalent stereotypes of German militarism demonstrated Washington's didactic intentions.

American observers cited German cityscapes as examples for a rational and predictable bureaucracy. Its work "truly charmed" Dreiser, when he exclaimed "Berlin is shot through with the constant suggestion of officialism and imperialism."[72] Already in 1897, Albert Shaw credited German bureau-cracy's scientific methodology for much of the "progress" in less than two decades after the empire's establishment:

> To this work of modern improvement, especially in public appointments, the Germans seem to have brought more of the scientific spirit and method than any other people. Their habits of thoroughness in research, and of patient, exhaustive treatment of any subject in hand, have fully characterized their new progress in the arts of civilized life. Above all, the Germans had already devel-oped a system of public administration more economical and more infallibly effective than could have been found elsewhere; and they were prepared [for] the growth of their cities and the new demand for modern improvements.[73]

Shaw's admiration for the German Beamten, lifetime civil servants, stemmed from three points: first, they applied the results of scientific research to their work. Second, their work kept the infrastructure's expansion in pace with urban growth. Third, their projects even anticipated future demographic trends in the Reich.

In his enthusiasm for the Beamten, Howe failed to recognize the author-itarian elements of the German *Obrigkeitsstaat*:

> Germany [is] almost alone building her cities to make them contribute to the happiness, health, and well-being of the people. This seems to be the primary consideration with officials and citizens. It is this that distinguishes the cities of this country from the other cities of the world. ... Far-sightedness characterizes Germany in all things.[74]

But Howe did not mention to his readers that census suffrage also applied to German municipal elections. These patrician features of German municipal administration might have even appealed to Howe in the context of contemporary American municipal politics. *Bosses* managed individual political machines that controlled city politics through elaborate patronage networks. Cincinnati's George B Cox or New York City's Richard Croker fascinated Max Weber as "political capitalist entrepreneurs," but galvanized the progressive movement as eponyms of corruption.[75] This context made American observers susceptible to idealizing German-style bureaucracy. It served as a positive counterexample to their own experience through meritocracy, incorruptibility, and dedication to the public good ascribed to German Beamten. Baker, however, tinged his admiration for the German Beamten class with doubts about its military ethos, when he noted acerbically "the spirit of the government is the military spirit."[76]

Universal conscription invited the most open criticism of the German interventionist state, which the American visitors viewed as a European peculiarity. The German military played a large role quantitatively in the perception of contemporary American observers.[77] While all observers deemed the peacetime draft and social status of the military as German peculiarities, its assessment proved controversial between the observers. Some viewed the German military as the culmination of authoritarian militarism, others perceived it as a symbol of perfect organization. The American observers' verdict depended on whether they concentrated on the German officers' caste or the common inductees.

Dreiser's dispatches exemplified American suspicions of the German military:

> I did not know then, quite, how intensely proud Germany is of her army, how perfectly willing the vast majority are to serve, how certain the great majority of Germans are that Germany is called of God to rule—beherrschen is their vigorous word—the world. ... What a clever custom thus to sugar-coat the compulsory pill. And, in a way, what a travesty.[78]

Dreiser diagnosed that universal conscription secured pervasive militarism in German society. In characteristic sarcasm, Dreiser congratulated the Reich's government for its ability to enthuse its subjects for service with chauvinistic emotions.

On the other side of the debate, the German military signified for "without doubt the greatest military system the world ever saw" for Baker.[79] While technological advances in armaments and equipment enthralled Baker as chronicler of innovations, Collier approvingly depicted the German military as social engineering avant la lettre:

Bismarck's words, "Ohne Armee kein Deutschland," meant to him, and mean to-day, far more than that the army is necessary for defence. It is the best all-round democratic university in the world; ... it is essential to discipline; it is a cement for holding Germany together.[80]

Collier tweaked the semantic meaning of "democratic" from a political ordering principle to "all-encompassing." Recurring on tropes such as the military as the school of the nation, the broadscale induction and training of recruits fascinated Collier with obsessive intensity:

[The German army] offers a brilliant example, in a material age, of men scorning ease for the service of their country; it keeps the peace in Europe; and until there is a second coming, of a Christ of pity, and patience, and peace, it is as good a substitute for that far off divine event.[81]

The former Unitarian minister's idolization of German soldiers sought to critique contemporary, modern American culture. Collier took the popular narrative of decadent modernity disfiguring masculinity as a portent of cultural decline to new extremes.[82] For Collier, German men had the privilege over their American cousins of proving their virility on the field of honor:

As yet the Germans have not been overtaken by the tepid wave of feminism, which for the moment is bathing the prosperity-softened culture of America and England. It is a harsh remedy, but both America and England would gain something of virility if they were shot over. We are all apt enough to become womanish ... when we are reaping in security the fields cleared, enriched, and planted by a hardy ancestry of pioneers. There were no self-conscious peace-makers; ... no devotees of third-sexism, in the days of Waterloo and Gettysburg, when we had men's tasks to occupy us.[83]

Aside from his argument's shaky plausibility of interpreting pacifism as dangerous "feminism," Collier's agitation showed a remarkable rhetoric. Wittingly or unwittingly, he drew on Roman writer Tacitus' argument in his ethnography "Germania." Through idealization of Germans, the author tried to construct a positive counterexample to his or her own society. Subsequently, Collier's perception of Germany served to criticize contemporary American culture.

American observers perceived the German educational system as decidedly less controversial, but at least as pertinent for their readers. Comparing the expansion of education across multiple European countries, Washington praised the German educational sector as an innovative pioneer.[84] But to the

probable surprise of contemporary German professors classically trained
in the Arts, American observers like Washington felt most interested in
German vocational schooling and organization of big science. For instance,
social scientist Earl Dean Howard introduced his readers to *Fortbildungs-
schulen,* vocational schools today known as *Berufsschulen,* as key reason for
German "industrial progress."[85] The German Empire succeeded in filling
the gap between elementary schooling and the increasing demands by the
labor force.

State funding for costly basic research became another popular example
for the willingness of the German public to invest in education. Berlin's
Physikalisch-Technische Reichsanstalt (PTR) impressed Baker deeply. The
concentration of ninety-five professors exclusively on "laying a deep and
solid foundation for future scientific discovery" convinced Baker of the need
for the generous funding. To his dismay, he found no American equivalent.
Anticipating rejection of American governmental funding, Baker called on
American philanthropists to compensate for the "lack of parental care on
the part of the governing power." Fearing that the Wilhelmine Empire could
reap the benefits of scientific progress in the future, Baker implored potential philanthropists: "May not some of them feel the need of such a scientific
establishment as the Reichsanstalt?"[86]

A STATIST PIONEER OF MODERNITY

American contemporaries viewed massive social dislocations as an iden-
tical problem for the United States and the German Empire in the fin de
siècle era. Thus they developed a particular interest for German strategies in *taming modernity.*[87] Unsettling years of large, but volatile economic
growth colored American observers' perceptions of Germany. Upon visiting Berlin's cutting-edge Physikalisch-Technische Reichsanstalt, Baker,
for instance, lamented the hard sciences' increasing inability to provide
definitive answers:

> Science, which sometimes seems the final standard of accuracy and complete-
> ness, in the light of these experiments appears unstable, without a sure founda-
> tion and without the possibility of a sure foundation. ... Thus everything about
> us is constantly changing relations, so that there is no standard of anything.

But the collective need for orientation persisted unabated. Empirical comparisons with other societies became particularly useful for locating one's
own position and for profiting from the experience of others. Baker com-

mented on the relevance of comparisons on the same page: "all measurement is merely a series of comparisons."[88]

American observations drew thus innumerable comparisons—implicitly and explicitly—between the United States and the German Empire, when writing on their experiences in Germany. Their comparisons also highlighted the comparability of challenges between Germans and Americans, regardless for them, whether these comparisons were positive or not. The externalization of American domestic debates onto the Reich further underscored the comparability of both societies. Roberts's and Collier's diverging opinions on German social policies, for instance, substantiated this comparability.

The transatlantic visitors associated the late German Empire with "modern life" and its challenges in an exclusivity that surprises present-day readers. They readily accepted the Wilhelmine Reich as a fellow pioneer in modernity. This acceptance had developed quickly, if compared with observations from the German-speaking lands a few decades before. Samuel Clemens's two visits epitomized this fundamentally altered perception: in 1878 he romanticized Heidelberg as a quaint college town in which time stood seemingly still.[89] Fourteen years later, he visited Berlin, global eponym of a mushrooming metropolis, to report on its street cleaning and mass transit systems in technical detail. In addition, observations on the Kaiserreich continuously expanded quantitatively between 1890 and 1914. The increasing American attention for the Wilhelmine Empire derived from a new appreciation of the German economy's dynamism. Howe suggested to his readers that "the German city, like our own, is the product of the last generation."[90] Multiple observers developed a fascination for the German example from their interest. The Kaiserreich seemingly better succeeded in channeling the ramifications of industrialization, even if its pace appeared even higher in Germany. Its capital Berlin became the primary exhibit for this argument, the growth of which dwarfed even American metropolises.

Despite its undisputed importance, the constant references to Berlin as pars pro toto for the Reich at large raise the question of thematic and geographic blind spots in American observers' perception. Next to the ubiquitous Berlin, their itineraries covered large cities and the booming industrial corridor along the Rhine, but decidedly less rural East Elbia. Hence American observers inevitably perceived the Wilhelmine Reich as more urban and economically expanding than its aggregate statistical indicators would suggest. This also concealed the considerable regional identities and tensions under the empire's umbrella. Two explanations competed to account for these blind spots: the Reich's rural areas were deemed either backward or familiar to the observers' American experiences. Howe described East Prussia as "divorced ... from the liberalizing influences of modern life." Noting that "the great landowners live upon their estates," the Prussian squires seemed eerily familiar to him.[91] Howe's disdain for the antebellum South colored his characterization of East Elbia as a German Dixie. Simultaneously, stark regional differences within the empire did not take American observers aback, as they accepted them as a condition of life from their own backgrounds.

The observer's continued to accentuate the Kaiserreich's homogeneity in their depiction of its political system. Thus they characterized it as a monolithic bloc domineered by Kaiser Wilhelm II. To Americans, his reign exhibited schizophrenic traits. Wilhelm II vigorously impelled the empire's future at the cutting-edge of modernity, while invoking royal prerogatives of bygone times. The German Empire's purported embrace of modernity fascinated American observers, while simultaneously disdaining its royal pretensions. Wilhelm II's mercurial political persona largely blocked pluralistic elements of the empire, such as the Reichstag or its federal structure from the view of American observers. Hence they could only locate opposition to him in the Socialist workers' movement. The SPD's advocacy of socialism triggered deep-seated fears of anarchist terror. Inevitably, the Social Democrats of the German variety that demanded political participation through parliamentary reform puzzled American observers. This reduction of the German workers' movement precipitated American perceptions of the SPD as a crisis phenomenon, instead of as a viable alternative to the established political system.

Regardless of their own political principles, all American observers equated the Wilhelmine Reich with a society that relied on an interventionist bureaucracy to confront the challenges of modernity. As the German Empire exemplified state intervention into the everyday lives of its subjects in hitherto unknown intensity, this paradigm determined American perspectives positively and negatively. When observers' reported, for instance, on Germany's burgeoning electrical and chemical industries as the high tech industries of the era, they explained their success through state-funded basic research. In the verdict of American observers, the Reich's socialized infrastructure outclassed any transatlantic equivalent in capacity and efficiency. They employed the German integrated railroad system as a positive counterexample to the privately held railroad trusts in the United States that held back economic growth in their minds.

American observers cited these examples for their argument that German leaders—in spite of their reactionary reputation and in contrast to the inaction of their American peers—deliberately attempted to face the challenges of modernity with its opportunities. American observers credited the German Beamtentum, the corps of lifetime civil servants, for the successes of this most positive interpretation of the German Empire's policies. Combining expertise and incorruptible thoroughness, the German Beamten implemented an ambitious mandatory pension system and channeled the rapid growth of the Reich's cities.

A striking contrast between the distrust of the German Empire's political personnel and admiration for some of their policies determined American perceptions. The paradox between the Hohenzollerns' royal pretensions and their bureaucracy's concern for the welfare of its subjects confounded American observers. In characterizing the Wilhelmine Empire as an authoritarian welfare state, American observers already anticipated the contradiction Hermann Beck has summarized.[92] The fundamental ambivalence toward the German example explained why not a single American observer of this sample fundamentally questioned the United States' political system. Moreover, none recommended the adoption of German policies. American observers rather debated their possible adaption to American contexts with nuance and detail. Roberts, for instance, envisioned a centralized, corporatist railroad direction, instead of German state-owned railroads. In their pursuit of answers to the social challenges wrought by modernity, the German Empire did not serve as an ideal to emulate for American observers, but rather as a unique trove of possible solutions.

This American esteem for the Wilhelmine Reich surprises in light of the decaying relations between both states in the following years. Without any reservations, American contemporaries accepted the German Empire as a fellow pioneer in modernity—albeit in a statist vein. Its combined volatility and dynamism attracted American observers as a familiar dilemma. Dreiser concluded in early 1914 that its domestic dynamism offered the German Empire the chance to "become internally so powerful that it will almost stand irresistible," only to qualify, "if it can keep its pace without engaging in some vast, self-destroying conflict."[93] The transmogrification of Germans from peers to the defining enemy image between 1914 and 1917 highlighted how quickly deep cultural bonds could be cut. Roberts perspicaciously identified the German Empire's volatility beneath the veneer of economic growth and brittle displays of imperial splendor. Only he could not know that Americans were less insulated from German developments than he hoped for:

> The observer from another continent, whatever his angle of observation, may allow another generation or two to pile up results before trying to forge a sure judgment. The German cannot wait. He is deep in the battle of ideas and is forced to conclusion because he must choose a side and act. He cannot avoid the urgencies and possibly the terrors of his progress.[94]

Scott H Krause studied at Göttingen, UC Los Angeles, and Freiburg, before receiving his doctorate at University of North Carolina at Chapel Hill, where he teaches European history. Scott has received fellowships of the German Academic Exchange Service (DAAD), American Council on Germany (ACG), Central European History Society (CEHS), and the German Historical Institute, Washington, DC (GHI). Publications include "Neue Westpolitik: Remigrés' and Americans' Clandestine Campaign to Westernize the SPD in Cold War Berlin, 1948–1958," *Central European History* 48 (2015) and "Inventing the 'Outpost of Freedom': Transatlantic Narratives and Actors Crafting West Berlin's Postwar Political Culture," *Zeithistorische Forschungen* 11 (2014; with Stefanie Eisenhuth).

NOTES

1. Mark Twain, "The German Chicago," in *The Complete Essays of Mark Twain,* ed. Charles Neider (Garden City, NY, 1963), 87–98. For Clemens's visit to Berlin, see from his biographies Fred Kaplan, *The Singular Mark Twain: A Biography* (New York, 2003), 460–69; Andrew J Hoffman, *Inventing Mark Twain: The Lives of Samuel Langhorne Clemens* (London, 1997), 371–76.
2. For the classic argument, see Hans-Ulrich Wehler, *Das deutsche Kaiserreich, 1871–1918* (Göttingen, 1973). For the most recent variation of the argument, see Hans-Ulrich Wehler, *Deutsche Gesellschaftsgeschichte, III: Von der "Deutschen Doppelrevolution" bis zum Beginn des Ersten Weltkrieges. 1849–1914* (Munich, 2008), 1250–95.
3. Joachim Remak, "Another Germany, A Summing Up," in *Another Germany: A Reconsideration of the Imperial Era,* ed. Jack R Dukes and Joachim Remak (Boulder, CO, 1988), 207. For the critique of Wehler, see David Blackbourn and Geoff Eley, *The Peculiarities of German History* (Oxford, 1984).
4. Sebastian Conrad and Jürgen Osterhammel, eds, *Das Kaiserreich transnational: Deutschland in der Welt, 1871–1914* (Göttingen, 2004). For the thesis of globalization leaving its imprint on the Kaiserreich, see Sebastian Conrad, *Globalisierung und Nation im Deutschen Kaiserreich* (Munich, 2006), 7–25.
5. See Arjun Appadurai, *Modernity at Large: Cultural Dimensions of Globalization* (Minneapolis, MN, 1996); Dipesh Chikrabarty, *Provincializing Europe: Postcolonial Thought and Historical Difference* (Princeton, NJ, 2000).
6. See Detlev JK Peukert, *The Weimar Republic: The Crisis of Classical Modernity* (New York, 1993), xiv.
7. Ulrich Herbert, "Europe in High Modernity. Reflections on a Theory of the 20th Century," *Journal of Modern European History* 5, no. 1 (2007): 9, 21.
8. Charles Emmerson, *In Search of the World before the Great War* (New York, 2013); Florian Illies, *1913: The World before the Storm* (New York, 2013).
9. Christopher Clark, *The Sleepwalkers: How Europe Went to War in 1914* (New York, 2013), xxxi.

10. This chapter consciously concentrates on the prewar years to avoid pre-determined conclusions. Until now, literature on the American perception of Germany has focused on the American perception of Germany between 1914 and 1917 in search for explanations for the American entry into World War I, see Ragnhild Fiebig von Hase and Ursula Lehmkuhl, eds, *Enemy Images in American History* (Providence, RI, 1997); Jörg Nagler, "From Culture to Kultur: Changing American Perceptions of Imperial Germany, 1870–1914," in *Transatlantic Images and Perceptions,* ed. David E Barclay and Elisabeth Glaser-Schmidt (Cambridge, 1997), 131–54.

11. Twain, "German Chicago," 91–93.

12. Christof Mauch and Kiran Klaus Patel, "Modernities: Competition versus Convergence," in *The United States and Germany during the Twentieth Century: Competition and Convergence,* ed. Christof Mauch and Kiran Klaus Patel (Cambridge, 2010), 5.

13. Lewis L Gould, ed., *The Progressive Era* (Syracuse, NY, 1974); Michael E McGerr, *A Fierce Discontent: The Rise and Fall of the Progressive Movement in America, 1870–1920* (New York, 2003) offer an overview of agenda and composition of the progressive movement. For an introduction to American progressives' interest in European social policies, see Daniel T Rodgers, *Atlantic Crossings: Social Politics in a Progressive Age* (Cambridge, MA, 1998). Axel R Schäfer, *American Progressives and German Social Reform, 1875–1920: Social Ethics Moral Control and the Regulatory State in a Transatlantic Context* (Stuttgart, 2000) meticulously traces the transfer of ideas on municipal government from German policies to progressive arguments.

14. Renate von Bardeleben, "A Traveler at Forty," in *A Theodore Dreiser Encyclopedia,* ed. Keith Newlin (Westport, CT, 2003), 376–79.

15. EL Burlingame, "Letter to Elmer Roberts," 18 October 1910, Elmer Roberts Papers, Collection 2243, Box 1, Folder 7, University of North Carolina at Chapel Hill, Wilson Library, Southern Historical Collection.

16. The sources have been selected according to the following criteria: (I) the authors had to have been socialized in the United States, ensuring their connection with contemporary American domestic debates. (II) The authors had to draw from personal experience of the German Empire or one of its parts. (III) Their experiences were published in monographs. These have the advantage over newspaper or magazine articles in that they allow for open personal coloring. Yet in contrast to private correspondence, monographs had a larger contemporary reach being published immediately. (IV) The monographs had to be published contemporarily between 1890 and 1914, to exclude retroactive coloring of Imperial Germany through the experience of war.

17. For their respective biographies, see for Baker: John E Semonche, *Ray Stannard Baker: A Quest for Democracy in Modern America, 1870–1918* (Chapel Hill, NC, 1969); for Dreiser: Richard R Lingeman, *Theodore Dreiser: An American Journey, 1908–1945* (New York, 1990); for Howe: John Braeman, "Howe, Frederic Clemson," in *American National Biography. Vol. 11, Hofstadter-Jepson,* ed. John A

Garraty (Oxford, 1999); for Roberts: Noah Huffman, "Guide to the Elmer Roberts Papers, 1835–1937," *University Libraries of the University of North Carolina at Chapel Hill* (2007); for Collier: Richard G Albion, "Collier, Price Hiram," in *Dictionary of American Biography: Vol. 2, Brearly-Cushing,* ed. Allen Johnson (New York, 1958), 305–6.

18. This chapter derives from my 2010 MA thesis at the Albert-Ludwigs-Universität Freiburg, entitled: *Das späte Kaiserreich in den Augen amerikanischer Beobachter.* I am indebted to Willi Oberkrome for his encouragement from the earliest stages of the thesis on, his perspicacious suggestions, and his continuing support. In Chapel Hill, Konrad Jarausch helped me immensely in thinking about different conceptions of modernities on a broader scale. All errors and omissions remain my own.

19. Quotes have been selected through the principle of Tertium Comparationis, or the third of comparison, for a historical comparison, see Thomas Welskopp, "Stolpersteine auf dem Königsweg. Methodenkritische Anmerkungen zum internationalen Vergleich in der Gesellschaftsgeschichte," *Archiv für Sozialgeschichte* 35 (1995): 339–67; Heinz-Gerhard Haupt and Jürgen Kocka, "Historischer Vergleich: Methoden, Aufgaben, Probleme. Eine Einleitung," in *Geschichte und Vergleich: Ansätze und Ergebnisse international vergleichender Geschichtsschreibung,* ed. Heinz-Gerhard Haupt and Jürgen Kocka (Frankfurt am Main, 1996), 9–45.

20. Jürgen Kocka pioneered the opportunities and feasibility of German-American comparisons in Jürgen Kocka, *Angestellte zwischen Faschismus und Demokratie: Zur politischen Sozialgeschichte der Angestellten: USA, 1890–1940 im internationalen Vergleich* (Göttingen, 1977), 39–49.

21. Ray Stannard Baker, *Seen in Germany* (London, 1902), 31.

22. William Jennings Bryan, *The Old World and Its Ways: Describing a Tour around the World and Journeys through Europe* (Saint Louis, 1907), 541.

23. Price Collier, *Germany and the Germans from an American Point of View* (New York, 1913), 601–2.

24. Collier, *Germany and the Germans,* 121, 592. Collier referred to the "Schwarzwälder Dorfgeschichten" [Black Forest Village Stories] by Berthold Auerbach, *Schwarzwälder Dorfgeschichten* (Lahr, 1952). Hamburg shipping magnate Albert Ballin directed HAPAG, or Hamburg America Line. HAPAG came to signify German industrial prowess and naval ambition globally as the largest shipping line of the world, see Gerhard A Ritter, "The Kaiser and His Ship-Owner: Albert Ballin, the HAPAG Shipping Company, and the Relationship between Industry and Politics in Imperial Germany and the Early Weimar Republic," in *Business in the Age of Extremes: Essays in Modern German and Austrian Economic History,* ed. Hartmut Berghoff, Jürgen Kocka, and Dieter Ziegler (Cambridge, 2013), 15–39.

25. See Section 3.

26. Dreiser, *Traveler at Forty,* 428.

27. Baker, *Seen in Germany,* 29–31, 55.

28. Dreiser, *Traveler at Forty,* 428.

29. Collier, *Germany and the Germans,* 581–82.

30. Ibid., 164, 509, 593–94.

31. Wilhelm II's actual political power has been debated stridently among historians. For an overview of the debate, see Wolfgang J Mommsen, "Wilhelm II. als König von Preußen und deutscher Kaiser," in *Der Erste Weltkrieg. Anfang vom Ende des bürgerlichen Zeitalters,* ed. Wolfgang J Mommsen (Frankfurt am Main, 2004), 64–78. For the opposing positions of the debate, see John CG Röhl, "Der Königsmechanismus im Kaiserreich," in *Kaiser, Hof und Staat. Wilhelm II. und die deutsche Politik,* ed. John CG Röhl (Munich, 1987), 116–40, who claimed to have identified a decisive "King's mechanism" and Hans-Ulrich Wehler, *Deutsche Doppelrevolution,* 1000–1006, who has interpreted the emperor as actor within a polycracy.

32. Collier, *Germany and the Germans,* 365–66.

33. Frederic C Howe, *European Cities at Work* (New York, 1913), 4–5.

34. Elmer Roberts, *Monarchical Socialism in Germany* (New York, 1913), 116.

35. Frederic C Howe, *Socialized Germany* (New York, 1915), 31. Howe insisted that he completed the manuscript before World War I's outbreak.

36. Collier, *Germany and the Germans,* 81.

37. Howe, *Socialized Germany,* 8.

38. Collier, *Germany and the Germans,* 62, 193.

39. Howe, *Socialized Germany,* 21.

40. Peter Fritzsche has highlighted the press importance for coping in rapidly expanding urban environments, see Peter Fritzsche, *Reading Berlin 1900* (Cambridge, MA, 1996).

41. For the clout of the press in the Wilhelmine Era and its strained relationship to the monarchy, see Martin Kohlrausch, *Der Monarch im Skandal. Die Logik der Massenmedien und die Transformation der wilhelminischen Monarchie* (Berlin, 2005), 45–83.

42. Roberts, *Monarchical Socialism, 117.*

43. Ibid., 120.

44. Baker, *Seen in Germany,* 129–30.

45. Collier, *Germany and the Germans,* 191–92.

46. Roberts, *Monarchical Socialism,* 106.

47. Baker, *Seen in Germany,* 118–19.

48. Ibid., 121–22.

49. Collier, *Germany and the Germans,* 208–9.

50. Ibid., 367–68.

51. Ibid., 208.

52. Bryan, *The Old World and Its Ways,* 541.

53. For the development of German waterways in the nineteenth century as an explicitly modern infrastructure project and resistance to it, see David Blackbourn, *The Conquest of Nature: Water, Landscape, and the Making of Modern Germany* (London, 2006), 113–78; Wolfgang König, *Wilhelm II. und die Moderne: Der Kaiser und die technisch- industrielle Welt* (Paderborn, 2007), 84–97.

54. Dreiser, *Traveler at Forty,* 468.

55. Ibid., 469–73.

56. For the organization of the German railways, see Lothar Gall, "Eisenbahn in Deutschland: Von den Anfängen bis zum Ersten Weltkrieg," in *Die Eisenbahn in Deutschland. Von den Anfängen bis zur Gegenwart,* ed. Lothar Gall and Manfred Pohl (Munich, 1999), 55–70. For Roberts's understanding of it, see Roberts, *Monarchical Socialism,* 18–21.

57. Ibid., 32.

58. For the intensity of connections between both economies, see Niels P Petersson, "Das Kaiserreich in den Prozessen ökonomischer Globalisierung," in *Das Kaiserreich transnational. Deutschland in der Welt 1871–1914,* ed. Sebatian Conrad and Jürgen Osterhammel (Göttingen, 2004), 49–68; Volker Berghahn, "Deutsche Industrie und amerikanische Geschäftswelt, 1900–1914," in *Das deutsche Kaiserreich in der Kontroverse,* ed. Sven Oliver Müller and Cornelius Torp (Göttingen, 2009), 441–454. For the transnational dimension of German economic policy, see Cornelius Torp, *Die Herausforderung der Globalisierung. Wirtschaft und Politik in Deutschland 1860–1914* (Göttingen, 2005).

59. Baker, *Seen in Germany,* 201–4.

60. Ibid., 53.

61. Roberts, *Monarchical Socialism,* 17.

62. Baker, *Seen in Germany,* 161, 199–200, 202, 207.

63. Roberts, *Monarchical Socialism,* 45.

64. Ibid., 59, 66–69, 71–72.

65. Collier, *Germany and the Germans,* 368–70.

66. Roberts, *Monarchical Socialism,* 12, 64, 75.

67. See Howe, *European Cities,* 3. For Howe's motivation, see Stanley P Caine, "Origins of Progressivism," in *The Progressive Era,* ed. Lewis Gould (Syracuse, NY, 1974), 17.

68. Dreiser, *Traveler at Forty,* 466.

69. Howe, *European Cities,* 22–23, 45–46. Research has shown that Berlin's expansion policies had not exclusively the well-being of in inhabitants in mind, see Michael Erbe, "Berlin im Kaiserreich (1871–1918)," in *Geschichte Berlins: Von der Märzrevolution bis zur Gegenwart, 3rd ed.,* ed. Wolfgang Ribbe (Berlin, 2002), 732–44.

70. Howe, *European Cities,* 7.

71. Booker T Washington, *The Man Farthest Down. The Struggle of European Toilers* (Garden City, NY, 1912), 218.

72. Dreiser, *Traveler at Forty,* 467–68.

73. Albert Shaw, *Municipal Government in Continental Europe* (New York, 1897), 290–91.

74. Howe, *European Cities,* 4.

75. Max Weber, "Wissenschaft als Beruf 1917/1919–Politik als Beruf, 1919," in *Gesamtausgabe, vol. 1/17,* ed. Wolfgang J Mommsen and Horst Baier (Tübingen, 1992), 215. For the clout of urban political machines, see Nell Irvin Painter, *Standing at Armageddon: The United States, 1877–1919* (New York, 2008), 8.

76. Baker, *Seen in Germany,* 62.
77. For an overview of the usage of the term *militarism* in its transatlantic context, see Jörn Leonhard, *Bellizismus und Nation: Kriegsdeutung und Nationsbestimmung in Europa und den Vereinigten Staaten 1750–1914* (Munich, 2008).
78. Dreiser, *Traveler at Forty,* 443.
79. Baker, *Seen in Germany,* 92.
80. Collier, *Germany and the Germans,* 459.
81. Ibid.
82. Collier's argument closely echoed the contemporary German *Kulturkritik,* whose cultural skepticism Gerhard A Ritter identified as a facet of cultural modernity, see August Nitschke, Detlev JK Peukert, and Rüdiger vom Bruch, *Jahrhundertwende. Der Aufbruch in die Moderne 1880–1930* (Reinbek, 1990), 309.
83. Collier, *Germany and the Germans,* 419–20.
84. Washington, *The Man Farthest Down,* 383–84.
85. Earl Dean Howard, *The Cause and Extent of the Recent Industrial Progress of Germany* (Boston, 1907), 96, 100.
86. Baker, *Seen in Germany,* 161–64, 171, 190, 193. For the development of big science in Germany, see Gerhard A Ritter, *Großforschung und Staat in Deutschland: Ein historischer Überblick* (Munich, 1992). For the history of the PTR, see David Cahan, *An Institute for an Empire. The Physikalisch-Technische Reichsanstalt, 1871–1918* (Cambridge, 1989).
87. See Konrad Jarausch, *Out of Ashes: A New History of Europe in the 20th Century* (Princeton, NJ, 2015).
88. Baker, *Seen in Germany,* 174–76.
89. For Samuel Clemens's first visit to the German Empire, see Klaus-Jürgen Popp, ed., *Mark Twain in Deutschland* (Munich, 1977).
90. Howe, *European Cities,* 7.
91. Howe, *Socialized Germany,* 39.
92. Hermann Beck, *The Origins of the Authoritarian Welfare State in Prussia: Conservatives, Bureaucracy, and the Social Question, 1815–1870* (Ann Arbor, MI, 1995).
93. Dreiser, *Traveler at Forty,* 430.
94. Roberts, *Monarchical Socialism,* 133–34.

SELECTED BIBLIOGRAPHY

Baker, Ray Stannard. *Seen in Germany.* London, 1902.
Bryan, William Jennings. *The Old World and Its Ways: Describing a Tour around the World and Journeys through Europe.* Saint Louis, 1907.
Clark, Christopher. *The Sleepwalkers: How Europe Went to War in 1914.* New York, 2013.
Collier, Price. *Germany and the Germans from an American Point of View.* New York, 1913.
Conrad, Sebastian. *Globalisierung und Nation im Deutschen Kaiserreich.* Munich, 2006.

Dreiser, Theodore. *A Traveler at Forty*. New York, 1914.

Elmer Roberts Papers, University of North Carolina at Chapel Hill, Wilson Library, Southern Historical Collection.

Fritzsche, Peter. *Reading Berlin 1900*. Cambridge, MA, 1996.

Herbert, Ulrich. "Europe in High Modernity. Reflections on a Theory of the 20th Century." *Journal of Modern European History* 5, no. 1 (2007): 5–20.

Howard, Earl Dean. *The Cause and Extent of the Recent Industrial Progress of Germany*. Boston, 1907.

Howe, Frederic C. *European Cities at Work*. New York, 1913.

——. *Socialized Germany*. New York, 1915.

Mauch, Christof, and Kiran Klaus Patel, eds. *The United States and Germany during the Twentieth Century: Competition and Convergence*. Cambridge, 2010.

Peukert, Detlev JK. *The Weimar Republic: The Crisis of Classical Modernity*. New York, 1993.

Roberts, Elmer. *Monarchical Socialism in Germany*. New York, 1913.

Rodgers, Daniel T. *Atlantic Crossings: Social Politics in a Progressive Age*. Cambridge, MA, 1998.

Shaw, Albert. *Municipal Government in Continental Europe*. New York, 1897.

Twain, Mark. "The German Chicago." In *The Complete Essays of Mark Twain*, edited by Charles Neider, 87–98. Garden City, NY, 1963.

Washington, Booker T. *The Man Farthest Down. The Struggle of European Toilers*. Garden City, NY, 1912.

Chapter 2

The Dual Training System
The Southwest's Contributions to German Economic Development

Hal Hansen

One of the most pronounced features of Germany's social-economic develop-ment, one distinguishing it from that of almost all other advanced capitalist societies, derives from the prominence of artisans and their institutional lega-cies. The crafts (*Handwerk*) survive in Germany as a series of legally defined occupations (*Berufe*) that operate under a craft code (*Gewerbeordnung*) that is distinct from the laws regulating other firms, particularly industrial ones. Whereas a discrete class of handicraft producers disappeared in the face of industrial competition in most other places, the German crafts were reorga-nized and revitalized over the last half of the nineteenth century, a process in which the German Southwest played a formative role. Furthermore, because of the success of the Southwestern system of schools and certification prac-tices that grew up to supplement and regulate apprenticeship training, they not only spread to Prussia and the rest of the empire, they eventually dif-fused to the industrial and service sectors of the economy as well.

Unfortunately, historiographic portrayals of backward late nineteenth-and early twentieth-century artisans leave us no way to explain the exis-tence of a prosperous *Mittelstand* (small and medium-sized companies) today, or of an apprenticeship-based education and training system that has proven itself as modern and effective as any in the world.[1] It is true that German artisans inherited a system of corporate organization that, despite its degradation, vagaries, and internal diversity, served to preserve a distinctive, collectively reproduced identity. Yet, while conventional wisdom

has identified modern handicraft organization with premodern guild traditions and practices, this view too glibly passes over nineteenth-century organizational change. Moreover, Germany's modern training system was not
the product of chance, cartelization, or—as some of its academic supporters
now claim—the educational ideas of Woldemar Pache or Georg Kerschen-
steiner.[2] Rather, it, and the restructuring of *Handwerk* more generally, were
products of concerted economic and social policies: bootstrapping efforts
to render small-shop craft and cottage producers competitive at market,
thereby relieving Southwestern states of threats to their political stability
and pressures to provide public relief to economically distressed areas.[3]

Modern vocational schools, which gradually transformed *Handwerk* and
its training practices, trace their origins to these regions. Geographically isolated from the most dynamic, large urban areas driving nineteenth-century
German industrialization—such as Berlin, Hamburg, and the heavy-industry
districts of the Ruhr—the small-scale, dispersed urban settlements of Baden
and Württemberg lacked the natural exchanges of information that made
large cities such dynamic centers of learning, economic growth, wealth, and
culture.[4] They found it difficult to keep up with emergent innovations in production strategies and design, technology, tools, materials, market demand,
business practice, marketing, credit, and the law. Further, settlement disper-
sion and the capital scarcity characteristic of the small- and medium-sized
craft and cottage industry that dominated these areas made keeping abreast
of these developments more difficult still. They lacked both the natural commercial, social, and cultural links that made metropolitan areas so vibrant
and the capital that allowed large, capital-intense autarkic firms in areas of
industrial urbanization to gather information on their own.[5]

To these social-geographic drawbacks, the Southwestern states
responded with a system of collectively organized and funded institutions,
above all, industrial, trades, and technical continuation schools (*Fortbildungs-
schulen*), institutional centerpieces of the Southwest's "trades promotion policies." The Southwest's innovative trades and industrial continuation schools
embraced several functions at once. In addition to vocational instruction,
they provided instruction in reading, arithmetic, drawing, science, and some
cultural subjects as well. Further, they functioned as clearinghouses for best
practice in the trades for producers in the areas in which they were established, building technical collections of products from abroad, assembling
the latest machines and materials in model workshops, dispensing technical and commercial advice, and offering workshops, lectures, and demonstrations in the evenings for local employers and workers alike. Instructors
were also required to report regularly to state trade ministries on local
developments and needs. A raft of other self-help institutions emerged to

complement the work of the schools: industrial associations, central trades offices, savings banks, marketing cooperatives, technical *Hochschulen,* and other technically oriented higher schools.[6]

Designed to stimulate job growth, these initiatives were buttressed by other collective goods and services on which craft shops depended but could not individually supply for themselves: research and development; mechanisms for the collection and diffusion of the latest product designs, production methods, and business practices; sources of guidance and instruction on technological, financial, and legal matters; viable forms of collective representation in their interactions with the state; and so on. If they hoped to countenance market competition, craft firms not only had to improve their products and manufacturing methods, they also had to master marketing, credit, industrial relations, business planning, contracts, safety codes, taxes, and the like. Because these imperatives were new and continually changing, traditional cycles of apprenticeship and informal reproduction in the workplace no longer sufficed.

Thus, the Southwestern states built institutions designed to compensate small producers in these regions for the economic disadvantages of geographic isolation, low agglomeration densities, and small shop development. In doing so, they addressed problems faced by skill-using, small-shop craft producers everywhere. However, because Germany's industrial social geography varied widely, trades promotion policies of this type proved difficult to adopt in other regions, especially those dominated by big-city and large-firm development, where the legal and policy interests of the dominant producers were quite different from those in the Southwest.[7] This is why the continuing presence of the craft sector, operating under a legal code separate from industry's, proved such an important part of the continued strength of *Mittelstand* production in Germany. Its distinct regulatory law, *Gewerberecht,* insulated craft producers from a legal landscape designed by and for large industrial firms, one in which collective goods, on which craft firms depend, were far less important. Moreover, it permitted the gradual development of an education and training system in the craft sector that diffused to industry, agriculture, and services once it had matured.

THE HANDICRAFT LAW OF 1897 AND SOUTHWESTERN REVISIONS

Although *Sonderweg* interpretations of modern German development have generally lost traction,[8] they persist when it comes to explaining the *Gewerbeordnung* (GO) of 1897, cornerstone of modern German craft law, training, and *Handwerk* itself.[9] This legislation was actually an amendment (*Novelle*) to the North German Union GO of 1869 that eliminated all craft licensing within the Prussian-led federation. Extended to the empire in 1871 during unification, it was widely believed to need modification by the 1890s, above all because of its negative effects on craft organization and apprenticeship training. Often mistakenly called the "Handicraft Protection Law," the final bill created an elaborate system of formalized craft training, a mandatory certification process for both journeymen and masters, and an associational framework to administer and finance both. Contrary to standard accounts, it was carefully weighed and heavily bargained, producing a progressive self-help and training initiative influenced at every turn by Southwestern ideas and interests.

Historians of Germany still generally construe compulsory guilds and associations as backward-looking, tradition-bound organizational forms, or they consider these as much ado about nothing.[10] However, many German liberals had, by the 1880s, come to see classical liberal doctrine as passé. Contemporary monographs make clear that obligatory associations faced few a priori objections from policy makers or scholars in the late nineteenth century.[11] A liberal order required, they believed, both liberty and order. Moreover, policy makers understood that the organizational design of an association fundamentally shaped its character, goals, and viability, and that slight variations in rules often made the difference between robust, effective organizations and frail, ineffectual ones.

Such details were clearly the focus of representatives from Baden and Württemberg, Dr. Karl Schenkel and Karl von Schicker, respectively, within the committee system of the Federal Council (Bundesrat). The bill had begun as a cooperative project of Karl Heinrich von Boetticher, State Secretary of the Imperial Interior Ministry, and Hans Hermann Freiherr von Berlepsch, Prussian Minister of Trade and Industry. It ended as the private work of von Berlepsch, almost certainly due to his disagreements with von Boetticher over his desire to rescue Prussia's marginal, mostly regressive *Innungen,* or voluntary craft guilds.[12] Thus, Schenkel and Schicker worked closely with Prussian Trade Ministry officials, although it was imperial legislation, to alter Berlepsch's draft. This took place within a joint Bundesrat workgroup consisting of members—including allies from Hesse and Bavaria—of the committees for Commerce and Transportation and for Judicial Affairs.[13]

However much of Prussia's *Innungen* suffered from high organizational costs and modest resources, enhancing their organizational capacity through legal prophylactics hardly assured their transformation into progressive self-help organizations dedicated to improving production and business methods or ensuring rigorous training. Indeed, Southwestern officials feared the initial proposals might well intensify these groups' demands for anticompetitive protections. They insisted that organizational capacity was a necessary but insufficient condition for self-help and self-government. Effectiveness depended upon how public law corporations were constituted, they maintained, as well as the broader institutional setting in which they existed.[14]

Consequently, Schenkel and Schicker pursued two successful strategies in revising the Handicraft Bill. First, they offered a federal solution, one allowing the various German states to conserve and strengthen those craft organizations that predominated in their own territories instead of imposing a one-size-fits-all policy they feared would undermine their own industrial associations (*Gewerbevereine*). These were progressive, market-oriented voluntary groups dominated by larger craft employers. Second, they worked to place newly created craft chambers at the center of the legislation to mediate among the resulting regional diversity of organizational forms. This, in effect, subordinated *Innungen,* few of which existed in the Southwest but were abundant in Prussia, to the progressively structured craft chambers, which the legislation made responsible for regulating and administering training and certification within the crafts.[15] Throughout the negotiations, Schenkel and Schicker used "Prussian wishes" as the formal basis for discussions, but kept them secondary to these fundamental organizational and policy principles.[16]

Thus, in addition to making journeyman training and certification a prerequisite for employment in the crafts, the GO of 1897 made membership in the craft chambers obligatory for all practicing artisans. From the perspective of the framers, this compulsion had nothing to do with "illiberal" protections. Rather, it was a pragmatic response to the limitations of voluntarism in organizing and enforcing collective standards, regulations, self-help organizations, and other forms of social solidity. Since the mid 1980s, several social scientists have emphasized that public law corporations are more than monopolies; these also possess a "self governing" or "collective action" face.[17] In their preoccupation with the continuities of inherited institutional forms, historians of Germany have paid insufficient attention to transformative changes within them, and of the role of federalism in shaping these.

THE DIFFUSION OF VOCATIONAL SCHOOLS
AND TRADES PROMOTION

At the time of its passage, public commentators and scholars broadly saw the 1897 legislation as another in a long line of revisions to the GO. Its significance as the legal cornerstone of modern *Handwerk* and the German training system only became apparent in retrospect. To talk of a dual system of workplace training and school-based supplementary education in 1897 is to ignore the fact that large parts of the empire, especially Prussia, lacked the requisite complement of schools. Moreover, most continuation schools in existence were remedial in intent and cultural in orientation. Moonlighting common school teachers typically staffed them. Wilhelm Stieda, an influential political economist, predicted that the Handicraft Bill would have little effect since it failed to provide for an active trades promotion policy of the sort that Baden had developed.[18]

Stieda's prophecy was perceptive but wrong. For as a result of their collaboration with Southwesterners within the Federal Council, prominent officials within the Prussian Trade Ministry began to take an interest in Southwestern trades promotion practices and their effects. Indeed, newly appointed Prussian Trade Minister Ludwig Brefeld's speech introducing the 1897 Handicraft Bill before the Imperial Diet (Reichstag) implied that this would be the ministry's goal:

> Southwestern Germany saw to it that no handicraft controversy existed there. The administrations [of those states] have taken care of their artisans to a greater extent than has been the case [in Prussia]. In fact, it is not to be denied—I am sorry to have to admit—it would have been very desirable if the Prussian state had done something more for the handicrafts; and I hope that in the future that will happen.[19]

The archival record richly confirms the Southwestern roots of the Prussian trade ministry's subsequent activities. Two elements of Southwestern practice in particular caught the attention of these officials: the extensive system of lower trades and industrial continuation schools; and the establishment of central trades offices to oversee and coordinate trades promotion activities, particularly those aimed at handicraft uplift.

Consequently, between 1885 and 1904, the number of state-subsidized trades continuation and special trades schools in Prussia grew from 715 to 2,065. Over the same period, state subsidies to these schools grew from 0.9 to 7.4 million marks.[20] Attendance jumped from 83,772 to 175,100 students between 1899 and 1904, just as Prussian trade ministry officials were explicitly embracing Southwestern practice.[21] Moreover, Prussian officials began a broad array of educational initiatives designed to increase the exchange of economically fungible information, knowledge, practices, and skills: exhibits of materials, small electric motors, machines, and tools whose diffusion promised to benefit the handicrafts; regional trades offices supplying practical information on materials use, power tools, innovative work methods, new technologies, and the like; master courses, public lectures, roving exhibitions, and other opportunities for further trades education and training; public exhibitions to display and promote the work of apprentices; and other institutions designed to formulate, administer, and oversee trades promotion. Prussian efforts explicitly targeted the handicrafts in an effort to give them as many of the advantages enjoyed by industry as possible.[22]

The passage of the Handicraft Code of 1897 had two unforeseen but critical repercussions for German training. First, by granting craft employers exclusive control over publicly certified training and licensing, it prevented Germany's emergent unions from pursuing a trade union strategy based on the monopolization of skills.[23] Because organized labor lacked the capacity to control access to skilled work, it embraced an industrial organizational strategy, one that led to large encompassing unions. By the 1920s, these had become leading advocates of extending the craft training and certification system to the industrial sector, for they were tired of seeing qualified craft journeymen move into skilled industrial jobs. These were jobs they naturally sought to reserve for their own recruits in industry.[24]

Second, craft control of skill certification led to conflict between skill-intensive industrial firms, especially in the metalworking and machine-building sectors, and *Handwerk* in the interwar years. The former had difficulty recruiting first-rate apprentices for its training programs, though by all accounts, the quality of these was superior to anything craft firms offered. Ambitious apprentices preferred craft to better industrial training because publically recognized licensing permitted them access to skilled work throughout Germany in either sector. The private certificates industrial firms issued depended solely upon firm reputation. This diminished their portability and, hence, value.[25]

Consequently, Germany's skill-using industrial employers and its industrial unions had a mutual interest in promoting skill formation and certification. They worked hard throughout the Weimar years to transfer the craft system of training regulation and certification to industry.[26] However, this came to pass only upon the Nazis' rise to power in the 1930s, when it diffused on to agriculture and services as well. Two factors proved essential to this breakthrough. Most pressing was an emergent shortage of skilled labor projected to constrain economic growth as it intensified, a product of low birthrates from 1914 through the depression. It became especially palpable in metalworking and machine building as Germany's military buildup began to take hold. Also crucial was the capacity of the Nazis to weaken labor organizations to the point where they could have little say in training policy—a point that persuaded large, Ruhr-based industrial employers to retreat from their historic opposition to Weimar era industrial training schemes.[27] Only in 1969 was labor given legal parity within the training system, finally realizing the plans of Weimar era officials, many of whom were holdovers from the Prussian Trade Ministry in the prewar years.[28]

These elaborate institutional developments kept the education, training, and socialization of the average German youth where it had always been: in the workplace. It accomplished this by formalizing and systematizing what had become an increasingly inappropriate method of informal, unregulated learning. In effect, it transformed a practice—apprenticeship—whose primary function had been to facilitate the productive employment of juvenile labor into a dedicated training relationship.[29] It did so by imposing— through parapublic bodies—public duties and responsibilities on private training firms, and uplifting the crafts through trades promotion policies, especially the establishment of multifunctional industrial, trades, and technical schools. By regulating and documenting learning, certification proved indispensable to this process.[30] Moreover, the GO of 1897 cleared up much of the organizational turmoil in *Handwerk* that had undercut other forms of self-help and self-governance in the crafts.

THE OCCUPATION, SOCIAL THEORY, AND HISTORICAL SELF UNDERSTANDING

Historical memory and self-understanding are key contributors to policy-making. It is hard to imagine a country in which they have been more central to it than Germany since 1945. Moreover, just as two world wars, national socialism, and the Holocaust have dominated German self-understanding and policy for half a century, Germany's current economic and political vigor, advances in social science, and the events of 1989 and their repercussions have begun reshaping them anew. This book reflects that evolution.

Different Germans, Many Germanies?, however, is also a product of change on the other side of the Atlantic. The postwar self-assurance and self-understanding of Americans, which informed postwar historiography of Germany, have evolved over the intervening decades as well. Shifting experience and perspective have increasingly raised questions about earlier American per-ceptions of some German institutions and traditions, particularly "salvage-able" ones. *Handwerk* and the apprenticeship system, however, have always been "tough sells" to Americans. Like the champions of the *Sonderweg* approach, most of whom studied or taught for periods in the United States, Americans have typically considered them backward-looking, illiberal, and protectionist.

This was certainly the case during the US administration of its zone during the Occupation of Germany, when American officials did their best to uproot both. Interestingly, since the American zone consisted principally of Hesse, Bavaria, and northern portions of present-day Baden-Württemberg, these initiatives affected precisely those regions in which *Handwerk,* and the training system it built, were most advanced, organized, and entrenched. Two issues especially disturbed US authorities: the power of craft chambers to regulate craft entry through craft licensing and compulsory membership; and the parapublic character of these chambers, which from an American point of view improperly blurred the boundaries between the public and private spheres.[31] Both contravened the American idea of freedom.

Consequently, in 1946, over the strenuous objections of the assorted German organizations consulted, occupation authorities transferred super-vision of the journeyman and master exams from the craft chambers to the state, a task for which it possessed no particular competence. In 1947, they further undermined the *Handwerk* system of self-governance by doing away with all forms of compulsory associational membership. They also made it illegal for craft organizations to exercise any parapublic functions—such as the imposition of mandatory fees to finance *Handwerk*'s many self-help activities—and removed their status as public law corporations. Finally, in 1948, unable to win the cooperation of any of the major German stake-holders, American authorities simply decreed an end to all occupational licensing in the crafts, and put a simple system of registration by postcard in its place. They took these actions in part, of course, because they did not understand the rationale behind the development of these institutional structures or how they functioned.[32] American practice led them to suppose the market the best regulator of qualifications.[33] Besides, they found such practices deeply undemocratic.

Predictably, once they were free to do so, Germans wasted no time in rebuilding these institutions, beginning in 1953.[34] Their reasons were fundamentally those that had informed the development of the system in the first place: the dependence of small and medium-sized firms on the collective goods—like skills, information, and self-help institutions—coop-eratively produced and financed through collective action. Naturally, these institutions have continued to evolve. Germans undertook a major revision of this system in 1969 and have continued to tweak it regularly since.[35]

What both *Sonderweg* scholars and American occupation authorities generally failed to see was how these corporatist practices served to enhance civil society, rather than concentrate power within the state. Industrial, handicraft, and agricultural chambers minimized the necessity for the elaborate, hierarchically organized bureaucratic controls that developed in France. Heinrich von Treitschke pointedly observed that while the French had invented the word sovereignty, they never learned to acknowledge the notion of self-government.[36] Before him, Lorenz von Stein had argued that in contrast to "pure democracy"—in which the nation disappears into a pond of unconnected atoms—self-government is properly grounded in "organized division." Reflecting the differences of society's various stakeholders [and the social-geographical diversity of the country], "industrial, trade and community associations develop ... through which a comprehensive representation of all significant interests are fashioned."[37] This corporative conceptualization of self-government became a fundament of the German notion of public administration.[38]

Still, it is the compulsory character of these organizations that most disturbs classic liberals. Three considerations derived from hard-won experience, however, convinced the drafters of the GO of 1897 that compulsion made sense. First, legal coercion reduced the costs of organization and extended associational coverage far beyond what voluntary organizations had ever achieved. Free associations were nearly impossible for small producers to organize and sustain.[39] They possessed limited resources. Their needs and interests diverged by region, trade, and income. The cost of organizing large numbers of heterogeneous actors was high. The average maintenance expense of an industrial chamber in the 1890s ran between seven and eight thousand marks a year.[40] Given the relatively meager return small producers could expect from their organizational investments, combined with the odds against success, incentives to organize voluntarily were paltry, so most marginal artisans declined to get involved.

Second, compulsion enabled the resulting bodies to enforce collective rules, undertake joint activities, and to distribute more fairly the burdens of both. Without it, self-government was impractical. Voluntary organizations proved congenitally constrained by free riders—people who profited from collective goods to which they did not contribute—and the practice and threat of defection since their members were free to leave organizations with which they disagreed. Consequently, voluntary associations were unable to discipline members who broke rank or refused to share in the costs of producing collective goods, classic "collective action" problems that

Mancur Olson famously detailed decades ago.[41] Experience had shown that meaningful self-governance of the kind necessary to regulate systematic apprenticeship training, administer demanding certification programs, and fund collectively financed trades promotion policies simply would not work on a voluntary basis.

Third, where policing was weak or ineffective and rule breaking prevalent, economic incentives built pressure on rivals to do likewise. Thus, compulsion further facilitated the implementation of collective responsibilities and rules by encouraging mutual monitoring and policing. In turn, collective enforcement abated free riding and other incentives to cheat by, increasing the likelihood of detection. It also tended to remove the unscrupulous and their competitive advantage, because their license to produce could be suspended or withdrawn.[42] Finally, where suitably organized, compulsory associations offered the additional advantage of exposing small employers with limited horizons—a group that had proven extremely resistant to voluntary organizations—to new ideas, procedures, and techniques by pushing them into contact with groups with which they would not otherwise have interacted. In this way, marginal employers could learn from their larger and more progressive counterparts.[43]

The force of these ideas is evident in the continued vitality of *Handwerk* as captured in a few figures. In 2010, there were just under a million craft firms, half of which had fewer than five employees and 97 percent fewer than twenty. They employed 4.75 million people or 11.8 percent of the German workforce, nearly half of whom worked in firms with between five and twenty employees. Moreover, craft firms engaged 462,000 apprentices or 29.3 percent of all dual system trainees.[44] The dynamism and general health of this sector, and that of the German *Mittelstand* more broadly, is unfathomable without the institutional framework within which they function, the origins of which track back to the late nineteenth century and to the German Southwest.

CONCLUDING REMARKS

Alone, the vigor of the crafts justifies having salvaged *Handwerk,* along with the institutions and practices buttressing it, from the dustbin of history. This, Germans have done at least twice: first, in the late 1890s and, again, in the early 1950s. Moreover, the reverberations of these actions extend far beyond the crafts. *Handwerk* institutions underlay an education and training system that diffused to industry, agriculture, and services, gradually evolving into a central component of Germany's educational system. Further, the workforce skills thus generated reinforced Germany's historic manufacturing strategy of producing diversified, high-quality goods, cornerstone of the "German economic model." Furthermore, the institutionalization of work certification within the crafts in the 1890s precluded unions from pursuing craft-based labor relation strategies in the crucial decades of the early twentieth century, pushing them instead toward industrial organizational strategies and their political alliance with the Social Democratic Party. In short, no account of modern German economic, social, or political history can dispense with the seminal contributions of artisans and their institutions.

The political-economic development of the German Southwest, particularly Baden and Württemberg, is of historiographic interest for several reasons. It underscores the variety of German social geography and demonstrates the capacity of the non-Prussian periphery in the 1890s to shape institutional development within the politically dominate Prussian core and, in turn, the empire as a whole. Further, the Southwest's bootstrapping trades promotion policies provide an important counterpoint to a large historiographic literature characterizing *Handwerk* institutions of the German Kaiserreich as backward-looking, protectionist, and rent-seeking.[45] However, thanks to the craft uplift practices of the Southwest, they were transformed into an original response to the needs of the small and medium-sized producers to mounting large-firm competition, institutional developments that help to explain the number and vitality of *Mittelstand* firms there today. Finally, because of the central role of the state and collective action in the construction of this social-economic order, Southwestern experience cautions one against the embrace of a facile economic liberalism that disparages the capacity of government and collective institutions to contribute to economic growth and social welfare.

I thank the Berlin Program, the Social Science Research Council, the Woodrow Wilson and Spencer foundations, Harvard's Center for European Studies, and the National Endowment for the Humanities for their support of parts of this research, and Edmund Clingen and David Bills for helpful critiques of this essay.

Hal Hansen has taught at Suffolk University, the University of Massachusetts Boston, and the Kobe University of Commerce in Japan. He is no longer teaching, but retains an active interest in comparative economic, political, and educational history.

NOTES

1. For instance, Hans Rosenberg, "Political and Social Consequences of the Great Depression of 1873–96 in Central Europe," *Economic History Review* 13, no. 1/2 (1943): 58–73; Hans Rosenberg, *Grosse Depression und Bismarckzeit. Wirtschaftsablauf, Gesellschaft und Politik in Mitteleuropa* (Berlin, 1967); Hans-Ulrich Wehler, *Das Deutsche Kaiserreich, 1871–1918* (Göttingen, 1973), especially 48–59; Heinrich August Winkler, *Mittelstand, Demokratie und Nationalsozialismus. Die politische Entwicklung von Handwerk und Kleinhandel in der Weimarer Republik* (Cologne, 1972); and Shulamit Volkov, *The Rise of Popular Antimodernism in Germany: The Urban Master Artisans, 1873–1896* (Princeton, NJ, 1978). For a brief summary and contextualization of some of this literature, see Charles S Maier, *The Unmasterable Past: History, Holocaust, and German National Identity* (Cambridge MA, 1988), 100–15; Helga Grebing, *Der deutsche Sonderweg in Europa 1806–1945: Eine Kritik* (Stuttgart, 1986); and Oded Heilbronner, "From Antisemitic Peripheries to Antisemitic Centres: The Place of Antisemitism in Modern German History," *Journal of Contemporary History* 35, no. 4 (2000): 559–76.
2. See Wolf-Dietrich Greinert, *The "German System" of Vocational Education: History, Organization, Prospects* (Baden-Baden, 1994), 501.
3. Hal Hansen, "Rethinking the Role of Artisans in Modern German Development," *Central European History* 42, no. 1 (2009): 33–64.
4. Hal Hansen, "Caps and Gowns: Historical Reflections on the Institutions That Shaped Learning for and at Work in Germany and the United States, 1800–1941" (PhD thesis, University of Wisconsin–Madison, 1997), 124–79; Alfred Marshall, *Principles of Economics* (New York, 1890), chapter 10.
5. Gary Herrigel, *Industrial Constructions: The Sources of German Industrial Power* (New York, 1996), 33–71; Hansen, "Caps and Gowns," 169–79.
6. Hansen, "Rethinking," 56–62; Frank Haverkamp, *Staatliche Gewerbeförderung im Grossherzogtum Baden: Unter besonderer Berücksichtigung der Entwicklung des gewerblichen Bildungswesens im 19. Jahrhundert* (Freiburg [Breisgau], 1979).
7. In the United States, large, national mass-production firms reshaped the legal-institutional landscape in ways that made it difficult for smaller craft firms to prosper. Michael J Piore and Charles F Sabel, *The Second Industrial Divide: Possibilities for Prosperity* (New York, 1984), 19–49.
8. *Sonderweg* critics have argued: (1) that while old German elites dominated political power at the national level, the bourgeoisie controlled social, economic, and cultural life; (2) that the aristocracy continued to play a more prominent role in nineteenth-century England and France than in Germany; and (3) there was no standard course of political development in Europe against which Germany could be singled out as having lagged. David Blackbourn and Geoff Eley, *The Peculiarities of German History: Bourgeois Society and Politics in Nineteenth-Century Germany* (New York, 1984).

9. See Matthias Kreysing, "Berufsausbildung in Deutschland und den USA—Institutionalisierung des dualen Berufsbildungssystems in vergleichender Perspektive" (PhD thesis, University of Göttingen, 2003), 296; Kathleen Thelen, *How Institutions Evolve: The Political Economy of Skills in Germany, Britain, the United States, and Japan* (New York, 2004), 43*ff.*

10. An example of the former is Hans-Peter Ullmann, *Interessenverbände in Deutschland* (Frankfurt am Main, 1988), 43. An instance of the latter is David Blackbourn, *The Long Nineteenth Century: A History of Germany, 1780–1918* (New York, 1998), 348–49.

11. Thilo Hampke, *Handwerker- oder Gewerbekammern? Ein Beitrag zur Lösung der gewerblichen Organisationsfrage* (Jena, 1893), 98.

12. See Boetticher's testimony in *Stenographische Berichte über die Verhandlungen des Reichstags*, VIII. Legislaturperiode, I. Session 1890/92 (Berlin: Norddeutsche Buchdruckerei und Verlagsanstalt, 1892): V, 3019–20.

13. Hansen, "Caps and Gowns," 367*ff.*

14. Ibid., 363–94.

15. Bundesrath, Session von 1897: "Antrag der Ausschüsse für Handel und Verkehr und für Justizwesen zu dem Entwurf eines Gesetzes betreffend die Abänderung der Gewerbeordnung—Drucksache des Bundesraths Nr. 97 von 1896 (Nach den Beschlüssen der Subkommission.)" General State Archive-Karlsruhe, 237 / 24656. Also see the oral report and discussion in the Imperial Diet of the Subcommission's proposals: *Stenographische Berichte*, IX. Legislaturperiode, IV. Session 1895/97, 179th Sitting (Berlin: Norddeutsche Buchdruckerei und Verlagsanstalt, 1897): VII, 4774*ff.*

16. Schenkel, 26 November 1896 (No. 1453), General State Archive-Karlsruhe, 237/24656: 333*ff.*

17. See Philippe C Schmitter and Wolfgang Streeck, *Private Interest Government: Beyond Market and State* (Beverly Hills, CA, 1985).

18. William Stieda, "Handwerk," in *Handwörterbuch der Staatswissenschaften,* ed. Johannes Conrad et al. (Jena, 1892), 1112–13.

19. *Stenographische Berichte über die Verhandlungen des Reichstags*, IX. Legislaturperiode, IV. Session1895/97 (Berlin, 1892), VII, 5427, my translation.

20. "Denkschrift über die Begründung eines Landesgewerbeamts und eines ständigen Beirats," Geheimes Staatsarchiv, Merseburg, Rep. 151 (Finance Ministry) IC, Nr 9368: 12–13.

21. Ibid., 12–13.

22. Ibid., 14–15.

23. Thelen, *How Institutions Evolve,* 22; Kathleen Thelen and Ikuo Kume, "The Rise of Nonmarket Training Regimes: Germany and Japan Compared," *Journal of Japanese Studies* 25, no. 1 (1999): 33–64.

24. Hansen, "Caps and Gowns," 581*ff.*

25. Ibid., 579–94.

26. Ibid., 579–618.

27. For accounts of this process, see Hansen, "Caps and Gowns," 603–18; Frederick McKitrick, "Old World Craftsmen into Modern Capitalists: Artisans in Germany from National Socialism to the Federal Republic, 1939–1953" (PhD thesis, Columbia University, 1994), 36–128; Thelen, *How Institutions Evolve,* 219–39; David Meskill, *Optimizing the German Workforce: Labor Administration from Bismarck to the Economic Miracle* (New York, 2010), 141–82.

28. Women represented a small percentage of apprentices in *Handwerk* in 1900. Their numbers substantially increased in the 1930s, as the craft system diffused to industry and, especially, services. Because they predominate in the service sector, young women now outnumber young men in full-time vocational schools, while the reverse is true in the dual system. Still, 41 percent of trainees were women in 2000. Federal Ministry of Education and Research, *Germany's Vocational Education at a Glance* (Bonn, 2003), 3, 11.

29. Hansen, "Caps and Gowns," 56–64.

30. See Hal Hansen, "Rethinking Certification Theory and the Educational Development of the United States and Germany," *Research in Social Stratification and Mobility* 29, no. 1 (2011): 31–55.

31. McKitrick, "Old World Craftsmen," 238.

32. Ibid., 236–54.

33. For a critique of this idea, see Hansen, "Rethinking Certification."

34. McKitrick charts the political footwork of *Handwerk* and the passage of the *Handwerk* Act of 1953 in "Old World Craftsmen," 327–501.

35. For instance, see Zentralverband des Deutschen Handwerks, "Die neue Handwerksordnung und ergänzende gesetzliche Vorschriften nach dem Stand vom 2. Januar 2006," http://docplayer.org/11587976-Die-neue-handwerksordnung.html.

36. Heinrich von Treitschke, "Frankreichs Staatsleben und der Bonapartismus," in *Historische und Politische Aufsätze,* ed. Heinrich von Treitschke (Leipzig, 1886), III, 137.

37. Quoted from Jürgen Schriewer, "Intermediäre Instanzen, Selbstverwaltung und berufliche Ausbildungsstrukturen im historischen Vergleich," *Zeitschrift für Pädagogik* 32, no. 1 (1986): 77.

38. See Schmitter and Streeck, *Private Interest Government.*

39. Thilo Hampke, "Das neue badische Gewerbekammergesetz," in *Jahrbuch für Gesetzgebung, Verwaltung, und Volkswirtschaft im Deutschen Reich,* ed. Gustav Schmoller (Leipzig, 1894), 154.

40. Hampke, *Handwerker- oder Gewerbekammern?,* 153.

41. Mancur Olson, *The Logic of Collective Action; Public Goods and the Theory of Groups* (New York, 1965).

42. Hampke, *Handwerker- oder Gewerbekammern?,* 121, 127, 132, 206.

43. Gustav von Schmoller, *Jahrbuch für Gesetzgebung, Verwaltung und Volkswirtschaft im Deutschen Reich* (Leipzig, 1877), 190*ff.*

44. Zentralverband des Deutschen Handwerks (2010): Daten und Fakten, http://www.zdh.de/daten-und-fakten.html.

45. As we have seen, Americans took a similar view during the occupation and did their best to eliminate them. This view of *Handwerk* institutions has proved quite persistent, nowhere more so than in economics. See, for instance, the recent econometric study by the sociologist, Thijs Bol, "Economic Returns to Occupational Closure in the German Skilled Trades," *Social Science Research* 46 (2014): 9–22. Explicitly extending American research approaches to a European context, Bol compares earnings from regulated and nonregulated occupations of "a similar human capital." However, he does this on the basis of school-leaving certificates. Moreover, he ignores the fact that master certification not only authorizes the independent practice of a regulated trade but also the gives a master the right to take apprentices and train them. Thus, it functions as training certification, ensuring that apprentices receive a competent trainer. Finally, Bol overlooks the collective action functions of occupational regulation. His study concludes the latter to be a rent-seeking practice.

SELECTED BIBLIOGRAPHY

Crossick, Geoffrey, and Heinz-Gerhard Haupt. *The Petite Bourgeoisie in Europe, 1780–1914: Enterprise, Family, and Independence.* New York, 1995.

Georg, Walter, and Andreas Kunze. *Sozialgeschichte der Berufserziehung: Eine Einführung.* Munich, 1981.

Greinert, Wolf-Dietrich. *The "German System" of Vocational Education: History, Organization, Prospects.* Baden-Baden, 1994.

Hall, Peter, and David Soskice. *Varieties of Capitalism: The Institutional Foundations of Comparative Advantage.* New York, 2001.

Hampke, Thilo. "Das neue badische Gewerbekammergesetz." In *Jahrbuch für Gesetzgebung, Verwaltung, und Volkswirtschaft im Deutschen Reich,* edited by Gustav Schmoller, 161–94. Leipzig, 1894.

Hansen, Hal. "Caps and Gowns: Historical Reflections on the Institutions that Shaped Learning for and at Work in Germany and the United States, 1800–1945." PhD dissertation, University of Wisconsin–Madison, 1997.

——. "Rethinking Certification Theory and the Educational Development of the United States and Germany." *Research in Social Stratification and Mobility* 29, no. 1 (2011): 31–55.

——. "Rethinking the Role of Artisans in Modern German Development." *Central European History* 42, no. 1 (2009): 33–64.

Haverkamp, Frank. *Staatliche Gewerbeförderung im Grossherzogtum Baden: Unter besonderer Berücksichtigung der Entwicklung des gewerblichen Bildungswesens im 19. Jahrhundert.* Forschungen zur oberrheinischen Landesgeschichte. Vol. 29. Freiburg [Breisgau], 1979.

Herrigel, Gary. *Industrial Constructions: The Sources of German Industrial Power.* New York, 1996.

Maier, Charles S. *The Unmasterable Past: History, Holocaust, and German National Identity.* Cambridge, MA, 1997.

Olson, Mancur. *The Logic of Collective Action; Public Goods and the Theory of Groups.* New York, 1965.

Schmitter, Philippe C, and Wolfgang Streeck. *Private Interest Government: Beyond Market and State.* Beverly Hills, CA, 1985.

Streeck, Wolfgang. "German Capitalism: Does It Exist? Can It Survive?" In *Political Economy of Modern Capitalism: Mapping Convergence and Diversity,* edited by C Crouch and W Streeck, 33–54. Thousand Oaks, CA, 1997.

Thelen, Kathleen. *How Institutions Evolve: The Political Economy of Skills in Germany, Britain, the United States, and Japan.* New York, 2004.

Chapter 3

The German Forest as an Emblem of Germany's Ambivalent Modernity

Jeffrey K Wilson

Widely vaunted in the nineteenth century as a national symbol, *der deutsche Wald* (the German forest) has been cast in a harshly negative light. The radical, *völkisch* nationalists' embrace of the woods—an *Urwald* (primeval forest) inhabited by rooted peasants descended from tree-worshiping Teutonic warriors—supposedly attested to Germany's atavism, irrationality, and flight from modernity.[1] Yet scholars recently have become skeptical of modernity itself, recognizing its ambivalent nature. Rather than believing a deficit of modernity lead to fascism, historians have concentrated their attention on the ways that the embrace of modernity contributed to the catastrophes of the twentieth century.[2] The German forest was itself a modern invention, a product of the era of nation-states. This was true both as a mental construct and as a material reality. Although many liked to envision the woods as a pristine ancient space, and imagined trees as relics of the past, many also recognized that Germany's forests were orderly, scientifically managed spaces—a far cry from the mythical *Urwald*. And like any modern invention, the German forest had both its positive and negative characteristics. The highly managed, fast-growing pine monocultures delivered steady supplies of timber for expanding German markets, yet at the same time inaugurated environmental damage and social displacement, as the monocultures fell more easily to disease and insect infestations, and peasants lost their traditional use-rights to the woods.[3] The same ambivalent outcomes also apply on the cultural and political levels. The widespread invocation of the German forest idea led in many different directions; in some circles, it stimulated a genuine concern with environmental issues, but in others it fostered racist notions of the national community. Indeed, many different groups mobilized the concept for disparate aims, leading to competing claims on this national symbol.

The late nineteenth and early twentieth centuries saw a proliferation of books and articles discussing the fabled German forest. These works generally agreed on a common set of ideas, comprising the sylvan discourse. Those engaged in this discourse shared several core beliefs. First, Germans shared a common reverence for the woods, rooted in their barbarian past. Second, this special relationship with the forest had been preserved in Germany until at least the late eighteenth century, despite the encroachment of feudal rights on once commonly held woodlands. Third, forests came under pressure with the arrival of capitalism, as many unscrupulous landowners (including perhaps the state) transformed their stands of timber into profits. Fourth, the loss of woodlands carried costs for the nation, whether environmental (greater erosion and flooding), medical (less clean air and declining opportunities for healthy recreation, especially for the urban populace), social (fewer sources of income and resources for peasants), economic (dwindling source of wood at a time of rampant worldwide consumption), cultural (less opportunity for artistic inspiration and scientific investigation), or political (waning attachment to the *Heimat* [region] and the nation). Fifth, Southern European cultures had already decimated their forest in ancient times and declined a result; it might only be a matter of time before Western Europeans—and further in the future, the Americans and the Russians—would suffer a similar fate. Sixth, Germany's continued success relied on defending the forest against the threat posed by unbridled capitalism. The notion of the German forest, and its importance for the nation, achieved near universal assent; it was open enough to encompass a broad range of political and economic attitudes, yet specific enough to be meaningful.

Yet precisely because the German forest was such a widely disseminated symbol of Germandom, a disparate array of groups attempted to mobilize it for their own ends. Landowners, hunters, timber producers, peasant-rights activists, hikers, charitable organizations, and state officials all deployed the idea of the German forest for widely divergent purposes, illustrating the ways nationalist and environmentalist language could be used for material aims. Thus, perhaps more interesting than the fact that Germans invested their landscape with national meaning are the ways in which this symbol—intended to unite the nation—became an object of bitter contention in the Kaiserreich. Perhaps the best way to assess the wide divergence of contemporary views of the German forest is to examine the radically different articulations of the sylvan discourse on the eve of World War I: on one hand, a vision for social change penned by *völkisch* forester, and on the other, the proceedings of a congress aiming to save a beloved urban forest from real estate development.

RUDOLF DÜESBERG'S SOCIAL DARWINISM

Those who emphasize the antimodern and irrational strains of the German sylvan discourse usually highlight the work of Rudolf Düesberg. Düesberg gained attention on the radical right with his 1910 book, *Der Wald als Erzie-her* (*The Forest as Educator*). The book—half forestry manual and half social reform blueprint—championed a new kind of sylviculture and a new kind of society. The German forest, Düesberg claimed, arose from the same environment as the German people, and both suffered under the alien forces of capitalism. Praising the social order of woodlands undisturbed by commercial forestry, Düesberg argued they provided a social model for a Germany liberated from industrial capitalism. "The dominant laws for the cultivation of a forest apply equally to the rationally organized human community," he insisted, noting "in this way the forest becomes an educator."[4] Although his studies led him to advocate a traditional social hierarchy and a rejection of much of the trappings of modernity, he remained critical of agrarian elites and clung to the liberating potential of science.

Echoing social Darwinist efforts to draw conclusions about the character of human society from observations of nature, Düesberg explicitly advocated the German forest as a model for German social relations. "All the imperfections of human institutions," he maintained, "arise from the misunderstanding of immutable natural laws." Thus the true German forest, as a product of nature, would reveal the kind of social conditions nature intended for the German people. In Düesberg's formulation, the forest was more than a metaphor for society, it was an organic companion shaped by the same environmental forces. "As descendants of a settled *Volksgemeinschaft* (people's community) of peasants, made great by the iron drive to hard labor in a tough climate on soil of little fertility, the Germans are comparable to the nordic forest trees," he claimed.[5] Düesberg believed cooperation was the key to this model. "The forest in its original condition is the lasting life-community of a great circle of plant and animal life," he explained, "which is ruled less by the struggle for existence than by the friendlier picture of mutual adjustment and help." Düesberg envisioned the woods not as the site of ruthless competition by individuals, but as a place where each tree contributed to the whole. In commercial forests, trees grew to great heights, "not as individuals, but only as members of a highly developed community."[6]

The German people, Düesberg asserted, had once belonged to such a com-munity—defined by race and governed by laws corresponding to their racial character—but industrial capitalism destroyed it. Thus he demanded, "the social order of the German forests must be a model for the institutions in the economic and social life of the German people."[7]

Just as the "essence of the forest" was "not compatible with the capital-istic means of valuing land," neither was the essence of the German people suited to capitalism, Düesberg insisted. Capitalism, he claimed, eroded the natural order of both. Drawing on anti-Semitic discourse, he argued capital-ism sprang from a "nomadic" (read Jewish) mentality, which allowed one to accumulate mobile wealth (first livestock, then money) largely divorced from the land. "The German race," by contrast, was rooted in the soil, tending "towards settled agriculture." Thus the introduction of "alien" capitalism to Germany led to a fundamental disruption of the "natural" social order, he contended.[8] Like woodland trees suffering under current forestry methods, which ignored their "species characteristics," the Germans labored under an "equally incompatible ... worldview governing economic and social life." Capitalism had regimented social relations in the forest as it had in society, he explained; whereas trees thrived when allowed to grow of their own volition in natural forests, capitalist forestry forced trees into competition with one another, planting them close together in order to drive them to ever greater productivity (i.e., timber yields) in the struggle for survival (i.e., light). Ultimately, this practice reduced the productive elements of sylvan society to "miserable specimens." In much the same way, capitalist industries exploited German workers, Düesberg claimed, forcing them into regimented urban lives dominated by competition for survival. Thus he con-cluded: "The nomadic worldview, hostile to the German spirit, has over the long term overcome the fundamentally opposed view of the settled peasant and pushed it into the background."[9]

As a society and a state divorced from its origins and organized around capitalist industry, Imperial Germany earned Düesberg's condemnation. "The basis of the modern state and the institutions of public life are neither Christian nor Germanic," he maintained, "they represent a nomadic, Jewish *Weltanschauung*." The ruling "Jewish and Roman" concepts of property had eroded German "law and custom," driving the rooted German peasant from the land. Düesberg therefore demanded "the recognition of egoism as the driving force behind human economic and social life, the unbinding of the free play of forces is responsible for all the neediness and disgraces, from which the German *Volk* suffers." Rather than serving the needs of the German people, the state catered to the interests of industry and trade, spending exorbitant funds on the quest for world markets. Specifically, he cited military spending, which he claimed soared to three times the amount necessary for national defense in order to project Germany's influence around the world and subsidize the armaments industry. The industrial order supported by the German state had produced an enormous growth of wealth, Düesberg admitted, but it had also polarized society, resulting in the proletarianization of the "masses robbed of a *Heimat*" and the spread of socialism.[10]

Rather than supporting Germany's industrialization and the progressive erosion of natural social relations, Düesberg advocated a state-sponsored return to the land, in particular a vigorous investment in forestry and wood processing. Like rural reformers who emphasized the value of woodworking in the rural life, Düesberg regarded the forest as a great social benefactor, providing raw materials and sources of employment for the peasant economy. Indeed, he hoped to shift the German economy toward renewable raw materials to avoid the crisis of dwindling resources industrial economies were bound to face. Peasant woodworking, centered on the farm, would stem the tide of laborers going to the cities. Along with widespread landownership, Düesberg predicted, artisanal production would counteract the corrosive influence of capitalism, preventing proletarianization and negating the socialist threat.[11]

Opposed to capitalism's competitive and socially divisive character, Düesberg drew on nature to find models of social cooperation, where they were more visible than "in the confusion of human affairs." He did not try to deny the role of struggle, but rather to contextualize it. "The goal of struggle is not so much the benefit of the single being as the welfare of the whole," he observed, thus the "social order serves the otherwise senseless, chaotic struggle for existence." He concluded that, for humans as well as plants, "all institutions of economic and social life must be directed to the highest goal: to maintain and ennoble the species," and posited the "national family" (*Volks-familie*) as a model for both. In the forest, each member of the community had a special role to play. So too in society, where the differences in strength and ability between men and women, old and young, all complemented one another in the "labor community of the family." This conservative notion formed "the basis for an aristocratic order," a hierarchy "with the monarch at the top." Düesberg called upon the Junkers to revive this national family, which appeared as a strategy to restore Germany's feudal order.[12]

While Düesberg regarded Germany's landed elites as crucial allies in dismantling industrial capitalism, he did not wholeheartedly endorse them. Indeed, he criticized "many large landowners" for a lacking "consciousness of social duties," and charged the Agrarian League, the aggressive agricultural lobby, with the pursuit of landowners' self-interest above the common good. Neither of these traits was compatible with Düesberg's harmonious national family. Furthermore, the Junkers' manors, often employing hundreds of landless and seasonal laborers, violated their employees' "personal freedom," he charged. The very structure of East-Elbian agriculture ran counter to Düesberg's vision of a Germany dominated by small landholders and artisans. Labor only had meaning when one worked for oneself, he insisted; thus he called for the return of workers to the land to counter industrial alienation and the socialism it bred. Only with widespread landownership, Düesberg claimed, would rootedness and patriotism flourish. "Therefore," he concluded, "the possession of land by a few is hurtful to everyone."[13] Although unlike many agrarian reformers (and out of deference to his prospective Junker allies) he did not propose the break-up of large estates, he did insist on a progressive income tax and the abolition of interest group politics.[14] He recommended that large landowners mechanize their production to avoid recruiting landless laborers. Land for the expanding German population could be won through the purchase of Russian Poland; the Poles (who were chafing under Russian rule anyway) could be resettled in South America in a "peaceful exchange."[15] Modern means—including wholesale population transfers—would return Germans to the land and restore the *Volksgemeinschaft*.

Düesberg's belief in science also tempered his antimodernism, setting him apart from true reactionaries. Although his title drew on Julius Langbehn's 1890 *Rembrandt als Erzieher* (*Rembrandt as Educator*) for inspiration, Düesberg did not share Langbehn's hostility to science. Langbehn rejected science, according to Fritz Stern, "because it presumed to penetrate the mystery of life and nature, to make comprehensible a universe that [he] wanted left shrouded in poetic obscurity."[16] Düesberg, on the other hand, whole-heartedly embraced the benefits of science, devoting the first half of his work to calculating the efficiency of various sylvicultural methods, and the second to plumbing the forest's mysteries to understand its laws. Düesberg condemned medieval Scholasticism, dismissing it as the source of "the petty spirit of bureaucracy, pedantry, and belief in authority." Particularly in the forest, one could observe the effects of imposing rigid mathematical models on nature, inspired as they were by commercial interests. The natural sciences, by contrast, offered new methods of "unconditional critical observation, exact experimentation, and the investigation of connections, interactions, and transformations in the phenomena of the environment," which defeated this narrow tendency, Düesberg insisted. These new insights inspired his recognition that "so-called progress is often, if not always, a return to nature, to the recognition of the eternal laws."[17] For Düesberg, the natural sciences opened the path to enlightenment, revealing immutable natural principles and providing solutions to modern problems. While he embraced an essentially reactionary social order, he did so (at least ostensibly) neither out of deference to tradition or authority, nor out of a fundamental hostility to technology and science, but out of a belief that such a society conformed to scientifically discernible natural laws.

Düesberg's racialized image of the woods, and the social conclusions he drew from it, arose not from aesthetic considerations but scientific ones. He clearly desired to unlock the mysteries of nature through scientific investigation. He demanded the translation of his dendrological research into social policy. While the society he imagined looked remarkably similar to that of agrarian romantics, he justified his arguments in (pseudo-) scientific terms. Thus his plea for a return to nature emanated more from a belief in the inherent good of organic social relations (whether for plants or humans) than from nostalgia or a concern with history or aesthetics. Indeed, when Hugo Conwentz (the founder of the Prussian nature protection authority) surveyed German foresters in 1900, Düesberg (already eleven years at his post in a state forest) responded he had undertaken no efforts to preserve rare trees or rural beauty in his reserve.[18] Thus Düesberg demonstrated little interest in the widespread passion for sylvan beauty that dominated the German forest discourse at the turn of the century. There was little evidence in his work of the kind of historical or aesthetic interests that animated the *Heimatschutz* (*Heimat* protection) movement's preservation efforts, for example. Instead, his inspiration was drawn from the popular science tropes of social Darwinism.

Düesberg's book was embraced by the radical right (it was included on a list of recommended nationalist books), but attained little popularity.[19] His work was far too fantastic, dark, and explicitly political to earn much consideration from mainstream readers. Indeed, his employer, the Prussian Minister of Agriculture Bernd von Arnim-Kriewen, gave a particularly scathing review in a private assessment, dismissing his work as commonplace and "in part worthless," concluding "I do not believe that Düesberg's often evident eccentricity and lack of clarity will win his work the regard he hopes for." However, in his capacity as Chief Forester of the royal hunting ground at Groß Mützelburg, Düesberg did succeed in gaining the attention of Crown Prince Wilhelm, which in turn prompted an internal investigation. Officials from the crown prince's staff, seeking to reduce the influence of radical nationalists on their impressionable charge, sought to remove the errant forester from his position. Although they did not succeed, it was clear that they eyed his work with suspicion.[20] While this kind of radical social Darwinism would attain significant appeal after the cataclysm of World War I, before 1914 it was odd and eccentric.

THE WALDSCHUTZTAG'S SOCIAL REFORMISM

Far more representative of the sylvan discourse on the eve of World War I was the work of social reformers in the campaign to save the Grunewald, a forest popular with Berliners as a site of recreation. The Prussian Ministry of Agriculture, owner of the forest, had sought since 1902 to sell off significant parts of the Grunewald for real estate development. The value of the land had been rising with the development of luxury suburbs on the edge of the forest, and the prospect of selling land on the Havel River, which bounded the Grunewald on the west, held out the opportunity to realize significant profits for the ministry. The Berlin public had mobilized against this effort starting in 1904, although in five years it had failed to gain anything other than vaguely worded "guarantees" from the ministry. In 1909, frustrated by state intransigence, a wide range of Berliners expressed their demands for the protection of the Grunewald at a *Waldschutztag* (forest protection conference). The speeches given at the meeting, by representatives of over thirty groups representing teachers, housing reform advocates, public health officials, and *Heimat* enthusiasts, among others, elucidate the significance of the idea of the German forest for the middle classes.

Medical professor Dr Karl Anton Ewald—the chairman of the Berliner Waldschutzverein—opened the *Waldschutztag* describing the changing role of his organization. Although it had been founded for "purely aesthetic reasons"—specifically, to prevent littering in the forests surrounding Berlin— the political situation had moved Ewald's club from combating *Schmutz* (filth) in the woods to advocating public *Schutz* (protection) of them. The preservation of the forests around Berlin, Ewald argued, furthered the social, cultural, aesthetic, and public health agendas of all the groups participating in the *Waldschutztag*.[21]

Besides Ewald's association, an additional five groups sponsored the meeting, each representing differing interests in the conservation of the Grunewald: the Bund Deutscher Bodenreformer under the leadership of the property reform advocate Adolf Damaschke; the Büro für Sozialpolitik, a coalition of liberal social reformers, represented by its founder Ernst Francke, a prominent liberal; the Deutsche Gartenstadt-Gesellschaft, a group promoting more affordable suburban living to counterbalance the increasing density of cities, headed by the moderate socialist Bernhard Kampffmeyer; the Brandenburg branch of the Bund Heimatschutz, led by the left liberal Prussian Landtag representative, nature enthusiast, and school principal Karl Wetekamp; and the Zentralkommission der Krankenkassen Berlins und der Vororte, represented by a Herr Simanowski.[22] Joining the organizers of the conference were a further thirty groups representing several clusters of interests. Twelve focused on social concerns: five stressed urban issues, four were liberal labor unions, two social reform associations, and the last a league of women's groups.[23] Another ten of them addressed themselves to public health issues: four groups were dedicated to public health generally, three to combating alcoholism, two with athletics, and one with holistic medicine.[24] These two clusters of associations comprised the majority of the interest groups at the conference, reflecting the dominance of social and public health concerns at the organizers' level. In addition, a further five groups represented youth and educational interests: three were teachers' associations, one promoted science education, and the last was a youth welfare organization.[25] A final three represented academic interests: the Verein für Geschichte Berlins, the Deutsche Botanische Gesellschaft, and a scientific society promoting the preservation of the Grunewald's moors.[26] While each of these diverse groups approached the Grunewald problem from a different angle, the need to maintain workers' access to nature held the conference together. As the representative of the liberal Verband der Deutschen Gewerkvereine, Karl Goldschmidt, argued "the interest of the workers is closely connected with the preservation of woodlands around Berlin," stressing this issue would determine the "national future."[27]

Participants in the *Waldschutztag* all agreed on the importance of workers' access to nature as an important means to overcome the problems of urbanization that threatened their health, morality, and patriotism, and approached the topic from their diverse perspectives. Property reform advocates, concerned with rising rents and poor housing conditions, sought to prevent the state from selling its land to real estate speculators, a move they felt would avert a further escalation of land prices throughout the region. Moreover, they sought to preserve the forest for the use of this impoverished constituency, otherwise confined to crowded apartments. In a fiery speech, Karl von Mangoldt, a prominent land reformer, demanded a heavy municipal tax on profits from real estate transactions (the *Wertzuwachssteuer*) to discourage land speculation. Speaking for "those battalions of workers upon whom to a great extent the future and hope of our *Volk* rests, those who have been packed into the *Mietskasernen* (rental barracks), those whose access to nature has been blocked," Mangoldt insisted that "every capitalist interest that stands in the way must be thrown to the ground!"[28] Mangoldt's rousing speech generated an enthusiastic response from the audience and illustrated the links between urban reform, social policy, and the forest.

Reducing urban density and preserving woodlands naturally appealed to public health interests. Several medical doctors regarded the preservation of Berlin's forests as a crucial public health issue. Dr Karl Beerwald, editor of the weekly *Sozialreform* and representative of the Deutsche Zentrale für Volkshygiene, identified the Grunewald as the lungs of the capital, and argued that workers could "balance out the detrimental influence of the metropolis," especially the effects of air pollution, "by spending time in free nature."[29] Albert Kohn of the Zentralkommission der Krankenkassen Berlins und der Vororte, which insured about one million residents of the capital, concurred, noting that as more forests fell to the axe, "all the more so grows the social misery of a wide strata of the proletariat."[30] Acting on these beliefs, the Vaterländische Frauenverein had already opened a *Waldschule* (forest school) in the Grunewald for working-class and petite bourgeois children suffering from lung ailments in 1904.[31] The need to preserve the forest around Berlin pressed urgently on these public health activists.

A healthier population with better access to recreation would also contribute to the goals of social reform, ameliorating the misery of Berlin's working class and thus alleviating the social tensions liberal reformers felt fueled political radicalism. The temperance movement, for instance, stressed the forest as an alternative to drink.[32] Speaking as one of the chief organizers of the conference, Dr Ludwig Jablonski worried the worker without access to nature "will go to a musty bar for a little pleasure after work, and entrust himself to alcohol." Moreover, Jablonski argued that a worker immersed in spirits "will, instead of exercising his body outdoors, willingly visit prostitutes."[33] In order to combat the lure of beer gardens in "God's free nature," the Guttempler Orden and the Frauenverein gegen Alkoholismus established alcohol-free refreshment halls in the Grunewald by 1914.[34] Thus, according to social reformers, a lack of healthy recreational opportunities necessarily led to physical and moral degeneration, shattering stable family life.

Delegates to the *Waldschutztag* also endorsed the idea that the Grunewald could strengthen the Berliners' ties to their *Heimat* and the nation. Jablonski distanced Berliners' love of *Heimat* from "all giddy sentimentality and ... hateful chauvinism." Unlike rural residents, who often lived in one house all their lives and associated this intimate space with memory and tradition, Berliners regularly moved every few years, losing a sense of place and of history. "He has no *Heimat*," Jablonski fretted; yet at the same time "the forest is really, as paradoxical as it might sound, the *Heimat* of the Berliner." Maintaining this tie to the wooded *Heimat* was important, he asserted, for should one "take away the forest from him, and he will lose feeling. Make it so that only a few lucky beneficiaries get the pleasure that has been denied him, and you raise him to become a person without a *Heimat*, without a Fatherland." Jablonski clearly meant to invoke the threat of socialism here; thus Berlin's forests made the difference between national unity and class war. Likewise Professor Karl Wetekamp, a representative of the Brandenburg branch of the Bund Heimatschutz and a left-liberal member of the

Prussian Landtag, emphasized the connection between the preservation of the *Heimat* and patriotism. "What we want is to protect our *Heimat*," he demanded, "not as an end in itself, but rather ... to preserve for the *Volk* something that will constantly rejuvenate its love of the *Heimat*. Love of the *Heimat* is the best foundation for the virtue upon which alone the welfare of the state depends: the love of the Fatherland." True patriotism, according to Wetekamp, had to be rooted in the *Heimat*. Only the love of *Heimat* would be capable, he contended, of generating a patriotism that "in moments of danger mobilizes everything, life and limb, for the Fatherland." While ideally the love of *Heimat* would be best fostered by universal land owner-ship, he noted urbanization had rendered that goal impossible. Instead, Wetekamp proposed that the municipalities acquire land in order to create a "common possession" in which all urbanites could share, "and we could have a no more beautiful common possession than our lovely nature, in which all of us, high and low, rich and poor, can move about and find new energy and joy. I believe we are all united in this thought."[35] A poster produced by the Forest Protection Association at the time of the conference similarly stressed the public claim to woodlands. "Fellow citizens," it proclaimed, "help us pre-serve our woods!" Thus, the *Waldschutztag* made patriotic appeals to assert the public's right to the forest.

Overall, the *Waldschutztag* stressed the importance of the woods for securing the health and loyalty of the working class. A wide range of socially active groups, representing the diversity of Berlin's associational life, came together to champion their cause. As the Berliner Waldschutzverein summa-rized in its annual report that year: "The destruction of the woodlands and the excessive herding together of people endangers and damages the public health, leads to a disavowal of all moral connections to the *Heimat*'s soil, and aggravates the job of raising the culture of the urban population above its present level." The meeting therefore ended with a long petition to the Kaiser, asking him to preserve the Grunewald for these reasons.[36] Behind this appeal stood dozens of organizations with local and national member-ships, representing a broad and politically active public that endorsed the German forest discourse, but in a way quite distinct, if not completely at odds with, Düesberg's social Darwinist visions. And while Düesberg's work raised the eyebrows of his employers and did not find enough public interest to merit another print run, the proceedings of the meeting proved such popular reading in social reform circles (both in Berlin and in other German cities) that the Berliner Zentralausschuß für die Wald- und Ansiedlungsfrage issued another edition the following year. The *Waldschutztag*, standing at the opposite end of the political spectrum from Düesberg, was more in tune with the public sentiment of the day.

CONCLUSION

Germans on the eve of World War I had differing views of the woods. The *völkisch* nationalist forester Düesberg saw the forest as the antidote to modern urban society. He rejected the city because it undermined the traditional social order and corroded the strength of the nation; he hoped to radically alter German society by reorienting state investment from the city to the countryside, building up the rural economy as a counterbalance to urban industrialism, and ultimately resettling German workers on the land. Quite by contrast, the left-liberal social reformers gathering in Berlin's *Waldschutztag,* mainly urban professionals, accepted the necessity of urbanization and industrialization, and instead sought to temper its worst features—overcrowding, declining public health, and social and political alienation—by encouraging forest preservation. In short, they proposed bringing the forest to the worker, while Düesberg hoped to put the worker in the forest and keep him there.

Of course, both Düesberg and those campaigning to save the Grunewald shared a desire to rekindle German patriotism as well as a hostility to revolutionary socialism, and this fact has often led scholars to simply dismiss both, with their talk of a return to nature, as antimodern. Yet these two tendencies differed significantly in their means of challenging what they perceived as the socialist threat. On one hand, for Düesberg, socialism was simply another evil produced by contemporary modernity, one that could only be exorcised with the conditions that engendered it: urban life, industrial labor, and capitalism. He aimed to create a radical new world, one based on both tradition *and* science, which returned Germans to their woodland origins. Berlin social reformers, on the other hand, did not reject capitalism, industry, and urban life in principle, but sought instead to reconcile them with humanity in myriad ways, in particular by bringing workers into contact with nature. They aimed to undermine revolutionary socialism not by demolishing the current economic, social, and political order, but by addressing socialist concerns with quality of life directly. These social reformers, active in a city where the SPD held almost all of Berlin's seats in the democratically-elected Reichstag and controlled a significant proportion of Berlin's representatives in the Prussian Landtag and the Berlin city council, felt pressured to address the concrete demands of their socialist neighbors in realistic ways. Their program embraced a modernity that included the familiar elements of capitalism, industry, and urban life, but sought to mitigate the worst aspects of each.

While social reformism of the *Waldschutztag* stood at odds with Düesberg's social Darwinism, the two ends of this political spectrum could nonetheless agree on the forest as an important tool for addressing the problems of Germany's modernization. Both identified the German *Volk* as suffering from urbanization and industrialization; both saw the city as a site of disease and dissolution threatening the nation; and both believed a return to nature could save Germany from the catastrophes of degeneration and revolution. Yet this core belief in nature's ability to counteract the turmoil brought about by modernity could lead in a variety of directions, from Düesberg's efforts to dismantle the cities and return workers to the land, to the *Waldschutztag*'s desire to create a belt of woods around Berlin. Both plans were modern attempts to harness nature to address the problems of modern urban society, and as such, the German forest stood as an emblem of Germany's ambivalent modernity.

Jeffrey K Wilson, Associate Professor of History at California State University, Sacramento, is an historian of modern Germany, with a particular interest in the intersection of nature and nationalism. He recently published a book entitled *The German Forest: Nature, Identity, and the Contestation of a National Symbol, 1871–1914,* the research for which was funded in part with a grant from the Berlin Program for Advanced German and European Studies. His current project explores the timber trade in Central Europe during World War I and its aftermath.

NOTES

1. This view has a long pedigree dating back at least to George Mosse and continues to echo in recent works. See George Mosse, *The Crisis of German Ideology: Intellectual Origins of the Third Reich* (New York, 1964), 15–19; *The Nationalization of the Masses* (New York, 1975), 35–41, 93–94; Wolfgang Theilemann, *Adel im grünen Rock. Adliges Jägertum, Großprivatwaldbesitz und die preußische Forstbeamtenschaft 1866–1914* (Berlin, 2004); Michael Imort, "A Sylvan People. Wilhelmine Forestry and the Forest as a Symbol of Germandom," in *Germany's Nature: Cultural Landscapes and Environmental History,* ed. Thomas Lekan and Thomas Zeller (New Brunswick, NJ, 2005), 55–80; Johannes Zechner, "Politicized Timber: The 'German Forest' and the Nature of the Nation 1800–1945," *The Brock Review* 11, no. 2 (2011): 19–32; Johannes Zechner, *Der deutsche Wald. Eine Ideengeschichte zwischen Poesie und Ideologie 1800–1945* (Darmstadt, 2016).

2. "The Genesis of the 'Final Solution' from the Spirit of Science," in *Reevaluating the Third Reich,* ed. Thomas Childers and Jane Caplan (New York, 1993), 234–52; Kevin Repp, *Reformers, Critics, and the Paths of German Modernity: Anti-Politics and the Search for Alternatives, 1890–1914* (Cambridge, MA, 2000); Thomas Rohkrämer, *Eine andere Moderne? Zivilisationskritik, Natur und Technik*

in Deutschland 1880–1933 (Paderborn, 1999); Thomas Rohkrämer, *A Single Communal Faith?: The German Right from Conservatism to National Socialism* (New York, 2007).

3. James C Scott, *Seeing Like a State. How Certain Schemes to Improve the Human Condition Have Failed* (New Haven, CT, 1998), 11–21.
4. Rudolf Düesberg, *Der Wald als Erzieher* (Berlin, 1910), 138–39.
5. Ibid., 202, 138.
6. Ibid., 17, 42.
7. Ibid., 138–39.
8. Ibid., 193, 182.
9. Ibid., 138–43.
10. Ibid., 147–52.
11. Ibid., 152–54, 185.
12. Ibid., iii–iv, 144–45, 158.
13. Ibid., 157, 145–46.
14. Ibid., 158–73, 183–84.
15. Ibid., 192–93. Elsewhere, Düesberg regarded a lack of settlement space as justifiable grounds for war. Ibid., 146.
16. Fritz Stern, *The Politics of Cultural Despair: A Study in the Rise of the German Ideology* (Berkeley, CA, 1961), 122.
17. Düesberg, *Der Wald als Erzieher,* 141, 202.
18. Survey submitted by Düesberg to Conwentz, 12 October 1900. In Staatsbibliothek Preussischer Kulturbesitz, Nachlass Conwentz.
19. See Rudolf Rüsten, *Was tut not? Ein Führer durch die gesamte Literatur der Deutschbewegung* (Leipzig, 1914).
20. The effort to remove Düesberg foundered on the reluctance of the Ministry of Agriculture to transfer him. The ministry feared crossing the prince, who had previously promised Düesberg could stay in his position, despite its apparent subsequent approval of Düesberg's reassignment. See correspondence between the Ministry of Agriculture and the Hofmarschallamt, 22 April 1909 to 1 July 1912. In Geheimes Staatsarchiv Preussischer Kulturbesitz, I HA Rep.87D, Nr.969, Düesberg.
21. Der Berliner Zentralausschuß für die Wald- und Ansiedlungsfrage, ed., *Der Kampf um unsere Wälder* (Berlin, 1909), 6.
22. Ibid., 5. On Damaschke and the *Bodenreform* movement, see Nicholas Bullock and James Read, *The Movement for Housing Reform in Germany and France, 1840–1914* (Cambridge, 1985), 159–63, 178–79; Elisabeth Meyer-Renschhausen and Hartwig Berger, "Bodenreform," in *Handbuch der deutschen Reformbewegungen, 1880–1933,* ed. Diethart Kerbs and Jürgen Reulecke (Wupperthal, 1998), 265–76; Josef Seemann, "Bund Deutsche Bodenreformer (BDB) 1898–1945," in *Lexikon zur Parteiengeschichte,* ed. Dieter Fricke et al. (Leipzig, 1983), 282–88; Brian Ladd, *Urban Planning and Civic Order in Germany, 1860–1914* (Cambridge, 1990), 177–78. On Kampffmeyer and the Gartenstadt movement, see Klaus Bergmann, *Agrarromantik und Grossstadtfeindschaft* (Meisenheim, 1970), 135–64;

Kristiana Hartmann, *Deutsche Gartenstadtbewegung: Kulturpolitik und Gesellschafts-reform* (Munich, 1976); Kristiana Hartmann, "Gartenstadtbewegung," in *Handbuch der deutschen Reformbewegungen, 1880–1933,* ed. Diethart Kerbs and Jürgen Reulecke (Wupperthal, 1998), 289–300. On Francke and the *Büro für Sozialpolitik*, see Rüdiger vom Bruch, ed., *Weder Kommunismus noch Kapitalismus: bürgerliche Sozialreform in Deutschland vom Vormärz bis zur Ära Adenauer* (Munich, 1985), 130–39; Holger J Tober, *Deutscher Liberalismus und Sozialpolitik in der Ära des Wilhelminismus* (Husum, 1999).

23. Included here were the Ansiedlungsverein Groß-Berlin, Berliner Zentralaus-schuß für die Wald- und Ansiedlungsfrage, Freie Vereinigung Grunewald, Mieterbund Groß-Berlin, Verein der Vororte Berlins zur Wahrung gemein-samer Interessen; the Gewerk-Verein der Heimarbeiterinnen, Hirsch-Duncker Gewerbeverein, Verband der Deutschen Gewerkvereine, and the Kartell der Christlichen Gewerkschaften Berlins und Umgegend; the Berlin branch of the Gesellschaft für soziale Reform and the Jacob Plaut-Stiftung Berlin; and the Verbündete Frauenvereine Groß-Berlin.

24. Included here were the Berliner Medizinische Gesellschaft, the Berlin branch of the Deutsche Zentrale für Volkshygiene, the Verein öffentlicher Gesund-heitspflege, and the Vereinigung der Walderholungsstätten vom Roten Kreuz; the Berliner Zentralverband zur Bekämpfung des Alkoholismus, Branden-burgischer Distrikt des Internationalen Guttempler Ordens, and Deutscher Verein gegen Mißbrauch geistiger Getränke; the Ausschuß der Berliner Turn-gaue and Berliner Hochschulsportvereinigung; and the Bund der Verein für Naturgemäße Lebens- und Heilweise (Naturheilkunde).

25. Included here were the Berliner Gymnasiallehrer-Verein, Berliner Gymnasi-allehrer-Gesellschaft, Berliner Lehrerverein; the Berlin branch of the Verein zur Förderung des mathematischen und naturwissenschaftlichen Unterrichts; and the Deutsche Zentrale für Jugendfürsorge.

26. Included here were the Verein für die Geschichte Berlins, Deutsche Botanische Gesellschaft, and the Ausschuß der wissenschaftlichen und gemeinnützigen Vereine zur Erhaltung der Grunewald-Moore.

27. Berliner Zentralausschuß, ed., *Der Kampf um unsere Wälder,* 32.

28. Ibid., 21–26. Besides campaigning to preserve Berlin's woodlands, Man-goldt stood as a major housing reformer in Imperial Germany. As head of the Deutsche Verein für Wohnungsreform, the Institut für Gemeinwohl, and the Ansiedlungsverein Groß-Berlin, he allied himself with the Büro für Sozialpolitik to champion a federal housing reform law. In Berlin, he and his Ansiedlungsverein gained prominence in the fight to save the Tempelhofer Feld military parade grounds from development. See Werner Hegemann, *Das steinerne Berlin: Geschichte der grössten Mietskasernenstadt der Welt* (Berlin, 1930), 449–57; Felix Escher, *Berlin und sein Umland* (Berlin, 1985), 312–15; Bullock and Read, *The Movement for Housing Reform,* 255–56.

29. Ibid., 30.

30. Ibid., 31; on Kohn, see Wolfgang Stargardt, Florian Tennstedt, and Heinz Umrath, "Albert Kohn, ein Freund der Kranken. Rückblick auf das Wirken eines frühen Kämpfers für die Krankenversicherung," *Die Ortskrankenkasse* 58 (1976): 810–16.

31. On the Grunewald *Waldschule*, see Arnold Hirtz, "Waldschule und Kindererholungsstätte," *Das Schulhaus* 15 (1913): 449–50; W Lange, "Die Waldschule," *Pädagogische Warte* (1908): 1098–99; Regine Deutsch, "Charlottenburger Waldschule," *Deutsche Kultur* 3 (1907): 598–601; Karl König, "Einrichtungen von Waldschulen," *Pädagogische Warte* (1910): 938; letter from Ausschuss für den zweiten Berliner Waldschutztag to Berlin Magistrat, February 1909. In Landesarchiv Berlin, STA Rep.01-02 Nr.1814 b.92-93.

32. The Guttempler sought to save individuals from alcoholism and were dedicated to the "moral improvement and ethical perfection of humanity" through the "elimination of alcoholic beverages as a source of pleasure." The Deutscher Verein gegen Mißbrauch geistiger Getränke, by contrast, sought to establish state regulation of drunkenness. See Satzungen der Distriktsloge Nr.14 (Brandenburg) von Deutschlands Grossloge II des I.O.G.T. In Amtsgerichtsrat Charlottenburg, 95 VR 924 NZ, Bd. 1, b.42; on the campaign against alcoholism in Imperial Germany, see James S Roberts, *Drink, Temperance, and the Working Class in Nineteenth-Century Germany* (Boston, 1984); Alfred Heggen, *Alkohol und Bürgerliche Gesellschaft im 19. Jahrhundert* (Berlin, 1988).

33. Berliner Zentralausschuß, ed., *Der Kampf um unsere Wälder*, 8.

34. See *Nachweisung aller Pachtrechte, Grunddienstbarkeiten und sonstigen Rechte dritter, welche sich auf diejenigen forstfiskalischen Flächen beziehen, die an den Verband Groß-Berlin veräußert werden sollen.* In Landeshauptarchiv Brandenburg, Pr. Br. Rep.2A III F Nr.3094.

35. Berliner Zentralausschuß, ed., *Der Kampf um unsere Wälder*, 28.

36. This campaign did not end with a mere petition to the Kaiser. Confronted by rising demands from urban social reformer groups and municipal governments, the Prussian state relented, allowing for Berlin and its suburbs to buy the Grunewald and other forests around the city at prices far below their real estate value. For more on this campaign, see Jeffrey K. Wilson, *The German Forest: Nature, Identity, and the Contestation of a National Symbol, 1871–1914* (Toronto, 2012), 86–131.

SELECTED BIBLIOGRAPHY

Bergmann, Klaus. *Agrarromantik und Großstadtfeindschaft*. Meisenheim, 1970.

Berliner Zentralausschuß für die Wald- und Ansiedlungsfrage, ed. *Der Kampf um unsere Wälder*. Berlin, 1909.

Deutsch, Regine. "Charlottenburger Waldschule." *Deutsche Kultur* 3 (1907): 598–603.

Düesberg, Rudolf. *Der Wald als Erzieher*. Berlin, 1910.

Hirtz, Arnold. "Waldschule und Kindererholungsstätte." *Das Schulhaus* 15 (1913): 449–59.

Imort, Michael. "A Sylvan People. Wilhelmine Forestry and the Forest as a Symbol of Germandom." In *Germany's Nature: Cultural Landscapes and Environmental History,* edited by Thomas Lekan and Thomas Zeller, 55–80. New Brunswick, NJ, 2005.

König, Karl. "Einrichtungen von Waldschulen." *Pädagogische Warte* 17 (1910): 932–38.

Lange, W. "Der Waldschule." *Pädagogische Warte* 15 (1908): 1096–1107.

Mosse, George. *The Crisis of German Ideology: Intellectual Origins of the Third Reich.* New York, 1964.

——. *The Nationalization of the Masses.* New York, 1975.

Peukert, Detlev. "The Genesis of the 'Final Solution' from the Spirit of Science." In *Reevaluating the Third Reich*, edited by Thomas Childers and Jane Caplan, 234–252. New York, 1993.

Repp, Kevin. *Reformers, Critics, and the Paths of German Modernity: Anti-politics and the Search for Alternatives, 1890–1914.* Cambridge, MA, 2000.

Rohkrämer, Thomas. *Eine andere Moderne? Zivilisationskritik, Natur und Technik in Deutschland 1880–1933.* Paderborn, 1999.

——. *A Single Communal Faith?: The German Right from Conservatism to National Socialism.* New York, 2007.

Rüsten, Rudolf. *Was tut Not? Ein Führer durch die gesamte Literatur der Deutschbewegung.* Leipzig, 1914.

Scott, James C. *Seeing Like a State. How Certain Schemes to Improve the Human Condition Have Failed.* New Haven, CT, 1998.

Stern, Fritz. *The Politics of Cultural Despair: A Study in the Rise of the German Ideology.* Berkeley, CA, 1961.

Theilemann, Wolfgang. *Adel im grünen Rock. Adliges Jägertum, Großprivatwaldbesitz und die preußische Forstbeamtenschaft 1866–1914.* Berlin, 2004.

Zechner, Johannes. "Die grünen Wurzeln unseres Volkes. Zur ideologischen Karriere des deutschen Waldes." In *Völkisch und national. Zur Aktualität alter Denkmuster im 21. Jahrhundert,* edited by Uwe Puschner and G Ulrich Großmann, 179–94. Darmstadt, 2009.

——. "Politicized Timber: The 'German Forest' and the Nature of the Nation 1800–1945." *The Brock Review* 11, no. 2 (2011): 19–32.

Chapter 4

Health as a Public Good
The Positive Legacies of *Volksgesundheit*

Annette F Timm

How involved should the state be in the provision, organization, and ethical foundations of health care provision? How does state involvement increase tendencies toward social control, medicalization, and the juridification of the private sphere? How might systems of social and medical insurance *also* improve health outcomes and provide individuals with greater access to care? I phrase these opening questions in such general terms to highlight the fact that our perceptions of the history of health care in Germany are inevitably colored by our present-day ideologies of the politics of health. How to achieve the appropriate balance between state intervention and individual choice in health care is among the most politically contested debates in the domestic politics of all nations with the luxury to have moved beyond the most existential worries. The German case has provided fodder for those arguing that state intervention and what Americans often refer to as "socialized" medicine inevitably strip individuals of choice and create mechanisms of social control that are politically undesirable or even ulti-mately evil.

I use the word evil self-consciously. In a deliberate effort to create good-versus-evil analogies, conflations of the concepts of public health, eugenics, and state-sponsored euthanasia still color the debates about health care reform in the United States, and polemics about what Sarah Palin called "death panels" rely upon the precedent of the Third Reich to score political points with ill-informed voters.[1] Let me cite just one example. In August 2009, Glenn Beck used his show on the Fox News Channel to run a series of episodes on American health care reform in which he disingenuously juxtaposes President Obama's plan to Nazi eugenics. The series included a short documentary on the history of eugenics that haphazardly traced both the American and German roots of the plan to weed out "deficients" in the name of public health. Beck's voice-over asserts:

> WWI and the flu pandemics basically turned doctors into social planners, and Hitler and the Nazis took the logic of public health to totalitarian extremes. ... The same year Hitler joined the Nazi party, in 1920, the Nazis rounded up hundreds of thousands of disabled, elderly, and mentally ill and exterminated them as, quote, "useless bread gobblers" or "life of unworthy of life." The Nazi eugenic idea evolved naturally into the eventual Holocaust, and the deaths of six million Jews.[2]

Beck makes the case that reactions to an emergency—the post–World War I influenza epidemic—combined with serious economic crisis led Germans down a path from public health, through eugenics to genocide. He places "social planners" and Nazis in the same category, because he wants to depict the Nazis as the apotheosis of a kind of modernity that devalues life. It is not difficult to find flaws and massive historical inaccuracies in his argument, of course. But we must recognize that historians have made similar arguments with, needless to say, far more sophistication and attention to historical accuracy. The history of health care in Germany has been understandably overshadowed by Nazi crimes and the need to explain them, and the essential modernity of Nazi strategies—their continuity with the Enlightenment project of controlling human destiny after the erosion of religious certainty—has been remarked upon at least since Max Horkheimer and Theodor Adorno's *Dialectic of Enlightenment*.[3] While still controversial, the "modernity" argument is most common in discussions of all matters related to health and "racial health" in the Third Reich.[4] It is also true that directly integrating the longer history of eugenics and the early Nazi practice of euthanasia into the story of the Holocaust has become a virtually uncontested commonplace of the historiography of the Third Reich. My goal in introducing the easily discredited arguments of Glenn Beck is *not*, however, to place him in the same company as scholars like Detlev Peukert and Zygmunt Bauman, who have made the link between Nazi racial policy and modernity in ways infinitely more sensitive to the moral and historiographical quandaries that this creates.[5] I quote the words of someone I consider to be a dangerous propagandist simply to highlight how politically charged this history still is and how vulnerable the story of the world's first public health care system is to distortion and political appropriation.

One could of course argue that the misappropriation of a given historical issue for political polemical purposes should not unduly disturb historians. The Rankian ethos that still partially reigns in our discipline would have us respond with a resigned shrug and send us back to our meticulous and supposedly nonideological investigations of the past. But I would like to argue that the rantings of Glenn Beck and others like him reveal something that should give us pause about how our narratives have filtered down into public consciousness. We have spent so much time investigating how Weimar modernity contained the seeds of the Holocaust that we have failed to properly appreciate some of its most important achievements. We have viewed these achievements (such as liberalized attitudes toward gender and sexuality, the provision of social welfare and insurance, and the construction of efficient measures of preventive health) as utopian, temporary, and ephemeral: inevitably to fall victim to economic crises and Nazi ideology. The term *Volksgesundheit* (public health)—the idea that a nation should be interested in health as a joint, communal enterprise—appears in italics in our writing and in our teaching as an obviously ideological and racially undermined concept. My purpose here is to argue for a different teleology, one that understands the legacies of *Volksgesundheit* as Janus-faced and contradictory. I am not making an argument for the word itself. As we have seen in various recent controversies, even the word *Volk* has not lost its power to call racist assumptions to mind.[6] But understanding the promotion of health as a collective responsibility that transcends the treatment of individuals, includes preventive measures, and ensures universal access is not inherently racist, nor need it be intertwined with nationalistic causes. The focus on the trajectory that leads from Rudolf Virchow, through Otto von Bismarck and Ernst Haeckel to Adolf Hitler has occluded the dramatic improvements to aggregate health that Germany's system of social and medical insurance had achieved long before the Nazis' co-optation of the term *Volksgesundheit.*

Making this case comprehensively would of course entail an investigation of how certain currents of thought and practice in Imperial and Weimar Germany *can* be seen as precursors to Nazi racial hygiene. I and many other historians have pointed to these continuities in investigations of the history of eugenics, population policy, reproductive health care, and disease control measures.[7] But in the limited space available to me, I will address the historiographical arguments about modernity, *Volksgesundheit,* and the Nazis only briefly before concentrating on the ways in which a notion of collective responsibility for the health of the population helped to foster progressive developments in economic structures, public hygiene, and attitudes toward gender and sexuality, particularly in the Weimar Republic. I will conclude with an argument that the achievements of the Imperial and

Weimar periods were not simply nullified by the murderous and genocidal goals that governed health care in the Third Reich. Legacies of an earlier ethos were eventually integrated into both post–World War II German states, and along with extra safeguards against abuses, contributed to an even more comprehensive system of health care provision, which has made access to medical care an effective right of German citizenship.

HEALTH CARE AND GERMAN MODERNITY

The question of whether the Third Reich represented a fundamentally reactionary development or whether we should view the rise of the Nazis as part of the story of European modernity has provoked voluminous debate. Rather than rehearsing this debate here, I will take issue with only one recent contribution that seems particularly likely to promote the kind of one-sided view that I have critiqued. In a recent contribution to a collection of essays about eugenics and nationalism in Europe, Aristotle Kallis asserts that two interdependent modern visions were fused in Nazi racism: a "biomedical totalitarianism" with its roots in nineteenth-century scientific discourses and medical practice; and a "more nebulous and uncertain" vision of a "racially pure" society in specifically Nazi ideology. Of the two, he insists, the biomedical impulse to control human destiny was more sure of itself, more consistent in its methods, and more "holistic and 'total.'" From the late nineteenth century onward, Kallis asserts, German society reached a consensus that only scientists and doctors should be tasked with explaining "human perfectability" and making life-and-death decisions for individuals and society as a whole. This "totalitarian biomedical paradigm" concentrated on the elimination of "deviance" and "extend[ed] the biomedical domain of jurisdiction from fighting disease on an individual basis to promoting 'health' at a collective level."[8] Although he admits that pre-Nazi public health measures were enshrined in a "project of liberal modernity [that] was predicated on a set of checks and guarantees of individual freedom," Kallis argues that late nineteenth- and early twentieth-century German efforts to improve the collective health of the nation were "inextricably" linked to the extremes of Nazism. The transition from the "liberal" Weimar health regime to the murderous racism of the Third Reich was simply a failure "to curb radical, counter-paradigmatic trends, or to ensconce sufficient safeguards" to combat the dangers of its "supremely modern space."[9] While citing a few "modern but decidedly contradictory possibilities" of the Weimar system—"sexual liberation, the novel sense of social tolerance, political pluralism, and progressive social engineering"—Kallis ultimately argues that all it took for these positive impulses to be negated was the "intersection of different strands of totality." The Nazis escalated Weimar tendencies, bringing about a "shift from pluralism to singularity, from the individual to the national body, from multidimensional social intervention to principles of prescription." The very openness of liberalization efforts—their contribution to a "loss of meaning" and social anchoring—aided the process and "afforded racial utopia."[10]

According to Kallis, the individualist stance of liberalism was no match for the collectivism of "biomedical totalitarianism." This interpretation leaves little room for the possibility that Wilhelmine and Weimar social health and welfare measures might also have had progressive effects and legacies or that a collectivist attitude toward public health care could be something other than totalitarian in intent and practice. Unlike Detlev Peukert, Kallis does not even explain how specific economic crises weakened these progressive possibilities, and he ignores the fact that it was primarily the state's financial inability to live up to socially progressive promises that fed extremism in the later years of the republic.[11] Kallis has made more nuanced arguments elsewhere,[12] and there is some truth in what he says about the normalizing impulses of state-sponsored medicine and the tendencies toward pathologization that they create.[13] But this kind of highly theoretical view—an interpretation that is more concerned with theoretical conceptions of fascism and totalitarianism than with an empirical investigation of the social and cultural mechanisms of political legitimacy—misleadingly describes the role of health care in Imperial, Weimar, and even, though more problematically, Nazi Germany.[14] Attitudes toward health care and *Volksgesundheit* are framed only in terms of their ideological content, which is represented as exclusively nationalist and ultimately racist. Without any investigation of actual practice it becomes a relatively simple matter to suggest that totalitarian tendencies were built into the very idea of collectivist health care—that only very strong safeguards could have prevented an almost inevitable radicalization. I would now like to give a few examples of how investigations of the economic and social impact of universal access to medical care problematizes this easy teleology.

HEALTH AS AN ECONOMIC GOOD

It is a well-known though easily obscured fact that the German health care system began neither as an entirely biomedical nor a socialist enterprise but rather as a primarily political and economic strategy. In 1883, the German Reichstag passed legislation to create the world's first national health insurance program in the form of a sickness insurance plan for workers.[15] This Bismarckian policy, which was aimed both at stealing the thunder of the growing socialist movement and at responding to the pressures of very rapid industrialization and urbanization, greatly expanded the scope of medical involvement in society.[16] Part of this story is certainly the immense prestige that German medicine was gaining at the time; Robert Koch's discovery of the tuberculosis bacillus in 1882 and his proof of the contagious nature of cholera in 1884 were universally hailed as momentous achievements both in Germany and abroad. These medical discoveries influenced health care policy, however, not only because they meshed well with the nationalist aspiration of an imperial state, but also because they enabled dramatic improvements in human health. As Richard J Evans has demonstrated in reference to the nineteenth-century cholera epidemics in Hamburg, medical science settled long-standing debates in urban (and national) politics about the rational degree of government intervention in urban hygiene and health care.[17] An understanding of the precise mechanisms of the spread of disease led to massive public works projects to improve sanitation and water treatment systems. Leaving aside the increasingly popular rhetoric of Social Darwinism and eugenics—trends that we can more easily link to later racist currents—German public health care measures were instituted in late nineteenth-century Germany as extremely pragmatic acts. They were adopted even by traditionally laissez-faire jurisdictions, like Hanseatic Hamburg, because they worked.

A second important aspect of the Bismarckian legacy that is often obscured in accounts like Kallis's is the extent to which the universalization of health care and social insurance that began in the Whilhelmine period created a sense of entitlement amongst the general population, an understanding that they had been granted new rights. Greg Eghigian has explored this issue in detail, arguing that "by institutionalizing compensation and making it compulsory [nineteenth-century social insurance] had transformed compensation into an individual right."[18] To have enshrined health and welfare provision as part of the day-to-day functioning of the state meant that citizens began to recognize access to treatment and compensation for injury as one of the rewards of German citizenship.

Many doctors reacted to these circumstances by calling to mind Rudolf Virchow's famous response to the revolutions of 1848: the insistence that doctors are "the natural lawyers of the poor" and that "the social question falls for the most part within their jurisdiction."[19] The most prominent advocate for social medicine of the late Imperial and early Weimar era was the Social Democratic doctor Alfred Grotjahn, whose research stemmed from a compassionate concern for the plight of the working classes, and whose many books emphasized the social causes and consequences of disease. Having begun writing in the late nineteenth century about the need to shift the medical view away from the laboratory and to include economic and social considerations in the study and practice of medicine, Grotjahn argued that "the social/political wind that blew during the years around the turn of the century" had created a new orientation, making it possible to see how health and economics were intertwined.[20] Understanding this and reorienting medical practice around social circumstances would, he argued, improve living standards and increase freedom for individual Germans:

> The individual as such is once again becoming valuable. No longer the "goods" but rather the people are beginning to move into the center of public participation. Finance and industrial politics no longer claim the first place in political discussions and measures, but rather population politics (*Bevölkerungspolitik*), the "human economics," the economization of people, are topics of forceful national demands.[21]

Grotjahn was not alone in assuming that both economic and social improvements were only to be achieved through thorough analyses of aggregate health. Both the medical profession and state health agencies, such as the Kaiserliches Gesundheitsamt (Imperial Health Bureau, founded in 1876 and renamed Reichsgesundheitsamt in 1918), and the Kommission zur Vorbereitung einer Reichsmedizinalstatistik (Commission for the Preparation of Imperial Medical Statistics, established in 1871) had begun tracking rates of disease, births, and deaths in the 1870s.[22] These institutions were grounded in a growing consensus that the "public good" (*Gemeinwohl*) required more attention. We can certainly understand them as biopolitical institutions interested in improving the aggregate human capital of the nation.[23] But the fact remains that along with the kinds of medical practices that Grotjahn advocated, these institutions were also instrumental in bringing about a dramatic decline in infectious illnesses. Between 1880 and 1933, a "sustained mortality decline" was evident, and degenerative diseases replaced infectious diseases as the most common cause of death.[24] While evaluations of the health status of the population as a whole were certainly motivated by militaristic concerns about a falling birth rate, medicalized efforts addressing infectious diseases most certainly decreased suffering for hundreds of thousands if not millions of Germans.

New health challenges arose during and after World War I. Aside from injured veterans, public health officials on the home front had to cope with the effects of starvation and the worldwide influenza epidemic.[25] In October and November 1918, death rates more than doubled from where they had been just a month earlier, and the highest civilian mortality rates of the entire war were registered.[26] During the immediate postwar years, rising rates of tuberculosis, typhus, scarlet fever, diphtheria, and other illnesses prompted the Reichsgesundheitsamt to proclaim a health crisis.[27] Government officials and Social Democratic Party (SPD) members called for dramatic increases in public health and welfare measures, often insisting on the importance of recognizing the social causes of disease. As one author in the SPD newspaper *Vorwärts* put it, the focus of efforts to protect *Volksgesundheit* had to shift "from medical police tutelage to much more emphasis on educating the population ... Without the cooperation of the individual, comprehensive protections against illness are impossible to implement."[28] Even the Reichsgesundheitsamt recognized the importance of acting upon the social and economic consequences of the war; a 1922 report insisted that wartime famine had produced "diminished resistance [*Widerstandsfähigkeit*] in the population," leading to high rates of infection and deaths from influenza and other infectious diseases. The recognition of federal agencies that women had experienced far greater hunger than soldiers at the front and were thus less resistant to disease led to specific policies to support family and maternal health.

There were certainly strong biopolitical implications to these reactions to the post–World War I health care crisis. As I and others have argued, constant references to the national tragedy of a falling birth rate and the consequences for Germany's position of international strength were common across the political spectrum.[29] But it is worth pausing to consider what these fears actually produced in terms of health care measures. In large cities like Hamburg, Berlin, Düsseldorf, and Cologne, urban health bureaus were established to coordinate an extremely broad spectrum of health care provisions. Clinics to educate and treat victims of tuberculosis, venereal disease, alcoholism, and psychiatric illness, along with efforts to promote maternal, infant, and children's health became fixtures of the urban landscape.[30] The marriage counseling clinics that opened in large cities across the republic were certainly inspired by eugenic principles and desires to increase the birth rate and prevent genetic illness, but they also provided information about birth control along with psychological, legal, and economic advice that was gratefully accepted by those suffering the lasting effects of the war on family life.[31] Dramatic efforts were made to reintegrate injured veterans into the workforce through the development of work-appropriate prosthetics and occupational therapy.[32] Much ink has been spilled about the normalizing tendencies of these bureaucracies and the degree to which they presumed public authority to influence private decisions and life choices, particularly for the working classes. But there can be no doubt that they also provided services that prevented disease, lessened individual suffering, and provided access to information about preventive health care. As Greg Eghigian has argued, when services were cut back in the wake of escalating inflation in the mid 1920s, the competition for scarce social and medical resources was fierce. It became "necessary to prove that one's needs were more pressing, one's predicament more dire, one's sacrifice far greater than anyone else's" in order to gain access to needed and desired medical services.[33] The fact that these services had come to be perceived as a right of citizenship caused enormous dissatisfaction with the government when access became more competitive, a fact that eventually threatened the legitimacy of the republic.

As social insurance and access to medical care became ever more universal, a sense of entitlement—what Claude Lefort has described as an "awareness of rights"—was created. Rights, Lefort argues, do not simply "exist," but are created as "publically recognized principles" that are only partly embodied in law and are based on actual practice within the space of civil society; these principles are not *entirely* under the control of the state.[34] German citizens conceived of these new services as something they were owed. This sense of entitlement must be acknowledged alongside our studies of the normalizing and racializing tendencies of medicalization, rationalization, and racialization. We must recognize that the universalization of health care in the Weimar years opened up spaces for the inclusion of a much broader swath of society in the practical benefits of citizenship. The degree to which this is true is most evident in the sphere of gender and sexuality.

GENDER AND SEXUALITY

The expansion of health and welfare services massively expanded both the services available to working-class women and the involvement of middle-class women in the provision of this care. Attention to the birthrate inevitably meant attention to women's health, and particularly to pregnancy and childbirth.[35] Eugenic concerns vastly increased the attention paid to birth control. We know that these efforts were generally directed at those considered less desirable as contributors to the national gene pool. But access to birth control also provided women with the means of preventing unwanted pregnancies. A doctor or a welfare worker in a state agency may well have evaluated the future children of a mother of five with an alcoholic husband as genetically undesirable. But this mother was also desperately happy to receive advice and gain access to birth control so that she could prevent the birth of a sixth child. This iconic example also makes evident another salutary effect of the emphasis on aggregate population health: it included men as reproductive agents. This shift in focus helped create policies that increased both men's and women's ability to control their reproductive lives. A heated debate in Berlin in 1930 about the use of vending machines to sell condoms was eventually settled with the argument that given men's inability to entirely control their sexual urges, condoms would have to remain freely available to prevent the spread of venereal diseases and the consequent threat to the birthrate.[36] While it is fairly easy to decry such decisions as a one-sided preservation of male access to sex, women also certainly benefited from the prophylactic and contraceptive benefits of the continued availability of condoms, a situation that endured through the Third Reich.

I am not alone in arguing that access to birth control and the involve-ment of women in health and welfare services in the Weimar Republic pro-vided significant benefits for women and families. (See in particular the work of Atina Grossmann and Michael Schwartz.) It is far less common to point out that social insurance and an expansive understanding of *Volksgesundheit* also made possible the flowering of sexological discourse and practice. Less than a year after the founding of the republic, Magnus Hirschfeld, a sexologist and cofounder of the world's first gay rights organi-zation, opened the Institute for Sexual Science. This was a place of research, political advocacy, counseling, and public education. Closely allied with the women's movement and with other sex reform organizations, Hirschfeld's institute sought to educate the broader public about the spectrum of human sexualities (he used the term *sexuelle Zwischenstufen*—sexual intermediaries). The institute's various medical and welfare experts provided counseling to people they called hermaphrodites, transvestites, and homosexuals, but also to married couples seeking to improve relationships and sexual satisfac-tion.[37] Hirschfeld was influenced by the Darwinian rhetoric of his day, but he deployed his biologically deterministic and medicalized understanding of human sexual preference to advocate for tolerance, decriminalization, and access to sexual counseling and medical treatment for sexual minorities and individuals whom we would today refer to as intersex. His dream of integrating sexology into medical education and having his institute directly funded by the state were dashed. Nevertheless, the institute managed to treat 3,500 individuals in the first year of its operation alone, and many of the psychologists and medical doctors who worked at the institute part-time had practices that were funded by the social insurance system.[38]

In general, the activities of the institute and Hirschfeld's tireless political advocacy for the rights of sexual minorities stand as a significant challenge to the argument that biomedical tendencies were necessarily totalitarian or that overarching campaigns for *Volksgesundheit* necessarily entailed racialized, nationalistic logic. Hirschfeld was a strong advocate for the nationalization of health care provision, and together with Alfred Grotjahn and Julius Moses (the founder of the Social Democratic Doctor's Association), he crafted an ultimately unsuccessful petition to the new Social Democratic government for the creation of a national health ministry.[39] Arguing that free access to health care was as important as free education and free legal aid for the creation of a just society,[40] Hirschfeld viewed universal access to medical care not as a means of creating an exclusionist state, but rather as a path to creating a society that encompassed the full spectrum of human difference. His was an expansive understanding of *Volksgesundheit* that emphasized the importance of being sensitive to individual psychosocial needs while still viewing these individuals as equal members of a larger *human* collective.

It is no accident that the Nazis viewed Hirschfeld as a key enemy of their plans to create a racial utopia. Having already slandered him as a degenerate Jew in their political publications, the National Socialist Students Association plundered the Institute of Sexual Science on 10 May 1933 and burned its library's books at Berlin's Opernplatz. It is quite clear that this part of the story of *Volksgesundheit* in twentieth-century Germany is not likely to make it into a Glenn Beck video any time soon. But Hirschfeld's reliance on the ideal of a state-funded system as a means of providing refuge and encouraging the acceptance of sexual minorities is as much a part of the long history of German public health care as are Nazi arguments that a collective notion of health requires the purposeful exclusion and even murder of such "deviations" from the norm.

THE NAZI CO-OPTATION OF *VOLKSGESUNDHEIT*

Hirschfeld and the entire Weimar sexual reform movement were convenient targets of Nazi derision. Yet it is misleading to assume that the attack on Social Democratic figures and institutions meant that the sense of health care as a right entirely disappeared in the Third Reich. The public perception that the state owed its citizens access to health and welfare services was strong enough to curtail the maneuverability of Nazi policy makers after the *Machtergreifung* (seizure of power). As Leonardo Conti, who later became Reichsgesundheitsführer, put it in the early months of the regime, plans for genetic and racial welfare measures (*Erb- und Rassenpflege*) were so advanced that laws (like the sterilization law) could be immediately implemented after the *Machtergreifung,* while for more general health politics there "was not even an idea for the general outlines of a worked out organizational program ... for the duties of *Volksgesundheit.*"⁴¹ Having attacked social insurance as a socialist ploy during the 1920s and early 1930s, the Nazis found that they could not easily combat the public's sense of entitlement to state-organized health and welfare benefits. Different factions to the right and left in the Nationalsozialistische Deutsche Arbeiterpartei (NSDAP) never found a new consensus, and the party's own rhetoric about the long suffering *Volksgemeinschaft* only increased public expectations of rewards for sacrifices suffered during World War I and its economically disastrous aftermath.⁴²

We must, then, carefully separate the notion of universal health care from the racial exclusions of its Nazi variant. Winfried Süß warns us to beware of assuming that there was something in the logic of social insurance that inevitably led to the racial state—that Nazi health politics simply radicalized the collectivist urge of a universal system to produce a "final solution for the social question" in its exclusionary and ultimately genocidal racial hygiene policies. This explanation of the radicalization of health policy in the Third Reich, Süß claims is too "global" while being historically imprecise. It suggests that what we have thus far understood as somehow truly unique about the Third Reich—the "physical annihilation of the excluded [*Ausgegrenzten*]"—is actually an "inherent element of all capitalistically organized industrial societies." Racism as the driving force of Nazism actually recedes as a causal factor in these arguments.⁴³ In other words, insisting upon the link between the idea of collectivist health care and Nazism actually radically underestimates the degree to which Nazi racism was responsible for the worst crimes of the regime, including but not limited to the Holocaust. (One suspects, in fact, that this underplaying of race might also explain the fondness of right-wing propagandists like Glenn Beck for this line of argument.) At the same time, the focus on medical care as virtually exclusively associated with racial policy has underemphasized the degree to which it was also a factor in creating the sense of belonging that made nonmarginalized Germans feel at home in the *Volksgemeinschaft*—the feelings, in other words, that made it possible for them to look the other way when others were excluded from the benefits of belonging.⁴⁴ It is simply naïve to believe that the benefits of citizenship are an ideologically neutral good. The fact that some citizens of a murderous regime benefit from its crimes has no bearing upon our debates about these benefits in a democratic context.

CONCLUSION

Germans' sense of entitlement to health care continued into the post–World War II period and became part of the founding ethos of both German states. While I have not been able to fully explore these legacies here, it is worth mentioning that in the post–World War II period, Allied occupiers immediately ceded authority in matters of urban hygiene, medical insurance, and disease control to German authorities. British health officials were particularly likely to argue that elements of the Weimar system that they had so admired could be reinstituted and that reforming rather than replacing the German health and welfare system was the best way of overcoming the second war-induced health crisis of the twentieth century.[45] Once again, desperate requirements for the efficient provision of care to a vast number of Germans in need called for a comprehensive and state-run effort. Efforts to reinstitute specifically eugenic laws, such as a sterilization law, were thwarted by constitutional protections in the West and fierce antifascism in the East. Both states made universal access to medical care a politically unassailable tenet of citizenship.

The challenge in historicizing this development is to track the trajectory from the beginnings of social insurance in the 1880s, through the racist co-optation of *Volksgesundheit* under Nazism, to the current situation of almost universal support for a public system. The story that Kallis tells simply ends in 1945, making it relatively easy to depict Nazi health care as the apotheosis of trends toward "biopolitical totalitarianism" that are supposedly inherent in a state-funded and administered system. But the narrative is far more complex. We need to rethink the place of health care in the longue durée of German history for two reasons. First of all, depicting *Volksgesundheit* as *inherently* exclusionary is a simplification of a far more differentiated historical reality. Despite some undeniable continuities, the Nazi seizure of power represented a dramatic rupture that cut off progressive possibilities that we can still call ahead of their time. Underplaying this rupture obscures the degree to which health care had become an aspect of lived citizenship that continued to influence Germans' understandings of their place in the *Volksgemeinschaft* into the Nazi era. But second, and more controversially, I would argue that a one-sided view of this history also damages the credibility of a concept that is vital to the future well-being of all civilized nations: the concept of a right to health care that can only be guaranteed through active state intervention and a system of publically supported insurance.

Annette F Timm is Associate Professor of History at the University of Calgary and editor of the *Journal of the History of Sexuality*. Her publications include *The Politics of Fertility in Twentieth-Century Berlin* (Cambridge, 2010) and *Gender, Sex, and the Shaping of Modern Europe: A History from the French Revolution to the Present Day* (coauthored with Joshua A Sanborn, 2nd ed., London, 2016). She is currently completing a book entitled *Lebensborn: Myth, Memory, and the Sexualization of the Nazi Past,* and she is engaged in an ongoing collaborative research project about the transmission of knowledge about sexuality and transsexuality from Germany to North America.

NOTES

1. For a description of Palin's discredited argument, see Justin Bank, "Palin vs. Obama: Death Panels," FactCheck. Annenberg Public Policy Center, August 14, 2009, http://www.webcitation.org/mainframe.php.
2. There are numerous clips of this series available on YouTube. This quote was taken from the episode on 11 August 2009, at http://www.youtube.com/watch?v=OTwRLbgcdOE. Beck argues that eugenics originated with American and British socialist thinkers and that Hitler personally wrote to the president of the American Eugenics Society for advice and then implemented polices that caused "an American eugenicist" to complain that "the Germans are beating us at our own game." In Beck's various rants, he disingenuously insists that he is not claiming that eugenics "are coming back," and yet the editorial linkages between his presentation of history and his arguments about the present are undeniable.
3. Theodor Adorno and Max Horkheimer, *Dialectic of Enlightenment: Philosophical Fragments,* ed. Gunzelin Schmid Noerr, trans. Edmund Jephcott (Palo Alto, CA, 1987).
4. The modernity debate is now extremely wide ranging. For overviews see Saul Friedlander, "The Extermination of the European Jews in Historiography," in *Thinking about the Holocaust: after Half a Century,* ed. Alvin H Rosenfeld (Bloomington, IN, 1997), 3–17; Edward Ross Dickinson, "Biopolitics, Fascism, Democracy: Some Reflections on Our Discourse about 'Modernity,'" *Central European History* 37, no. 1 (2004): 1–48; and Dennis Sweeney, "Reconsidering the Modernity Paradigm: Reform Movements, the Social and the State in Wilhelmine Germany," *Social History* 31, no. 4 (2006): 405–34. For specific reference to social welfare, see David F Crew, "The Ambiguities of Modernity: Welfare and the German State from Wilhelm to Hitler," in *Society, Culture, and the State in Germany, 1870–1930,* ed. Geoff Eley (Ann Arbor, MI, 1996), 319–44; and Young-Sun Hong, *Welfare, Modernity, and the Weimar State, 1919–1933* (Princeton, NJ, 1998). For rejections of the modernity thesis see Michael Burleigh and Wolfgang Wippermann, *The Racial State: Germany, 1933–1945* (Cambridge,

1991); Yehuda Bauer, *Rethinking the Holocaust* (New Haven, CT, 2001); and Yehuda Bauer, "Conclusion: The Significance of the Final Solution," in *The Final Solution: Origins and Implementation,* ed. David Cesarani (London, 1996), 300–9.

5. Detlev Peukert, *The Weimar Republic: The Crisis of Classical Modernity* (New York, 1989); Zygmunt Bauman, *Modernity and Ambivalence* (Ithaca, NY, 1991).

6. I am thinking of debates surrounding Hans Haacke's Reichstag piece "Der Bevölkerung" and its implicit protest against the Reichstag inscription "Dem deutschen Volke."

7. Annette F Timm, *The Politics of Fertility in Twentieth-Century Berlin* (New York, 2010); Gabriele Czarnowski, *Das kontrollierte Paar: Ehe- und Sexualpolitik im Nationalsozialismus*, Ergebnisse der Frauenforschung (Weinheim, 1991); Atina Grossmann, *Reforming Sex: The German Movement for Birth Control and Abortion Reform, 1920–1950* (Oxford, 1995); Michael Schwartz, *Sozialitistische Eugenik: Eugenische Sozialtechnologien in Debatten und Politik der deutschen Sozialdemokratie, 1890–1933* (Bonn, 1995); Paul Weindling, *Health, Race and German Politics between National Unification and Nazism, 1870–1945* (Cambridge, 1989); and Cornelie Usborne, *The Politics of the Body in the Weimar Republic: Women's Reproductive Rights and Duties* (Basingstoke, 1992).

8. Aristotle A Kallis, "Racial Politics and Biomedical Totalitarianism in Interwar Europe," in *"Blood And Homeland": Eugenics And Racial Nationalism in Central And Southeast Europe, 1900–1940,* ed. Paul Weindling and Marius Turda (Budapest, 2007), 390–91.

9. Ibid., 409.

10. Ibid., 409–10.

11. Peukert, *The Weimar Republic,* 136–37.

12. See Aristotle A Kallis, "Race, 'Value' and the Hierarchy of Human Life: Ideological and Structural Determinants of National Socialist Policy-Making," *Journal of Genocide Research* 7, no. 1 (2005): 5–29.

13. See for example Wolfgang Ayass, *"Asoziale" im Nationalsozialismus* (Stuttgart, 1995); and David F Crew, *Germans on Welfare: From Weimar to Hitler* (New York, 2001).

14. Recent investigations suggest that it will always be historiographically problematic to remain on this level of purely theoretical investigation. See Michael Geyer and Sheila Fitzpatrick, eds, *Beyond Totalitarianism: Stalinism and Nazism Compared* (New York, 2008).

15. Accident insurance followed in 1884, invalid and old-age insurance in 1911 (by which time 67 percent of the population was covered by one form or the other). Each branch of the three types of insurance was separately administered through regionally organized employee/employer boards. In 1927, unemployment insurance was also available. For more precise statistics see Greg A Eghigian, "Bureaucracy and Affliction: The World of German Social Insurance and the Birth of the Social State, 1884–1929" (PhD thesis, University of Chicago, 1993), 7–9.

16. Donald W Light, "State, Profession, and Political Values," in *Political Values and Health Care: The German Experience,* ed. Donald W Light and Alexander Schuller (Cambridge, MA, 1986), 3. On Bismarck's antisocialist strategies, see Hans-Ulrich Wehler, *The German Empire 1871–1918* (Leamington Spa, 1973).

17. Richard J Evans, *Death in Hamburg: Society and Politics in the Cholera, 1830–1910* (Oxford, 1987).

18. Greg A Eghigian, *Making Security Social: Disability, Insurance, and the Birth of the Social Entitlement State in Germany* (Ann Arbor, MI, 2000), 227.

19. Quoted in Alfred Grotjahn, *Soziale Pathologie: Versuch einer Lehre von den sozialen Beziehungen der menschlichen Krankheiten als Grundlage der sozialen Medizin und der sozialen Hygiene,* 2nd ed. (Berlin, 1915), 3.

20. Ibid., 4.

21. Grotjahn, *Soziale Pathologie,* 520.

22. See Axel C Hüntelmann, *Hygiene im Namen des Staates: Das Reichsgesundheitsamt 1876–1933* (Göttingen, 2008) and Johanna Blekker, "Die Stadt als Krankheits-faktor: Eine Analyse ärztliche Auffassungen im 19. Jahrhundert," *Medizin-historisches Journal* 18, no. 1/2 (1983): 127. The *Deutsche Medicinische Wochenschrift,* published in Berlin beginning in 1875, provided weekly statistics on deaths and illnesses in Berlin, listing detailed explanations of the exact diseases and the extent of epidemics.

23. Hüntelmann, *Hygiene im Namen des Staates,* 11.

24. Hallie J Kintner, "Recording the Epidemiologic Transition in Germany, 1816–1934," *Journal of the History of Medicine and Allied Sciences* 54, no. 2 (1999): 167 and 170.

25. Belinda Davis, *Home Fires Burning: Food, Politics, and Everyday Life in World War I Berlin* (Chapel Hill, NC, 2000).

26. Richard Bessel, *Germany after the First World War* (Don Mills, 1993), 224.

27. Reichsgesundheitsamt, Denkschrift über die gesundheitlichen Verhältnisse des deutschen Volkes im Jahre 1920/21 (Berlin, 1922).

28. Anon, "Neue Wege der Volksgesundheitspflege," *Vorwärts* (1919), incompletely cited clipping in "Sammlung Rott," Freie Universität Berlin, F12.

29. Timm, *The Politics of Fertility*; Schwartz, *Sozialistische Eugenik*; Grossman, *Reforming Sex*; Weindling, *Health, Race and German Politics.*

30. Hermann Bolzau, "Gesundheitsämter," in *Handwörterbuch der Wohlfahrtspflege,* ed. Oskar Karstedt et al. (Berlin, 1924), 168. On venereal disease clinics, see Timm, *The Politics of Fertility.*

31. Timm, *The Politics of Fertility.*

32. Michael Geyer, "Ein Vorbote des Wohlfahrtstaates. Die Kriegsopferversorgung in Frankreich, Deutschland und Großbritannien nach dem Ersten Weltkrieg," *Geschichte und Gesellschaft* 9, no. 2 (1983): 230–77; and Deborah Cohen, *The War Come Home: Disabled Veterans in Britain and Germany, 1914–1939* (Berkeley, CA, 2001).

33. Eghigian, *Making Security Social,* 227.

34. Claude Lefort, *The Political Forms of Modern Society: Bureaucracy, Democracy, Totalitarianism* (Cambridge, 1986), 23 and 261.
35. By far the most detailed account of these services is to be found in Patricia R Stokes, "Contested Conceptions: Experiences and Discourses of Pregnancy and Childbirth in Germany, 1914–1933" (PhD thesis, Cornell University, 2003).
36. Timm, *The Politics of Fertility*, 76–77.
37. For general overviews of Hirschfeld and his institute see Tracie Matysik, "In the Name of the Law: The 'Female Homosexual' and the Criminal Code in Fin de Siècle Germany," *Journal of the History of Sexuality* 13, no. 1 (2004): 26–48; Ralf Dose, "The World League for Sexual Reform: Some Possible Approaches," *Journal of the History of Sexuality* 12, no. 1 (2003): 1–15; and Rainer Herrn, *Schnittmuster des Geschlechts: Transvestitismus und Transsexualität in der frühen Sexualwissenschaft* (Giessen, 2005).
38. Herrn, *Schnittmuster des Geschlechts*, 115.
39. Elena Mancini, *Magnus Hirschfeld and the Quest for Sexual Freedom: A History of the First International Sexual Freedom Movement* (New York, 2010), 114.
40. Magnus Hirschfeld, "Verstaatlichung des Gesundheitswesens," *Flugschriften des Bundes Neues Vaterland* 10 (Berlin, 1919).
41. Quoted in Winfried Süß, *Der "Volkskörper" im Krieg: Gesundheitspolitik, Gesundheitsverhältnisse und Krankenmord im nationalsozialistischen Deutschland 1939–1945* (Munich, 2003), 32.
42. Ibid., 275–77.
43. Ibid., 25–26.
44. Although some of his arguments have certainly proven controversial, the evidence that Götz Aly provides in *Hitler's Beneficiaries: Plunder, Racial War, and the Nazi Welfare State* (New York, 2006) attests to the material gains that many Germans experienced during the Third Reich.
45. George Foggon, "Alliierte Sozialpolitik in Berlin," in *Sozialpolitik nach 1945: Geschichte und Analysen,* ed. Reinhart Bartholomäi et al. (Bonn-Bad Godesberg, 1977), 33–36. Foggon came to Berlin in 1945 as head of Labor Affairs for the British Military Government. He argues that the occupying powers all agreed on the question of German expertise in the health care field.

SELECTED BIBLIOGRAPHY

Crew, David F. "The Ambiguities of Modernity: Welfare and the German State from Wilhelm to Hitler." In *Society, Culture, and the State in Germany, 1870–1930,* edited by Geoff Eley, 319–44. Ann Arbor, MI, 1996.

Czarnowski, Gabriele. *Das kontrollierte Paar: Ehe- und Sexualpolitik im Nationalsozialismus. Ergebnisse der Frauenforschung.* Weinheim, 1991.

Dickinson, Edward Ross. "Biopolitics, Fascism, Democracy: Some Reflections on Our Discourse about 'Modernity.'" *Central European History* 37, no. 1 (2004): 1–48.

Eghigian, Greg A. *Making Security Social: Disability, Insurance, and the Birth of the Social Entitlement State in Germany*. Ann Arbor, MI, 2000.

Grossmann, Atina. *Reforming Sex: The German Movement for Birth Control and Abortion Reform, 1920–1950*. Oxford, 1995.

Grotjahn, Alfred. *Soziale Pathologie: Versuch einer Lehre von den sozialen Beziehungen der menschlichen Krankheiten als Grundlage der sozialen Medizin und der sozialen Hygiene*, 2nd ed. Berlin, 1915.

Herrn, Rainer. *Schnittmuster des Geschlechts: Transvestitismus und Transsexualität in der frühen Sexualwissenschaft*. Gießen, 2005.

Hirschfeld, Magnus. "Verstaatlichung des Gesundheitswesens." *Vorwärts* 36, no. 43 (1919).

Hong, Young-Sun. *Welfare, Modernity, and the Weimar State, 1919–1933*. Princeton, NJ, 1998.

Hüntelmann, Axel C. *Hygiene im Namen des Staates: Das Reichsgesundheitsamt 1876–1933*. Göttingen, 2008.

Kallis, Aristotle A. "Racial Politics and Biomedical Totalitarianism in Interwar Europe." In *"Blood and Homeland": Eugenics and Racial Nationalism in Central and Southeast Europe, 1900–1940*, edited by Paul Weindling and Marius Turda. Budapest, 2007.

Peukert, Detlev. *The Weimar Republic: The Crisis of Classical Modernity*. New York, 1989.

Schwartz, Michael. *Sozialistische Eugenik: Eugenische Sozialtechnologien in Debatten und Politik der deutschen Sozialdemokratie, 1890–1933*. Bonn, 1995.

Süß, Winfried. *Der "Volkskörper" im Krieg: Gesundheitspolitik, Gesundheitsverhältnisse und Krankenmord im nationalsozialistischen Deutschland 1939–1945*. Studien zur Zeitgeschichte; 65. Munich, 2003.

Timm, Annette F. *The Politics of Fertility in Twentieth-Century Berlin*. New York, 2010.

Part II

Democratic Transformation

Chapter 5

Antifascist Heroes and Nazi Victims

Mythmaking and Political Reorientation in Berlin, 1945–47

Clara M Oberle

This essay on the reconfiguration of postwar German antifascism investigates one of the key ways in which Allies and Germans alike formed and negotiated understandings of "different Germans, many Germanies." Focusing on the immediate postwar years predating the foundation of the German Democratic Republic (GDR) and Federal Republic of Germany (FRG), it looks at the changing characterization of a country of aggressive Nazis or fascists into one of antifascists.[1] This study does not present a fundamental revision of German culpability in war, ethnic cleansing, or genocide. Instead, it offers an inquiry into the processes by which many Germans during the immediate postwar years would come to identify themselves with and as "victims," "anti-Nazis," and "antifascists." It is to the concrete case of Berlin (1945–47) that this chapter turns. Presenting evidence from two very different realms—cultural policies vis-à-vis youth as well as housing legislation—it suggests we expand our understanding of places of myth-generation and political reorientation, to go beyond well-studied and important sites such as the classroom, official youth groups, election campaigns, the press,

Special gratitude for valuable commentary to Konrad Jarausch, Martin Sabrow, Sean Forner, Annette Timm, Brian Puaca, Dan Diner, Atina Grossmann, Anson Rabinbach, Frank Mecklenburg, and Andreas Huyssen. Some parts of this chapter build on earlier work, published in *New German Critique* 118 (2012). The author wishes to thank the journal for permission to publish these here.

and the war crimes trials. Further, the evidence challenges us to expand our understanding of the cast of actors involved in giving the myth its eventual form. As shall be shown, it went through numerous iterations and was influenced by some of the most unlikely contenders, in response to diverse and sometimes even contrary intentions. Thus, rather than engaging in an exercise of debunking what historians have called the "myth of antifascism," the chapter proposes we consider seriously the emergence and functioning of this very myth, as myth.

The immediate post-catastrophe setting, that of the rubble-strewn, broken city in which old hierarchies, values, and norms were no longer stable, mattered greatly. "I know it is not easy for youth to orient themselves in the intellectual [geistigen] and political chaos with which Nazism has left us," Max Fechner, later GDR minister of justice, empathized with Berlin and German youth in an address delivered in 1946.[2] He then acknowledges the lukewarm interest in his speech, observing that in the turmoil, youth and adults alike are preoccupied with the material and social chaos around them, pressed to find a way to make a living amid the rubble, finding themselves "without firm ground," "unsettled," "confused," and "shocked in defeat."[3] Key functions of myths, as scholars since Durkheim and Lévi-Strauss have observed, have been to uphold social order, to integrate societies, and to serve as a pragmatic moral and political guide.[4] Examining the emergence of modern political myths, Münkler and before him Cassirer have noted that contexts of economic and political crisis, disorientation, and uneasy transformations provide "the natural soil upon which political myths ... grow up and ... find ample nourishment."[5] As Jan Assmann has reminded us, myths first and foremost provide orientation as to who we are, and where in the greater cosmos we stand.[6] Order, social cohesion, guidance, orientation: these, as countless witnesses of the time attest, appeared sorely absent in rubble-strewn, immediate postwar Berlin.

Indeed, the physical and demographic setting alone would have appeared to many as disorienting. Thus, the city's population was continuously in flux and substantial parts unsettled. By April 1945, a third of Berlin apartment dwellings were damaged beyond repair.[7] While we lack entirely reliable figures for the numbers of Berliners rendered homeless, they approximated a million.[8] At the same time, there was a visible influx of large numbers of other persons into Berlin. These included not only Soviet and later US, British, and French military and civilian personnel, but also recently freed so-called displaced persons, returning evacuees, some released prisoners of war (POWs), and unsettled ethnic Germans from places farther east and southeast; by February 1946 half a million of the latter entered Berlin per month.[9] The material surroundings likewise called for reorientation. With 50,000 tons of shells dropped over the center of the city, Berlin had received the heaviest load of destructive materials in all of Europe.[10] With an estimated 55 to 75 million cubic meters of rubble, the streets appeared to be dominated by debris, buildings ruinous and disfigured.[11]

When reading the records of Allied and German descriptions of the Berlin cityscape, one is struck by actors' preoccupation with the destruction and chaos. Were it not for statistics and housing records that tell us otherwise, one might be left to believe that rather than about two thirds inhabitable, Berlin was instead completely destroyed, no more than (in Bertolt Brecht's words) a "rubble heap near Potsdam."[12] Apocalyptical language abounds, even though for resident Berliners, the surprise would not have been as great in 1945 since they had had several years to get used to it. What were temporary and long-term Berlin residents seeing by May or June 1945? The pictures painted in the first postwar months were particularly dark. And this not just because, at first, not a single one of the 100,000 street lanterns were working.[13] Letters and diaries of the time show Berliners focusing on that which was altered and broken, not that which was intact, including entire districts virtually intact. Allies and Berliners alike had to engage in habitual reconnaissance walks, physically reorienting themselves in a "sea of rubble" and houses.[14] Many observers, pointing to rubble and broken housing, describe a landscape of catastrophe and grave disorientation.[15]

It is important to keep in mind that myths, including the myth of antifascism, are generated in particular settings. Berlin and Germany in 1945, recently defeated, rubble-strewn, its inhabitants not yet fully housed or controlled, presented Germans, Allied and German officials with a great task: to position and orient themselves. In the process of the Allies and local population addressing both material and political concerns within this very particular setting, they formed a public German antifascist myth, and this within a very few years, between 1945–47.

What is this so-called myth of antifascism, so prominent in postwar German history? Especially in its later version under the auspices of the GDR, it had two important elements. On the one hand, it propagated tales of the heroic German resistor, a sort of action-hero against fascism. On the other hand, this antifascist myth held that Germans across the board were Hitler's first victims and thus naturally antifascist. In brief, it exonerated Germans and exaggerated the antifascist resistance while ignoring the wide support national socialism had enjoyed in Germany.[16] Several scholars, including Catherine Epstein, Antonia Grunenberg, Dan Diner, Annette Leo, and Herfried Münkler have shown how this myth functioned throughout the forty years to legitimize the Socialist Unity Party (SED) regime.

Jürgen Danyel, Olaf Groehler, and Lutz Niethammer among others have looked at what was conveniently left out of this myth; they have studied the double-victimhood, double-perpetrators, and crossovers between the two that marked GDR society.[17]

One key question has received less attention though:[18] how was this postwar myth of German antifascism adopted and shaped in the first place? In what areas and by whom?

At first glance, Moscow seemed to have shaped much. On 10 June 1945, Marshal Zhukov, governor of the Soviet Military Administration in Germany (SMAD), proclaimed its primary task the "final extermination of remnants of Fascism."[19] The goal of all activities was to reach and win over "wide masses of the population."[20] SMAD thus encouraged a wide range of antifascist organizations. At the same time, it subjected these organizations to close scrutiny; all, for example, had to provide membership lists and register with SMAD.[21] The decree, then, set down the terms for Soviet and their collaborators' policies: it demanded that existing antifascists cast their net as widely as possible in order to win support. This was the classic popular front approach which the Soviet leadership had officially pursued with Georgi Dimitrov since the Seventh Komintern Congress in 1935.[22] It also reflected the SMAD's concern that Germans were to be feared, that fascism, despite Nazi Germany's military defeat, still had to be "exterminated." Even expectations of armed resistance after June 1945 were running high, particularly amongst members of the Soviet occupation.[23] Similar distrust and even expressed fear of Nazis or fascists (the terms were used interchangeably, sometimes within one and the same document) could be found among the Western Allies abroad and in Germany. This was the case especially once reports and photographs of German extermination camps and the underlying "cruelty, bestiality, and savagery" had started to circulate and once members of the occupation had begun to tour sites of Nazi crimes.[24]

Was there evidence for continued fascist, Nazi, and anti-Allied sentiments? The period 1945–47 sees a flourishing of Allied opinion surveys, in all realms. Not just in the realm of politics—also in cultural affairs, education, sports, youth affairs, medicine, transportation, or housing—wherever the Soviets and Western Allies looked, they keenly, fearfully, noted evidence of remaining national socialist ideology and language. Repeatedly, they issued orders "for the eradication of directives, terms, and figures of speech ... of fascist nature."[25] And yet, as became evident, decrees alone could not stamp out the remnants of Nazism and fascism. How else could these be countered? Here myths could play an important function.

This study suggests that practical concerns of the immediate postwar years also shaped the myths. One such concern, presented here, was the so-called "problem of youth," another was the negative popular opinion vis-à-vis the Allies in light of a most urgent housing crisis. In both cases, we see the genesis of an antifascist myth, arising out of the Allied attempt to create an antifascist consensus or at least a language of antifascism among the German population.[26] The first example is one of initial failure, the second eventually one of a troubling success. These are by no means the only sites of myth generation. They also are not an exhaustive history of Allied and municipal policies vis-à-vis youth or responses to the postwar housing crisis. Rather, the focus rests on these two cases as they allow more nuanced insights into the mechanisms and practices of shaping and adapting the myth.

"GOOD GERMAN TRADITIONS," YOUTH, AND THE KULTURBUND

The story of the founding of the Kulturbund and the role of the Soviet cultural commissars and the writer Johannes R Becher is well-known. In brief, under the leadership of Becher, who had returned in June 1945 to Berlin from years of Soviet exile, Berlin's intellectuals had been quickly gathered to form a cultural organization with the programmatic name Cultural League for the Democratic Renewal of Germany (Kulturbund zur demokratischen Erneuerung Deutschlands). The organization was officially founded on 3 July 1945, a day before the arrival of the Western Allies in Berlin. The idea to form a central and nonpartisan cultural organization was not novel in 1945. Communist popular front approaches of the 1930s (in Paris, in 1935, Willi Münzenberg had already called for an "antifascist cultural league"), Jewish, and exile cultural leagues in centers of German emigration such as England, Mexico, or Sweden, had come before.[27] The immediate postwar Kulturbund in Berlin served multiple purposes. Supported by Soviet and Western Allies, it was able to provide those working in the realm of culture (artists, poets, playwrights, musicians, actors) with audiences, paper, ration cards of the highest level, and frequently a home to return to in more ways than one. It also provided audiences with publications, concerts, and exhibits. And in turn, it legitimized the regimes of the occupying powers. In addition to these instrumental functions, many members shared in the idea that cultural activity served a political purpose. The programmatic name itself—for the democratic renewal of Germany—proclaimed as much. The goal, Becher announced in June 1945, was "to create a movement ... willing to annihilate all remnants of fascism and reactionary forces."[28] Similarly, Lev Dubrovitski, Soviet cultural commissar and head of the Soviet Military

Administration's Berlin information unit, later remembered: "the military struggle perhaps had come to an end, but that did not necessarily mean that fascist ideology had been eradicated."[29] The fight against fascism now continued in the realm of culture, and the defeat of fascism "alone was the criterion for our decisions."[30] Dubrovitski's statement implies a willingness to embrace unorthodox means as long as they served the ends. Visiting Germany in the fall of 1945, Isaac Deutscher observed the remarkable degree to which, in his view, the Soviet authorities on the ground were abstaining from "totalitarian methods," allowing for a "certain freedom of expression" of which intellectuals in the Soviet Union could only dream.[31] As shall become evident, the Kulturbund's interaction with youth indicates a similar flexibility in combating national socialism.

In its founding manifesto of 3 July, the Cultural League already proclaimed its primary goal was to be the "fight for the moral regeneration of our nation in particular by influencing ... German youth."[32] The scholarship on the Kulturbund's pre-1947 history has grown impressively over the past two decades. Interestingly, the role of youth seems to have been given little attention.[33] Yet in the Kulturbund's published documents and official announcements, youth is a central group, linked throughout with the concepts of rebirth and regeneration. Youth would be the ones "to turn [their] home (*Heimat*), Germany, into a real democracy."[34] Germany's redemption would come from the new generation who would be "truly human," who would "succeed in ridding Germany of disgrace," and who would, one day "regain the respect of the world."[35] Youth, in brief, is celebrated as the redeemer, the builder of a new and better epoch, of "a new and happier Germany."[36] Was this mere rhetoric? The Kulturbund's internal correspondence and exchanges with the Allied Kommandatura's education commission indicate its members were aware of discrepancies between optimistic representations of youth as the harbinger of a bright future and what they considered the grimmer realities on the ground. Many expressed deep concern with the role of the younger generation. They considered male students dangerous, the universities veritable hotbeds of national socialism. Reflective of a wider postwar discourse by the older generations, youth appeared within the correspondence of the Kulturbund and SMAD as a malleable group, one that had proved particularly susceptible to Nazi indoctrination—and now presented a serious problem.[37] German youth was not equipped to lead themselves or others out of fascism. As one Friedrichshain report from August 1945 concluded, they "possess none, or scarcely any, of the prerequisites for antifascist youth work."[38]

How could young Germans be led out of national socialism, turned into trusted anti-Nazis and antifascists? If wrong ideas were the problem, the right ones might be the solution. Censoring and purging libraries or school curricula of Nazi material, as was repeatedly done by the Allies, would not suffice.[39] This only left a gap. A dominant, though not exclusive, Kulturbund policy had been to invoke the active memory of the "good German traditions" that had existed before the Third Reich.[40] Here, they could also rely on similar invocations made by Germans in exile, works reminding the reader of the existence of that "other" German culture. Thus, Becher's poem "Tränen des Vaterlandes anno 1937" ("Tears of the Fatherland"), written in Soviet exile, and republished after 1946, invoked the cantatas and fugues of Bach, the art of Grünewald, the poetry and prose of Gryphius and Hölderlin as representative of the "mighty," and "radiant" German culture.[41] Cultural League programming, memorials, and publications likewise invoked these and of course the works of Goethe and Schiller as representative of that German culture that could now guide the way.[42] Indeed, this approach of highlighting the "good German" culture they were helping resurrect fit the program prescribed by Tiulpanov himself: work in the realm of culture was to remain flexible and cater to German needs and to those of the intelligentsia in particular.[43] Like conservative historians at the time (for instance Friedrich Meinecke's conclusion to his work *The German Catastrophe: Reflections and Recollections,* originally published in 1946), the publications and programming of the Cultural League often suggested a return to the ideas and spirit of Weimar. For only a few, this meant the Weimar Republic. For most, it meant the Weimar of Goethe.

Many contemporaries, however, feared that this approach of awakening a dormant memory of Weimar, of humanist or democratic German culture would not work for youth, given their experiences and often lack of ties to either of these traditions.[44] While surely exposed to the Weimar classics, following decades of attack on the humanist framework, these youth would have received the classics mainly within a nationalist, even volkish framework.[45] Likewise, among those born in the late 1920s and 1930s, democracy may have come with negative connotations. "Most of you have known democracy for only half a year while, in contrast, you have known dictatorship for twelve years," the aforementioned Max Fechner thus acknowledged in the 1946 address delivered to Berlin youth.[46] In his view, youth equated democracy with the experience of severe emotional and material hardship. It had become associated with postwar "turmoil," the return to a "devastated homeland (*Heimat*)," unemployment, lack of education or professional training opportunities, hunger, homelessness, the "shock of defeat," and "disorientation."[47] Like a number of his contemporaries, Fechner worried that many youth still clung to a view of the world based on the "corrupting false doctrine" (*verderbliche Irrlehre*) of the "heinous prophets" of national socialism.[48] Indeed, in Allied and German public discourse alike, youth were commonly characterized as the most fanatical supporters of national socialism, and therefore the greatest problem in postwar Germany.[49] Simply reviving older humanist and democratic traditions would not work. A greater task of reeducation lay at hand.

Some of the best scholarship on the so-called Hitler Youth cohort has since challenged the postwar characterizations of youth as the most Nazi-fied, ideologically charged contingent in 1945. Jaimey Fisher has thus read the discourse around youth and reeducation as a narrative device by which adult Germans denied their own significant role in Germany's Nazi past and negotiated for themselves a new position in the postwar order.[50] Kim-berly Redding suggests that many Allied personnel as well as returning exiles—both groups which discussed Cultural League policies—held false assumptions, having been out of touch with German youth, their image of youth instead relying heavily on national socialist prescriptive literature.[51] Given the youth's experiences of trauma, material, and psychological depri-vation during the last years and months of the war, partial distancing from national socialist ideology and politics had begun already prior to German defeat.[52] Perceptions by and about youth therefore differed significantly. By the warm summer of 1945, many Berlin youth displayed rather a clear preference to Swing dancing, finding work and food, or learning a craft than to mobilizing along national socialist or any political lines. Many may have experienced what the young Martin Broszat recalled as an "impatient yearning ... finally to live privately again."[53] They hesitated to engage in public debates or memorializations of the immediate past.[54] And, as von Plato has shown, the disillusionment of youth with national socialism led to a "widespread rejection of collective organizations."[55] Even when engaged with unions, with the Social Democratic Falcons, the Christian Democratic youth groups, the German Youth Activities, or the FDJ (Freie Deutsche Jugend), young Berliners seemed to prefer operating on their own terms. Youth, in short, did not easily let themselves be mobilized and directed from above. Meanwhile, frustrated municipal and district youth commit-tee (Jugendausschuß) officials, staffed by SMAD in first postwar weeks, as well FDJ leaders in Berlin and elsewhere, repeatedly commented on enroll-ment and attendance problems at events of a cultural and political nature. Increasingly, they resorted to legislation and participation requirements to reach these youth.[56]

Soviet and Kulturbund members likewise realized that the greater problem for reeducation was not simply the youth's lacking ties to dem-ocratic traditions, nor even their supposed national socialist fanaticism. Rather, it was the youth's missing interest in the Kulturbund and its programs that proved increasingly troubling.[57] The youth were not interested in hearing Becher or, for that matter, Hauptmann, drone on about the past or the need to create a better Germany. Some even took the Kulturbund to be "an administrative office or political party," a characterization to which its members naturally objected.[58] The frequent presence of Soviet officials, such as the head of the SMAD Propaganda Administration Sergeij Tiulpanov, did not help draw in youth either.[59] Unlike their counterparts in district youth committees, the Cultural League refrained from making attendance mandatory. If they wanted a mass audience among youth, they had to appeal to its needs and interests.

Heroes, the Kulturbund members subsequently suggested, were what German youth needed. Lieselotte Thoms of the league's radio unit told educators that youth wanted to emulate others; she refers to "the yearning for role models."[60] And she observes that these yearnings were expressed by youth themselves. Indeed, this is also attested in oral histories of the 1926–33 cohort, with interviewees recalling their longing for guiding figures in a context of lessened stability and social cohesion.[61] Many of the traditional authority figures had retreated or been removed. In the accounts of the youth cohort, mothers, far from the determined *Trümmerfrau* heroine they were later made to be, are often portrayed as exhausted, "incapable of providing security, sympathy, or advice."[62] Many fathers, to the extent that they were physically present, are presented as withdrawn and estranged.[63] The teacher as role model had also been greatly compromised.[64] In this context new heroes had to be introduced, Thoms thus suggested in 1946, who "through their personality [would] have an almost magnetic effect on young people."[65] Not ideas, for instance of humanism, but emotional ties were the key to solving the problem of reeducation.[66] This appears to be in response to the immediate postwar context described above. It also appears to be directly in line with another strand of early Kulturbund characterizations of national socialism. For these early Kulturbund descriptions had also emphasized psychological factors or group behavior over ideas and economic frameworks. None of the surviving texts produced by the Berlin-based Kulturbund between 1945 and 1947 give the classical Komintern explanation of fascism as the ultimate imperialist form of finance capitalism.[67] So if fascism was rather a phenomenon of mass emotions, and militarist hero tales had led to an emotional embracing of nationalism, could that very same genre not become the weapon with which to beat national socialism?[68]

While the construction and celebration of antifascist heroes took up much of the league members' interest, youth, by and large, still were not interested. Indeed, there were hardly any youth among the league members.[69] They also remained absent from league events. Most youth preferred going to the movies (*Gone with the Wind* was the number one blockbuster, *Der Untergang der Titanic* also highly popular), and they were emulating sportsmen, singers, movie actors, perhaps even foreign literati, but not antifascist heroes of the Nazi era. Sending prominent authors on school tours to beg for youth interest, or having musicians and actors enhance Kulturbund programming of antifascist poetry readings, "to make it, if possible, more interesting" attest to the Kulturbund leaders' awareness of continuing disinterest.[70] As Kulturbund members noted, most Berlin youngsters preferred reading adventure stories, trashy novels, and pulp fiction (*Schund- und Kitsch-Literatur*) to attending panels and lectures at which political victims of national socialism, concentration camp martyrs, and resistance poets were invoked.[71] Interestingly, the Kulturbund mostly ignored youth interest and political involvement elsewhere, even at the level of student government, which of course did exist.[72]

Subsequently, the myth went through further transformations: anthologies for youth, focusing on the heroic actions of clandestine resistance fighters and intelligence units, Harald Hauser suggested, were to be published, rather than simple martyr stories.[73] Oppositional writers, in this case French writers who had died in Nazi prisons, were to be cast in chivalric roles, to be depicted as having fought "for all freedom-loving mankind," their "sharp florette" delivering "wounds to stupidity and malice."[74] Indeed, not only Cultural League writers or those living in Berlin had noted the importance of form. In Munich, writer Ernst Wiechert thus noted the important role of literature of "the cheap sort" (*das Billige und Tingeltangelhafte*) in fabricating heroes, mobilizing, and intoxicating the masses.[75] Meanwhile, Becher in Berlin argued that "true pathos" was necessary to develop "true passion."[76] And Peter Huchel, among his fellow members of the Kulturbund's literature commission, thus proposed new narrative forms such as romance novels, written "with the means of shallow literature," intended "to combat the ideologically dangerous rubbish" which still enjoyed a wide readership.[77] Thus literary and political elites embraced this so-called shallow literature form, both to provide guidance and to reach a mass audience. They seem to have also responded to precedents from the immediate past, for example Berlin's flourishing *Dreissig Pfennig Roman* (*Thirty Penny Novel*), a series that had churned out best sellers for youth between the years 1935 and 1944. With their tales of adventure, their action hero stories, situated in far and exotic places, their tales of trials, mysteries, battles, and heroic deeds, often underscored by national socialist ideology, these Nazi-era pulp novels had been highly popular.[78] The anti-Nazi, antifascist heroes clamoring for the attention of the youngsters from 1945 to 1947 may have been intended to compete with them. Indeed, during this period, in form, the official antifascism embraced an ever-more shallow, ever-more schmaltzy myth of the heroic antifascist warrior.[79] The initially more serious and nuanced publications, for instance *Verbannte und Verbrannte: Schriftsteller, die wir nicht lesen durften* (*The Banned and Burnt: Writers We Weren't Allowed to Read*) or poorly attended events on the works of Heinrich Mann or Carl von Ossietzky, were now accompanied by publications of the Soviet-sponsored Aufbau Verlag, Verlag Junge Welt, Vorwärts Verlag, and Verlag Neues Leben with titles such as N Solotovskij's, *Abenteuer eines Tiefseetauchers* (*Adventures of a Deep-Sea Diver*), or *Das Eismeer ruft* (*The Arctic Sea Is Calling*).[80] Here, as in numerous other youth books, biographies of, for example, Thälmann, we see the emergence of the antifascist adventurer, the male action hero as the most dominant form of myth.[81] The myth also became shallow in content: full of pathos, it seemed devoid of serious analyses of national socialism, fascism, or antifascism. Most youth during those years, as the evidence would show, remained untouched.

Here then we have a case of initial failure concerning the attempted reach of reeducational policies. Yet, the evidence suggests the myth was indirectly influenced by youth. While Berlin's youth remained largely disinterested in the official antifascist myth, precisely with its lack of positive response in 1945, 1946, and 1947, and through its identification with other role models—sports and movie heroes, the heroes of boys' stories and shallow literature—they influenced both the form and content of antifascist narratives.

HOUSING

If German youth gave Soviet and local Kulturbund members cause for concern, the adult population presented an even greater problem. And the adult population, too, came to influence the official shape and meaning of "antifascist." This becomes particularly evident in the realm of housing.

Surveying of popular opinion on housing started in July 1945, the moment all Allies were in Berlin. Following Soviet initiative, the Allied Control Council had created a joint housing committee. Its members embarked on addressing the grave housing crisis, first by surveying the housing stock in Berlin and noting public opinion, then by changing housing legislation.[82] Much of the research here is based on records of this housing committee, which met at least once a week for two years. If this chapter periodically refers to "the Allies," making it sound as if they acted in unison, it is because in this very early period, 1945–47, there *was* a great deal of agreement and joint activity in the area of housing (as opposed to, for example, the questions of education and youth work, transportation, travel, rearming of the municipal police, the return of POWs, or the use of railway stations). For several weeks, these housing committee surveyors—for the most part trained architects and urban planners—visited actual apartments, block by block, across Berlin.

The surveys present the following dynamic between Allies and Germans: over and over again, the surveyors noted, Germans were resentful. In veritable litanies about their living conditions (leaking roofs, broken windows, crowded rooms, lack of plumbing, ubiquitous debris and ruins), they identified the antifascist Alliance as culprits, and this with great vehemence. Members of the military administration were still addressed as military opponents. "Der Iwan," "Der Russe," "Die amerikanische Wehrmacht," and "Feindeinwirkungen" (enemy impact) were responsible for these conditions.[83] Though none of those surveyed and quoted address rapes directly, the language they use is strongly suggestive. Allied housing officers who had entered the houses of Germans to survey or administer housing did not just "invade" them; they also were reported to have "defiled" and "penetrated" them.[84] The rather indignant views vis-à-vis the Allies were widely held and also come out in the records of numerous housing court cases.[85]

Even more troubling, many Berliners framed their suffering in a comparative way, using fascism/national socialism as their standard. These comparisons may have come to the beholder merely based on life experience and chronology. They also, however, reflect several years of propagandistic comparisons. Long before Khrushchev and Nixon's famous kitchen debates, competing Soviet and national socialist regimes had invited comparisons. Housing standards could serve as welcome, material exhibition of the superiority of one system and the inferiority of another. national socialist propaganda had thus emphasized its mission and supposed ability to provide good, "livable" space for the volkish community, starting with the building of affordable *volkswohnungen* (volk apartments), the reallocation of forcefully confiscated Jewish property, all the way to war and colonizing policies.[86] And throughout, they had contrasted good living and housing conditions under national socialism with poor housing elsewhere. For instance, descriptions of tremendously overpriced, "terribly unimaginative housing fortresses" of Manhattan and the "slums" of the Bronx, Brooklyn, and other parts of New York, with conditions whose appearance "[could] let a human heart freeze," had served to illustrate the flaws of the New Deal regime.[87] Widely circulating images from the 1942 Nazi propaganda exhibit *Das Sowjetparadies*—presented in Berlin and across the Reich in the form of traveling exhibits, postcards, film, pamphlets, and books—had portrayed Soviet subjects residing in constantly deteriorating conditions, eventually residing in living caves (*Wohnhöhlen*), like cavemen.[88] In brief, housing conditions were frequently compared and invoked as measure of regime legitimacy.

Within this framework then, many Berliners observed that by 1945, compared with 1942 and before, their living conditions had deteriorated. Now they themselves were dwelling in living caves. Some speculated that for generations the German people would suffer.[89] Moreover, they were comparing life under the Nazis to that under the Soviets or other occupiers.[90] And, like the Nazi propagandists, many implied that national socialism was the better system. As Allied housing, intelligence, transportation, and foreign offices noted with considerable concern, Berliners felt that their life had turned terrible thanks to the Allies. Should the housing crisis continue, there might be "serious discontent, and even ... popular unrest."[91] Many Germans cast themselves in the role of victims of "Allied bombing terror" and its results, the latter being unbearable, disorderly living conditions.[92] This was the phrasing in the majority of the lamentations of fall 1945 and thus iterated earlier, Nazi-era tropes of Germans as victims.[93] The conclusion of the Germans appeared to echo the national socialist propaganda: the "peace would be terrible," the Allies brutish and uncivilized.[94]

POLICIES AND RESPONSES

Did the Allies take these lamentations and expressions of resentment seriously? The evidence suggests they took these as more than a simple manifestation of the clichéd Berliner proclivity to complain. Throughout the immediate postwar years, they report on these lamentations with urgency and a sense of crisis, not least regarding German-Allied relations, governability, and the long-term prospects of peace.[95] Indeed, Paul Betts and, more recently, Eli Rubin in the case of Berlin-Marzahn, have shown that public opinion and letters to officials (*Eingaben*) regarding housing would continue to be keenly monitored by the GDR regime, taken as indicator of regime-subject relations and of the extent to which the making of socialist modern man was any success. [96] What policies did the Allies on the ground then devise in response to the resentment publicly displayed by Berliners in written and oral form during the very first years of occupation?

Crude Reeducation Attempts: Rubble Posters

One method, adopted already in the summer of 1945, reminded the local population directly that the Allies were *not* responsible for the postwar disorder and housing crisis. One might call this approach rather *plakativ,* that is, direct, literally eye-catching, and simple. Thus the Allies in all four zones of Berlin painted signs quoting Goebbels' proclamation, "You will no longer recognize Berlin," announcing, "this you owe to Hitler," or proclaiming, "Shame on Hitler and his work: rubble, rubble," and placed these on the ruins of prominent public buildings and apartments alike.[97] The message, unapologetic as to Allied bombings, seemed to extend a hand to ordinary Germans, letting them know: they, the Germans, were not responsible. What was fascism then?—Hitler, occasionally Goebbels. While the message was clearly intended to teach Germans a lesson as to who was responsible for the postwar rubble and sufferings (and by implication, who was not), the desired effect of changing German opinion, turning Germans into antifascists, was likely not achieved.

New Housing Law

Another measure to counter the resentment of Berliners proved rather more effective. The Allies jointly rewrote housing legislation in a concerted effort to address the housing crisis, which, all sides agreed, was serious. In the process, it changed the way Germans spoke of the Allies. The new housing law (Control Council Law No. 18) eventually provided housing for everyone. How was this to be ensured? Ultimately, all sides agreed that the best possible solution was to redistribute housing.[98] The law for Germany thus regulated the surveying, "inspection, allocation, and use of existing dwelling space."[99] And it created new categories of Germans.

While *not* addressing forced Aryanization of Jewish property during the Third Reich[100]—the law contained a clause that promised preferential treatment in allocating housing to all Berliners who had "suffered from the measures of the Nazis."[101] In anticipation of misuse, the next article of the law specified that only those who could officially prove their victim status would be eligible.[102] As such, it originally aimed to help the victims of fascism gain ground.

What this May 1946 law accomplished, however, was quite another thing: from the summer of 1946 on, Germans shifted their self-identification and lamentations—in court rooms, letters to housing officers, and on housing application forms—from "victims of Allied terror bombings" to "victims of the war," "victims of Hitler's war," and, ultimately, "victims of fascism/Nazism," or of "the Hitler regime."[103] For very practical reasons: they now fit a category that merited material benefits. Again and again, they highlighted their suffering, their health concerns, their trauma, and their victim status, not just in court cases, but also in letters of appeal to German and Allied authorities alike.[104] Taken in isolation, the passage listing entitlement priorities was ambiguous as to when the suffering was to have taken place, noting preference was to be given to persons who "had suffered through the measures of National Socialism."[105] Now "through its measures" could be interpreted to have such consequences as might only be felt in the postwar present. Hitler's ultimate victims, in this version, were the Germans themselves.

This change in German self-characterization, oft rehearsed and repeated, was of course much noticed by the Allies, hotly debated, but finally accepted. The Allies actually accepted this new way Germans told their personal history, well knowing that this was hardly a city or nation of resisters and antifascists.[106] Yet the Allies also wanted to shape public narratives and the way history was told: for fascism/Nazism had waged an aggressive war, and these people were suffering the consequences. It was thus only in Allied interests to have Germans now classify fascism/Nazism rather than the Allies as the villain. If Germans were to continue being resentful, at least the hatred should not be directed against the Allies.[107] At the same time, the policy suggested that everyone willing to embrace the Allied version of history would be treated in a preferred way, would be embraced by them, assured housing and security. It was a way to appease an unrepentant population, and, so some Allies hoped, one which might actually help them wean Germans of their fascism and make them *post-facto* antifascists.

But now fascism/Nazism, though it was associated with war and war-related suffering in Germany, had become an amorphous concept, more shallow than the hero myths devised for youth: erased were time frames, erased was the memory of the vast support it had enjoyed (save for Hitler, Goebbels and the Nazi elites, who were invoked), erased was the memory of individual responsibility and participation, erased was mention of the Nazi ideology, and missing was of course also the memory of persecutions and genocide.

Concluding, this study may have implications for our thinking about the process by which fascists could become antifascists, about postwar antifascism as myth, the importance of the material setting in European perspective, and finally, the question of reeducation and emerging German self-characterizations after the war.

CONCERNING THE PROCESS

First, in this study on the adaptation and spread of postwar antifascism, there are interesting structural similarities to earlier Bolshevik policies for building popular support: in both cases, we see a process by which popular feedback is incorporated into literary production, in the new political leadership's attempt to mobilize and reeducate a wide readership.[108] Faced with the challenge of leading a proletarian revolution in a Russian empire largely devoid of classic industrial proletarians, the Bolsheviks had further-more responded by creating what Gregory Massel has called a "surrogate proletariat" of unlikely agents: peasants and Muslim women.[109] In opening up the term "proletarian revolution" to the widest possible body of con-tenders, the original ideology produced most unorthodox blossoms. The postwar German case seems to be one of surrogate antifascism in a country largely lacking antifascists. Interestingly, in the post 1917 Soviet case, the very process of deideologization and diversification that accompanied the substantial widening of the party base may help explain the party purges, as Sheila Fitzpatrick has suggested.[110] In the postwar German case, it is of course also precisely at this moment of unorthodox opening of antifascism for a mass base that we see the greatest crackdown within the Communist Party leadership and vis-à-vis the non-Stalinist antifascists in the Soviet zone, not least with the outlawing and persecution of all antifascist orga-nizations and committees not officially approved by Soviet authorities.[111]

Second, as with other cases of attempted "revolutions from above," the process of myth generation and ideology transfer appears not all that diri-gible from above as one might expect from the so-called big powers. Thus, the actors involved in the generation of the antifascist tales (with hero as well as victim emphasis), in both cases presented here included Nazi perpe-trators as well as victims, ordinary Germans as well as Allies. And just as in the early years of the GDR that Lokatis and Barck have studied, literary production and the generation of the antifascist hero tales retained a consid-erable element of improvisation, revision, and contestation.[112] Furthermore, the cases in which the Allies and Kulturbund members tried to consciously construct an operative myth and used more crude, direct approaches for spreading the new narratives—adventure stories, rubble posters—appear to be a history of initial failure. The Kulturbund case then could be placed alongside other recent studies that have turned to histories of experimen-tation and failure, such as Christoph Classen's superb study on antifascism and fascism in Sowjetische Besatzungszone (SBZ, Soviet Occupation Zone) early GDR radio.[113] In turn, where the new narratives were adopted by larger parts of the population, as was the case in the realm of housing, they came as the not always intended, but ultimately welcomed result of the interplay between material conditions, local mentalities, and Allied welfare policies and language. They were also narratives that would be continuously rehearsed in everyday settings.

CONCERNING THE MYTH

Both the victim and the hero-based narratives generated in the immediate postwar performed key functions of myth *qua* myth. As Jan Assmann suggests, myths emerge in contexts of great deficiency and in periods of transition.[114] This study of the early postwar transition years in Berlin has attempted to reinscribe the physical and social context into our understanding of emerging redemption narratives. The sources from youth and housing cases alike paint an image of Germans profoundly—often literally—unsettled and disoriented, yearning for guidance, struggling to find their place. The evidence however also reinforces Münkler's findings that not all myths take off.[115] In this case as well, whether a myth resonated also depended on the different generational experiences and yearnings.[116] Yet all sources point to a disorientation, across the generations. In this context, the myths offered the possibility to imagine a different kind of German. Partaking in them would allow the narrators to position themselves anew, not least vis-à-vis the new regimes. And myth offered a shorthand, a highly stylized but graspable view of what to many still appeared an unfathomable, indecipherable, chaotic world.[117] In brief, they promised order and renewed stability in a context that still sorely lacked these. As such, they responded to basic yearnings "from below," and were shaped by these. The Kulturbund members, Soviet political and cultural officers, and Allied housing personnel alike understood the importance and power of myths, not least having studied their functioning within fascism. Shaping new myths and popularizing them was in the Allies' interest. If we take Barthes' understanding of well-functioning myths, the new myths thus served ideology and, ultimately, those seeking to maintain or establish power. Barthes, however, also accounts for the type of myth we saw generated in the case of the antifascist hero myth crafted for youth by Soviet and Cultural League officials: a myth which fails to deliver, "produced on order, ... invented with difficulty, ... stiff and literal, ... indiscreet, clumsy in appropriation," eventually "reduced to litany."[118] Interestingly in our case, precisely where myths were proscribed as strategy, they failed to take root. On the other hand, where they appeared as a welcome but unintended consequence of negotiations between new regimes and citizens, they were most successful. Here, the emerging myths arguably served as key components of consensus-building.[119]

CONCERNING THE EUROPEAN CONTEXT

Concerning the wider European setting, this study has suggested the importance of local material conditions or what one might call the dialectic of the rubbled space. Material conditions, the Allies observed, fueled the continued fascist sentiments of the Germans. So to alter these material conditions was eventually one way in which the Allies responded. And the situation in which parts of the city were destroyed—but not every structure—posed most urgently the question of the allocation of resources. The immediate postwar period was thus about redistribution and not reconstruction, which is how much of the postwar city and occupation historiography still is posited. Redistribution was surely not the only cause for the adaptation of victimhood tales and eventually, anti-Nazi and antifascist tales. But it did affect the manner in which Berliners portrayed themselves and narrated their immediate past.

This connection of local material conditions, and redistribution of resources (including housing), with antifascist narratives seems to parallel other European cases. For example in the cases on Eastern and Central Europe examined by Eagle Glassheim, Mark Mazower, Katherine Lebow, and Philipp Ther, all authors tie the establishment of postwar communist regimes (and with it, the embracing of antifascist rhetoric by local populations) to the redistribution of land and material in the immediate postwar period.[120] Antifascism was, furthermore, now linked with victimhood. The scholarship on redistribution and victimhood debates in Western European cities also indicates that redistribution proved a litmus test for the new, self-proclaimed antifascist regimes.[121] Though not explicitly examining the effect of law on memory narratives, these studies also seem to indicate that the wording of the laws had a lasting influence on the way urban dwellers of all political backgrounds narrated their stories about the past.

The construction of antifascist myths, featuring highly stylized heroes, likewise was not unique to the Berlin or German setting alone. Recalling the Italian context of 1946, Italo Calvino would later remember the pressures during those times on writers to "create a 'positive hero,' to provide images that were salutary in terms of social behavior and revolutionary militancy."[122] Similar to the Cultural League's heroes, the called-for polemical literary "socialist heroes" had "very little influence or following in subsequent years."[123] This raises the question of what the newly emerging myths accomplished.

AND FINALLY, CONCERNING REORIENTATION
AND THE DIFFERENT GERMANS

Do the new narratives themselves qualify as evidence of denazification? The Allies themselves expected that denazification, pacification, and democratization of Germany would take decades. While the narratives did indeed change within a short period of time, it would make little sense to speak of conversion by 1947. But the cases presented here indicate that in the immediate postwar, a new framework and narrative structure was created. This, as the study of the more clumsy aspect of the myth has shown, did not come out of new books or posters mirroring and mocking Nazi propaganda. Rather, it was a myth embraced and shaped by Germans as well, tied to material conditions and thus repeatedly rehearsed and adapted in the everyday. The new myths moreover, especially in the version coming out of housing laws, allowed Germans to narrate their own biographies and experiences in a new tone, as victims of fascism, Hitler, and Hitler's war, and therefore aligned with the Allies.

The evidence presented here may thus be reflective of a process of reorientation, not yet of reeducation or conversion. It would have to be placed alongside long-term economic and political changes, restructuring of institutions, and reeducation evident, for instance, in the long-term effects of new school curricula or foreign exchange programs. With these cases then, we have seen a story of intense German and Allied interactions, with the myth of antifascism evolving from responses vis-à-vis the far from silent local population in a context of partial material destruction. It is a story of nonresponses to the new myth, of competing versions, as well as signs of visible impact, noticeable in shifts in popularly expressed attitudes, following the occupiers' commitment to solve the housing crisis. It is also the story of Berliners embracing Allied, especially Soviet terminology, for their own purposes, shaping and transforming the stories of victimhood and antifascism or anti-Nazism. And it is the story of the occupiers' often earnest ambition to improve the city and its citizens. Ultimately, their hope had been to teach Germans about the danger and destructiveness of fascism, thereby, they hoped, turning fascists into antifascists. It was a story Allies and Germans could share, one which would unite victors and conquered. The cost for this consensus and new antifascism, constructed by Germans and the Allies together: a skewed version of the most recent German past, a partial amnesia and general amnesty. It would take several decades to move from this type of myth and *Bewältigung* of the past to new forms of approaching and engaging with it.[124]

Clara M Oberle (PhD, Princeton University, 2006) is Associate Professor in the Department of History at the University of San Diego, and an affiliate with its programs in architecture and Italian studies. Her work on housing, health, and postwar intellectual history has appeared in the *Journal of Military History, Hygieia Internationalis,* and *New German Critique.* A recipient of numerous awards, including the Jefferson Davis Prizes in History, Carnegie Mellon, and MacArthur Foundation grants, she has been Visiting Scholar at Humboldt University and Research Fellow at Berlin Program for Advanced German and European Studies, Technische Universität Berlin, and New York University's Remarque Institute.

NOTES

1. The terms "fascist" and "antifascist" are used in reference to the discourse, not as analytical category.
2. Max Fechner, *Jugend und Politik* (Berlin, 1946), 4.
3. Ibid., 4–5.
4. Émile Durkheim, *Les formes élementaires de la vie réligieuse: le système totémique en Australie* (Paris, 1968); Claude Lévi-Strauss, *Structural Anthropology* (New York, 1975), 206–30; Matthias Wächter, *Der Mythos des Gaullismus: Heldenkult, Mythospolitik und Ideologie, 1940–1958* (Göttingen, 2006).
5. Herfried Münkler, *Die Deutschen und ihre Mythen* (Bonn, 2010), 11, 27. Ernst Cassirer, *The Myth of the State* (New Haven, CT, 1946), 278.
6. Jan Assmann, *Das Kulturelle Gedächtnis: Schrift, Erinnerung und politische Identität in frühen Hochkulturen* (Munich, 2002), 142–43.
7. Hauptamt für Statistik und Wahlen des Magistrats von Groß-Berlin, ed., *Berlin in Zahlen, 1946–1947* (Berlin, 1949), 185–89.
8. Ibid.
9. Atina Grossmann, *Jews, Germans, and Allies: Close Encounters in Postwar Germany* (Princeton, NJ, 2007); Angelika Königseder, "Durchgangsstation Berlin: Jüdische 'Displaced Persons' 1945–1948," 1997 *Jahrbuch zur Geschichte und Wirkung des Holocaust*; SMAD Befehl No. 15, Berlin, 17 July 1945, in *Inventar der Befehle des Obersten Chefs der Sowjetischen Miltärverwaltung in Deutschland,* ed. Jan Foitzik (Munich, 1995), 16; Jürgen Danyel and Phillip Ther, eds, "Flucht und Vertreibung in europäischer Perspektive," *Zeitschrift für Geschichtswissenschaft* no. 51 (2003); Frank Biess, *Homecomings: Returning POWs and the Legacies of Defeat in Postwar Germany* (Princeton, NJ, 2006); Reinhard Rürup, *Berlin 1945: eine Dokumentation* (Berlin, 1995), 124.
10. Rürup, *Berlin 1945,* 13.
11. Berlin Magistrate Housing Office Files, "Angaben über Trümmerbeseitigung in verschiedenen Städten," by Tiefbauamt Stadt Mainz, n.d. [ca. 1946–47], held at Akademie der Künste, Abteilung Baukunst, Scharoun Nachlaß; Günter

Peters, "Ausgewählte Schwerpunkte der Gesamtberliner Stadtentwicklung von 1945 bis 1990," in *Wirtschaft im geteilten Berlin, 1945–1990*, ed. Wolfram Fischer and Johannes Bär (Munich, 1994), 124; Gerhard Keiderling, "'Mindestens 20 Jahre …' Der Beginn der Enttrümmerung Berlins," *Berlinische Monatsschrift* 1 (1999): 36–39.

12. Quoted in Klaus Wilczynski, "Auf einmal sollst Du ein Fremder sein," *Berlinische Monatsschrift* 9 (2000): 212. Destruction levels differed within buildings themselves, within districts, and significantly between central and peripheral districts. See Magistrat der Stadt Berlin and Hauptamt für Statistik, *Mitteilungen des Hauptvermessungsamtes* (Berlin, 1946).

13. Klaus Scheel, ed., *Die Befreiung Berlins 1945: Eine Dokumentation* (Berlin, 1985), 198. Laurenz Demps, ed., *Luftangriffe auf Berlin: Die Berichte der Hauptluftschutzstelle* (Berlin, 2013).

14. Margret Boveri, *Tage des Überlebens: Berlin 1945* (Munich, 1985), 76.

15. Ursula von Kardorff, *Berliner Aufzeichnungen aus den Jahren 1942 bis 1945* (Munich, 1962), 309; Boveri, *Tage des Überlebens*, 130, 131, 139.

16. See definition by Mary Nolan, "Antifascism under Fascism: German Visions and Voices," *New German Critique* 67, special issue "Legacies of Antifascism" (1996): 33; and Mary Fulbrook, *German National Identity after the Holocaust* (Cambridge, 1999), 48–78.

17. Annette Leo, ed., *Mythos Antifaschismus: Ein Traditionskabinett wird kommentiert* (Berlin, 1992), Introduction; 7; Thomas Flierl, "Das antifaschistische Traditionskabinett als ideologischer Staatsapparat," in *Mythos Antifaschismus: Ein Traditionskabinett wird kommentiert*,13; Antonia Grunenberg, *Antifaschismus–ein deutscher Mythos* (Hamburg, 1993); Jürgen Kocka, ed., *Historische DDR-Forschung: Aufsätze und Studien* (Berlin, 1993); Lutz Niethammer, ed., *Der "gesäuberte" Antifaschismus: Die SED und die roten Kapos von Buchenwald* (Berlin, 1994); Jürgen Danyel, "Die Opfer und Verfolgtenperspektive als Gründungskonsens? Zum Umgang mit der Widerstandstradition und der Schuldfrage in der DDR" and Olaf Groehler, "Verfolgten-und Opfergruppen im Spannungsfeld der politischen Auseinandersetzungen in der SBZ und DDR," in *Die geteilte Vergangenheit: Zum Umgang mit Nationalsozialismus und Widerstand in den beiden deutschen Staaten*, ed. Jürgen Danyel (Berlin, 1995), 31–46, 17–30; Eric D Weitz, *Creating German Communism, 1890–1990: From Popular Protests to Socialist State* (Princeton, NJ, 1997); Jeffrey Herf, *Divided Memory: The Nazi Past in the Two Germanys* (Cambridge, 1997); Annette Leo and Peter Reif-Spirek, eds, *Helden, Täter und Verräter: Studien zum DDR-Antifaschismus* (Berlin, 1999); Alan L Nothnagle, *Building the East German Myth: Historical Mythology and Youth Propaganda in the German Democratic Republic, 1945–1989* (Ann Arbor, MI, 1999); Bernd Faulenbach, Annette Leo, and Klaus Weberskirch, eds, *Zweierlei Geschichte: Lebensgeschichte und Geschichtsbewußtsein von Arbeitnehmern in West- und Ostdeutschland* (Essen, 2000); Catherine Epstein, *The Last Revolutionaries: German Communists and Their Century* (Cambridge, 2003); Herfried Münkler, *Die Deutschen und ihre Mythen* (Bonn, 2010).

18. Leo and Reif-Spirek, *Helden, Täter und Verräter*, 10.
19. Sowjetische Militärverwaltung in Deutschland, *Befehle des Obersten Chefs der Sowjetischen Militärverwaltung in Deutschland* (Berlin, 1946); Befehl no. 2, 10 June 1945.
20. Ibid.
21. Ibid.
22. Rabinbach, *Begriffe aus dem Kalten Krieg: Totalitarismus, Antifaschismus, Genozid* (Göttingen, 2009), 33.
23. See documents in Bernd Bonwetsch and Robert W Thurston, eds, *The People's War: Responses to World War II in the Soviet Union* (Urbana, IL, 2000); reprinted SMAD and Soviet Secret Service sources in the appendix of Antony Beevor, *The Fall of Berlin 1945* (New York, 2003); Norman Naimark, *The Russians in Germany: A History of the Soviet Zone of Occupation, 1945–1949* (Cambridge, 1995).
24. Norbert Frei, "'Wir waren blind, ungläubig, und langsam,' Buchenwald, Dachau, und die amerikanischen Medien im Frühjahr 1945," *Vierteljahrshefte für Zeitgeschichte* 35, no. 3 (1987): 385, citing George Marshall, 24 April 1945. See also Melissa Willard-Foster, "Planning the Peace and Enforcing the Surrender: Deterrence in the Allied Occupations of Germany and Japan," *Journal of Interdisciplinary History* 40, no. 1 (2009): 46–48.
25. Landesarchiv Berlin (hereafter cited as LAB), C Rep 309 A 4990, RB File Personalbüro, Schriftwechsel mit Besatzungmächten, 30 December 1945, "Betr: Ausmerzen von Bestimmungen, Redewendungen usw. faschistischer Wesensart." See also Clara Oberle, *City in Transit: Railways, Ruins, and the Search for Order in Berlin, 1945–1947* (PhD dissertation, Princeton University, 2006), 185–210.
26. Note that the term "antifascist" is used in this chapter to reflect the discourse and language of the sources, not as historical category of analysis.
27. Volker Gransow, *Kultur und Politik in der DDR* (Berlin, 1975), 52; Magdalena Heider, *Politik–Kultur–Kulturbund: Zur Gründungs- und Frühgeschichte des Kulturbundes zur demokratischen Erneuerung Deutschlands 1945–1954 in der SBZ/DDR* (Cologne, 1993), 16–33.
28. Johannes R Becher, "Aufruf zur Gründung des Kulturbundes (Entwurf), [20] June 1945, Document 2 in Horst Möller, Alexandr Tschubarjan, Jan Foitzik and Natalja Timofejewa, eds, *Die Politik der Sowjetischen Militäradministration in Deutschland (SMAD): Kultur, Wissenschaft und Bildung, 1945–1949: Ziele, Methoden, Ergebnisse: Dokumente aus russischen Archiven* (Munich, 2005), 82.
29. Quoted in Rüdiger Bernhardt, "Maßstab Humanismus: Sowjetische Kulturoffiziere und demokratischer Neubeginn," *Neue Deutsche Literatur* 24, no. 4 (1976): 156–57.
30. Ibid.
31. Isaac Deutscher, *Reportagen aus dem Nachkriegsdeutschland*, quoted in Christoph Kleßmann, *Die Doppelte Staatsgründung* (Bonn, 1991), 375.
32. "Kulturbund zur Demokratischen Erneuerung Deutschlands," in *The League of Culture in Berlin: A Memorandum*, ed. Johannes R Becher (Berlin, 1948), 9.

33. For example, Heider, *Politik–Kultur–Kulturbund*; David Pike, *The Politics of Culture in Soviet Occupied Germany, 1945–1949* (Stanford, CA, 1992); Anne Hartmann and Jürgen Eggeling, *Sowjetische Präsenz im kulturellen Leben der SBZ und frühen DDR 1945–1953* (Berlin, 1998); Bernard Genton, *Les Alliés et la culture: Berlin, 1945–1949* (Paris, 1998), 50–51; Rüdiger Bernhardt, "Le role des officiers culturels soviétiques dans la diffusion d'une litérature antifasciste, démocratique et sociale," in *La Dénazification par les Vainqueurs: la Politique Culturelle des Occupants en Allemagne, 1945–1949*, ed. Rüdiger Bernhardt and Jérôme Vaillant (Lille, 1981); Manfred Jäger, *Kultur und Politik in der DDR, 1945–1990* (Cologne, 1995); Wolfgang Schivelbusch, *Vor dem Vorhang: Das geistige Berlin 1945–1948* (Munich, 1995); Sean A Forner, "'Deutscher Geist' und demokratische Erneuerung: Kulturbünde in Ost und West nach 1945," in *Rückblickend in die Zukunft: Politische Öffentlichkeit und intellektuelle Positionen in Deutschland um 1950 und 1930*, ed. Alexander Gallus and Axel Schild (Göttingen, 2011), 221–37. See also Sean Forner, *German Intellectuals and the Challenge of Democratic Renewal: Culture and Politics after 1945* (Cambridge, 2014).

34. R Littauer, ed., *Georg Büchner: Ein Dichter und Kämpfer* (London, 1945), 10.

35. See, for example, Hedda Zinner's poem, "Ihr nicht!" invoked by Cultural League, BA SAPMO DY/27-1479, the Neukölln district Jugendausschuß, Summer 1945 "Aufruf," BA SAPMO DY 30/IV 2/16/211, and reprinted in Freie Deutsche Jugend, ed., *Wir rufen die Jugend: Die gesamte Jugend muß es sein: Aufbau unseres Vaterlandes, Ehrensache der gesamten Jugend* (Dresden, 1946), 24.

36. BA, SAPMO, DY/27-1479, Kulturbund Generalsekretär to "Berliner Schüler und Schülerinnen!" The original text refers to "ein glücklicheres Deutschland."

37. BA, SAPMO, DY/27-1479, Letter Generalsekretär des KB An die Alliierte Kommandantur, Kommission für Erziehung, 13 September1946, Betr.: Schülerveranstaltungen der Stadtleitung Berlin des Kulturbundes zur demokratischen Erneuerung; see also Jaimey Fisher's chapter "The *Jugendproblem*," in Fisher, *Disciplining Germany: Youth, Reeducation, and Reconstruction after the Second World War* (Detroit, 2007), 59–88.

38. "Bericht über die bezirkliche Jugendarbeit," 9 August 1945, cited in Kimberly A Redding, *Growing Up in Hitler's Shadow: Remembering Youth in Postwar Berlin* (Westport, 2004), 39.

39. See, for example, Befehl Nr. 29 des Obersten Chefs der SMAD über die Arbeit des Sektors Propaganda und Zensur, Berlin,18 August 1945 and Befehl Nr. 39 des Obersten Chefs der SMAD über die Konfiskation nazistischer und militaristischer Literatur, Berlin, 8 September 1945, printed and translated in *Die Politik der Sowjetischen Militäradministration in Deutschland (SMAD): Kultur, Wissenschaft und Bildung, 1945–1949: Ziele, Methoden, Ergebnisse: Dokumente aus russischen Archiven*, ed. Horst Möller and Alexandr Tschubarjan (Munich, 2005), 85–88; Kontrollratsbefehl Nr. 4: Einziehung von Literatur und Werken nationalsozialistischen und militaristischen Charakters, Berlin, 13 May 1946. Note that this document uses both terms, *faschistisch* and *nationalsozialistisch*. In Alliierter Kontrollrat, *Amtsblatt des Alliierten Kontrollrats* (Berlin, 1945–49), 151.

40. Forner, "'Deutscher Geist' und demokratische Erneuerung.'"
41. Johannes R Becher, "Tränen des Vaterlandes anno 1937," reprinted in *Jugend-Gedichtsbuch: Wir rufen die Jugend: Die gesamte Jugend muß es sein: Aufbau unseres Vaterlandes, Ehrensache der Jugend,* ed. Freie Deutsche Jugend Kreisleitung Dresden (Dresden, 1946), 7.
42. Ibid.
43. Letter Tiulpanov [German transliteration: Tjulpanow] to Karaganov, 3 November 1945, in Horst Möller et al., *Die Politik der Sowjetischen Militäradministration in Deutschland (SMAD): Kultur, Wissenschaft und Bildung, 1945–1949* (Munich, 2005), 341–42.
44. Manfred Jäger, "Kultureller Neubeginn im Zeichen des Antifaschismus," in *Studien zur Geschichte der SBZ/DDR,* ed. Alexander Fischer (Berlin, 1993), 118.
45. For example in E Sablotny and A Schmudde, eds, *Ewiges Volk: ein Lesebuch für höhere Schulen* (Leipzig, 1941), 108–33. Georg Bollenbeck, "Das Ende des Bildungsbürgers. Normative Höhe, tiefer Fall: Wie der Geist der deutschen Klassik in Weimar mit sehnsüchtigem Blick auf den rettenden Führer ausgetrieben wurde," *Die Zeit* (14 January 1999): 19–20. See also Ine van Linthout, "Das Volk der Dichter und Denker," in *Das Buch in der Nationalsozialistischen Propagandapolitik* (Berlin, 2012), 48–51.
46. Max Fechner, *Jugend und Politik* (Berlin, 1946), 3.
47. Ibid., 4–5.
48. Ibid., 3–4.
49. See Jaimey Fisher, *Disciplining Germany: Youth, Reeducation, and Reconstruction after the Second World War* (Detroit, 2007), 66.
50. Fisher, *Disciplining Germany,* 4, 63–65.
51. Kimberly A Redding, *Growing Up in Hitler's Shadow: Remembering Youth in Postwar Berlin* (Westport, 2004), 14, 44.
52. Ibid., 27–32; Dorothee Wierling, "Mission to Happiness: The Cohort of 1949 ...," in *The Miracle Years: A Cultural History of West Germany, 1940–1968,* ed. Hanna Schissler (Princeton, NJ, 2001).
53. Martin Broszat in Werner Filmer and Heribert Schwan, eds, *Mensch, der Krieg ist aus! Zeitzeugen erinnern sich* (Düsseldorf, 1985), 55.
54. Rolf Schörken, *Jugend 1945: Politisches Denken und Lebensgeschichte* (Opladen, 1990), 23–39, 44.
55. Alexander von Plato, "The Hitler Youth Generation and Its Role in the Two Post-War Germanies," in *Generations in Conflict: Youth Revolt and Generation Formation in Germany 1770–1968,* ed. Mark Roseman (Cambridge, 2003), 218.
56. Alan McDougall, "A Duty to Forget? The 'Hitler-Youth Generation' and the Transition from Nazism to Communism in Postwar East Germany, ca. 1945–1949," *German History* 26, no. 1 (2008): 25–28. Redding, *Growing Up in Hitler's Shadow,* 37, 42, 45, 80–89.
57. For example, BA, SAPMO, DY/27-1497, Generalsekretär des KB to Alliierte Kommandantur, Kommission für Erziehung.

58. BA, SAPMO, DY/27-1497, Bertolt Brecht, "Brief an Schulkinder über ein Gedicht Johannes R. Bechers," 1947, in *Johannes R. Becher: Lyrik, Prosa, Dokumente,* ed. Max Niedermayer (Wiesbaden, 1965).

59. BA, SAPMO, DY/27-34, Büro des Bundessekretär A. Abusch, "Schriftwechsel mit Schriftstellern und Künstlern, Verlagen, Institutionen und Ämtern, 1946–1949," f. 179; SAPMO, DY/27-Kulturbund Fotografien 1945–1949.

60. BA, SAPMO, DY/27-1477. Manuskripte 1946. File Lieselotte Thoms.

61. Redding, *Growing Up in Hitler's Shadow,* 85.

62. Ibid. This is not surprising, given fourteen- to eighteen-hour work days for more than 50 percent of mothers, Redding notes.

63. Ibid., referencing sociologist Thurnwald's study from 1947.

64. Fisher, *Disciplining Germany,* 69–70.

65. BA, SAPMO, DY/27-1477. Manuskripte 1946. File Lieselotte Thoms. Note the relation to "charisma" and "aura" theories since Max Weber, see Joshua Derman, "Max Weber and Charisma: A Transatlantic Affair," *New German Critique* 113 (2011): 51–88.

66. This focus on emotions and psychology has parallels in the immediate postwar historiography from the West (e.g., George Mosse, Hannah Arendt), which had explained the rise and functioning of fascism with leader cults, political aesthetics, authoritarian personalities, and mass emotions. In and among the Berlin radio stations, there was an even more engaged debate about how to frame antifascism. See Christoph Classen, *Faschismus und Antifaschismus: die nationalsozialistische Vergangenheit im Ostdeutschen Hörfunk, 1945–1953* (Cologne, 2004).

67. On pre-1945 communist narratives of fascism and antifascism, see Eric D Weitz, *Creating German Communism, 1890–1990: From Popular Protests to Socialist State* (Princeton, NJ, 1997); Herf, *Divided Memory,* 13–39; Rabinbach, *Begriffe aus dem Kalten Krieg.*

68. BA, SAPMO, DY/27-1497, Generalsekretär des KB to Alliierte Kommandantur, Kommission für Erziehung, Berlin-Dahlem, Kaiserwerther str. 8–10, 1 September 1946, Betr.: "Schülerveranstaltungen der Stadtleitung Berlin des Kulturbundes zur demokratischen Erneuerung," f. 1.

69. BA, SAPMO–Kulturbund Archiv–Nr. 10/112. See also Schivelbusch, *Vor dem Vorhang,* 128–29, and Weitz, *Creating German Communism,* 323–24.

70. BA, SAPMO, DY27-224, Kulturbund Sitzungen, Kommission Literatur 1946, Günter Weisenborn, 14 March 1947, f 10.

71. BA, SAPMO, DY/27-224, Kulturbund, Kommission Literatur.

72. Brian Puaca, *Learning Democracy: Education Reform in West Germany, 1945–1965* (New York, 2009); Fisher, *Disciplining Germany.*

73. BA, SAPMO, DY/27-1477, Abteilung Presse und Funk, Kulturbund, Manuskripte 1946, "Die Französische Literatur der Widerstandszeit."

74. Ibid.

75. Ernst Wiechert, *Rede an die Deutsche Jugend* (Zurich, 1946), 8–11.

76. Johannes R Becher, "Auferstehen!" [June 1945], in *Publizistik II, 1939–1945* (Berlin, 1978), 462, calls for "eine echte Leidenschaftlichkeit und Begeisterung, ein wahres Pathos."

77. BA, SAPMO, DY/27-224 of the Kulturbund Kommission Literatur, anonymous and Huchel, f. 103.

78. Titles of the 30 Pfennig Roman Series, published 1935–1945 by Aufwärts in Berlin included for example Peter Rauenberg, *Gefährliche Fahrt*; Kossak-Raytenau, *Die Männer mit den harten Herzen*; Anatol Maly, *Ein Cowboy unter Banditen*; Orest Bjern, *Ein Mann Rechnet Ab*; Alfred Herzog, *Die Dame mit den Glücksfingern*. For examinations of the 30 Penny Novel and the SA Youth Novel in popular national socialist culture, see Helga Geyer-Ryans, "Trivialliteratur im Dritten Reich: Beobachtungen zum Groschenroman," and Rainer Stollman, "Die krummen Wege zu Hitler: das Nazi-Selbstbildnis im SA-Roman," in *Kunst und Kultur im deutschen Faschismus,* ed. Ralf Schnell (Stuttgart, 1978), 217–60, 191–215.

79. See Karin Wieckhorst, *Die Darstellung des "antifaschistischen Widerstandes" in der Kinder- und Jugendliteratur der SBZ/DDR* (Frankfurt am Main, 2000), appendix of titles, 107–29.

80. Berlin: Verlag Neues Leben, 1946 and 1947; Wieckhorst, *Die Darstellung,* 107–29.

81. Karin Wieckhorst, "Der Typus des Widerstandshelden," in *Die Darstellung des "antifaschistischen Widerstandes" in der Kinder- und Jugendliteratur der SBZ/DDR* (Frankfurt am Main, 2000), 69–73.

82. For example, British National Archives, Public Record Office (PRO), FO 1051/803, Housing Reports I, June 1946, signed Foggon; See also Deutscher Städtetag, ed., *Statistisches Jahrbuch deutscher Gemeinden* 37 (Schwäbisch Gmünd, 1949), 380–81.

83. Lieselotte Lamp, "Die Beschlagnahmung unseres Hauses," *Zeitzeugen* 27 (June 2005): 4; LAB, C Rep 309, A 4990, RBD 3 August 1945; C Rep 309, A 2128, RBD 3, October 1945; Report Bornemann C Rep 303-9, US Headquarters, Berlin District Files, Unterlagen über Suchaktionen (UNRRA), 9 September 1946.

84. For example LAB, C Rep 309 A 4990, RB Personalbüro, RB Köpenick [outside Berlin], RB Lichtenberg, August 1945. Mention of actual rapes is not to be found in the housing surveys.

85. PRO, FO 1051/803, Housing Reports, 1945–1946.

86. See Susanne Willems, "Die Neugestaltung Berlins als Reichshauptstadt—auf Kosten der Berliner Juden 1938 bis 1942," *Bulletin für Faschismus- und Welt-kriegsforschung* 2 (1998): 3–22; and Susanne Willems, *Der entsiedelte Jude: Albert Speers Wohnungsmarktpolitik für den Berliner Hauptstadtbau* (Berlin, 2002); Harald Bodenschatz' chapter, "Die Mietskasernenstadt im 'III.Reich,'" in Boden-schatz, *Platz frei für das neue Berlin! Geschichte der Stadterneuerung in der "größten Mietskasernenstadt der Welt" seit 1871* (Berlin, 1987), 114–134; Ulrike Haerendel, *Kommunale Wohnungspolitik im Dritten Reich: Siedlungsideologie, Kleinhausbau und "Wohnraumarisierung" am Beispiel Münchens* (Munich, 1999); on the initial propa-

gandistic successes of *volkswohnungen* and their eventual failure, see Wolfgang König, *Volkswagen, Volksempfänger, Volksgemeinschaft: "Volksprodukte" im Dritten Reich: Vom Scheitern einer nationalsozialistischen Konsumgemeinschaft* (Paderborn, 2004).

87. Giselher Wirsing, *Der maßlose Kontinent: Roosevelts Kampf um die Weltherrschaft* (Jena, 1942), 94–97.

88. *Exhibition "Das Sowjetparadies"* Postcard (1942), verso, inscription: "Wohnhöhle eines Droschkenkutschers und seiner Ehefrau aus einer Grosstadt im ,Paradies der Arbeiter und Bauern.'" Reichspropagandaleitung der NSDAP, *Das Sowjetparadies: Ausstellung der Reichspropagandaleitung der NSDAP: Ein Bericht in Wort und Bild* (Berlin, 1943). See also Hans-Erich Volkmann, ed., *Das Russlandbild im Dritten Reich* (Cologne, 1994).

89. PRO, FO 1051/803, Housing I, "Interview with Dr. Ernst Runge," 1 August 1945. PRO, FO 1051/803. Housing I, "Poor Rebuilding Prospects" [n.d.], Press and Broadcast Unit, "Berlin's Housing Problem," 7 July 1945.

90. Ibid.

91. PRO, FO 1012/516, Letter "The German Housing Situation in the British Zone," 15 October 1946, f. 1.

92. LAB, C Rep 309 A 1912 RB Betriebsküchen et al., 22 October 1945, LAB C Rep 309 A 4990, RB Personalbüro, RB Lichtenberg, August 1945; C Rep 309 A 1912, RB Betriebsküchen et al., 27 August 1945.

93. See Jeffrey Herf, *The Jewish Enemy: Nazi Propaganda during World War II and the Holocaust* (Cambridge, 2006).

94. For example, NSDAP, "Ohne Sieg kein Wiederaufbau," *Redner-Schnellinformation* 63 (1943): 1.

95. PRO, FO 1051/803 Housing Reports I, for example, 4 September 1945, Major Nuttall to Colonel Watt, 10 September 1945, and FO 1051/150 Requisitioning and Housing, Letter to Deputy Chief Berlin, 24 March 1947.

96. Paul Betts, "Building Socialism at Home: The Case of East German Interiors," in *Socialist Modern: East German Everyday Culture and Politics,* eds. Katherine Pence and Paul Betts (Michigan, 2008), 96–132; Eli Rubin, *Amnesiopolis: Modernity, Space, and Memory in East Germany* (Oxford, 2016).

97. LAB, F Rep 290, SG1 NK Ruinenstraße A-L, Best. Nr. 6160; LAB, F Rep 290, SG1 NK Ruinenstraße M-Z, Best. Nr. 20538. For further images of these signs, see also photographs in Margaret Bourke-White, *"Dear Fatherland, Rest Quietly": A Report on the Collapse of Hitler's "Thousand Years"* (New York, 1946), 86.

98. PRO, FO 1051-720, Housing Law 18 and Drafts.

99. LAB, C Rep 309, A 5064, Kontrollrat Gesetz Nr. 18, Preamble.

100. Restitution claims were covered elsewhere, in different military law. See Constantin Goschler, "Jewish Property and the Politics of Restitution ...," in *Robbery and Restitution: The Conflict over Jewish Property in Europe,* ed. Martin Dean, Constantin Goeschler, and Philipp Ther (New York, 2007).

101. Kontrollrat Gesetz Nr. 18, Art. VIII 1 (a)

102. Kontrollrat Gesetz Nr. 18, Art. IX, 2 (a-b)

103. For example, LAB, C Rep 309, A 4990, 20 February 1946; LAB, C Rep 309, A 0550, November 1946 "durch die langjährigen Kriegseinwirkungen, besonders durch die verbrecherischen Maßnahmen des Hitlerregimes bei der sinnlosen Verteidigung Berlins." See numerous letters in LAB, C Rep 109, Nr. 392, Magistrat, Hauptamt für Bau- und Wohnungswesen, Einweisungen et al.

104. LAB, C Rep 109, Nr. 392, Magistrat, Hauptamt für Bau- und Wohnungswesen, Einweisungen. Brief an Oberbürgermeister Louise Schroeder; PRO, FO 1051/150 Housing and Requisitioning, letters of Herr Wieland, Berlin, to Sholto Douglas, Jan.–Feb. 1947.

105. LAB, C Rep 309, A 5064, Auszug aus dem Verordnungsblatt der Stadt Berlin Nr. 13 v. 18. 3. 1946, "Kontrollbehörde, Kontrollrat Gesetz Nr. 18," Article VIII 1 (a).

106. Archives de l'Occupation Française en Allemagne et en Autriche, GFCC, Caisse 3272/ P30, Comité de Logement, 26 Jul. 1946. Perhaps in response to concerns about the spirit of the law, one French housing officer suggested it would be best if the Control Council's Housing Office directly monitored the process of allocating preferential treatment, so "les anti-Nazi" would be given preference. Other agencies, such as the Allied Subcommittee on Industry and Building, were to refrain from interfering.

107. On the continuing issue of resentment, see especially Richard Bessel, "Hatred after War: Emotion and Postwar History of East Germany," *History and Memory* 17, no. 1 (2005): 195–216.

108. Simone Barck, Martina Langermann, and Siegfried Lokatis, *"Jedes Buch ein Abenteuer:" Zensur-System und literarische Öffentlichkeiten in der DDR bis Ende der sechziger Jahre* (Berlin, 1997), 318, 333.

109. Gregory J Massell, *The Surrogate Proletariat: Moslem Women and Revolutionary Strategies in Soviet Central Asia, 1919–1929* (Princeton, NJ, 1974).

110. Sheila Fitzpatrick, *The Russian Revolution* (New York, 1994), 98–102.

111. See Naimark, *The Russians in Germany,* 258ff.

112. Barck, Langermann, and Lokatis, *"Jedes Buch ein Abenteuer,"* 13–14, 34.

113. Christoph Classen, *Faschismus und Antifaschismus: die nationalsozialistische Vergangenheit im Ostdeutschen Hörfunk, 1945–1953*, Series: Zeithistorische Studien, 27 (Cologne, 2004).

114. Jan Assmann, *Das kulturelle Gedächtnis,* 78–79.

115. Münkler, *Die Deutschen und ihre Mythen,* 27.

116. Ibid.

117. On this function, see, for example, Friedrich Nietzsche, *Die Geburt der Tragödie aus dem Geist der Musik* (Leipzig, 1872), 132.

118. Roland Barthes, *Mythologies,* trans. Annette Lavers (New York, 1972), 147–48.

119. On the importance of such consensus-discourses, see Martin Sabrow, "Dictatorship as Discourse: Cultural Perspectives on SED legitimacy," in *Dictatorship as Experience: Towards a Socio-Cultural History of the GDR,* ed. Konrad H Jarausch (New York, 1999), 195–211, here 208.

120. Eagle Glassheim, "Ethnic Cleansing, Communism, and Environmental Devastation in Czechoslovakia's Borderlands, 1945–1989," *Journal of Modern History* 78, no. 1 (2006): 65–92; Mark Mazower, *Dark Continent* (London, 1998); Katherine Anne Lebow, *Nowa Huta 1949–1957: Stalinism and the Transformation of Everyday Life in Poland's "First Socialist City"* (PhD dissertation, Columbia University, 2002), 249–60; Philipp Ther, "The Integration of Expellees in Germany and Poland after World War II: A Historical Reassessment," *Slavic Review* 55, no. 4 (1996): 779–805.

121. David Kettler, "Exile and Return: Forever Winter," *Journal of Interdisciplinary Crossroads* 3, no. 1 (2006): 183–203; Leora Auslander, "Coming Home? Jews in Postwar Paris," *Journal of Contemporary History* 40 (2005): 237–59; Annette Wieviorka and Floriane Azoulay, *Le Pillage des Appartements et son Indemnisation* (Paris, 2000); Danièle Voldman, "La France après les ruines," *Vingtième Siècle* 30 (1991): 103–4; Danièle Voldman, *La reconstruction des villes françaises de 1940 à 1954: histoire d'une politique* (Paris, 1997).

122. Italo Calvino, Introduction (1964) to *The Path to the Spiders' Nests* (Hopewell, 1998), 16.

123. Ibid.

124. See for example Konrad Jarausch, *After Hitler: Recivilizing Germans, 1945–1995* (Oxford, 2008); Konrad Jarausch, "The Failure of East German Antifascism: Some Ironies of History as Politics," *German Studies Review* 14, no. 1 (1991): 85–102; Brian Puaca, "Teaching Trauma and Responsibility: World War II in West German History Textbooks," *New German Critique* 112 (2011): 135–53; Theodor Hamerow, "Guilt, Redemption, and Writing German History," *American Historical Review* 88, no. 69 (1983): 53–72; Martin Sabrow, "Die DDR erinnern," in Sabrow, ed., *Erinnerungsorte der DDR* (Munich, 2009), 23*ff*.

SELECTED BIBLIOGRAPHY

Barthes, Roland. *Mythologies.* Translated by Annette Lavers. New York, 1972.

Bernhard, Rüdiger, and Jérôme Vaillant, eds. *La Dénazification par les Vainqueurs: la Politique Culturelle des Occupants en Allemagne 1945–1949.* Lille, 1981.

Bessel, Richard. "Hatred after War: Emotion and Postwar History of East Germany." *History and Memory* 17, no. 1–2 (2005).

Bodenschatz, Harald. "Die Mietskasernenstadt im 'III. Reich.'" In *Platz frei für das neue Berlin! Geschichte der Stadterneuerung in der "größten Mietskasernenstadt der Welt" seit 1871.* Berlin, 1987.

Bonwetsch, Bernd, and Robert W Thurston, eds. *The People's War: Responses to World War II in the Soviet Union.* Urbana, IL, 2000.

Fisher, Jaimey. *Disciplining Germany: Youth, Reeducation, and Reconstruction after the Second World War.* Detroit, 2007.

Forner, Sean. *German Intellectuals and the Challenge of Democratic Renewal: Culture and Politics after 1945.* Cambridge, 2014.

Jarausch, Konrad H. *After Hitler: Recivilizing Germans, 1945–1995.* Oxford, 2008.

Leo, Anette. "Antifaschismus." In *Errinerungsorte der DDR,* edited by Martin Sabrow, 30–42. Munich, 2009.

Münkler, Herfried. *Die Deutschen und ihre Mythen.* Bonn, 2010.

Plato, Alexander von. "The Hitler Youth Generation and Its Role in the Two Post-War Germanies." In *Generations in Conflict: Youth Revolt and Generation Formation in Germany 1770–1968,* edited by Mark Roseman, 210–226. Cambridge, 2003.

Redding, Kimberly A. *Growing Up in Hitler's Shadow: Remembering Youth in Postwar Berlin.* Westport, 2004.

Schivelbusch, Wolfgang. *In a Cold Crater: Cultural and Intellectual Life in Berlin, 1945–1948.* Berkeley, CA, 1998.

Willems, Susanne. *Der entsiedelte Jude: Albert Speers Wohnungsmarktpolitik für den Berliner Hauptstadtbau.* Berlin, 2002.

Wierling, Dorothee. "Mission to Happiness: The Cohort of 1949 and the Making of East and West Germans." In *The Miracle Years: A Cultural History of West Germany, 1940–1968,* edited by Hanna Schissler, 110–128. Princeton, NJ, 2001.

Chapter 6

The Pen Is Mightier Than the Sword?

Student Newspapers and Democracy in Postwar West Germany

Brian M Puaca

Tensions between the staff of *Der Rundblick,* the student newspaper of the Kassel secondary schools, and the culture minister of the state of Hesse, Erwin Stein, heated up in August 1948. The paper's teenage editors were angered by Stein's decision to shorten the amount of time allowed for writing *Abitur* exam essays and chose to express their displeasure on the pages of their publication.[1] Under the headline, "Embarrassing, Embarrassing ... The Culture Minister and His Student Government," Ernst-Walter Hanack, one of the paper's leading writers, chided Stein for his disregard of the pupils' actions.[2] Apparently, Stein had failed to respond to a letter submitted to him by the student government of Hanack's school, the Realgymnasium Kölnische Strasse, asking him to repeal his decision. After repeated attempts to communicate with Stein failed, Hanack reasoned that the culture minister was ashamed of the student government organizations he had helped create in postwar Hesse. The eighteen-year-old even went so far as to claim Stein deemed student government to be a failure. He concluded his article, noting that he too was ashamed, but that he could not say for what reasons. He feared the reaction of Stein if he was more explicit, and, Hanack added, he did not want to lose the last flickers of hope that he still had in democracy.

The August criticisms certainly frustrated Stein, but it was the next issue of *Der Rundblick* that provoked an open confrontation. The editors of the paper placed Stein's recent decree on the front page. It lengthened the school year and delayed the *Abitur* exams and the beginning of the next school year until Easter 1949. Below the decree, Hanack authored another critique of Stein, titling it "Embarrassing, Embarrassing ... Once Again!"[3] His article asserted that Hessian pupils knew how necessary school reforms were, and he then pursued the question of why so many pupils were angered by the changes Stein proposed. Hanack rejected claims that Hessian pupils were conservative or that they desired a return to the educational policies of the Third Reich. He found fault with Stein, his directives, and most specifically, the means by which he put them into place. Hanack's parting shot was referring to Stein as the "so-called" Hessian culture minister. Certainly this scathing critique would serve as a test for the limits of a free press in the Hessian schools.

Stein's response was immediate and unwavering. On 22 September, just a week after the new issue appeared in the Kassel schools, Hanack and the paper's faculty advisor, Dr Ernst Anton, were called to a meeting at the culture ministry in Wiesbaden.[4] Questioned by culture ministry officials, Hanack was unrepentant, smoking cigarettes in the hallway and refusing to apologize for his criticisms of Stein. Although he admitted the tone and form of his second article were unfair, he stood by its central points. He would write the first article criticizing Stein again if he had the chance, he added. Hanack's impudence was documented in the final report delivered to Stein, but the culture minister had made up his mind about the youth even before the hearing began. In a note written two days before the meeting, Stein stated that he wanted Hanack expelled from his Kassel school and refused entry to any other *Gymnasium* in Hesse.[5] While this process might take time, Hanack and the paper's editor-in-chief, Reinhold Freudenstein, were to be removed from the paper immediately. In addition, Dr Anton received a verbal beating from culture ministry officials before being dismissed from his position as faculty advisor.[6] Stein, although a supporter of democratic school reform in many other arenas, believed that pupils must be prevented from publishing attacks in student newspapers that endangered the authority of culture ministry officials, school administrators, and teachers.[7]

The culture minister's vengeance, however, was not limited solely to the staff of *Der Rundblick*. Two days after the hearing in Wiesbaden, Stein issued a decree on student newspapers, placing stricter limits on the publications.[8] The new rules governing student newspapers were designed to prevent pupils from expressing their displeasure with the culture ministry or other educational authorities in such a public forum in the future. This decree required that faculty advisors supervise newspapers at all times and that each issue be subject to censorship prior to publication. Adding insult to injury, the culture minister also decided to limit the scope of student newspapers, requiring that they not circulate beyond the confines of the individual school. This decree was particularly troublesome for publications such as *Der Rundblick,* which served as the official publication for all of the secondary schools in Kassel—six of them, according to a 1948 request the editors directed to American military officials for assistance in securing paper.[9] In fact, many student newspapers throughout Hesse operated as citywide publications, in part to address a dearth of individual school newspapers owing to the high costs of printing. The situation thus looked grim for *Der Rundblick* in the days and weeks following Stein's decree. Günter Lehnigk, president of the Staatliche Wilhelmschule student government organization and member of the newspaper's staff, informed American officials that these new rules would reduce the circulation of *Der Rundblick* from 1,200 to 400 copies, translating into a three-fold price increase.[10] Stein's decree would make the paper too expensive for pupils to read and would thus mark the end of *Der Rundblick* and likely a similar demise for other student papers in Hesse.

THE PROMISE OF PEDAGOGICAL REFORM

For more than three years prior to the *Rundblick* incident, American military government officials had encouraged fundamental educational reforms designed to break authoritarian, nationalistic, and militaristic traditions in German schools within their zone of occupation. While structural changes proposed by American officials did not materialize in the West German school system in the late 1940s or 1950s, less visible curricular and extracurricular reforms did appear. Among the most important reforms was the introduction of student government and student newspapers, which American officials advocated as a means for providing pupils hands-on experience with democracy. Debating issues with peers, forming opinions, respecting the ideas of others, and expressing one's views were all ideals deemed fundamental to the preparation of young Germans for their future roles as citizens in a democratic state. American officials, whose ideas about the role of education in a democracy drew heavily from the work of John Dewey and other progressives, also lauded the values of group work, collaboration, and open discussion free from the confines of the teacher-centered classroom.[11] As they did throughout their zone of occupation, American officials directly informed Hessian teachers via circulation of a list of "Suggestions for Citizenship Education" of their belief that student publications assisted in the instruction of these practices. These suggestions, which first appeared in 1946 and were expanded in early 1947, underscored the pedagogical and democratic value of a school newspaper as a means for giving pupils "the opportunity to have their expressions published."[12] Student newspapers indeed served as a training ground for such activities, as postwar pupils had the opportunity to express their ideas, wishes, goals, criticisms, and frustrations in a public forum—in many instances for the first time.

Perhaps the most succinct summation of American views on the value of student newspapers comes from Halbert C Christofferson, an American military advisor in Hesse serving as a specialist on secondary school curricula and student affairs. In response to a letter from one of the Wiesbaden student publications requesting an American educator's opinion on the place and function of school newspapers, Christofferson elucidated three main points. First, he emphasized the "educational possibility for students on its staff."[13] Writing articles and managing finances were both important lessons, he noted, but learning good judgement, accepting responsibility, and cooperating with other students and the school's faculty were just as valuable. Second, Christofferson stressed the importance of the newspaper in enhancing the life of the school. Student newspapers could increase school pride, encourage other pupils to become more active, and offer constructive criticism for improvement. Last, Christofferson asserted that the third function of a student newspaper was "to print news about matters of interest to students and to provide a means for students to express their opinions." The publication, he added, is "both promoter and recorder, both announcer and critic, both designer and builder of a better school."[14] For Christofferson, the pedagogical value of student newspapers was virtually unlimited. At the same time, he also believed that these publications offered young Germans instruction in the requirements and responsibilities of citizenship in a new democracy.

The student publications that began to appear at this time provide evidence of significant efforts to introduce curricular and pedagogical reform in the postwar schools, as well as an acceptance of new democratic ideas on the part of many pupils. Created in the immediate postwar period, newspapers encouraged the active participation of pupils in the life of the school. The student newspapers of the postwar period also highlight the psychological and political changes that took place among Germany's youth. Many young people had undoubtedly grown more skeptical and disillusioned after 1945 due to their experiences in the Third Reich and the destruction of the war.[15] But, as we will see, in many instances they rapidly internalized the values of democracy. Criticizing the actions of once unassailable authority figures, demanding their right to be heard, and questioning the legitimacy of those who dominated their education, newspapers reflected changing attitudes in postwar West German schools.

It would be naïve to think that all pupils in the postwar schools equally enjoyed the new opportunities offered by student newspapers. There was undoubtedly a select group that could be characterized as "leaders" who were most involved in their school publications, such as Hanack at *Der Rundblick*. Likewise, there were "active participants" who might write letters or submit articles. A large number of pupils might best be classified as "tolerant observers." These individuals might read the newspaper when it appeared and talk about its content with others. Finally, there was without question a contingent of uninterested pupils who paid scant attention to these types of activities. Even though the number of pupils directly involved in publication might have been limited, the ideas they expressed, the questions they asked, and the atmosphere of discussion and debate they helped to foster benefited all members of the school community.[16] Simply reading student-authored criticisms of authority figures, encountering student government elections, and discussing school issues facilitated important, if subtle, changes in the pupils of the postwar era. Even those who were largely passive and engaged with the student press only peripherally prospered from the contributions of their more involved classmates. Thus, while the number of pupils authoring stories or editing the publication may be rather small, the impact of these newspapers in their schools should not be underestimated.

Historians of postwar Germany have fiercely debated the role of education after 1945 and its contributions to the creation of a new democratic state. Much of the scholarship on education in the early Federal Republic portrays the first two postwar decades as a "restoration" of pre-Nazi pedagogy. Focused on the three-tracked structure of the school system, many investigations of postwar German education have disregarded the curricular and pedagogical changes that gradually entered the classrooms after the war.[17] Those scholars who have written off the occupation era as a time of "failed reform" have disregarded key postwar innovations, such as the introduction of student government, the advent of social studies, and the publication of student newspapers, which began during the occupation and flourished throughout the 1950s and 1960s.[18] Challenging this large body of scholarship devoted to the shortcomings of postwar education reform is a handful of studies that suggest the emergence of small changes after 1945. "As it is well-known about other aspects of society," German historian Hermann-Josef Rupieper has written, "so too did the areas of youth policy and education politics arrive at a symbiosis of restorative and reformist tendencies."[19] He claimed that a "liberalization of content" occurred, even if the structures remained the same. Other scholars have recently begun to offer more balanced interpretations of the postwar educational situation in West Germany, citing the long-term effects of the postwar period on the schools.[20] Especially intriguing are the ideas of German historian Anselm Doering-Manteuffel, who has examined school reform as one component of the postwar westernization of Germany. Even though he claims that many postwar educational reforms were "marginal," Doering-Manteuffel highlights the advent of group-oriented classroom discussions and student self-government in fomenting broader educational and cultural changes.[21]

The West German Land (state) of Hesse serves as the case study for this examination of the student press in the Federal Republic. Because of the strong influence of the United States on postwar education, it was desirable to select an area occupied by American military forces from the end of the war. This limited the possible choices of postwar states to Hesse, Bavaria, Baden-Württemberg, the city-state of Bremen, and the former capital, Berlin, under quadripartite control by the four victorious powers. Strongly influenced by the Catholic clergy, Bavarian culture officials vigorously resisted American reforms.[22] Baden-Württemberg, officially established as an administrative and political entity in 1952 and also home to a disproportionately high Catholic population, reacted in a similar if less overtly confrontational manner to American proposals. Bremen and Berlin, on the other hand, were small areas, controlled by Social Democratic leaders, and the SPD had a long-established history of innovative pedagogy.[23] Hesse offers a much more moderate picture of German society, however. First, the state closely mirrors the confessional composition of the Federal Republic. Second, it is composed of a mixture of urban and rural areas, with Frankfurt as its metropolis, regional capitals such as Wiesbaden, Darmstadt, and Kassel, and smaller towns and rural areas. Finally, Hesse was more balanced politically than its conservative neighbors to the south and the more liberal areas of the north throughout the postwar era. A Christian Democratic (CDU)–Social Democratic (SPD) coalition governed Hesse into the early 1950s, with an SPD minister president and a CDU culture minister (the aforementioned Stein). While it is true that the SPD enjoyed strong support in Hesse throughout the 1950s and 1960s, the party never sought to initiate the sort of revolutionary educational reforms attempted in West Berlin or Hamburg.[24] In terms of religion, politics, and geography, Hesse is arguably the most representative of the West German Länder located in the American occupation zone.

With Hesse as its focus, this chapter proposes a number of new ways to enhance our understanding of postwar education reform in the Federal Republic. First, by broadening the definition of school reform, it concentrates on extracurricular and pedagogical changes instead of the ordering of the school structure. Content and method trump institutions and politics in this examination. Second, this chapter refocuses our attention on the actors most involved in the educational reform process at the local level: teachers, parents, and especially postwar pupils. Historians of education are often lulled into a comfortable complacency by limiting their investigation to culture ministry officials, school administrators, and political elites. In the case of West Germany, such approaches have reinforced the image of the schools as inflexible and unchanging. Finally, this chapter broadens our conception of the postwar period. Scholars of postwar Germany typically see the creation of the Federal Republic in May 1949 as a terminus—either as an end or as a beginning, depending on the perspective. This rigidity has caused many of those who have studied the West German schools to conclude that the reforms of the occupation era failed.[25] Evaluating the evolution of school reform over a longer period of time and across the divide of 1949 presents a much more complete picture. While this chapter concentrates primarily on the occupation era, it nevertheless argues that the evolution of student newspapers in Hesse was a gradual process that only completed its first phase in the 1960s.[26] The development of a student press in West Germany after the war serves as just one example of the subtle yet significant reforms that transpired within—and often in spite of—an admittedly restorative school structure.

THE EMERGENCE OF A VIBRANT STUDENT PRESS

Student newspapers emerged slowly in postwar Hesse, as was the case throughout the western zones of occupied Germany. By October 1948, Hessian officials had officially licensed twenty-three student newspapers.[27] While *Gymnasium* (most advanced secondary school) pupils published most newspapers at this early point, there were notable exceptions. At least a quarter of these licenses had been granted to elementary schools, girls' schools, or vocational schools. Three years later, there were thirty-eight officially sanctioned papers in the Hessian schools—an increase of almost seventy percent.[28] These statistics are misleading, though, insofar as they note the number of publications but not the number of schools involved in the process. As the case of *Der Rundblick* illustrates, several schools often joined forces in order to publish a newspaper. While the paper was headquartered in the Staatliche Wilhelmschule, which claimed an enrollment of over 350, the other schools that received *Der Rundblick* accounted for a potential readership of an additional 2,000 pupils. Another example is *Die Grosse Pause,* which the culture ministry approved in June 1949. This paper, as its application for a license indicates, involved pupils from five Wiesbaden

Gymnasien, together totaling almost 3,500 pupils.[29] The collaboration of pupils from a variety of schools on a shared publication was indeed common in this period, particularly since newspapers were both time-consuming to produce and required a wealth of production materials in the form of paper, ink, and a printing press.[30] In addition to multischool partnerships, culture ministry statistics are also misleading due to the fact that it is impossible to determine how many more schools had begun to publish without the proper permission from authorities—as *Der Rundblick* had done before 1948. Thus, while the number of officially licensed publications appears rather small, it obscures the much larger number of schools involved, the circulation of these papers, and those operating under the radar of the culture ministry.

Not all of the postwar student newspapers that appeared in Hesse were as confrontational and political as *Der Rundblick,* and a great deal of the content in these publications focused on less controversial issues. Student newspapers typically devoted much of their attention to a variety of intra-school activities and local happenings. The activities of student government received a prominent place in the paper, as did upcoming events in the life of the school. Editorials and letters from pupils addressed problems in the school ranging from disciplinary matters to cafeteria menu items. Sports garnered much attention in these publications too, with coverage of school teams and local clubs competing with national and international athletic news. Newspapers also included various other features, such as student essays, especially travel diaries from trips abroad, brief histories of the school and individuals related to it, and biographies of regional histori-cal luminaries. Notably, there was coverage of contemporary international news, if in a limited fashion. For example, *Die Glocke,* a citywide publica-tion operated by Frankfurt pupils, gave coverage to the developments in Palestine and published a lengthy examination of American education in 1947.[31] While there was an interest in national and world events, the large majority of the content in these student newspapers was directed toward the life of the school. These articles may not have been overtly political, but their production, distribution, and reception nonetheless contributed to the subtle process of democratization underway in the postwar schools.

The immediate postwar period was a time of enormous change, however, and pupils were not oblivious to the debates regarding school reform taking place around them. Contrary to the claims of culture ministry officials in the midst of the *Rundblick* affair, several other student newspapers entered into the fray with discussions on the state of postwar education during this period. Although not as brash as *Der Rundblick,* these papers did publish editorials on the potential benefits—and dangers—of school reform. *Das Tor,* one of Wiesbaden's two citywide student publications at the time, addressed these mixed sentiments in a May 1948 edition.[32] Distinguishing between the differing goals of the American and German school systems—the former to create good citizens and the latter to prepare an intellectual elite—the pupils embraced the introduction of some American pedagogical practices. At the same time, they rejected the idea that German youth should become part of some kind of "pedagogical experiment."[33]

Not to be outdone by its rival, the other Wiesbaden student publication, *Der Schlüssel,* published a front-page editorial expressing similar sentiments in its May 1948 issue. "The school has remained the same," it asserted. "The teachers have changed but the system has not."[34] In a conclusion that could have been written by American military officials, the pupils argued that "the schools must liberate youth from all the lingering effects of National Socialist ideas and educate them for true democracy. And that will be achieved largely through school festivals and celebrations, in which everyone has a specific task and the educator and youth come closer together."[35] These two examples from the Wiesbaden student press indicate both an awareness of the important educational questions of the period and a willingness to take action. The tone and content of these pieces makes it clear that pupils believed that they were entitled to a voice in decisions that affected them in the new postwar school.

The Hessian capital was not the only place where young Germans discussed these challenging questions of school reform. A July 1947 article published in Frankfurt's *Die Glocke* provides perhaps the best synopsis of the opinions of many postwar pupils.[36] The article's authors agreed that democratic change was necessary, but they took issue with what they deemed the flawed reforms of the previous two years.

> We want to get to know democracy differently. We want to see it in reality. But in this we are often disappointed. There are still too many teachers, who in fact teach democracy, but are often undemocratic. We know that teachers have the right to forbid and make demands. But the question is in what form this occurs. It is always said: Everyone will be heard, everyone has the right to freely express his opinion. And if someone wants to be heard, [the teacher] either gives a brief response or says "the question is so superfluous and time-consuming" that it is not worth discussion.[37]

The article concluded with a bold assertion that symbolized the dissatisfaction of many young pupils. "It is not right," the authors maintained, "that we gain the impression that democracy must continually be brought into being by others, while we ourselves need to do nothing."[38] While not a direct attack on school officials or the culture ministry, this article nonetheless expressed a tone of frustration similar to that of *Der Rundblick.*

Pupils in smaller towns were no less interested in these pedagogical issues than their big city counterparts. While the student newspapers of Kassel, Frankfurt, and Wiesbaden may have been the most visible to culture ministry officials, pupils in smaller areas also engaged in the pedagogical debates of the postwar period. Frustrated with the problems plaguing history instruction in his school, Otto Teplitzky of the *Schüler-Post,* the monthly publication of Dillenburg's Staatlichen *Realgymnasium,* questioned the goals of American demilitarization policies and, less directly, the integrity of many of the school's teachers.[39] He emphasized the importance of history in the education of young Germans. More importantly, he stressed the responsibility of the teacher—not the textbook—to convey the evils of war and the positive accomplishments of peaceful cooperation among neighboring peoples. His concluding plea must have resonated with his fellow pupils while at the same time irritating many experienced teachers in the school:

> History instruction must be true and objective above all, even if the truth is not in accordance with the ideas of the time. One must have the courage to give us so much trust. Our generation has grown up in a desert of filth and falsehoods. Because of this, we have a special right to the truth. The school provides the opportunity for this right to be given to us. One of its [the school's] most valuable means is history instruction. And it will remain up to the school whether we will learn something out of the past for the future.[40]

Teplitzky's article underscored the interest of pupils in the political and pedagogical questions of the occupation years, as well as a desire for change. It challenged teachers to address Germany's recent history, including the rise of national socialism and the war, as well as to trust pupils to make their own decisions about the country's past and its place in the postwar world.

Dillenburg was not the only small Hessian town in which an active student press evolved in the postwar years. Rotenburg, home to the Jakob-Grimm-Schule and its publication, *Die Ätherwellen,* provides yet another example. The minor conflict that erupted between the *Die Ätherwellen* and the culture ministry indicates that pupils were not only voicing louder and more biting criticisms of the schools and their administrators as the occupation came to a close, but that these tensions did not end with the *Rundblick* ruling in September 1948. The newspaper raised the ire of culture ministry officials through articles in two different issues in the spring of 1949. The first article was a critique of the new regulations for student publications that resulted in the aftermath of the *Rundblick* incident. The second piece was an interview with a regional school superintendent in which he criticized the plans for Hessian school reform. In a letter to Dr Seraphim, the school official who provided the interview, the culture ministry informed him that "the school newspaper is not the organ for a discussion of [these] problems, which undoubtedly surpass the ability of pupils to evaluate."[41] The letter went on to state that although similar to American practices, Hessian school reforms did not constitute an adoption of US educational policies. It concluded with the suggestion that Seraphim had been misquoted and encouraged a retraction or correction in a future issue.

Culture ministry officials also submitted two letters of protest to *Die Ätherwellen,* which prompted a response from the paper's editor and advisor in March 1949. The paper politely stated that it appreciated the attention and criticism and informed culture ministry officials of its intentions to produce an interesting and positive publication for its readers.[42] It rejected suggestions that it had misquoted or altered the interview with the district superintendent, however, stating that it had received written answers to its questions and published them verbatim. The newspaper's editor and advisor then argued that its articles were important because they analyzed the question of school reform from several sides.[43] Similar to *Der Rundblick,* the Rotenburg publication did not shrink in the face of challenges from the culture ministry. The paper's leadership defended its actions and presented the publication as a valuable—even necessary—resource in the postwar school.

CHALLENGING AUTHORITY AND DEBATING DEMOCRACY

Returning once again to the *Rundblick* incident, it is important to investigate the responses of pupils and parents to Stein's restrictive decree, as well as their broader significance. At an October 1948 meeting of the Secretariat of Hessian Student Newspapers in the Frankfurt *Amerikahaus,* the editors of the Land's student publications discussed their plight. The outcome of this meeting was an ingenious letter drafted by the head of the association, Hans Fieger, and submitted to the culture minister at the end of October 1948. In a clever maneuver, the pupils seized the moral high ground in the debate, arguing that their publications were more consistent with the spirit of democracy than Stein's decree. Their letter noted that "student newspapers mean an essential contribution to the development of democratic collaboration, exchange of ideas, [and] development of common interests of tolerance."[44] They added that, in accordance with American military government wishes, their publications "overcome the differences between the individual schools as high, secondary, part-time and full-time vocational, and elementary schools and thereby create an important basis for future school reform."[45] They further asserted that financial limitations often made the publication of a single-school newspaper fiscally impossible. The note concluded by explaining that the execution of the September decree would effectively end the student press in Hesse. In a succinct, one-page letter, Fieger had depicted the student press as the standard bearer of democratic school reform—both in the idea of a free press, as well as a bridge across the gaps created by the multitracked structure of the educational system. It is difficult to imagine pupils responding to school authorities in this manner in 1948; such an appeal would have been impossible five years earlier.

Stein's actions also elicited a second response two weeks later from an often-overlooked group in postwar education debates: parents. The Kassel Secondary School Parents Association presented a scathing nine-page letter to Stein in mid-November. The letter was a pointed attack on Stein's decree on student newspapers, comparing his decisions to authoritarian policies imposed on the schools during the Third Reich. They were even more irate with Stein's insistence that student publications should focus solely on school-related issues.

> Why does the school not want to contribute to the formation of the political citizen? We believe that you are pursuing a disastrous path, if you prevent students from studying a science whose neglect has brought the world immeasurable misery. It would be grotesque, if you tell young men—who have more experiences behind them than many old men will ever know and who have already seen one godless world sink—to make school menus, sports, fairy tales, music, and home economics clubs the subject of their thinking. That is romanticized fantasy, Mr. Minister![46]

The parents informed Stein that he would likely be shocked if he realized the scope of those who stood against him—not only the Land's pupils but his fellow adult citizens as well. After a derisive comparison of Stein's newspaper decree to the anti-socialist laws of "his ministerial colleague, Otto von Bismarck," the parents concluded their letter with the assertion that it was clear to them, in any case, that it was their job to remind the men who rule that "we live in a democracy."[47] Undoubtedly frustrated with the limitations Stein's policies placed upon the education of their children, these parents were also angry that they were not allowed to contribute to his decision. They demanded that their children learn the skills of "cooperation, responsibility, and critical thinking" so that they could become "future democrats and not the marionettes of a new authoritarian state."[48] While politics may have played a role in the ferocity of this letter—Stein was a CDU minister and Kassel a well-known Social Democratic stronghold—a sincere desire for reform in the school among postwar parents, even in an area as seemingly limited as student newspapers, should not be discounted.

In the end, *Der Rundblick* did not cease publication, nor were staff members discharged from the paper. After a November meeting in Kassel between Stein and Freudenstein, the student editor, the culture minister softened his stance considerably and allowed the publication to continue.[49] Even Hanack, who had sparked the controversy with his criticisms of Stein and the culture ministry, avoided expulsion and completed his Abitur examination a short time later.[50] Yet Stein's September decree remained in force, which placed all student publications under administrative censorship and prevented their circulation outside the schools. Additionally, the culture ministry remained steadfast in its insistence that pupils focus solely on intra-school issues and avoid broader social and political topics. In many ways, the schools of postwar Hesse were inhospitable to student newspapers, particularly through the early 1950s. Encountering only measured support from the culture ministry, student newspapers did not expand during the occupation as quickly as American officials and many German pupils hoped. The end of the occupation in 1949, however, did not mark the end of the Hessian student press.

THE EVOLUTION AND LEGITIMATION OF THE STUDENT PRESS

Despite hostility in some areas from conservative educators and anxious culture ministry officials, the student press experienced remarkable growth throughout the Federal Republic in the first full postwar decade. Student newspapers moved beyond the confines of *Gymnasien* and became increasingly commonplace in all of the different West German secondary schools during the 1950s. Nevertheless, the tension between support for these publications and the desire of administrators to control their impact, as displayed in Stein's decrees, was visible throughout the country. Virtually all of the West German states explicitly supported the creation of student government organizations and student newspapers in their schools as tools to complement classroom instruction.[51] Student newspapers in particular received praise for their contributions to the life of the school from educators and administrators alike in this period, yet there remained concerns that these publications could challenge traditional authority figures. In this way, the occupation and the decade that followed served as a time of negotiation between school officials and pupils, as both sides sought to delineate the appropriate limits of student publications. Other West German states may not have promulgated decrees as restrictive as those of Stein, yet they, too, struggled to define the appropriate role of student newspapers in the postwar school. The Hessian case thus represents both the boundless energies of critical student journalists and the conflicted feelings of many school officials throughout the Federal Republic.[52]

As was true of West Germany as a whole, the relationship between the culture ministry and student newspapers in Hesse continued to evolve throughout the 1950s. Perhaps the most obvious sign that the Hessian culture ministry was coming to terms with the new publications was the creation of an annual contest for student newspapers in 1957.[53] This display of greater support by the culture ministry, however, did not prevent Hessian student publications from continuing to challenge the limits placed upon them by Stein's decree. As student newspapers became ubiquitous in the Hessian schools during this period, their interests increasingly crossed the boundaries of the school and entered into broader debates on politics, culture, and society. In particular, a desire to address the rash of neo-Nazi activities occurring at the end of the 1950s added further irritation to pupils already chafing under the restrictions on content in student newspapers.[54] Again, the Hessian case illustrates the growth of student newspapers throughout the country and their increasing interest in broader political and social issues during this period. Pupils in several West German cities, including West Berlin, published critical analyses of contemporary political issues on their pages of their newspapers by 1960.[55]

After several challenges to the restrictions placed upon them, pupils in an Eschwege *Gymnasium* initiated a new newspaper whose criticisms finally prompted a reexamination of the rules governing student publications in 1964. These pupils claimed that their paper, although produced at the school using its press, should not be subject to Stein's restrictions because it was not the official organ of the school. Their collaboration, they asserted, was an independent publication distinct from the traditional school paper. Almost twenty years after the war, the arguments of these pupils found a more sympathetic audience. Student newspapers had gained the support of many teachers by the early 1960s, while the recent "Spiegel Affair" had reminded the German public that a free press was indispensable in a democratic state.[56] Because of the changes that had occurred in the political and educational landscape since Stein's decision, the Hessian culture ministry issued a new decree in 1964 differentiating between school newspapers (*Schulzeitungen*) and student newspapers (*Schülerzeitungen*). The landmark decree granted freedom of the press to the latter, exempting them from administrative censorship and thus overturning Stein's 1948 decision.[57] With this move, Hesse became the first West German state to declare unhindered freedom of the press to pupil-sponsored publications. This was an unprecedented act, which had an immediate impact on life in the schools. One historian has even argued that this decision, coupled with a 1965 decree enlarging the role of student government, marked the end of the postwar era in the Hessian schools.[58] By no means did this ignite a tidal wave of reform, but other states began to follow the Hessian lead by the end of the 1960s.

By way of conclusion, it would make sense to return to the question posed in the title of this chapter. The pen of postwar Hessian pupils proved to be mightier than the sword, or at least the disciplinary stick of Stein, other culture ministry officials, and school administrators. This is true of the immediate aftermath of the 1948 incident, as well as for the long-term development of the student press in Hesse. The responses of Kassel pupils and parents alike in the case of *Der Rundblick* illustrate subtle, but nonetheless significant, changes in the minds of postwar Germans regarding the role of education in the fledgling democracy. So, too, do the writings of pupils from Frankfurt, Wiesbaden, Dillenburg, and Rotenburg. Pupils demanded their rights to exercise free speech and publish a newspaper that represented their interests. They conceived of their publications as a valuable pedagogical tool, and at the same time, desirable, if not necessary, for a newly democratic society. Parents, too, indicated support both for the pedagogical value of their children's newspaper, as well as the democratic tenets upon which it was predicated. These beliefs were critical to the continuance and expansion of the student press in Hesse in the 1950s and early 1960s. Viewing the newspaper situation across the first two postwar decades, the promulgation of the 1964 decree underscores the significant, if gradual, change that occurred in the curriculum of the postwar schools. As an expanding cohort of postwar pupils acquired more experience with democratic values and a new generation of teachers embraced the concept, student newspapers cemented a place in the life of the school. Arguably a minor reform in terms of the postwar schools, the evolution of Hessian student newspapers in the first two postwar decades reflects a major change in the mentality of pupils. The case of *Der Rundblick* and the broader development of the Hessian student press after the war show that postwar pupils were far from passive, compliant youth. The publications they created gave them an outlet to voice their opinions and sharpen their skills as young citizens in a newly democratic state.

Brian M Puaca is Associate Professor of History at Christopher Newport University in Newport News, Virginia. He is the author of *Learning Democracy: Education Reform in West Germany, 1945–1965* (New York, 2009), which received the 2011 New Scholar's Award from the American Educational Research Association. He has published several articles and book chapters on German educational reform, cultural exchange, and postwar memory. His work has been supported by the Berlin Program for Advanced German and European Studies, Deutscher Akademischer Austauschdienst (DAAD), German Fulbright Commission, and the German Historical Institute.

NOTES

1. The *Abitur* is the finishing exam that marks the end of study in the *Gymnasium,* Germany's most advanced secondary school. Successful completion of this exam, taken after the final year of study, allows one to attend the university. The Hessian *Gymnasium* curriculum returned to thirteen years in the early 1950s after having been shortened to twelve years during the Third Reich.

2. Ernst-Walter Hanack, "Peinlich, Peinlich ... Der Herr Kultusminister und seine Schüler-Selbstverwaltung," *Der Rundblick* 2, no. 7 (1948): 1; Box 583; General Records, 1946–49; Education and Cultural Relations Division; Records of the Office of Military Government, Hesse; Records of State (Land) and Sector Military Governments Responsible to OMGUS 1945–51; Records of the US Occupation Headquarters, WWII, RG 260; National Archives, College Park (hereafter cited as NACP). Hanack, it is worth noting, went on to a successful career as a legal theorist and taught at the universities in Heidelberg and Mainz.

3. Ernst-Walter Hanack, "Peinlich, Peinlich ... Schon wieder mal!," *Der Rundblick* 2, no. 8 (1948): 1; Box 583; General Records, 1946–49; Education and Cultural Relations Division; Records of the Office of Military Government, Hesse; Records of State (Land) and Sector Military Governments Responsible to OMGUS 1945–51; Records of the US Occupation Headquarters, WWII, RG 260; NACP.

4. "Protokoll, Ernst-Walter Hanack," 22 September 1948, Abteilung 1178, File 146, Hessisches Hauptstaatsarchiv (hereafter cited as HHstA).

5. Letter from Dr Stein to Dr Kammer, 20 September 1948, Abt. 1178, File 72, HHstA.

6. "Protokoll, Dr Ernst Anton," 22 September 1948, Abt. 1178, File 146, HHstA.

7. "Information Report No. 392–Sociological. Student's Newspaper in Kassel," 8 October 1948, page 1; Box 585; General Records, 1946–49; Education and Cultural Relations Division; Records of the Office of Military Government, Hesse; Records of State (Land) and Sector Military Governments Responsible to OMGUS 1945–51; Records of the US Occupation Headquarters, WWII, RG 260; NACP.

8. "Schulzeitungen," Erlass vom 24.9.1948, *Amtsblatt des Hessischen Ministeriums für Kultus und Unterricht* 1, no. 7 (1948): 188–91.

9. "Request for Help in Securing Paper for School Newspaper," 17 June 1948, page 1; Box 583; General Records, 1946–49; Education and Cultural Rela-

tions Division; Records of the Office of Military Government, Hesse; Records of State (Land) and Sector Military Governments Responsible to OMGUS 1945–51; Records of the US Occupation Headquarters, WWII, RG 260; NACP.

10. "Information Report No. 392–Sociological Students' Newspaper in Kassel," 8 October 1948, page 1; Box 585; General Records, 1946–49; Education and Cultural Relations Division; Records of the Office of Military Government, Hesse; Records of State (Land) and Sector Military Governments Responsible to OMGUS 1945–51; Records of the US Occupation Headquarters, WWII, RG 260; NACP.

11. Dewey's *Schools of Tomorrow* (1915) and *Democracy and Education* (1916) were particularly influential for the New Deal liberals who constituted a majority of the American military officials working with the German schools.

12. Education and Religious Affairs, Office of Military Government (US) for Germany–Hesse, 14 January 1947, page 1, Abt. 1178, No. 81b, HHstA.

13. Letter from Prof. HC Christofferson, Secondary Education Specialist, Office of Military Government, US, to Hannelore Schätzel, 24 August 1948; Box 583; General Records, 1946–49; Education and Cultural Relations Division; Records of the Office of Military Government, Hesse; Records of State (Land) and Sector Military Governments Responsible to OMGUS 1945–51; Records of the US Occupation Headquarters, WWII, RG 260; NACP.

14. Ibid.

15. While the Nazis never achieved the level of control over education that they desired, they did succeed in reorganizing the curriculum, infusing it with militarism, anti-Semitism, and extreme nationalism, and reducing the years of schooling young Germans received. For further discussion of education in the Third Reich, see Gilmer Blackburn, *Education in the Third Reich* (Albany, NY, 1985); Harald Scholtz, *Erziehung und Unterricht unterm Hakenkreuz* (Göttingen, 1985).

16. For a more complete analysis of the impact of student newspapers—and student government more broadly—in the schools of the early Federal Republic, see Brian M Puaca, *Learning Democracy: Education Reform in West Germany, 1945–1965* (New York, 2009).

17. Despite protests from American officials, the West German educational system retained its three-track organization following World War II. The vast majority of pupils attended the *Volksschule,* which provided pupils with instruction through grade eight. This prepared them for their vocational training. The *Realschule* lasted one year longer and prepared pupils for careers in business and the civil service. The *Gymnasium* extended through grade thirteen and served as the gateway for university admission. See Christoph Führ, *Deutsches Bildungswesen seit 1945* (Bonn, 1996).

18. There is great consensus as to the "restoration" of pre-Nazi education after 1945. See Caspar Kuhlmann, "Schulreform und Gesellschaft in der Bundesrepublik Deutschland 1946–1966," in *Schulreform im gesellschaftlichen Prozeß,* Band I, ed. Saul B Robinsohn (Stuttgart, 1970), 1/155; Hans-Georg Herrlitz,

Wulf Hopf, and Hartmut Titze, *Deutsche Schulgeschichte von 1800 bis zur Gegenwart* (Regensburg, 1981); Arthur Hearnden, *Education in the Two Germanies* (Boulder, CO, 1974); Jutta-B Lange-Quassowski, *Neuordnung oder Restauration? Das Demokratiekonzept der amerikanischen Besatzungsmacht und die politische Sozialisation der Westdeutschen* (Opladen, 1979).

19. Hermann-Josef Rupieper, *Die Wurzeln der westdeutschen Nachkriegsdemokratie. Der amerikanische Beitrag 1945–1952* (Opladen, 1993), 172.

20. See James Tent, *Mission on the Rhine* (Chicago, 1982); HJ Hahn, *Education and Society in Germany* (New York, 1998), 91–112.

21. Anselm Doering-Manteuffel, *Wie westlich sind die Deutschen? Amerikanisierung und Westernisierung im 20. Jahrhundert* (Göttingen, 1999), 64.

22. For a detailed examination of the tensions between American occupation officials and the Bavarian culture ministry in regard to education reform, see Winfried Müller, *Schulpolitik in Bayern im Spannungsfeld von Kultusbürokratie und Besatzungsmacht 1945–1949* (Munich, 1995); Hubert Buchinger, *Volksschule und Lehrerbildung im Spannungsfeld politischer Entscheidung 1945–1970* (Munich, 1975).

23. There is a wealth of scholarship on education in Berlin following World War II. On the reforms of the early postwar period, see Marion Klewitz, *Berliner Einheitsschule, 1945–1951, Historische und Pädagogische Studien*, vol. 1, ed. Otto Büsch and Gerd Heinrich (Berlin, 1971); Karl-Heinz Füssl and Christian Kubina, *Mitbestimmung und Demokratisierung im Schulwesen. Eine Fallstudie zur Praxis von Beratungsgremien am Beispiel Berlins* (Berlin, 1984); Karl-Heinz Füssl and Christian Kubina, *Zeugen zur Berliner Schulgeschichte, 1951–1968* (Berlin, 1981).

24. For recent scholarship on the evolution of the Hessian schools in the postwar era, see Patricia Fedler, *Anfänge der staatlichen Kulturpolitik in Hessen nach dem Zweiten Weltkrieg 1945–1955* (Wiesbaden, 1993); Johann Zilien, *Politische Bildung in Hessen von 1945 bis 1965. Gestaltung und Entwicklung der politischen Bildung als schulpolitisches Instrument der sozialen Demokratisierung* (Frankfurt am Main, 1997). See also Birgitta M Schulte, ed., *Die Schule ist wieder offen: Hessische Schulpolitik in der Nachkriegszeit* (Frankfurt am Main, 1997).

25. The outbreak of the Cold War is most often cited for the failures of American education reform plans. For example, Karl-Heinz Bungenstab argues that 1947 marked the end of positive reforms, because the United States now shifted its priorities to containing communism. Henry Kellermann contends that reform, however limited through 1949, was not implemented based on Cold War ideological motives. See Karl-Ernst Bungenstab, *Umerziehung zur Demokratie? Reeducation-Politik im Bildungswesen der US-Zone 1945–1949* (Gütersloh, 1970); Henry Kellermann, "Von Re-education zu Re-orientation: Das amerikanische Re-orientierungsprogramm im Nachkriegsdeutschland," in *Umerziehung und Wiederaufbau: Die Bildungspolitik der Besatzungsmächte in Deutschland und Österreich*, ed. Manfred Heinemann (Stuttgart, 1981), 86–102.

26. For a general examination of postwar reform in all of the western Länder, with greater attention to Hesse, see Ludwig von Friedeburg, *Bildungsreform in Deutschland. Geschichte und gesellschaftlicher Widerspruch* (Frankfurt am Main, 1989).

27. "Liste der Schülerzeitungen veröffentlicht nach dem 1.Oktober 1948," Box 585; General Records, 1946–49; Education and Cultural Relations Division; Records of the Office of Military Government, Hesse; Records of State (Land) and Sector Military Governments Responsible to OMGUS 1945–51; Records of the US Occupation Headquarters, WWII, RG 260; NACP.

28. Listing of Licensed School Newspapers (title illegible), undated (circa 1951), Abt. 504, File 607, Fiche 3619, HHstA.

29. "Antrag auf Herausgabe einer Schulzeitung," 17 June 1949, Abt. 504, File 607, Fiche 3621, HHstA.

30. One should note that although Stein's 1948 decree formally forbade such partnerships, they continued unabated in the 1950s.

31. See "Heiliges Land–Land der Unruhen," and "Schulen in Amerika," *Die Glocke* 1, no. 2 (1947): 1–2; Box 583, General Records, 1946–49; Education and Cultural Relations Division; Records of the Office of Military Government, Hesse; Records of State (Land) and Sector Military Governments Responsible to OMGUS 1945–51; Records of the US Occupation Headquarters, WWII, RG 260; NACP.

32. "Schulreform," *Das Tor* 2, no. 2 (1948): 12; Box 583, General Records, 1946–49; Education and Cultural Relations Division; Records of the Office of Military Government, Hesse; Records of State (Land) and Sector Military Governments Responsible to OMGUS 1945–51; Records of the US Occupation Headquarters, WWII, RG 260; NACP.

33. Ibid.

34. "Die grosse Chance," *Der Schlüssel* 1, no. 2 (1948): 1; Box 583, General Records, 1946–49; Education and Cultural Relations Division; Records of the Office of Military Government, Hesse; Records of State (Land) and Sector Military Governments Responsible to OMGUS 1945–51; Records of the US Occupation Headquarters, WWII, RG 260; NACP.

35. Ibid.

36. "Unsere Sorgen!" *Die Glocke* 1, no. 4 (1947): 1; Box 583, General Records, 1946–49; Education and Cultural Relations Division; Records of the Office of Military Government, Hesse; Records of State (Land) and Sector Military Governments Responsible to OMGUS 1945–51; Records of the US Occupation Headquarters, WWII, RG 260; NACP.

37. Ibid.

38. Ibid.

39. Otto Teplitzky, "Geschichtsunterricht heute," *Schüler-Post,* no. 6 (1947): 2; Box 583, General Records, 1946–49; Education and Cultural Relations Division; Records of the Office of Military Government, Hesse; Records of State (Land) and Sector Military Governments Responsible to OMGUS 1945–51; Records of the US Occupation Headquarters, WWII, RG 260; NACP.

40. Ibid.

41. Letter from Dr Kammer, Hessian culture ministry, to Dr E Seraphim, *Landrat,* 10 March 1949, Abt. 504, File 607, Fiche 3619, HHstA.

42. Letter from "Die Ätherwellen" to Dr Erwin Stein, Hessian culture minister, 16 March 1949, Abt. 504, File 607, Fiche 3619, HHstA.

43. Ibid.

44. Letter from Hans Fieger, Secretariat of Hessian Student Newspapers, to Minister of Education of Land Hesse, 29 October 1948 (translated by JN Schramm, 9 November 1948), page 1; in Box 583, General Records, 1946–49; Education and Cultural Relations Division; Records of the Office of Military Government, Hesse; Records of State (Land) and Sector Military Governments Responsible to OMGUS 1945–51; Records of the US Occupation Headquarters, WWII, RG 260; NACP.

45. Ibid.

46. Letter from *Elternschaft der höheren Schulen Kassels* to Stein, 12 November 1948, page 6, Abt. 1178, File 146, HHstA.

47. Ibid, 9.

48. Ibid, 2.

49. Letter from Klaus Schäfer to Halbert C Christofferson, 27 November 1948; Box 583, General Records, 1946–49; Education and Cultural Relations Division; Records of the Office of Military Government, Hesse; Records of State (Land) and Sector Military Governments Responsible to OMGUS 1945–51; Records of the US Occupation Headquarters, WWII, RG 260; NACP.

50. It is worth noting that Hanack went on to a distinguished career as a professor of law in Mainz and retired in 1997. See Udo Ebert, ed. *Festschrift für Ernst-Walter Hanack zum 70. Geburtstag am 30. August 1999* (Berlin, 1999), xi–xiv.

51. Franz Schramm, Stein's predecessor as culture minister, sanctioned student government organizations in 1946. Stein, it should be noted, expressed complete support for student government organizations as an important component of political education. See "Lehrpläne für den politischen Unterricht in den Schulen des Landes Hessen," Erlass von 21.8.1948, *Amtsblatt des Hessischen Ministeriums für Kultus und Unterricht* 1, no. 6 (1948): 149–70.

52. The Hessian context provides further support for Dirk Schumann's claim that this period was one in which "conservatism prevailed, but this should not be mistaken for unquestioned acceptance of authority." See Schumann, "Authority in the 'Blackboard Jungle': Parents, Teachers, Experts and the State, and the Modernization of West Germany in the 1950s," *Bulletin of the German Historical Institute* 33 (2003): 65–78.

53. Zilien, *Politische Bildung in Hessen,* 401.

54. A wave of anti-Semitic graffiti in West Germany as the 1950s came to a close thrust education into the national spotlight once again. Seeking a scapegoat for these embarrassing crimes, politicians placed a large measure of responsibility on the schools. In many areas, these recriminations forced a reevaluation of the history and political education curriculum and further reforms to classroom instruction.

55. One such example comes from the Arndt-Schule in West Berlin, which began publishing its newspaper in 1946. Pupils published a special issue in 1959 on

anti-Semitism in German history in response to an outbreak of neo-Nazi incidents in the Federal Republic. See "Das Judenproblem," *Schülerzeitung der 10. Klasse der Arndt-Schule*, October 1959, B Rep. 015, No. 451, Landesarchiv Berlin.

56. The German news magazine *Der Spiegel* published an article in October 1962 on NATO military exercises that, according to the West German government, contained classified material. Police arrested the editor, on vacation in Spain, and searched the offices of the magazine. Several other journalists connected to the story were also arrested and had their homes searched. Many Germans viewed this incident as eerily similar to the actions of the Gestapo twenty years earlier. The "Spiegel Affair," as it has come to be known, ultimately contributed to the resignation of Konrad Adenauer after fourteen years as chancellor.

57. Zilien, *Politische Bildung in Hessen*, 407–8.

58. Ibid., 409.

SELECTED BIBLIOGRAPHY

Bungenstab, Karl-Ernst. *Umerziehung zur Demokratie? Reeducation-Politik im Bildungswesen der US-Zone 1945–1949*. Gütersloh, 1970.

Friedeburg, Ludwig von. *Bildungsreform in Deutschland. Geschichte und gesellschaftlicher Widerspruch*. Frankfurt am Main, 1989.

Führ, Christoph. *Deutsches Bildungswesen seit 1945*. Bonn, 1996.

Hahn, HJ. *Education and Society in Germany*. New York, 1998.

Hearnden, Arthur. *Education in the Two Germanies*. Boulder, CO, 1974.

Herrlitz, Hans-Georg, Wulf Hopf, and Hartmut Titze. *Deutsche Schulgeschichte von 1800 bis zur Gegenwart*. Regensburg, 1981.

Lange-Quassowski, Jutta-B. *Neuordnung oder Restauration? Das Demokratiekonzept der amerikanischen Besatzungsmacht und die politische Sozialisation der Westdeutschen*. Opladen, 1979.

Puaca, Brian. *Learning Democracy: Education Reform in West Germany, 1945–1965*. New York, 2009.

Rupieper, Hermann-Josef. *Die Wurzeln der westdeutschen Nachkriegsdemokratie. Der amerikanische Beitrag 1945–1952*. Opladen, 1993.

Tent, James. *Mission on the Rhine*. Chicago, 1982.

Zilien, Johann. *Politische Bildung in Hessen von 1945 bis 1965. Gestaltung und Entwicklung der politischen Bildung als schulpolitisches Instrument der sozialen Demokratisierung*. Frankfurt am Main, 1997.

Chapter 7

Human Rights, Pluralism, and the Democratization of Postwar Germany

Ned Richardson-Little

In 1945, the crimes of the Nazi regime served as a global symbol of the violation of human rights and the greater need for their protection. As representatives from across the world met at the newly formed United Nations to determine a new international system that could do so, in occupied Germany itself, the language of human rights was used to express the aspirations for the postwar era that would ensure the carnage unleashed by the Third Reich would never be repeated.[1] While Germans of all political stripes embraced the idea of human rights in the wake of World War II, the meaning of this concept was, however, fiercely contested among them. While almost all could accept that Nazi Germany represented the antithesis of human rights, how to undo and overcome this legacy proved divisive. Almost immediately after the conclusion of a war that came to represent the total negation of human rights, the very meaning of human rights and how they should be achieved became a site of struggle for moral legitimacy and political power.

By 1989, across both Germanies there existed a general consensus that pluralism, democracy, and the rule of law were essential elements of human rights. In the immediate postwar period, however, the interconnection of these values and systems was not seen as self-evident, and many used the concept of human rights to advance distinctly illiberal goals. In the Eastern zone of occupation, communists advanced the idea that human rights could only progress through a socialist revolution and "democratic centralism." In the Western zones, some political figures argued for a vision of human rights grounded in pluralistic democracy, but there were other prominent thinkers who used the idea to promote an agenda of conservative moral revival in opposition to the supposed failings of individualistic liberalism. Still others advanced an irredentist conception of human rights linking their realization to the reclamation of the lost German homeland in the East.

In West Germany, political competition, public debate, and an independent judiciary created space for a civic engagement with the problem of human rights resulting in public discourse moving away from the extremes toward a shared conception rooted in the principles of universality, individualism, and democracy. Human rights continued to serve as a means to advance particularistic causes, but pluralism and the rule of law emerged as the basic elements of human rights that almost all could agree on. In East Germany on the other hand, the monopoly on power held by the Socialist Unity Party (SED) allowed it to establish a hegemonic discourse of antiliberal, "socialist human rights" that endured for decades as a legitimization of its rule. Rather than challenge this hegemony, East Germans sought to either move to the West or to promote human rights within the conceptual boundaries set out by the SED. Only when activists and dissidents found it impossible to advance the antipolitical and moral goals of human rights and peace without legally guaranteed rights, did they embrace the idea that pluralism, democracy, and the rule of law were essential to the project of human rights. The embrace of the idea of human rights and its meaning was simply a natural reaction against the crimes of the Nazi era. The history of human rights, their relation to political and economic reform, and the role of the German people in their realization, were a socially and politically constructed set of ideas and ideals formed through public discourse and conflict.

HUMAN RIGHTS AS POLITICS IN POSTWAR GERMANY

The first major conflict over the meaning of human rights in postwar Germany began in October 1946, when elections held in the city of Berlin became a focal point in the competition for legitimacy between the Social Democratic Party (SPD) and the SED. In spite of the strenuous objections of SPD members in the Western zones of occupation, the SPD in the Soviet-run Eastern zone was merged with the West German Communist Party (KPD) in April 1946 to form the SED. While the SPD was barred from running in Länder (state) elections in the fall of 1946 in the Eastern zone, it was still able to run in Berlin, where the Allied authorities would be holding the first (and until 1990, only) election to include all four zones of occupation.

For both parties, the election presented a unique opportunity to demonstrate that their faction alone represented the popular choice of the working class of Germany. For the SPD, it was an opportunity to reveal the SED as an empty vehicle of the Soviet occupation. For the SED, it was a chance to undermine such SPD assertions and truly claim the mantle of a "united" socialist party. At a meeting of the SED executive in June 1946, party cofounder and former SPD leader Otto Grotewohl, asserted "this first election is a highly political event of great significance, not only for the Eastern Zone and the rest of Germany, but for the entire world where the campaign and the elections results will be closely followed and politically evaluated."[2] In this first free election since 1933, the support of the people would finally be revealed where before it had been only theoretical and speculative.

At the center of the SED's electoral campaign was a new manifesto, "The Basic Rights of the German People: The Path to German Unity," which sought to present the SED as the natural heir to the progressive German tradition.[3] The manifesto began with, "The German people cannot live without the restoration of German unity," the document promised to "eliminate the remaining vestiges of Nazism through the expropriation of militaristic great land-holders and war criminals." It further claimed that the SED would bring about a system of parliamentary supremacy, equality before the law, and the right to free expression, religion, and property. In short, the SED sought to co-opt the ideals of liberal democracy and nationalism and dissociate itself from the cause of revolution and radicalism.

The SPD responded with the electoral slogan "No Socialism without Human Rights!"[4] Beginning with the creation of the SED in the Eastern zone, antimerger activists in the SPD adopted the language of human rights to combat the perceived threat that Germany was exchanging one dictatorship for another. As one pamphlet to SPD members urging them to vote against the party merger argued, "dictatorships know no tolerance: human rights and cultural humanity perish ... Homogenized state parties are a plague of our social era."[5] The SPD translated these arguments from their internal party struggles out to the public sphere. During the campaign, the SPD's claims to support human rights rested on their simultaneous promises to relieve the suffering of the civilian population while denouncing the depredations of the Soviet occupation. As one SPD campaign leaflet read, "we make no promises on which we cannot deliver. We support nothing that cannot be realized. If the future of Berlin is to be secured, two major tasks of the present must be solved: ensuring the material needs of the population of Berlin and securing human rights for all."[6] While the resources of the Soviet authorities were crucial to the strength of the SED, the party's close connection to the occupying power linked the party to the hardships imposed by Soviet industrial reparations policy in addition to the epidemic of rape perpetrated by Red Army occupation soldiers.[7]

On 20 October 1946, the SPD routed the SED in Berlin, winning a decisive plurality of 48.7 percent in Berlin as a whole. In spite of the intense propaganda campaign and the coercion of the Soviet authorities, the SED finished third behind the Christian Democrats (CDU) with a paltry 20 percent.[8] Even in the Eastern zone of the city where Soviet influence was greatest, the SPD still won 43.6 percent of the vote with the SED trailing behind at less than 30 percent.[9] SPD leader Kurt Schumacher relished the results declaring "the new Germany wants to be democratic. Berlin has shown the face of the new Germany."[10] From the other side, the failure to gain even a plurality of the vote blindsided the SED. The party newspaper *Neues Deutschland* covered for the embarrassment as best it could by focusing on the results from the other Länder where, without the competition of the SPD, the SED had at least won a plurality if not outright majorities—the main headline boasted of the "Great Electoral Victory of the SED in the Zone"—but the weak showing in Berlin was still a major blow.[11] Instead of supporting the legitimacy of the SED, the election had actually revealed how shallow the party's actual support really was when up against SPD opponents in free elections.

At a meeting of the SED leadership in the wake of the elections, many saw the defeat as the result of genuine worker concerns over the problem of dictatorship and human rights. Richard Weimann, once a prominent Social Democrat in the Eastern zone, argued that hardliner rhetoric had exposed the SED to the attacks by the SPD. "The Social Democrats won the masses because they had the general postulates of humanity, human rights, and democracy in the foreground and placed them in opposition to dictatorship."[12] Whether this rhetoric was the deciding factor or whether it was simply a reaction to the abuses of the occupying Soviet troops, the SED leadership linked their loss to successful human rights propaganda.

CONTRADICTORY VISIONS OF HUMAN RIGHTS

The elections in 1946 sparked conflict over the meaning of human rights in postwar Germany, but the SPD and the SED were not the only voices claiming their own interpretations of this concept. Four significantly different and contradictory schools of thought on the idea of human rights arose in the late 1940s: the social democratic, the state socialist, the revisionist nationalist, and the Christian nationalist. While advocates of these varying ideals could agree that the restoration of human rights was essential to the future of Germany, the history of human rights in the immediate postwar years was one of conflict rather than consensus as various groups competed to define what human rights would mean in practice.

Across Europe and in international institutions, there was one current of broadly social democratic thought that linked human rights to the defense of liberal democracy alongside strong protections for social and economic rights.[13] In occupied Germany, SPD leader Kurt Schumacher represented the leading figure promoting such an interpretation. While Schumacher did not formally define the idea of human rights, from his speeches and writings, one can discern a conception of human rights centered on anti-communism, democratic participation, and economic egalitarianism. For Schumacher, human rights were primarily a matter of politics. He argued that human rights were not simply the rights of citizens in a bourgeois society or the special rights of workers, but they were the universal rights shared by all as inspired by the French Revolution.[14] He implicitly accepted Karl Marx's dismissal of the rights of man in a liberal society as the mere rights of the bourgeois citizen, but from this demanded a system of human rights that would truly honor the principles of "freedom, equality, frater-nity and humanity."[15] Although social and economic rights were essential to Schumacher's conception of human rights, he also held political freedoms to be of primary importance as "we will fight with great passion and dedi-cation for social benefits, [but] one is only prepared to die for the great idea of freedom."[16] All of the economic and social rights that social democracy stood for would flow from the first position of a genuinely democratic society.

While Germany had made progress toward this goal during the Weimar era, Schumacher argued that the German people had not fought hard enough to preserve this system and the Nazis were able to destroy it. This failure meant that a democratic system had to be reborn stronger than before with a greater commitment by the German people to a parliamentary democracy based on human rights. Postwar Germany needed to become a pluralistic democracy that accepted opposing viewpoints and political ideas to avoid repeating the mistakes of the past. Schumacher defended the existence of the far right-wing German party saying, "yet, we are in the position of any democracy: even 'Neanderthals' can enjoy human rights."[17] Ideological enemies needed to be defeated through democratic means just as social democratic policies need to be advanced through parliamentary tactics.

Other prominent figures in the SPD followed Schumacher's line and often spoke explicitly on the need for the rule of law and judicially enforced legal rights as the means of protecting human rights against a tyrannical concentration of power at the top. Writing in *Der Spiegel,* Hinrich Wilhelm Kopf invoked the crimes of the Nazis to argue for a strong system of independent courts to check administrative orders and a constitutional court "to ensure that German citizens are never again deprived of those elementary and inalienable rights that are recognized as universal human rights by all civilized nations."[18] From this experience under the Nazis, it was clear to Kopf that while the state was essential to providing human rights in the form of social benefits, the primary threat to human rights stemmed from the political sphere in the form of an unchecked dictatorship.

From the perspective of the SED and supporters of state socialism in the Eastern zone, such talk of human rights and pluralism reflected a failure to recognize the threat of resurgent fascism through liberal means. Following the SED's electoral defeat of 1946, legal scholar Karl Polak sought to reconcile the popularity of the idea of human rights with the necessity of centralized party control and socialist revolution. Polak preserved Marx's critique of the rights of man and citizen as a rhetorical ploy by the bourgeoisie to proclaim their class interests in the name of all humanity, but he expanded on this logic by claiming human rights as part of the superstructure of all societies over all historical eras, developing in relation to changes in the economic base. Just as all democratic systems of government from the bourgeois period of history would pale in comparison to the truly democratic society that would exist following the revolutionary cessation of class conflict, so too would the human rights of the socialist order outshine the sham human rights of bourgeois society. According to Polak, "Socialism is by definition the realization of human rights; and human rights are, if they are not to remain an empty principle, only realized insofar as socialism has been made a reality."[19] In practical terms, all forms of human rights would flow from the radical reform of the economic order rather than from any kind of purely political change.

Polak drew opposing conclusions in terms of human rights from that of the social democrats arguing that parliamentary democracy would simply lead back to fascist control. Liberal constitutionalism with its pluralism and social openness only provided opportunities for reactionaries to take control of the system to the detriment of all society. No matter the political reforms, the crucial problem would always remain economic and so long as capitalism reigned, so too would the problem of exploitation and the threat of a resurgence of fascism. Directly addressing the 1946 slogan of the SPD, Polak declared the exact opposite: there could be "no human rights without socialism."[20] Furthermore, he argued that SPD propaganda was inherently dishonest and sought to conceal that its true goal was nothing more than the inferior "bourgeois human rights" of the past. For Polak, this meant bringing about, "the expropriation of the expropriators, the overthrow of the capitalist social order and its system of the exploitation of man by man and the overcoming of capitalist oppression and rule through the free association of people."[21] Human rights would thus be the end result of a revolutionary change in the economic system of Germany as conducted by the SED as vanguard of the proletariat. Whereas the Social Democrats warned of concentrated political power as the greatest threat to human rights, Polak contended that only through the dictatorship of the proletariat could one realize the reforms needed for human rights to flourish.

Beyond this debate between whether it was political or economic reforms that would secure human rights, there lay the position of Christians, particularly those of the "personalist movement," who posited that what Germany truly needed was a moral revolution. Beginning in the 1930s, the personalist movement centered on the idea of the sanctity of the human person while rejecting both modern liberalism and totalitarian communism. When it came to human rights, as British Catholic thinker Christopher Dawson explained, "what we are defending, in short, is not democracy but humanity."[22] In Germany, the Christian personalist line of thought was expressed most clearly not by a theologian, but by the eminent historian Gerhard Ritter. He argued that the narrow view of human rights as a product of the bourgeois revolutions in the United States and France was inherently flawed and that the true origins of human rights lay with the fight for religious freedom in the sixteenth century.[23] Although many spoke of human rights in terms of political rights and the creation of a zone of liberty for the individual against the arbitrary actions of the state, Ritter argued that this early history pointed toward a conception of human rights grounded in Christian social ethics. For Ritter, the calamity of the Nazi era stemmed from the revolutions in America and France, which actually corrupted the idea of human rights, disconnecting it from eternal truths and making it synonymous with individualistic materialism. "If it was the point of human rights to restrict the sovereignty of the state in the name of an individual sphere of freedom, this problem could not really be solved with a radically interpreted sovereignty of the people that led directly to the submission to the masses."[24] This break from Christian-based human rights inexorably led to the murderous *Volksgemeinschaft* of the Nazis: the logical outcome of a democracy founded on materialism was "profoundly destructive, compromising the very freedom of the personality that it was alleged to secure."[25]

According to Ritter, the perversion of human rights and their diversion from Christian values to a vehicle for crass individualism, led not just to soulless liberalism but, ironically enough, to Soviet totalitarianism. He argued that the champions of materialism as the ideal basis for society had shifted from the United States to the Soviet Union, which now threatened to spread this destructive doctrine to the rest of Europe by force. A return to the political system of the Weimar era would not reestablish human rights in Germany as the rot was too extensive by the twentieth century for any such system to be of use. Instead, Germans had to devote themselves to reclaiming the original human rights of their Reformation era forebears. Ritter viewed the West German Basic Law as a crucial tool in such a program, not because it would create a system of legally guaranteed rights, but because it could be a force for the revival of Christian social ethics in the form of human rights.[26] For Ritter, the problem of human rights was one of moral rebirth from which all else would flow to act as a force against both modern liberalism and Soviet communism.

The final strand of the German human rights discourse originated in the mass deportations of Germans at the close of World War II. The massive influx of refugees and expellees from across Eastern Europe including areas that had historically large German populations inspired calls for restitution in the name of self-determination and human rights. The leading intellectual proponent of this cause was the legal scholar Rudolf Laun, who developed the concept of the right to a homeland. Whereas Schumacher, Polak, and Ritter aimed at achieving human rights through reforms within Germany, Laun focused on reconstituting German national territory as the means to realizing human rights.

According to Laun, the cultural rights of the individual could not be exercised in isolation, so individuals had the right to realize them as part of their larger national community. The essential right of the individual as a member of such a community was the "right to a homeland" (*Recht auf Heimat*).[27] As Lora Wildenthal has noted, in arguing for this right, he "did not seek a right to just any homeland ... but rather to a nationality's supposedly unique and irreplaceable homeland."[28] The essence of human rights was the right to one's ancestral homeland (*angestammte Heimat*) thus privileging those who had the earliest claim to a region.[29] Laun's history of human rights, like that of Ritter, began with religious freedom in the sixteenth century, but he claimed Germany's pioneering work steadily progressed to culminate in the "freest constitution in the world" under the Weimar Republic. While the Nazis violated human rights, Laun claimed that recent years were no evidence that the German masses had forfeited their earlier achievements. He argued that the German people "supported human rights even in the National Socialist period, just as before," but that many had also supported Hitler due to "gullibility, lack of judgment, ignorance of the facts and a sophisticated propaganda system that convinced many that Hitler's state was a *Rechtsstaat*."[30]

The terror of the Nazi regime, according to Laun, had nothing to do with capitalism, materialist individualism, or the failure to defend democracy, but was rather the poison fruit of the 1919 peace settlement imposed by the West upon the German people.[31] According to Laun, the stubborn and hateful refusal to allow true self-determination for the German speakers of the Habsburg lands resulted in the ongoing violation of these people's rights. The support of the Sudeten Germans for the German conquest of their land did not reflect an affinity with Nazism but the overwhelming desire to realize their human rights to self-determination, regardless of what political group had facilitated such a victory.[32] Laun's argument implied that the destruction of World War II could actually be placed at the feet of the Allies for having torn apart the German nation and putting Germans in a position where they would support a figure who promised to reunite their people.

According to Laun, the path forward on human rights required the reclamation of the German *Heimat*—namely East Prussia and Silesia from Poland and the Sudentenland from Czechoslovakia. As the Allies would never agree to such a proposal, he argued that in the meantime it was essential that individuals have the right to directly petition the allied powers to demand their human rights. The contemporary arrangement of total Allied power over Germans due to the unconditional surrender of 1945 represented an affront to human rights, and without the right to petition, Germans would continue to be the victims of massive human rights abuses. While Laun said almost nothing of the Holocaust or the rights of self-determination for European Jews (his work implied that they never really had a home in Europe anyways) he did, however, refer to the expulsion of Germans from Eastern Europe as genocide.[33]

Laun's ideas on human rights and self-determination were not fringe concern and gain widespread support, if not always in such stark terms. The 1953 program of the right-wing Deutsche Partei asserted, "the right to a homeland is the basis of all human rights."[34] On the other side of the West German political spectrum, the SPD also invoked the "right to a homeland" in political campaigns and included the idea in the famous Godesberg Program of 1959.[35] Kurt Schumacher in particular avoided the strong anti-Allied rhetoric of Laun in connection to this right, if only to avoid the impression that "Germans were now flocking to the cause of human rights now that their plans for tyranny had failed."[36]

The lessons of the Third Reich pointed away from fascism and racial hierarchy but for many, the path to human rights lay in dictatorship, irredentism, or spiritual renewal rather than a multiparty democracy, the division of powers, or an independent judiciary. It is likely that Kurt Schumacher, Karl Polak, and Rudolf Laun would have agreed with Gerhard Ritter's assertion that "on human rights depends in the end whether life on this old European continent will remain worth living."[37] But from their writings, it is clear that they would not agree as to what human rights meant and exactly how these rights would rescue Europe and Germany from the brink. For each, the embrace of human rights was essential to the rejection of the Third Reich and the rehabilitation of postwar Germany, yet their conflicting conceptions of human rights as a matter of politics, economics, morality, or territory demonstrate the diversity of the meaning of human rights in this period.

THE DEMOCRATIZATION OF HUMAN RIGHTS

The interconnection of democratization and the realization of human rights was tenuous in the immediate postwar years, but by 1989, liberal democracy and pluralism were seen almost universally as core tenets of the ideals of human rights. In West Germany, this change occurred beginning in the 1960s, while in East Germany it did not happen until the mid 1980s. The decisive factor in this difference was a matter of political and civic conflict rather than a naturally occurring consensus or process of moral epiphany. While illiberal strands of the human rights discourse steadily faded away in the Federal Republic as the result of public exchange, in the German Democratic Republic (GDR), the SED continued to maintain its hegemonic discourse of human rights through dictatorship well into the 1980s.

As Konrad Jarausch has argued, "West German pluralism permitted the conflicts that accompanied [modernization] to be resolved more constructively than did its Eastern counterpart of a welfare dictatorship."[38] Early West German democratic institutions, however, limited in their openness, allowed for activists and citizens who felt politically homeless in the Adenauer era, to come together to call for greater pluralism and democracy at home, not just abroad. By contrast, in East Germany, the language of human rights remained a tool of the SED in its propaganda against the West and in its ongoing efforts to legitimize one-party rule in the GDR. Only when East Germans recreated a nascent public sphere in the 1980s can one observe the emergence of a discourse of human rights centered on individual political rights and liberties.

While the West German state was a vocal critic of human rights abuses in the GDR regarding free speech, free association and freedom of belief, the early decades of the Federal Republic are marred by abuses of these same freedoms at home. The Federal Republic of Germany (FRG) banned the KPD and imprisonment of left-wing activists the name of preserving a constitutional state, but many West Germans had reservations about the contradictions between state rhetoric and practice. As Patrick Major has argued, this period of judicial anticommunism did not compare to the political oppression meted out by the Nazis or the mass surveillance conducted in East Germany, but it did represent a violation of the principles the West German state claimed to represent.[39] He writes, "there were so many judges of Nazi vintage still passing sentence in the FRG that it is very difficult to talk of an unprejudiced judiciary in the 1950s and 1960s," and it took a bout of liberal reform in 1968 to end "a period of political justice which did not reflect credit on the Federal Republic's legal system."[40]

This push for reform in the 1960s came primarily from civil society groups such as the Humanist Union and the International League for Human Rights and the West German chapter of Amnesty International that challenged the CDU government and the dominant anticommunist consensus of the 1950s. Amnesty International in particular brought together activists from a wide variety of political backgrounds, all of whom could work together through the nonpartisan language of human rights to increase the freedoms they could all enjoy.[41] Events such as the "Spiegel Affair" of 1962, in which the editors of the Hamburg-based newsmagazine were arrested in the name of protecting state secrets, helped to galvanize the public against such actions and raise awareness as to the dangers of unrestricted state power at home.[42]

The intellectual shift in West Germany from the 1940s to the 1970s can best be seen in the work of the prominent international legal scholar Otto Kiminich. While Kiminich supported the concept of a right to a homeland—he himself was an expellee from the East—he approached the problem as one of universal minority rights rather than from a purely German perspective in terms of territorial loss. Although he supported an active role for the Federal Republic in promoting human rights abroad, he saw that the Cold War critiques of communism were sometimes equally applicable at home. In his 1973 work, "Human Rights: Failure and Hope," he argued that "it is undeniable that in East and West, in North and South, in industrialized countries and in developing countries, the gigantic machinery of the state apparatus, regardless of whether it works silently or with the clatter of machine guns, threatens human rights."[43] For Kiminich, West Germany "is where our task and our opportunity for the struggle for human rights at the global level begins."[44] Through the public conflict over the meaning of human rights, syntheses of early thought began to emerge.

The ideas of people like Otto Kiminich brought the ideals of national rights and moral renewal together with the liberal democratic critique of West German Cold War propaganda for the purposes of advancing human rights at home.

As West Germans turned toward a more pluralistic and democratic conception of human rights in the 1960s, the SED and East German legal scholars were recommitting to the idea of human rights as a product of the dictatorship of the proletariat. In 1959, the SED founded the Committee for the Protection of Human Rights to campaign against West German abuses, in particular the banning of the KPD and the persecution of leftists.[45] After Karl Polak's death in 1961, the legal scholar Hermann Klenner continued to promote the ideal of human rights through "democratic centralism." On the fifteenth anniversary of the Universal Declaration of Human Rights in 1963, he wrote:

> The basic socialist rights derive from necessity out of the economic development of society and the possibilities of the dictatorship of the proletariat, which is the executor of historical necessity, and identifies its contents. It is not characterized by a state-free sphere in which the individual can pursue his private caprice—a petty-bourgeois illusion![46]

The language of human rights in the GDR remained dominated by an interpretation that confirmed the SED's right to rule without opposition. At the end of the 1960s, the organization expanded its campaign against human rights abuses in the capitalist world by speaking out against political repression in Greece, the Vietnam War, and civil rights issues in the United States, all the while being barred from addressing violations of human rights within the GDR itself.[47]

In spite of the clear contradiction between the lofty claims of the SED and its coercive practices, East German citizens did not take up the vocabulary of human rights to demand political reforms as they had in the West, but it did begin to trickle down into the language of popular protest. In 1968, the SED simultaneously sought public approval of a new socialist constitution for the GDR that would codify the one-party rule of the SED, while also using the United Nations Human Rights Year as an opportunity to promote their own record on the subject to gain international legitimacy.[48] Some citizens sought to use the idea of human rights to call for greater freedom to travel, fewer restrictions on free speech and more space for religious liberty. The only one of these demands to make an impact was that of Christians seeking protection for religious worship as church officials organized their congregants who sought to defend their tenuous position in the atheist East.[49] Without an open public sphere in which to voice dissenting views and mobilize coalitions of disaffected citizens, however, such calls for change in the name of human rights remained marginal.

In the 1970s in East Germany, the language of human rights served as utilitarian means of demanding exit papers after all other positions had failed. Those that did view political and civil rights as essential to human rights often sought to go to West Germany where they believed that these rights had already been realized instead of fighting for them within the GDR. As one Christian seeking to move to West Germany wrote: "I unreservedly declare my allegiance to the FRG, which I regard as my fatherland, now that the territory of the GDR has obviously been lost to Germany ... I am tormented by this yearning for the FRG, because this free, pluralistic welfare state is my intellectual and political home."[50] For those who believed in the idea of liberal democratic human rights, it made more sense to go to where those rights already were rather than to challenge the entrenched position of the SED.

Aside from those seeking to emigrate, East German Christians continued to employ the language of human rights as a means of pressing for increased religious freedom. They invoked the Universal Declaration of Human Rights and the United Nations Human Rights Covenants of 1966 to demand greater autonomy for the church, increased control over moral education for religious parents and protections from state harassment for believers.[51] According to church officials and East German Christians, however, there was a clear separation between socialism as a political and socioeconomic system and socialism as a worldview. They demanded space for a Christian *Weltanschauung* while affirming their support for socialism in general. Human rights and religious freedoms represented a private matter of belief that existed beyond affairs of state and was thus not a threat to SED rule. In the wake of the Helsinki Accords of 1975, lower-level clergy began to push for increased freedom of expression in the name of human rights but senior figures in the church leadership went out of their way to publicly proclaim the GDR's full compliance with international human rights agreements while disciplining those whose calls for human rights were deemed too political in order to avoid antagonizing the SED and state security.[52]

The dissidents who emerged from the ranks of the East German intelligentsia in the 1970s called for an increased freedom of expression and a greater room for criticism of the SED, but most often they avoided the language of human rights and rejected calls for parliamentary democracy and pluralism that would harm the socialist project. Although they demanded rights to free speech and sometimes, in the case of the famed chemist Robert Havemann, actually promoted the creation of an opposition party, they rejected any system that would undo the socialist revolution and return the country to capitalism. As Peter Schneider observed of the dissidents of the 1970s, especially those from the cultural elite, "they criticized the Socialist Unity Party's abuse of power, not its monopoly of it; their demands for more democracy were meant not to secure free elections and a ('bourgeois-reactionary') multiparty system, but to eliminate censorship and build a plurality of opinion within the socialist power structure."[53]

Rudolf Bahro, a dissident party functionary who was himself severely punished in 1977 following the publication of his eco-utopian treatise *Die Alternative* in the West, exemplifies the simultaneous rejection of the East German status quo along with the dismissal of the emerging human rights movement. While Bahro claimed to believe in the ideals of human rights and political democracy in general, he could not support the return of such backward "bourgeois" institutions advocated by international human rights activists. Bahro declared that the turn to human rights by dissidents in the rest of the Eastern Bloc, not to mention the West, represented a "position that is at the same time the broadest, and the most insipid, and, in any constructive sense, most vacuous."[54] The problems that the human rights movement sought to combat would naturally disappear from the "superstructure" once the economic "base" was sufficiently altered through long-term determined action. As such, "the conception of party pluralism seems to me an anachronistic piece of thoughtlessness."[55]

As Cold War tensions rose once again with the reignition of the nuclear arms race in the early 1980s, East German peace activists arose to campaign against further deployment of missiles in West Germany as well as to hold the SED accountable to its peace-loving rhetoric. Initially, these dissidents avoided criticizing the political order of the GDR by framing their cause as pacifistic rather than political. They targeted mandatory military education in schools and parades by the armed forces, not the SED monopoly on power. Yet, after several years of repression by the state apparatus, the peace movement shifted its focus from the arms race to human rights. As one activist later recalled, "we had simply realized that this was a 'must,' that without it we couldn't do anything ... only after we had begun to run into enormous organizing difficulties did our focus begin to change."[56] This turn toward human rights kept the moral goals of the peace movement front and center but also made the establishment of a pluralistic society and polity a precondition for the realization of these moral goals. The Initiative for Peace and Human Rights (IFM), the first independent human rights organization in the GDR, declared that "pluralism is an overarching value for the enforcement of fundamental human rights ... The essential tension between different approaches to human rights issues is productive and should not be destroyed by policy debates with the goal of unification."[57] Just as had occurred in West Germany, an emergent civil society produced new conceptions of human rights and diverse groups were able to agree on the principles of pluralism and democracy, if at times only due to mutual self-interest in the face of repressive state practices.

This turn was not universal and for a time produced a split amongst peace movement activists themselves. Splitting away from the IFM activists in 1986 a group called the Counter-Voices (*Gegenstimmen*) still argued, along similar lines to Rudolf Bahro, that pluralism as well as other "bourgeois" political and civil human rights were mere distractions from the necessary social revolution that would finally bring about the liberation of human-ity.[58] Writing to exiled peace activist Roland Jahn in 1987, the draft resister and founder of the *Gegenstimmen* Rheinhardt Schult disputed the claim that political pluralism was necessary for the implementation of basic human rights: "That is for me no more than ideology or religion. It is on the same level as Lenin's line: Marxism is all-powerful because it is true."[59] The turn to pluralism was again a political choice that did not stem from universal moral epiphany.

In a few short years, however, the IFM vision of human rights had clearly become dominant as small human rights organizations with similar values sprang up across the GDR. Human rights continued to serve as a means of pressuring the SED to allow greater access to exit visas, but by 1989 even GDR elites began to adopt the language of human rights to justify introducing greater freedom of speech, the rule of law and political plural-ism. Facing economic, social, and political crises, the elites of East Germany lost faith in their own hegemonic conception of human rights and came to adopt the principles of the dissidents in efforts to forestall collapse and usher in reforms. Shortly before the fall of the Berlin Wall, the same journal that had originally published Karl Polak's first works on human rights in 1946, now carried an article from the SED's two leading human rights scholars calling for a new GDR that would be "politically democratic, pluralistic and following the rule of law."[60]

CONCLUSION

The meaning of human rights in postwar Germany was not self-evident but evolved through discourse and conflict in the public sphere. The process of connecting the abstract ideals of human rights to concrete political and economic institutions and practices was, and continues to be, evolutionary as new threats to human rights appear and activists demonstrate the flaws and blind spots of the status quo. Although many political groups sought to instrumentalize the language of human rights to promote a sectarian or partisan agenda, without the monopoly on communications and power held by the SED, it was necessary to engage with competing discourses and appeal to broadly acceptable norms. Elites initially brought the idea of human rights into the public sphere, but the meaning of human rights was ultimately shaped by the social and political engagement of the German people. Civil society organizations and dissident groups brought to light the contradictions and hypocrisies endemic in both East and West Germany where the state failed to practice what it preached. Public pressure forced political leaders to move from particularist conceptions of human rights toward a pluralistic and democratic vision of human rights.

The embrace of the language of human rights alone did not transform Germany from a genocidal dictatorship to a liberal democracy and many advocates of human rights even fought to ensure that Germany would remain a one-party state. Yet, the idea of human rights was not just an empty vessel that any movement could adopt without consequence. Human rights were adopted for illiberal ends, but in both East and West Germany, the language of human rights served as the discursive means through which heterogeneous coalitions of activists, dissidents, and others could come together to fight for pluralism and democracy. In both countries, it served as a language of morality above the fray of politics and partisan division while, paradoxically, promoting a specific political vision of individualism, pluralism, and popular rule. The idea of human rights was crucial in the process of turning around Germany after the "break with civilization" during the Third Reich, but the path of human rights was both contested and historically contingent.

Ned Richardson-Little is Associate Research Fellow at the University of Exeter working on the Leverhulme Trust project "1989 after 1989: Rethinking the Fall of State Socialism in a Global Perspective." In 2013, he earned his doctorate in history from the University of North Carolina at Chapel Hill.

NOTES

1. Lora Wildenthal, "Human Rights Advocacy and National Identity in West Germany," *Human Rights Quarterly* 22, no. 4 (2000): 1051–59; Konrad Jarausch, *After Hitler: Recivilizing Germans, 1945–1995* (Oxford, 2008); and Konrad Jarausch, *After Unity: Reconfiguring German Identities* (New York, 1997), 87. On importance of the idea of human rights in reunified Germany, see Stuart

Taberner and Frank Finlay, *Recasting German Identity: Culture, Politics, and Literature in the Berlin Republic* (New York, 2002), 2; and Volker Rittberger, *German Foreign Policy Since Unification: Theories and Case Studies* (Manchester, 2001), 278.

2. Bundesarchiv Berlin-Lichterfelde (BArch-Lichterfelde) DY 30/IV 2/1/4 (Protokoll, 3. Tagung des Parteivorstandes vom 18. bis 20. Juni 1946.) 56.

3. Heike Amos, *Die Entstehung der Verfassung in der Sowjetischen Besatzungszone/DDR, 1946–1949* (Münster, 2006), 42–49.

4. Archiv der Sozialen Demokratie (AdSD), 6/PLKA000150, 'Kein Sozialismus ohne Menschenrechte' (20.10.1946).

5. AdSD, 6/FLBL001536, "An die Mitglieder der SPD!" (31.03.1946)

6. AdSD, 6/FLBL001419, "Berliner!" (20.10.1946).

7. Donna Harsch, *Revenge of the Domestic: Women, the Family, and Communism in the German Democratic Republic* (Princeton, NJ, 2007), 38; Norman Naimark, *The Russians in Germany: A History of the Soviet Zone of Occupation, 1945–1949* (Cambridge, 1995), 120.

8. Arthur Schlegelmilch, *Hauptstadt in Zonendeutschland: Die Entstehung der Berliner Nachkriegsdemokratie, 1945–1949* (Berlin, 1993), 363.

9. Dirk Spilker, *The East German Leadership and the Division of Germany: Patriotism and Propaganda 1945–1953* (Oxford, 2006), 101.

10. "Wahlsieg der SPD," *Sozialistische Mitteilung*, no. 92 (1946): 1.

11. "Großer Wahlsieg der SED in der Zone," *Neues Deutschland* (22 October 1946): 1.

12. BArch-Lichterfelde DY 30/ IV 2/1/10 (Protokoll, 6. Tagung des Parteivorstandes am 24. und 25. Oktober 1946) 2, 41.

13. On British Social Democracy and human rights, see Marco Duranti, "Curbing Labour's Totalitarian Temptation: European Human Rights Law and British Postwar Politics," *Humanity: An International Journal of Human Rights, Humanitarianism, and Development* 3, no. 3 (2012): 364. On connections between American liberalism and the social policies of Franklin Roosevelt with international human rights, see Elizabeth Borgwardt, *A New Deal for the World* (Cambridge, 2007).

14. "Hauptreferat Schumachers: 'Aufgaben und Ziele der deutschen Sozialdemokratie'" (9.5.1946), in Kurt Schumacher, *Reden, Schriften, Korrespondenzen 1945–1952* (Berlin, 1985), 414.

15. Ibid.

16. Ibid.

17. "Stellungnahme Schumachers zum Rechtsradikalismus in einer gemeinsamen Sitzung des Parteivorstandes und des Parteiausschusses der SPD" (14.3.1950), in Ibid., 996.

18. Hinrich Wilhelm Kopf, "Wozu brauchen wir eine Verfassung?," *Spiegel* 33 (1947).

19. Karl Polak, "Gewaltenteilung, Menschenrechte, Rechtsstaat: Begriffsformalismus und Demokratie," *Einheit* 1, no. 7 (1946) reprinted in Karl Polak, *Reden und Aufsätze: zur Entwicklung der Arbeiter- und Bauern-Macht.* (Berlin, 1968), 139–40.

20. Ibid., 140.

21. Ibid., 138.
22. Samuel Moyn, "Personalism, Community, and the Origins of Human Rights," in *Human Rights in the Twentieth Century,* ed. Stefan-Ludwig Hoffmann (Cambridge, 2010), 95.
23. Samuel Moyn, "The First Historian of Human Rights," *The American Historical Review* 116, no. 1 (2011): 63.
24. Quoted in Ibid., 65.
25. Quoted in Ibid.
26. Ibid., 67.
27. Lora Wildenthal, "Rudolf Laun and the Human Rights of Germans in Occupied and Early West Germany," in *Human Rights in the Twentieth Century,* ed. Stefan-Ludwig Hoffmann (Cambridge, 2010), 132, 136.
28. Ibid., 137.
29. Ibid., 140.
30. Rudolf Laun, *Die Menschenrechte* (Hamburg, 1948), 16.
31. Wildenthal, "Rudolf Laun," 141.
32. Ibid., 139.
33. Ibid., 141.
34. AdSD 6/FLBL003893 "Wahlkampfwerbung der Deutschen Partei zur Bundestagswahl am 6.9.1953; Darlegung ihres Programms für die zweite Legislaturperiode."
35. "Godesberger Programm, November 1959," http://www.hdg.de/lemo/html/ dokumente/DieZuspitzungDesKaltenKrieges_programmGodesbergerProgramm/.
36. "Bemerkungen zur allgemeinen Aussprache und Schlußworte Schumachers," in Schumacher, *Reden, Schriften, Korrespondenzen 1945–1952,* 421.
37. Moyn, "The First Historian of Human Rights," 66.
38. Jarausch, *After Hitler,* 183.
39. Patrick Major, *The Death of the KPD: Communism and Anti-Communism in West Germany, 1945–1956* (Oxford, 1997), 277–78.
40. Ibid., 281–82.
41. See Lora Wildenthal, *The Language of Human Rights in West Germany* (Philadelphia, PA, 2012), 63–100.
42. On the "Spiegel Affair" see, Ronald Bunn, *German Politics and the Spiegel Affair* (Baton Rouge, 1968).
43. Quoted in Lora Wildenthal, *The Language of Human Rights,* 232.
44. Ibid.
45. On the Committee, see Siegfried Forberger, *Das DDR-Komitee für Menschenrechte: Erinnerungen an den Sozialismus-Versuch im 20. Jahrhundert; Einsichten und Irrtümer des Siegfried Forberger, Sekretär des DDR-Komitees für Menschenrechte von 1959 bis 1989* (Berlin, 2000).
46. Hermann Klenner, "Fünfzehn Jahre Menschenrechtspraxis in Deutschland," *Deutsche Aussenpolitik* (Issue 12, 1964): 1157.
47. In 1969, the group changed its name to the *DDR-Komitee für Menschenrechte* as part of its reorganization.

48. Section 1 of the 1968 Constitution affirmed the primacy of the SED as the "working class and its Marxists-Leninist party" in leading the GDR. See also, Politisches Archiv-Auswärtiges Amt (PA-AA), MfAA C 487/76 "Vorbereitung des Anschlusses und Beitrittserklärung der DDR an die Konventionen über wirt. 1967–1968 UN Konventionen" and BArch-Lichterfelde DY 30/ J IV 2/3/ 1404 (Protokoll Nr. 43/68 Sitzung am 8. Mai 1968. Inhaltliche Konzeption für Maßnahmen aus Anlaß des von der UNO proklamierten "Internationalen Jahres der Menschenrechte") 1.

49. Ned Richardson-Little, "Dictatorship and Dissent: Human Rights in East Germany in the 1970s," in *The Breakthrough: Human Rights in the 1970s,* ed. Jan Eckel and Samuel Moyn (Philadelphia, PA, 2014), 57.

50. Quoted in Roger Wood, *Opposition in the GDR Under Honecker, 1971–85: An Introduction and Documentation* (New York, 1986), 177.

51. See the joint letter of East German Protestant Bishops to Walter Ulbricht (15.2.1968) in Evangelisches Zentral Archiv (EZA)104/687.

52. Ehrhart Neubert, *Geschichte der Opposition in der DDR: 1949–1989* (Berlin, 1998), 356–59. On the punishment of dissent, see Lothar Tautz, ed., *Friede und Gerechtigkeit heute: das "Querfurter Papier"–ein politisches Manifest für die Einhaltung der Menschenrechte in der DDR* (Magdeburg, 2002).

53. Peter Schneider, *The German Comedy: Scenes of Life After the Wall* (New York, 1992), 78.

54. Rudolf Bahro, "Ich werde meinen Weg fortsetzen," in *Rudolf Bahro: Eine Dokumentation* (Frankfurt am Main, 1977), 13.

55. Rudolf Bahro, *The Alternative in Eastern Europe* (London, 1978), 350.

56. Dirk Philipsen, *We Were the People: Voices from East Germany's Revolutionary Autumn of 1989* (Durham, NC, 1993), 54.

57. "Eingabe an den XI. Parteitag der SED," in*"Freiheit ist immer Freiheit–": die Andersdenkenden in der DDR,* ed. Ferdinand Kroh (Frankfurt am Main, 1988), 226.

58. Wolfgang Rüddenklau. *Störenfried: DDR-Opposition 1986–1989* (Berlin, 1992), 51.

59. Robert Havemann Gesellschaft (RHG). RJ 02. Letter from Rheinhardt Schult to Roland Jahn, 20. 4. 1987. See also, RHG RG/B 03 "Stellungnahme zu einer Eingabe an den XI. Parteitag der SED 1986" (Februar/März 1987)

60. R Reißig and F Berg, "Für eine moderne Konzeption des Sozialismus," *Einheit,* no. 12 (1989): 1081.

SELECTED BIBLIOGRAPHY

Caldwell, Peter C. *Dictatorship, State Planning, and Social Theory in the German Democratic Republic.* Cambridge, 2003.

Jarausch, Konrad. *After Hitler: Recivilizing Germans, 1945–1995.* Oxford, 2006.

Major, Patrick. *The Death of the KPD: Communism and Anti-Communism in West Germany, 1945–1956.* Oxford, 1997.

Moyn, Samuel. "The First Historian of Human Rights." *The American Historical Review* 116, no. 1 (2011): 58–79.

Neubert, Erhart. *Die Geschichte der Opposition in der DDR, 1949–1989.* Berlin, 1998.

Wildenthal, Lora. *The Language of Human Rights in West Germany.* Philadelphia, PA, 2012.

Chapter 8

African Students and Racial Ambivalence in the GDR during the 1960s

Sara Pugach

During the early 1960s, the Soviet Union and its allies made a concerted effort to provide scholarships for African students in order to forge alliances with newly independent nations across the African continent.[1] The Soviets had even founded Lumumba University, named after slain Congolese president Patrice Lumumba, to show their commitment to training African comrades. However, the presence of racism—which was not officially supposed to exist in the anticolonial, anti-imperial East—undercut Soviet endeavors to attract African allies.[2] Various prominent, racially motivated incidents contrasted starkly with the antiracial policies of the Soviets and their allies. In 1963, African students massed in Moscow's Red Square to express outrage at the death of a Ghanaian medical student who was engaged to a Russian woman, then died under suspicious circumstances. Their rallying cry of "Moscow is a Second Alabama!" clearly rejected Soviet claims that the USSR was antiracist.[3]

Like its senior ally, the German Democratic Republic (GDR) professed official antiracism and anti-imperialism. The GDR also bore the burden of being one of the successor states to the Nazis. This added a layer of complexity to questions of racial bias. The competition between the GDR and the Federal Republic of Germany (FRG) further complicated the issue of racism. Official rhetoric held that West Germany was the real inheritor of fascism. Yet GDR officials could not deny reports of racism in their country, even as they worked hard to ensure that they did not become available to the general public. The incidents in the USSR and elsewhere in communist Europe upset the African politicians that the GDR was trying to cultivate, and to convince of the imperialist nature of West Germany.

This chapter explores how ideas of race and racism did and did not surface in GDR debates over African students. It addresses how the FRG consistently appeared in accounts of racism in the GDR. Following Julie Hessler, who has examined how the USSR handled African claims of racism, I dissect the GDR's treatment of racial bias. I argue that East German racial policy, like that of the Soviets, was primarily about either denial or displacement. In the GDR, racism was often reframed as the result of "cultural confusion." After a lifetime of oppression in the colonies, Africans who accused East Germans of racism were considered simply skeptical of whites, and unable to recognize good from bad Europeans. Further, in other cases where racist behavior was noted, its perpetrators were cast as remnants, who belonged to a dwindling number of malcontents.

Deflecting racist critiques of the state and its citizens in this manner was crucial to East Germany, and used as a tactic to castigate the neighboring FRG. Throughout the 1960s, the two Germanys were locked in a political and ideological struggle. The FRG's Hallstein Doctrine dictated that nations having diplomatic relations with the West could not recognize the GDR. Therefore, although the GDR had trade missions in several African countries during the 1960s, it only had official ambassadorial representation in Zanzibar and Guinea,[4] at least until the doctrine was relaxed in 1970.[5] The GDR was thus compelled to maintain a public image as the Germany that showed solidarity with the developing, recently decolonized world.[6] Any hint of racism would tarnish that reputation.

The GDR was certainly never as free of racism as the historian Ulrich van der Heyden has claimed.[7] Yet students such as Mohammed Touré, a Malian who studied *Germanistik* (German Studies) at the Karl Marx University (KMU) in Leipzig during the 1970s, did have positive memories of the GDR. Touré even described his years in Leipzig as among the best in his life. He did not recall experiencing racism in East Germany, in sharp contrast to his later experiences in the FRG, where he moved in 1987.[8] Attitudes toward race in the GDR may thus best be described as ambivalent or, to use the German term, *zwiespältig*. Racism never disappeared, but it was both driven underground by strict antiracist policies, and diluted by frequent calls to solidarity and good will.

RACE AS A WEST GERMAN PROBLEM

Being a student in East Germany meant different things. Some African students attended university, while others went to vocational programs. Yet others were trainees who received an *Ausbildung*—an education—at a factory or other kind of business. There were also students who went to the GDR for short periods—usually no more than two years—to learn to be communist functionaries. These students took specific courses in political and practical communism at schools such as the Jugendhochschule Wilhelm Pieck (JWP), an academy of the Freie Deutsche Jugend (FDJ),[9] or the Hochschule der deutschen Gewerkschaften Fritz Heckert (HFH), which a South African student translated as "the College of Free German Trade Unions."[10] At the first, they would be trained as youth leaders; at the second, they would learn to become trade union representatives.

The students who went to JWP and HFH are particularly intriguing because they made more statements on race than their peers elsewhere. The Africans at these schools were not necessarily committed communists, even though the leaders of their liberation movements or political parties chose them for study in the GDR. Yet because they completed homework assignments that discussed their experiences in the GDR and their assessments of the "German Problem," gave speeches, and attended frequent meetings with their teachers, more of what they said about race in the two states has been preserved. Their testimonials must be read against the grain, since FDJ and Freier Deutscher Gewerkschaftsbund (FDGB) instructors likely influenced their work.[11]

The JWP and HFH began offering programs for African youths and labor leaders in 1960. The second group to come to the JWP arrived in 1961, in time to witness the construction of the Berlin Wall—which they applauded in a four-page shared declaration. The document was directed at "young Germans" in the GDR, and exhorted them to join the struggle to overthrow the corrupt and racist FRG regime. The African students urged East German youth "not to be fooled, because we can assure you that you live in very pleasant times; you are in an earthly paradise, if you compare it to the hell of Mr Adenauer and the others." Inside the FRG and its allies, "human dignity, above all that of the colored, is trampled underfoot." This was, the students explained, why progressive African forces and individuals from across the continent had joyfully greeted the Wall's construction.[12]

The JWP students depicted the FRG as a craven associate of the immoral United States. The group was indeed in the GDR during a period of heightened tension between East and West. The "West Berlin question" culminated in the building of the Berlin Wall on 13 August 1961. The GDR claimed that they wanted a peaceful resolution to the question of Berlin's status—whether it would become an independent city, remain under the control of the West, or have control transferred to the East. Meanwhile, Socialist Unity Party of Germany (SED) leader Walter Ulbricht and other politicians argued that the West's plan to involve NATO in Berlin's governance was a shameful continuation of the city's militarization following World War II, and a crass attempt to place West Berlin under further US control.[13]

The same group of students who celebrated the construction of the Berlin Wall, however, also commented on racism inside the GDR. An appraisal of a meeting between students and the administration reported that the visitors had three general outlooks on racial bias. Most of the students perceived a discriminatory "element" amongst the East German population, mainly exemplified through the use of the term *Neger* (negro) and pronounced curiosity. Nonetheless, they reassured their hosts that these attitudes were not typical. A smaller group of students claimed that there was absolutely no discrimination in the GDR. Finally, there were two students who believed the GDR had considerable educative work to do with its population on the question of race if the state wanted to avoid "flagrant conflict" with its African partners. The report described both as "overbearing" and "arrogant."[14]

Tellingly the report on the meeting, which was crafted by a JWP faculty member, echoed the general GDR response to racism: it was due either to African petulance or West German malfeasance. The report indicates that the African students still recognized racism as coming primarily from the FRG, and not comparable with the enormous biases of the West. Thus the Angolans in the group said that racism in the GDR was a "fascist residue," and doubtless the consequence of "infiltration from West Germany." The representative from Portuguese Guinea commented that such discrimination was a "remnant," and had nothing in common with "the situation in capitalist countries," where racism was rampant. Further, a Senegalese student opined that the existence of racism in the GDR was mainly in his colleagues' heads; he suggested that not all of his peers had reached the same "political level," hinting that some were blowing minor incidents of cultural misunderstanding out of proportion.[15]

Open discussion of discrimination in a supposedly anti-imperial state served a dual foreign policy function: first it censured the FRG; second, it burnished the GDR's own antiracist credentials with decolonizing African nations. Thus when a Kenyan student had to break off his studies at the JWP and return home in 1962, he did so with both regret and a newfound respect for socialism and East Germany. Before departing Kenya, he was informed that there were only "constraints" on the populations of socialist countries. After experiencing life in the GDR though, he was convinced that this impression was little more than a rumor spread by "imperialist forces," and that the GDR was a thoroughly pleasant place for people of all races. Indeed, "he had determined that there was no racial discrimination in the GDR, and that any discussions of such are related to [purely] personal matters." He would go back to Kenya and "spread the truth about the GDR." The audience was likely to be receptive since many members of the Kenya African National Union (KANU) had already visited socialist nations and come home with positive impressions.[16]

The faculties of the JWP and HFH were also eager to present the general East German public as antifascist and antiracist. The schools thus organized field trips to former concentration camps with the intention of reinforcing the view that Africans and East Germans had both suffered under fascist oppression. For instance, when participants in the JWP's African and Latin American program went to the mountains along the Czech border for a brief holiday in 1962, their visit also included an outing at the Jugendburg Hohenstein, a one-time concentration camp. A former prisoner gave a speech, and the students "enthusiastically" took part in a discussion of what they had seen.[17] In 1964, the head of faculty at the HFH requested that the school's director accompany the students on an excursion to Sachsenhausen. The former inmate had to go along, because "visitors are always more impressed when someone who was once a prisoner provides commentary on their tours."[18] These visits offered a dialogue on Germany's Nazi past while demonstrating that the GDR citizenry were also the victims of fascism.

The explicitly racial, anti-Semitic component of the Holocaust was likely not included in the speeches African students heard on fascism and resistance. Because the GDR claimed it was not the successor to the Nazis, the SED also held that it had no special responsibility to the Jews.[19] Because the significance of Jews as the primary victims of the Holocaust virtually disappeared from the GDR narrative on Nazism, communists and antifascists were depicted as its main targets.[20] The East German discourse on the Holocaust as an antifascist persecution rather than an anti-Semitic atrocity underscores the complex, ambivalent nature of the GDR's attitude toward race, and exposes the opportunistic side of antiracist ideology. In the 1960s, shoring up ties with African nations was important to both the expansion of the Soviet Bloc and countering the Hallstein Doctrine. Positioning East Germans as victims of the Holocaust—who resembled the African victims of colonialism—was a strategy to emphasize solidarity in suffering.

Whether or not this strategy worked, the HFH did cement relationships with alumni. The directorate of the school made a concerted effort to send alumni a stream of news on both the GDR and the goings-on at the college.[21] HFH administration envisaged producing a regular newsletter that would contain not only reports from the GDR, but incorporate updates from former students.[22] The HFH was particularly interested in knowing how May Day was celebrated in different African nations, and asked its alumni to write about the festivities in their countries, presumably for publication.[23] Correspondence to the HFH further contained requests from students for books that were unavailable to them at home, and which the school then tried to procure.[24]

The letter exchanges sometimes went beyond platitudes or requests for materials. One Ghanaian student, who had returned to Accra and was representing a union for the timber and woodworking industry, described how his training in the GDR had contributed to his success in getting a severance package written into the contract of the union's members. "This training of our youth have [*sic*] sealed the healthy relationship between our two countries. ... Dear Comrade, I have never stopped brooding over the happiest days I had in your wonderful country—the GDR. If I have the means and the will, I would make it a point to visit your country to meet your friendloving [*sic*] people once more."[25] The Ghanaian's sentiments were echoed in letters from students throughout Africa.[26]

In their letters, former students occasionally elaborated on the question of West German imperialism, which had been a central theme in their courses. Shortly before Kenyan independence, for example, a student railed against the FRG, which he claimed was always trying to entice him and his union colleagues to study there. The Goethe Institute in Nairobi was responsible for this West German propaganda.[27] Elsewhere, Kenyan students who had defected to the West during their training were cast as traitors not only to the GDR, but to Kenya as well.[28]

Other students, however, made it clear that they saw their former colonizers as greater threats than the FRG. A Cameroonian pointed out that the French were his principal enemies.[29] While a Zambian did mention the "Bonn Warmongers" in correspondence with the HTH, he did so with regard to FRG threats on Berlin, not West German imperialism. In the last months before Zambian independence on 24 October 1964, he foregrounded the duplicity of the British, Zambia's colonial rulers.[30] Clearly far more acquainted with the conditions in their own nations than their East German professors, the students understood the FRG as only a minor threat.

Student letters demonstrate the depth of the personal ties with HFH faculty and staff. Because the letters were written after the students had either returned home from the GDR, or moved on to another European country, they may be more reliable barometers of opinion than the reports produced in East Germany. The letters from the Cameroonian student were, for example, full of concerns not only for the future of his country, but for his life. He wrote from Accra, the Ghanaian capital, where he was living in exile. The student was likely a member of the Union of the Peoples of Cameroon (UPC), a popular, nationalist political party that the French had labeled communist during the 1950s.[31] Ahmadou Ahidjo, the first post-colonial Cameroonian leader, continued the struggle with the UPC, which had been banned and persecuted.[32] In one letter, the student thus spoke bitterly of the recent execution of fellow union members who remained trapped in Cameroon, and the death sentence levied on others.[33] In another, the student described himself as a refugee, and worried about the fate of his family because he could not get any news from them.[34]

The Cameroonian's letters are revealing of the difficulties of post-colonial development as well as of the evolving relationship between former students and their East German teachers. Their correspondence depicts a similar, shared goal: solidarity with the oppressed, opposition to colonialism and pro-Western leaders such as Ahidjo, and reliance on trade unionism and Marxism as solutions to postindependence corruption. Solidarity was one of the watchwords of GDR foreign policy regarding the developing world; the idea of brotherhood and friendship with those striving for independence was deeply embedded in official East German rhetoric. This propaganda was certainly pragmatic in countering the Hallstein Doctrine and linked to the desire that solidarity with the GDR might engender Marxist politics on the ground in Africa and elsewhere.[35] Yet in some cases, this sense of solidarity was evidently mutual, as former African students saw in their East German professors an audience sympathetic to their hopes and frustrations.

RACE AS AN EAST GERMAN PROBLEM

Students at other kinds of schools also took classes emphasizing the superiority of socialism, and the bankruptcy of the capitalist FRG. They often criticized discrimination in the FRG as well. For example, in the 1960s, the Nigerian president of the Union of African Students in the GDR condemned West German racism in reaction to written attacks on the GDR from another Nigerian, former student Aderogba Ajao who had written a scathing memoir of his experiences in the GDR with financial support from the Central Intelligence Agency (CIA).[36] To counter Ajao's negative portrayal, the union president drew on comparisons between race relations in the East and West. A Ghanaian medical student had told him that he and other Africans were barred from observing operations on female patients; in the GDR, this would be impossible, "because all forms of racial discrimination are forbidden." In West Germany, including West Berlin, "rowdy groups" of students roamed the streets, making life "unbearable." But in the GDR, German and foreign students were friends who showed each other mutual respect.[37]

On occasion, even loyal defenders of the GDR pointed out racist incidents. Such was the case with AE Ohiaeri. He was Nigerian, and one of the first African students to come to the GDR in 1951.[38] Ohiaeri studied medicine at the KMU in Leipzig. He became a doctor in the GDR and stayed in the country through at least the mid 1960s. But when he was back in Nigeria, he published a novel, *Behind the Iron Curtain*. The book was a thinly veiled autobiographical account of his experiences in Eastern and Western Europe. His criticism was not for the Soviet Bloc; it was for Great Britain, whom he claimed had detained him in London while he was visiting from the GDR, and refused to let him return.[39]

In 1965, after Ohiaeri had been in the GDR approximately fourteen years, he had a meeting with the African student contingent in Rostock. The meeting addressed their general unhappiness, reflected in the behavior of their dormitory director. The director had been Ohiaeri's German teacher in the 1950s, and he thought he might have better luck approaching him. He was wrong. The director met him with the same gruff, condescending rudeness. Ohiaeri was flummoxed, saying that in his entire time in the GDR, he had never before been treated this way, implying a racial bias on the director's part.[40]

Other accounts show that African students generally complained about racism in the 1960s. For example, in February 1965 another organization, the Committee of African Students and Workers in the GDR, wrote a letter to Ulbricht. The letter claimed that tensions between African and East German students were growing and leading to brawls. Its authors wanted to address the situation immediately, before things escalated and racially motivated incidents inside the GDR became anticommunist fodder for the Western press.[41]

The writers explained that there were four possible solutions to the issues raised by the existence of minority groups in an ethnically cohesive majority state like the GDR: accommodation of difference, isolation, assimilation, or partial assimilation. Only the last of these—partial assimilation—could really work. Most of the students were only in the country temporarily, and so partial assimilation could occur as long as "there was understanding [for this] on the part of the German people." In accordance with the overarching GDR discourse that African students were often responsible for their own problems, the committee did admit that there were students who provoked negative reactions from East German citizens. These cases often involved alcohol, a lack of appreciation for German culture and customs, or a dearth of "ideological clarity" about Marxism and its goals.

The committee's letter was heavily informed by Pan-Africanism. Its writers asserted that some Africans overreacted to "teasing" because of "historical and psychological factors." They wrote that, "the colonial barbarity under which Africans have long suffered, alongside all the humiliations that the black race has had to and continues to endure, can be bound together with mistrust and touchiness towards whites."[42] This argument was reminiscent of the work of scholars such as Cheikh Anta Diop and Frantz Fanon, who maintained that Europeans had degraded Africans so much that the Africans had come to believe the lies about black inferiority.[43]

According to the GDR narrative, the existence of racism inside its borders was also consistently blamed on the FRG. If a specific racist incident could not be attributed to the West, it had either never really existed, or stemmed from an underdeveloped African political awareness. The 1962 report on the conversation about discrimination between students and administrators of the JWP insinuated as much, with its criticism of the most vocal students as pompous troublemakers. Additionally, accounts of progress among the students demonstrate that the executives of the JWP believed African students had a generally weak understanding of politics and ideology. African "friends" were described as being "incapable of understanding the [political] problems discussed in class."[44] Race was not explicitly mentioned as a factor, but Africans were deemed less able to grasp complex ideas than the Latin American and European students.[45]

The friendly letters between former students and HFH administration were also not free of classically colonial, paternalistic rhetoric. For instance, a boilerplate letter that the HFH director sent to Ghanaian students in 1964 held that, "we now see ... the Ghanaian people expressing a moral and political maturity (*Reife*) that is able to strike a blow against the forces of the opposition that are trying to compel the country down a capitalist path. ... This political maturity proves that the Ghanaian people are ready to follow the course of progress, democracy, and socialism."[46] This statement may seem relatively benign, but within the overall context of European colonial discourse, it appears less sanguine. The word "maturity" is the key. Throughout the colonial era, Africans were consistently referred to as children, or being in a stage of development prior to that of Europeans. It was one of the justifications for why European colonization was necessary; Africans needed Europeans to evolve. The idea of Africans as childlike or immature persisted into the postcolonial era; indeed Germans continued to view Africans through a developmental lens well after most African nations had become independent.[47]

Seen from this perspective, the HFH's director's warm statement that Ghanaians were currently demonstrating moral and political "maturity" can be interpreted as meaning that they had lacked this quality in the past. But with the assistance of individuals trained abroad in socialist countries, they were now on the correct developmental path toward socialism. The word "moral" is also notable. In 1958, Ulbricht announced his "Ten Commandments of Socialist Morality." These included points on maintaining solidarity with the working class and peoples fighting for independence, but also incorporated the exhortation to live cleanly and decently, and to have respect for the family.[48] Some Africans were found wanting in this regard. Already in 1959, a report from the Vice Rector of the KMU expressed explicit concern that Africans were having morally inappropriate relationships with East German women. Improved "cultural work" on the part of the FDJ was needed to correct their sexual promiscuity.[49]

More disturbing was a 1963 attempt by an HFH professor to reject asylum for a Kenyan student because he and his fiancée, an East German interpreter, intended to live in the dorms together after their marriage. Allowing them to do so would have deleterious political and moral effects on other students. The student had originally applied for asylum on grounds that he was a member of KANU and persecuted by the British in colonial Kenya. However, the professor suggested that because Kenyan independence was a *fait accompli* by late 1963, the student not be granted asylum. Yet the rejection clearly had little to do with Kenya's impending decolonization; the professor's internal correspondence proves that the Kenyan was instead to be denied asylum expressly because of the poor moral example that he and his wife would present to other students.[50]

Race was considered as a West German problem or associated with poor African morality, an underdeveloped Marxist political consciousness, or an overweening sensitivity to all white behavior. Yet with regards to unifying African students and making them feel at home, the "imperialist" West sometimes appeared to be doing *better* than the GDR in some respects. According to the 1965 letter by the Committee of African Students and Workers in the GDR discussed above, the FRG had established meeting spaces for international students, which allowed them to connect with each other in a way that was not possible in the GDR. The committee thus recommended emulating the FRG, and setting up clubrooms specifically for African students.[51]

African students additionally questioned the GDR's standard explanations for racism. The Committee of African Students and Workers maintained that the racism of the Nazi period had not been as thoroughly expunged as the GDR wanted students to believe. "Some of the [Africans], including some older students, do not take the ... historical developments in Germany since the end of World War II into account; therefore they do not know that there are certain subversive elements in the GDR, which are still connected to the infamous Hitlerism." While the African students were somewhat to blame for their lack of historical knowledge, the fault also clearly lay with East Germany itself, where fascism stubbornly remained even twenty years after World War II. These reactionary elements were not helped by the films of Deutsche Film AG (DEFA), which "only showed colonial barbarism" and made no mention of African achievements gained since independence. If these were the only images of Africa that existed, it was no wonder that East Germans continued to ask Africans questions such as "do you still live in trees?," or "do you still eat people?"[52]

A 1961 letter from another student organization, the Committee for Afro-Asian Students in Leipzig, was more direct in its condemnation of East German racism. Its members wrote to protest the treatment of two Ghanaian business trainees. The trainees were at home when a car came to collect them and bring them to their office. Their German colleagues at the company said they wanted to "try something," and as a practical joke covered the trainees' heads with a depilatory cream that left them bald.[53]

The Leipzig Committee was furious. Their letter stated that, "We have been invited here to learn, not to be mistreated and exploited by German fascists and militarists. Such capitalist methods and racial hatred must be immediately purged from a socialist nation." They did not have to be treated like "apes, dogs, and mice" simply to have goods from the GDR delivered to Africa. East Germans had committed a grave, violent, insulting injustice against the Ghanaians. The letter concluded by saying that the committee would ensure that politicians and newspapers throughout the Third World heard of this outrage.[54]

Everyday racism recurs often in the records of African students' lives. An especially appalling example involved a Guinean woman who had come to the GDR to take a special training program at the Deutsche Hochschule für Körperkultur (DHfK) in Leipzig.[55] On an April morning in 1968, she purchased a round-trip ticket from Leipzig to Radebeul, a Dresden suburb. On her return trip, the conductor brusquely informed her that her ticket had expired, then walked away without saying another word. She fell asleep. When she awoke, a different conductor was pulling at the collar of her jacket, demanding that she get off the train. When she asked why, he told her she had not paid a supplemental fare. She was affronted and insisted that he treat her like other passengers and simply let her buy the supplement and finish her trip. He ignored her and repeatedly said "Get out!" Then he made the cryptic statement that "Africans are all alike"; when she asked him how, he did not reply.

Although socialist states were theoretically supposed to be antiracist, the above incidents concerning the Ghanaian trainees and the Guinean DHfK student demonstrate that reality did not reflect dogma. Even if there were good Germans, racism persisted.

THE LURE OF THE WEST

The clearest indication that African students did not accept the argument that the FRG and other Western states were racist hotbeds is that they often left East Germany for the FRG or one of its allies. They did so despite GDR propaganda concerning Western racism and imperialism.

While East Germans were largely unable to travel to the West, especially after the construction of the Berlin Wall, there were few if any restrictions on African students.[56] To the dismay of the GDR, this opened up the possibility of contact with the West.[57] Even the future African "socialist leaders" at the JWP or HFH were not immune to Western temptation. In April 1961, two Congolese students defected to West Berlin. The FDGB clearly feared further departures to the West. In order to prevent a repetition, a union bureaucrat recommended that there be a "general meeting of all African students at the school ... to ensure that both of the Congolese students who left for West Berlin and did not return are branded as traitors by the others, since they have crossed over to the side of West German imperialism, which works against the liberation of the African people."[58] Even after the Wall went up, officials at the party schools continued to dread the possibility of defection; in 1963, the JWP tried to stop its Kenyan contingent from going on vacation in Bonn, and its representatives fretted that one of their Ghanaian students was receiving private mail from Marburg.[59]

The GDR pictured the FRG as an evil counterpart to the crusading East. Yet for African students it was also an object of desire, and primarily for financial and educational reasons; the West simply offered more varied opportunities. In 1964, a student from Niger left the "Schule der Solidarität," part of the Institut für Journalistik, and moved to West Berlin. While it is unclear exactly why he left, the opposition Nigerien Sawaba party that had delegated him for study in the GDR did so without regard for his interests. He and three other Nigeriens had been shifted from studying veterinary medicine in the USSR to journalism in East Germany, without having a propensity for either.[60] The student may have believed there were better prospects for choice in the West. In general, the governments of independent African countries delegated students to study particular subjects in the GDR, ones that were deemed necessary to the construction of their fledgling states. Usually, the governments refused to let students deviate from these fixed plans. This did not always please the students, who had their own aspirations.[61]

On occasion, former GDR students living in the West also threatened its antiracist image. Such was the case with Adelani, and also with George Sapara-Arthur. He was Ghanaian and came to the GDR around 1960 to learn a trade. He quickly ran into problems and was identified as a malcontent. In June 1961, Sapara-Arthur left the GDR not for the FRG, but for a London Polytechnic university. There he gave interviews depicting the GDR and USSR unfavorably to the Western press, including the West German newspaper *Die Welt*. According to Sapara-Arthur, African students throughout the Eastern bloc were unhappy; unless they were communists, they were poorly treated. The GDR dismissed his report, and claimed that it was full of lies. In his interviews, Sapara-Arthur said he had been a student at the KMU, when he had really been an apprentice in the building industry. There was undeniable concern that Sapara-Arthur would threaten the GDR's anti-imperialist image with the Ghanaian government, as an agitated letter from the GDR Department of Vocational Training to the Office of the High Commissioner for Ghana in London attests.[62] Sapara-Arthur may well have been lying about some things in his interview with *Die Welt*. He was an apprentice builder, not a student at the KMU—but he did try to get admitted, and was continually rebuffed.[63] Yet, his conversation with Western reporters suggests that he saw more options for study in the West, as did the Nigerien student.

CONCLUSION

Official GDR rhetoric presented the East German state as antifascist, anti-imperialist, and antiracist.[64] The SED did back up its antiracist rhetoric through mechanisms that included scholarships for African students and trainees, the work of the East German Solidarity Committee in support of development schemes and liberation movements,[65] and aid to new African nations.[66] This antiracist rhetoric served important political ends. It bolstered relationships between East Germany and emergent African nations, and challenged the FRG and its Hallstein Doctrine. In depicting the FRG as racist, the GDR also identified itself as the "good" Germany, the progressive and modern half of a people whose other remained sunken in fascist, imperialist, and capitalist depravity.[67]

In private intragovernmental communications, however, bureaucrats from the Foreign Office, FDJ, and FDGB clearly recognized racism's existence. Even the infamous Ministerium für Staatssicherheit (MfS or Stasi colloquially) reported racist incidents during the 1960s. In 1963, for instance, the Stasi reported that a group of five young GDR citizens had "stalked ... attacked, and beaten" two Guinean students in Wismar as they returned home from a dance. While their friends egged them on, two of the German men had sneered: "Filthy niggers, what do you want in Germany, there's nothing for you here. You have to wash first if you want to dance with our women."[68] The Stasi planned to hold a preliminary hearing on the case, but it is unclear what, if anything, happened to the alleged perpetrators. In 1964 and again in 1968 the Stasi related similar, racially motivated assaults on African students in Blankenburg and Arnstadt/Erfurt, respectively.[69]

When the Stasi reported racial attacks, its officials attempted to deny that the GDR was responsible for the behavior of its citizens. In the 1968 case, which took place between two Congolese students and 100–150 GDR youths, the informant insinuated that the Congolese men were known for their bad behavior, and had likely started the altercation.[70] In general, GDR bureaucracy placed blame for racist incidents either on the machinations of the FRG, the Africans themselves, or a minority of backward citizens who were, in any event, probably also under West German influence. No efforts were made to investigate the possibility of the survival of a more widespread, ingrained racism amongst the citizenry; per policy, such was considered impossible.

The racial tensions underlying East German society did not disappear during the 1970s and 1980s; incidences of racism continued, still papered over by the official rhetoric of solidarity, anti-imperialism, and antiracism.[71] The repression of the existence of racism in the GDR may in some part account for the intensity of racism noted in the former East after the *Wende,* and for the definite increase in race-related violence in this period. Extremist far-right movements had begun to form in the East even before German reunification in 1990,[72] and demonstrate that the official SED denial of racism in the GDR was always piecemeal, if not outright illusory.

Defining racism in the 1960s GDR is not easy. It existed in the lived reality of African students, who sometimes became the victims of crude epithets and physical violence, and in the worried memos of GDR bureaucrats who privately acknowledged that racism survived in their country even as they presented an antiracist face to the world. Racism could have a direct impact on foreign relations with African states and challenge GDR assertions of solidarity with the developing world, as well as its superiority to the

FRG. At the same time, the connections formed between GDR citizens and African students show that the issue of race was complex. Good impressions of Africans existed, as did positive assessments of the GDR. The state and its population are most accurately described as ambivalent toward racism, which was sometimes destabilized by calls to solidarity and friendship. However, its presence never vanished completely.

Sara Pugach is Associate Professor of African History at California State University, Los Angeles. She is the author of *Africa in Translation: A History of Colonial Linguistics in Germany and Beyond, 1814–1945,* which appeared with the University of Michigan Press in 2012. Currently, she is working on a new project concerning the history of African students in the German Democratic Republic.

NOTES

1. Maxim Matusevich, *No Easy Row for a Russian Hoe: Ideology and Pragmatism in Nigerian-Soviet Relations, 1960–1991* (Trenton, NJ, 2003), 80–85.
2. Maxim Matusevich, "Black in the USSR," *Transition,* no. 100 (2008): 56–75; Sean Guillory, "Culture Clash in the Socialist Paradise: Soviet Patronage and African Students' Urbanity in the Soviet Union, 1960–1965," *Diplomatic History* 38, no. 2 (2014): 271–81.
3. Julie Hessler, "Death of an African Student in Moscow: Race, Politics, and the Cold War," *Cahiers du Monde Russe* 47, no. 1/2 (2006): 33–63.
4. Britta Schilling, *Postcolonial Germany: Memories of Empire in a Decolonized Nation* (Oxford, 2014), 93; Gareth M Winrow, *The Foreign Policy of the GDR in Africa* (Cambridge, 1990), 64, 81. Moreover, representation in these countries was uneven, and not continual.
5. Olivier Podevens, "Zwischen Hallstein-Doktrin und sozialistischer Solidarität: Das französische Schwarzafrika in den aussenpolitischen Konzeptionen der beiden deutschen Staaten," *Revue d'Allemagne* 31, no. 3–4 (1999): 377–90; Winrow, *The Foreign Policy of the GDR,* 42, 76.
6. Toni Weis, "The Politics Machine: On the Concept of Solidarity in East German Support for SWAPO," *Journal of Southern African Studies* 37, no. 2 (2011): 351–67.
7. Ulrich van der Heyden, "Mosambikanische Vertragsarbeiter in der Hauptstadt der DDR," in *Black Berlin: Die deutsche Metropole und ihre afrikanische Diaspora in Geschichte und Gegenwart,* ed. Oumar Diallo and Joachim Zeller (Berlin, 2013), 133–50.
8. Personal Interview, Mohamed Touré, Cologne, 11 August 2014.
9. Kurt Müller, *The Soviet Bloc and the Developing Countries* (Bonn, 1962), 29.

10. Stiftung Archiv der Parteien und Massenorganisationen der DDR im Bundes-
    archiv (hereafter referred to as SAPMO) DY 79/2510, Gewerkschaftshoch-
    schule Bernau, Institut für Intern. Gewerkschaftspolitik, AS, poem, "The
    College of Free German Trade Unions," 15 October 1963.

11. SAPMO DY 24/6707, Intern. Verbindungen FDJ, letter of the Leiter der Arbeits-
    gruppe Intern. Lehrgang to the Zentralrat der FDJ, Lamberz, 2 January 1962.

12. SAPMO DY 24/22720, Zentralrat der Freien Deutschen Jugend Abt. Inter-
    nationale Verbindungen, Internationale Lehrgänge an der Jugendhochschule
    "Wilhelm Pieck," 1962–63, *Abschlußerklärung des II. Afrikanischen Lehrganges an
    der Jugendhochschule "Wilhelm Pieck,"* 20 October 1962.

13. Deutsche Gesellschaft für Auswärtige Politik, Forschungsinstitut, *Dokumente
    zur Berlin-Frage*, "Note der Regierung der DDR vom 7. Januar 1959 an die
    Regierung der Sowjetunion zur Lage Berlins" (Berlin, 1987), 363–72; Manfred
    Wilke, *The Path to the Berlin Wall: Critical Stages in the History of Divided Germany*
    (New York, 2014), 206.

14. SAPMO DY/24/8752, Zentralrat der FDJ, Zentralarchiv, Bestand: Intern.
    Verbindungen, 1961–1965, "Einschätzung der Aussprachen mit den Delegati-
    onen des II. Internationalen Halbjahreslehrganges—Afrika—1962," 14 August
    1962.

15. Ibid.

16. SAPMO DY 24/6707, "Aktennotiz über eine Aussprache mit K. aus Kenia am
    26.6.62 (G Bornschein-H Eggert)."

17. SAPMO DY 24/6707, Aktennotiz, Urlaub Afrika- und Lateinamerikalehrgang
    in Hohenstein/Bebnitz. D.J.N. vom 29.7 bis 5.8.1962, 9 August 1962.

18. SAPMO DY 79/573, FDGB Bundesvorstand Archiv, 1964–1966, letter from
    Deutschland, Fakultätsleiter, to Prof. Dir. Karl Kampfert, 19 October 1964.

19. Michael Meng, "East Germany's Jewish Question: The Return and Preser-
    vation of Jewish Sites in East Berlin and Potsdam, 1945–1989," *Central European
    History* 38, no. 4 (2005): 606–36.

20. Jeffrey Herf, *Divided Memory: The Nazi Past in the Two Germanys* (Cambridge, 1997).

21. For instance, letters sent in 1964 mentioned that the college had recently
    formed an *Afrikanische Kulturensemble*. This group gave performances to East
    German youth and the general Berlin population, allowing "glimpses into
    Africa's rich cultural heritage." See SAPMO DY/79/613, H.D. to A.M.T., 1 June
    1964, among others.

22. Ibid, "Lieber Kollege Charlie," 28 May 1964.

23. Ibid.

24. Ibid, HFH Administration to E.K.G., Ghana, 28 April 1964, among others.

25. Ibid, J.A.O. to the Director of the HFH, 12 February 1964.

26. This included alumni from Kenya, Mali, Nigeria, and Zanzibar, for example.
    SAPMO DY/79/613, H.K. to the Director, 10 December 1963; SAPMO DY
    79/2510, M.C. to his former teacher, G.H., 23 December 1963; S.E. to Kollege
    F., 11 February 1964; A., Hanoi, to the Directorate, 25 February 1964.

27. Ibid, H.K. to the Director, 10 December 1963.

28. SAPMO DY 79/2512, Gewerkschaftshochschule Bernau, Institut für Intern. Gewerkschaftspolitik, O. to his former teacher H.R., 1 May 1963.
29. SAPMO DY/79/613, O.M., Accra, to the Director, 10 March 1964.
30. SAPMO DY 79/2510, C.B., Kitwe, to the Director, 31 January 1964.
31. Meredith Terretta, *Nation of Outlaws, State of Violence: Nationalism, Grassfields Tradition, and State Building in Cameroon* (Athens, OH, 2013), 100.
32. Thomas Sharp, "France and Cameroon's Hidden History," unpublished conference paper, University of Portsmouth, "1960: The 'Year of Africa' and French Decolonisation Revisited," 7 September 2010; Frank M Stark, "Persuasion and Power in Cameroon," *Canadian Journal of African Studies* 14, no. 2 (1980): 273–93.
33. SAPMO DY/79/613, OM, Accra, to the Director, HFH, 17 January 1964.
34. Ibid, O.M., Accra, to the Acting Director, HFH, 10 March 1964.
35. Hubertus Büschel, *Hilfe zur Selbsthilfe: Deutsche Entwicklungsarbeit in Afrika, 1960–1975* (Frankfurt am Main, 2014), 59–60.
36. Aderogba Ajao, *On the Tiger's Back* (London, 1962); John M Crewdson, "Worldwide Propaganda Network Built by the CIA," *The New York Times,* 26 December 1977.
37. SAPMO DY 24/6822, Zentralrat der FDJ, Zentralarchiv, Bestand: Intern. Verbindungen, 1958–1962, O.O., "The Fairy-Tales of Aderogba Ajao alias 'Adelani' and the Truth," c. 1960.
38. Universitätsarchiv Leipzig (Hereafter known as UAL), Arbeiter-und Bauern-Fakultät (ABF) 077, "Gesamtanalyse der Vorbildung der Kolonialstudenten in der deutschen Sprache bei Eintreffen in Leipzig," 15 May 1951.
39. AE Ohiaeri, *Behind the Iron Curtain* (Enugu, 1985).
40. Politisches Archiv des Auswärtigen Amtes, Ministerium für Auswärtige Angelegenheiten der DDR (Hereafter referred to as PAAA MfAA), B1263/75, Abt. Afrika, Sektion Gesamtafrikanische Fragen, Aktennotiz 8 Juli 1965. Other complaints included poor accommodations, the privileging of German students over foreigners, and the lack of African representation on dormitory committees.
41. PAAA MfAA B1263/75, Abt. Afrika, Sektion Gesamtafrikanische Fragen, letter from "Das Komitee der afrikanischen Studenten und Arbeiter in der DDR," with regards to "Besorgnisse der afrikanischen Studenten und Arbeiter in der DDR," to Walter Ulbricht and other leading GDR officials, February 1965.
42. Ibid.
43. Cheikh Anta Diop, *The African Origin of Civilization: Myth or Reality* (New York, 1974), 10*ff.*; Frantz Fanon, *Black Skin, White Masks* (New York, 2008).
44. SAPMO DY 24/6707, Lamberz, 2 January 1962.
45. JWP, HFH files from Bundesarchiv.
46. SAPMO DY/79/613, Director, HFH, to 14 former Ghanaian students, 12 February 1964.
47. Thomas Dekan, "Serengeti Shall Not Die: Bernhard Grzimek, Wildlife Film, and the Making of a Tourist Landscape in East Africa," *German History* 29, no. 2 (2011): 224–64.

48. Walter Ulbricht, "10 Gebote der sozialistischen Moral und Ethik, 10 July 1958," in *DDR, Dokumente zur Geschichte der Deutschen Demokratischen Republik, 1945–1985,* ed. Hermann Weber (Munich, 1986), 237.

49. UAL Pror. Stud. 17, Report, Dr. Moehle, Prorektor für Studienangelegenheiten, to the Regierung der DDR, Staatssekretariat für das Hoch- und Fachschulwesen, Sektor Ausland, Auslandsstudium, Betr.: Ausländische Studierende, 20 January 1959.

50. SAPMO DY 79/396, FDGB Bundesvorstand Archiv, Fakultät für Ausländerstudium, Schriftverkehr mit Deutsch-Afrikanische Gesellschaft, Bundesvorstand d. FDGB Ausland und Direktion der Hochschule 1963–1968, Professor K. to the Bundesvorstand des FDGB, Abt. Internationale Verbindungen, 20 August 1963.

51. PAAA MfAA B1263/75, Abt. Afrika, Sektion Gesamtafrikanische Fragen, letter from "Das Komitee der afrikanischen Studenten und Arbeiter in der DDR" to Walter Ulbricht and other leading GDR officials, February 1965.

52. Ibid.

53. PAAA MfAA 14396, Ausbildung von ghanesischen Facharbeiter und Fachschülern in der DDR, 1957–1962, Protest of the Komitee der Afro-Asiatischen Studenten in Leipzig, 15 June 1961.

54. Ibid. Indeed, the committee asserted that it would relate the story to "Staatsmänner" and "Zeitungen" in India, Ghana, Nigeria, Guinea, Egypt, Yugoslavia, and Indonesia, as well as to the United Nations. It is unclear whether they ever did.

55. UAL, Deutsche Hochschule für Körperkultur Leipzig, Sonderlehrgang 4 Frauen aus Guinea, 1966–1968, Archivnummer 545; see also Jay Straker, *Youth, Nationalism, and the Guinean Revolution* (Bloomington, IN, 2009), 83, 99. passim.

56. Attempts were made to prevent African students crossing the border, but these were largely unsuccessful. See PAAA MfAA A14594, Einschätzung der politischen-ideologischen Arbeit mit afrikanischen Studenten in der DDR, Jan., März 1964, letter of Schwab to Willi Stoph, 16 March 1964.

57. PAAA MfAA A14594, Einschätzung der politischen-ideologischen Arbeit mit afrikanischen Studenten in der DDR, Jan., März 1964, G.L., "Einschätzung der politischen-ideologischen Arbeit mit afrikanischen Studenten in der DDR," 29 January 1964.

58. SAPMO DY/34 24618, Büro des Präsidiums, Protokollbüro Präsidiums- u. Sekretariatsbeschlüsse des Bundesvorstands betr. Afrika allg. 1960–1963, Bericht über die Aussprachen mit Afrikanern in Kairo," 17 April 1961.

59. SAPMO DY 24/6707, "Wocheninformation," 26 July 1963. Further, as mentioned above there were also Kenyans who defected; see DY 79/2512, O. to H.R., 1 May 1963.

60. PAAA MfAA A16000, Aufnahme nigrischer Bürger zum Studium und zur Facharbeiterausbildung in der DDR, 1961–1964, Horst Voight, Sekretär Verband Deutscher Journalisten (VDJ), to Gottfried Lessing, betreffend "Kader an der Schule der Solidarität," 6 April 1964.

61. See for instance UAL ZM 3923, Schritfwechsel Studenten Mali, von 1963 bis 1985, Dipl.-Lehrer Fischer, Referent f. Ausländerstudium, to the Technische Universität, Dresden, 19 December 1963, rejecting a change of universities and subjects of study.

62. PAAA MfAA 14396, Ausbildung von ghanesischen Facharbeiter und Fach-schülern in der DDR, 1957–1962, letter from Neidhardt, Sektorleiter, Abt. Berufsbildung, Sektor Aus- und Weiterbildung ausländischen Bürger, to the Office of the high commissioner für Ghana, Technical Education Section, London, 29 June 1961.

63. Ibid, letter of Hasler, MfAA, to Rolf Seidel, Handelsvertretung der DDR in Ghana, 23 March 1961, concerning the continued career training of Ghanaian citizens.

64. See among others Anja Lemke, *Die Konstruktion nationaler Identität in Ost- und Westdeutschland während des Mauerfalls: Eine Diskursanalyse deutsch-deutscher Gegen-bilder* (Hamburg, 2011), 7.

65. Ingrid Muth, *Die DDR-Aussenpolitik 1949–1972* (Berlin, 2000), 91–92.

66. Winrow, *The Foreign Policy of the GDR*, 175–176; Young-Sun Hong, *Cold War Germany, the Third World, and the Global Humanitarian Regime* (Cambridge, 2015), 4ff.

67. Paul Grasse, "No More Fascism—No More War! East German Reflections on Political Remembrance in Unified Germany," in *Dissonant Memories—Fragmented Present: Exchanging Young Discourses between Israel and Germany,* ed. Charlotte Misselwitz and Cornelia Siebeck (Bielefeld, 2009), 17–26.

68. Der Bundesbeauftragte für die Unterlagen des Staatssicherheitsdienstes der ehemaligen Deutschen Demokratischen Republik (hereafter referred to as BStU), MfS ZAIG Nr. 803, E.J. über das provokatorische Auftreten von DDR-Bürgern gegenüber zwei Studenten aus Guinea, 2 October 1963.

69. BStU, MfS ZAIG Nr. 896, E.J. über tätliche Auseinandersetzungen mit aus-ländischen Bürgern in der Nacht vom 7. zum 8.5.1964, 8 May 1964; BStU, MfS ZAIG Nr. 1578, E.I. über eine Schlägerei zwischen afrikanischen Bürgern und Jugendlichen in Arnstadt/Erfurt, 18 September 1968.

70. BStU, MfS ZAIG Nr. 1578, E.I. über eine Schlägerei zwischen afrikanischen Bürgern und Jugendlichen in Arnstadt/Erfurt, 18 September 1968.

71. Van der Heyden, "Mozambikanische Vertragsarbeiter," 133–150.

72. Gideon Botsch, "From Skinhead Subculture to Radical Right Movement: The Development of a 'National Opposition' in East Germany," *Contemporary European History* 21, no. 4 (2012): 553–73.

SELECTED BIBLIOGRAPHY

Ajao, Aderogba. *On the Tiger's Back.* London, 1962.

Büschel, Hubertus. *Hilfe zur Selbsthilfe: Deutsche Entwicklungsarbeit in Afrika, 1960–1975.* Frankfurt am Main, 2014.

Guillory, Sean. "Culture Clash in the Socialist Paradise: Soviet Patronage and African Students' Urbanity in the Soviet Union, 1960–1965." *Diplomatic History* 38, no. 2 (2014): 271–81.

Hessler, Julie. "Death of an African Student in Moscow: Race, Politics, and the Cold War." *Cahiers du Monde Russe* 47, no. 1/2 (2006): 33–63.

Heyden, Ulrich van der. "Mosambikanische Vertragsarbeiter in der Hauptstadt der DDR." In *Black Berlin: Die deutsche Metropole und ihre afrikanische Diaspora in Geschichte und Gegenwart,* edited by Oumar Diallo and Joachim Zeller, 133–50. Berlin, 2013.

Matusevich, Maxim. "Black in the USSR." *Transition,* no. 100 (2008): 56–75.

———. *No Easy Row for a Russian Hoe: Ideology and Pragmatism in Nigerian-Soviet Relations, 1960–1991.* Trenton, NJ, 2003.

Muth, Ingrid. *Die DDR-Aussenpolitik 1949–1972.* Berlin, 2000.

Ohiaeri, AE. *Behind the Iron Curtain.* Enugu, 1985.

Podevens, Olivier. "Zwischen Hallstein-Doktrin und sozialistischer Solidarität: Das französische Schwarzafrika in den aussenpolitischen Konzeptionen der beiden deutschen Staaten." *Revue d'Allemagne* 31, no. 3–4 (1999): 377–90.

Schilling, Britta. *Postcolonial Germany: Memories of Empire in a Decolonized Nation.* Oxford, 2014.

Weis, Toni. "The Politics Machine: On the Concept of Solidarity in East German Support for SWAPO." *Journal of Southern African Studies* 37, no. 2 (2011): 351–67.

Winrow, Gareth M. *The Foreign Policy of the GDR in Africa.* Cambridge, 1990.

Part III

Searching for a New Model

Chapter 9

The German Model in Renewable Energy Development

Carol Hager

INTRODUCTION–THE GERMAN MODEL

The German model is most commonly defined in political science in terms of a collaborative relationship between the German government and key societal forces, particularly industry and organized labor, in order to promote economic growth and social well-being. The term was first used to describe the political and economic pattern of postwar West Germany, which achieved spectacular economic success and social stability.[1] Despite the neoliberal trend since the 1980s in much of the developed world, and the upheavals resulting from German unification in the 1990s, the unified German state retains much of its interventionist character.[2] Today's German model features market-oriented but coordinated capitalism, with significant concessions made to organized labor in return for workplace stability. Both industry and labor are organized in networks of associations, with peak associations negotiating on behalf of entire sectors. Germany has a corporatist policy making style, in which policy decisions are reached consensually among elites from government ministries, industry, and labor in advance of national legislation (see Figure 9.1). This setup was designed to minimize and depoliticize conflict.[3] It is a centralized model with power in the hands of political and economic elites.

At first glance, German energy policy making appears to fit this model. The energy sector was traditionally dominated by a relative few powerful, large utilities, which enjoyed territorial monopolies and close, cooperative

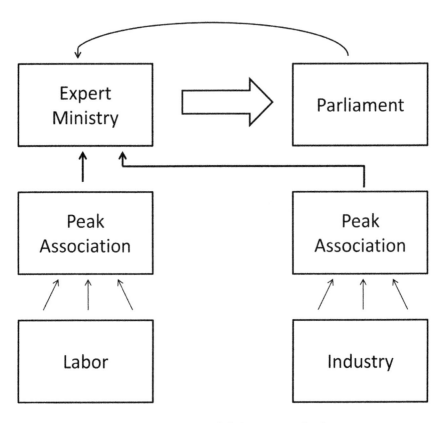

Figure 9.1. Classic Corporatist Model. Source: Author's image.

relationships with government. Policy changes in the late 1990s resulted in a wave of mergers that centralized the sector even more.[4] In the area of renewable energy, however, the model falls short. The Electricity Feed-in Law of 1990 (*Stromeinspeisegesetz*) and the Renewable Energy Act of 2000 (*Erneuerbare Energien Gesetz*) are widely credited with helping propel Germany to the forefront of renewable energy development. Figure 9.2 shows the mix and growth of renewable energies in Germany from 1990 to 2014. Germany's success is all the more impressive when contrasted with the US government's sporadic efforts to shift the energy mix toward renewables. Comparative explanations tend to credit the collaborative nature of Germany's industry/state relationship for enhancing its ability to behave proactively. But the partners in the corporatist trifecta were notably absent from this development. Neither the federal government nor the traditional energy sector initiated the move to renewables. On the contrary, the big utilities resisted investing in renewables and, with the aid of key ministries, tried to keep new entrants off the market.[5] There was no coordinated push from organized labor for renewables, either. Conventional accounts focusing on the German model cannot explain Germany's emergence as a leader in this sector.

The missing piece of the puzzle, I argue, is the particular pattern of German citizen activism over time. Mass mobilization against state-sponsored energy projects helped push the German government in the direction of supporting renewables over the objections of the traditional energy suppliers (coal and nuclear). Moreover, the green movement helped popularize an alternative energy paradigm more in keeping with decentralized, environmentally friendly energy generation.[6] Popular support for renewables has held up in the face of changing coalition governments and numerous attempts to walk back the laws. The development of renewables was thus much more bottom-up, local, and conflictual than the German model would predict. The story of renewable energy in Germany suggests that social movement protest was and remains a key driver of technological innovation. I conclude that, in this sector at least, it is the underlying potential for conflict that has made the collaborative German model work.

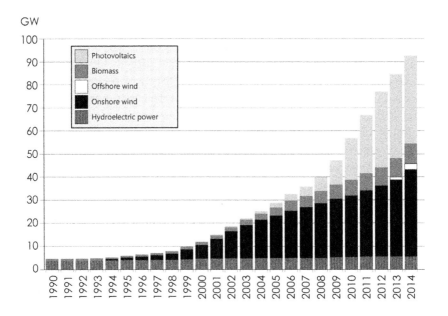

Figure 9.2. Renewable Energy Generation Capacity in Germany.
Source: Adapted from Quaschning, 2016, www.volker-quaschning.de.

FOUR PHASES OF CITIZEN ACTIVISM AND RENEWABLE ENERGY DEVELOPMENT

Phase 1–1970s to Early 1980s: Energy Crisis and New Social Movements

Mass mobilization over energy issues and the evolution of renewables occurred in four phases. The first phase began in West Germany with the oil crisis of the 1970s and lasted into the 1980s. The West German government reacted to the crisis by increasing support for coal and nuclear power. Many citizens objected, however, and public protest against nuclear and coal-fired power plants grew. "Citizen initiatives" began as local groups attempting to procure community services such as day care. From the mid 1970s on, however, they arose overwhelmingly in opposition to large, state-sponsored industrial projects. The protest was not simply about the environmental degradation or risk that such projects would entail. Citizen initiatives targeted these projects as symbols of a system of planning that bypassed local residents and promoted economic growth to the exclusion of quality of life considerations. These considerations were first articulated on a national scale during the massive, ultimately successful protest against a planned nuclear power plant at Wyhl in southwestern Germany.[7]

While the energy issue evoked the most strident critiques of the growth mentality, energy protest was embedded in a larger array of citizen movements (including the women's movement and the peace movement) concerned with the quality of life and critical of what Jürgen Habermas termed the economic and administrative "system."[8] Disgruntled citizens began to question not only the substance of government decisions, but also the legitimacy of the inaccessible form of decision making that produced them. Many protesters blamed the tight relationship between government and industry for policy decisions unrepresentative of the values of much of the population. These activists came to believe that the problems indicated "a long-term structural crisis, whose cause lies in the industrial-technocratic growth society itself."[9] Their protest thus began to connect themes of environmental protection and democracy.

At first, the federal government tried to suppress social movement activity, putting down demonstrations with force and attempting to curtail the citizen participation provisions of the planning process.[10] The government played its "German model" card, citing its monopoly on expertise as well as the need for order. Rather than quelling the unrest, this response seemed to confirm the meta-level concerns of the protesters. For example, one West Berlin group opposing a proposed energy project wrote: "political mandate does not mean ruthless promotion of ... industry interests, but rather concern for the well-being of the citizenry. And political mandate does not mean legitimation on the grounds of estimates given by technicians and experts who cannot separate their own expert knowledge from economic and industrial interests."[11]

By the mid 1970s, more West Germans identified themselves as members of grassroots citizen initiatives than of all political parties combined.[12] Citizen activism, much of it around energy projects, led to the founding of Green and alternative parties and networks of citizen groups throughout West Germany. The national-level Greens, formed in 1980, were conceived not as a conventional political party, but as the parliamentary arm of the citizen initiative movement.[13] The Greens entered the Bundestag in 1983, where they worked to achieve more transparency and openness in policy making. One of their early actions was to force the formation of two special parliamentary commissions on energy issues. The many local and regional parties and voting lists, along with the national-level Greens, brought the concerns of the citizen movements directly into government.

It was against this backdrop that the German renewable energy industry arose. Sustainable production using renewable resources was already a focus for the movements; renewable energy also fit well with their emphasis on decentralized, community-based decision making. The early participants were not just left-leaning political activists. Socially conservative farmers became local energy entrepreneurs: "In Northern Germany wind energy emerged successfully not because the planners, scientists or administrators gave rise to this spectacular boom, but due to the subtle interplay of individual initiatives, regional routines in balancing people and things and external forces that regulate the process, often in retrospect."[14] Wind power was developed by farmers, supported by environmentalists, and helped along by people building prototypes in backyards. In other words, grassroots initiatives were key to embedding alternative technologies in society *before* there was a federal policy framework. There was no push from traditional energy suppliers; indeed, as David Toke argues, these technologies were a poor fit for them: "an idealistic belief in a new alternative technology set up the conditions for a niche to develop in ways in which conventional industry, with its patent-based secrecy and expectation of early commercial returns, would find very difficult to replicate."[15]

The federal government's contribution to this early phase came mostly in the form of research and development (R&D) funding through the Ministry of Education and Research. This funding provided opportunities for universities, institutes, and some firms to experiment with renewables on the condition that these remain in a premarket phase.[16] The Ministry of Economics generally supported the established utilities' desire to keep new producers off the market and showed little interest in developing a "strategic framework" for expanding the renewables sector.[17] Nevertheless, write Jacobsson and Lauber, "in spite of the fringe status of that R&D, a broad academic *cum* industrial knowledge base began to be built up ... for both wind turbines and solar cells."[18]

Small producers formed umbrella associations to promote renewables at the national and European levels. In the field of solar energy, for example, these included the German Solar Energy Industries Association (Bundesverband Solarindustrie), the German Association for the Promotion of Solar Power (Solarenergie-Förderverein), and the European Association for Renewable Energy (Eurosolar), whose aim was to bring politicians, scientists and other professionals, and citizens together to advance the cause of renewable energy. Importantly, centers of scientific "counterexpertise" such as the Eco-Institute Freiburg arose. The Eco-Institute was founded as an independent research and advisory institution by people who had protested against the Wyhl nuclear power plant project—in this way it grew directly from the citizen initiative movement.[19] A nascent advocacy coalition took shape, with its own sources of practical and academic expertise outside the corporatist network. It tried to demonstrate that prosperity and environmentally sound energy production could go hand in hand.

Phase 2–Mid 1980s to Mid 1990s:
Decline of Nuclear Power, Rise of Climate Change Issue, German Unification

The second phase spanned the period from the mid 1980s through the early 1990s. Ongoing antinuclear protests gradually turned the tide of West German public opinion against nuclear power. After the Chernobyl accident in 1986, the remaining public support evaporated.[20] This was a crucial development because nuclear power was often cited, in Germany and elsewhere, as the main alternative to carbon-based energy sources. The industry also enjoyed the kind of entrenched power that raised the ire of the grass roots. Secretive, heavily subsidized, dismissive of public concerns about risks and waste storage, it epitomized for many the threat monopoly capitalism represented to democracy.[21] These suspicions played out most dramatically at Gorleben in Lower Saxony (see Figure 9.3). Gorleben was proposed as the site for a permanent nuclear waste storage facility in the 1970s and currently hosts an interim waste storage site. It has been a magnet for antinuclear protest for three decades, as the project's political support has waxed and waned, and a testament to the difficulty of finding a politically acceptable solution to the nuclear waste issue. The fact that public

Figure 9.3: Entering Gorleben, Leaving Democracy.
Source: Picture Alliance dpa.

opposition prevented nuclear power from becoming the go-to alternative was critical for the eventual success of renewables.

Nuclear power was not the only concern of citizen movements. Widely publicized cases of forest die-off (*Waldsterben*) from acid rain dramatized the negative impacts of coal-fired power plants as well. The issue of climate change also began to gain traction at this time, helped along by grassroots groups like Robin Wood and several scientific reports, one of whose warnings of impending "climate catastrophe" got wide play in the West German press. By the end of the 1980s, all of the major political parties cited the issue as one of their priorities.[22] The Kohl government responded to the demands for federal leadership on environmental issues by creating a Ministry of Environment in 1986. In contrast to the United States, climate change and energy discourses were linked early on in Germany, with the result that both remained higher on the national agenda over time.

A coalition of alternative energy advocates, including the expert institutes and organizations representing small solar and hydropower producers, proposed the first German feed-in tariff law. Federal laws are generally formulated in the ministries, but in this case it was parliamentary backbenchers connected with the advocacy coalition who wrote the law. In doing so, they bypassed bureaucratic and parliamentary opponents. Pressured by the public unrest and by vocal renewables advocates in the Bundestag, the government "more or less reluctantly" passed this law and other measures to support renewable energy.[23] According to Christoph Stefes, those who supported the feed-in law on environmental grounds "gained allies among politicians who had long distrusted the political and economic dominance of the energy utilities, blaming them for distorting the energy market and undermining the democratic foundation of the Federal Republic."[24] The major utilities opposed the feed-in law but, distracted by the challenges of reunification and the takeover of East German utilities, they did not devote much energy to stopping it.[25] In the end, all political parties in the Bundestag supported its passage in 1990.

The feed-in law permitted access to the grid for renewable energy producers at a guaranteed price. In setting a price, the law lowered the perceived risk for investors in renewables and led to a boom in capacity in the 1990s. "Learning networks" emerged more strongly, where the various participants in the new energy forms could communicate and new entrants could receive advice.[26] Renewable energy production also gave a boost to manufacturing and employment during the very difficult period after reunification,[27] especially in eastern Germany. Participants in the new forms of energy production built communication networks through which they shared information and gave advice to new entrants.

The big utilities challenged the feed-in law through their political connections and in the courts. The Ministry of Economics dragged its feet on implementing the law, but continuing citizen mobilization prevented it from being rolled back entirely.[28] When the government proposed reducing the feed-in tariff in 1997, for example, the German Wind Energy Association staged a large demonstration that included, in addition to renewable energy associations, major environmental groups such as Greenpeace and Bund für Umwelt und Naturschutz Deutschland (BUND), the metalworkers' union, farm groups, and church groups. The largely successful defense of the law made it clear that support for renewable energy had taken hold in German society. This distinguished Germany from its neighbors France, which doubled down on nuclear power, and the United Kingdom, which promoted its oil resources.

Local-level actions helped ensure a continuing market for renewables. Local activists petitioned municipal governments to enforce cost-covering contracts between utilities and suppliers of renewable energy. The city of Aachen approved an additional citywide solar tariff to encourage the expansion of solar energy locally. Several dozen other cities followed suit, and the

"Aachen model" became the foundation for subsequent federal legislation.[29] These local citizen initiatives, along with the growing national advocacy coalition and rising public demand for alternative energy, helped set in motion a positive feedback loop for renewables.

Phase 3–Late 1990s to Late 2000s:
Red/Green Coalition, Withdrawal from Nuclear Power

The third phase began in the late 1990s, when the Kohl government gave way to a Red-Green government led by Social Democrat Gerhard Schröder. The advocacy coalition for renewables had grown to include some state-level politicians, labor unions, and the German Engineering Association. It now had the ear of a more sympathetic governing coalition, some of whose members had entered politics through participation in the green and alternative movements of earlier decades. Still, the Ministry of Economics hesitated on the planned reform of the feed-in law, forcing pro-renewables parliamentarians once again to write the bill and push it through the Bundestag themselves.[30] The Renewable Energy Act (2000) expanded support for renewable energy and fixed compensation rates over a twenty-year period.

In its second term, the Red-Green coalition made important changes in national-level institutions. Green gains in the 2002 elections led to a transfer of competency for renewable energy from the Ministry of Economics, led by the Social Democratic Party of Germany (SPD), to the Environment Ministry, led by the Greens, with a corresponding shift in the responsible parliamentary committees. This change took renewable energy out of the purview of the more skeptical economic authorities and into the competency of the more sympathetic environmental authorities. It also shifted the frame from economic efficiency and marketability to ecological impact, which was more in keeping with public opinion. The alternative "small is beautiful" energy paradigm that emerged from the citizen movements of the 1970s now had a place in national government. In 2006, the Environment Ministry was included for the first time in the Chancellery's "energy summits," regular meetings with the Ministry of Economics, the big utilities, and other energy sector players. "It thereby found its way into the last bastion of oligarchic policy-making in the energy sector, opening the doors for other interests and alternative voices," writes Christoph Stefes.[31] The Red-Green coalition's signature achievement was a negotiated commitment to withdrawal from domestic nuclear power generation, which became law in 2002.

The major industry advocates of the traditional top-down, growth-focused energy paradigm, the coal and nuclear industries, "consistently opposed the substantial deployment of renewable electricity in general, and [the feed-in tariff] in particular," especially after the unexpectedly rapid growth of renewables following the passage of the 1990 law. They challenged the 1990 and 2000 laws in both national and European courts, the latter challenge mainly on grounds that the feed-in tariff constituted a hidden state subsidy and thus violated internal market rules.[32] The European Court of Justice ultimately found against the plaintiffs in 2001. Although the traditional utilities still dominated the energy sector, their challenges fell short in large part because environmental groups were able to mobilize the advocacy coalition in defense of the law. Much of the technical expertise on renewables was now in their corner, and public support for the energy transition grew along with the number of renewable energy installations during this decade. By the time the European Union adopted its "20/20/20" framework in late 2008, Germany had become a European leader in renewables.[33]

Phase 4–2009 to the Present: Fukushima, Commitment, and Critique

The Red/Green coalition gave way to a "grand coalition" government in 2005 and then a conservative-led (CDU/CSU-FDP) coalition government in 2009, which was more skeptical of alternative energy.[34] Chancellor Angela Merkel, who opposed the Renewable Energy Act when she headed the CDU in 2000, was viewed with suspicion by renewables advocates. Her government seemed to confirm that suspicion by announcing that it would lengthen the timetable for Germany's transition from nuclear power, extending the life of some plants. The announcement proved costly to the CDU-FDP government. It provoked a new wave of protest mobilization, which swelled following the Fukushima nuclear disaster in Japan in spring 2011. Merkel's subsequent announcement of a temporary hold on the extension for select plants seemed only to inflame public sentiment against the government, resulting in the CDU's loss of two state elections and the selection of the first ever Green minister president in traditional CDU stronghold Baden-Württemberg.[35] The Merkel government was compelled to rescind the extension and commit to a withdrawal from nuclear energy production by 2022, along with 80 percent energy generation from renewable sources by 2050. Protest mobilization continues to be a powerful tool for renewable energy advocates.

The Baden-Württemberg case reinforces a further point about citizen unrest in Germany. Just as in the first phase, the energy protests of recent years are embedded in a larger array of movements advocating for a renewed emphasis on noneconomic quality of life and critical of the government-industry growth coalition. These groups unite themes of environmentalism, community integrity, and grassroots democracy. In Baden-Württemberg, the Greens' 2011 electoral victory was aided by ongoing protest surrounding a huge project to enlarge and revamp the Stuttgart train station. "Stuttgart 21" became for many a symbol of corporatism run amok, a self-interested behind-the-scenes alliance between subnational politicians, German Railroad personnel, and railroad-affiliated technical experts. Opposition to Stuttgart 21 followed the two-pronged pattern of activism described here for energy protest, with citizen initiative groups mobilizing the grassroots and the Greens fighting the project in state and local parliaments, aided by counterproposals prepared by independent experts. The activists succeeded in forcing a referendum on the project, in which their position ultimately lost.[36] This, too, illustrates a broader point: often the proximate goal—the defeat of particular projects or policies—is not realized. But the protest propels longer-term changes that, while more subtle, may be more profound.

One such change is that today, even the anticipation of public unrest influences the range of policy alternatives considered by government and the investment decisions considered by firms. A case in point is carbon capture and storage (CCS) technology, promoted as a means to prolong the viability of the coal industry while Germany pursues further reductions in carbon emissions. Interviews with power company representatives reveal a reluctance to invest in the technology for fear of public protest.[37] In September 2011, the Bundesrat blocked a law for pilot CCS projects; fear of citizen protest was reportedly a major motivation.[38]

A study of the German biotechnology industry has similar findings. The issue is not that critical citizens have gained direct access to industry planning decisions. Rather, it is that they have changed the internal conversation in firms, making particular investments look riskier and strengthening certain players over others.[39] In his study of Berlin land use planning, Uwe Altrock finds that some planning alternatives are rejected out of hand by the Berlin state government in order to avoid citizen objections. This practice, says Altrock, distinguishes recent planning from that of previous decades; compromises are now made in anticipation of public protest.[40]

Another important change is the way that counterexpertise has given legitimacy to participants outside the corporatist networks. In the CCS case, representatives of fossil fuel interests "are well aware of this fact, consistently articulating concern that NGOs may launch a public debate on safety or environmental issues, stifling acceptance for CCS. The case of nuclear energy is often cited as a disconcerting example."[41] The Eco-Institute Freiburg has become a leading European research and consultancy institution with well over 100 employees in three locations. It produces scientific studies and provides information to policy makers, environmental nongovernmental organizations (NGOs), and companies interested in environmental sustainability.[42] The network for renewables has professionalized and become adept at advocating through regular political channels as well as protest. Representatives of the traditional energy paradigm can no longer simply dismiss the Greens and their allies as Not-In-My-Back-Yard (NIMBY) protesters standing in the way of progress. The German model of an expert bureaucracy collaborating with political and economic elites no longer enjoys the legitimacy it once had in the eyes of the public. A revised German model, which takes account of the influence of grassroots citizen movements, Greens and their parliamentary allies, and counter-experts, is depicted in Figure 9.4.

That is not to say that the traditional corporatist networks have been displaced. The large conventional utilities remain at the center of the policy making structure. Having failed to block the emergence of renewables, they

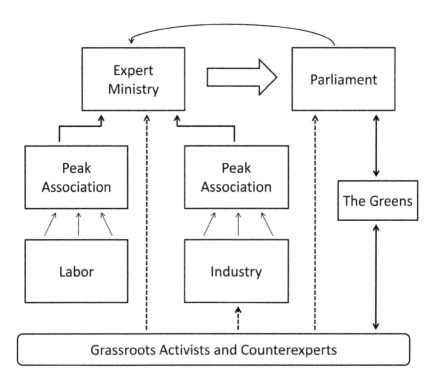

Figure 9.4. New German Model. Source: Author's image.

are making more of an effort to get in the game.[43] The Economics Ministry, renamed Ministry of Economics and Energy in 2013, has taken charge of changes to the law. Centralized collaboration between government and big industry still characterizes the German model, but it appears increasingly to clash with the bottom-up, participatory nature of the renewables industry up to now and the grassroots democratic ambitions of its Green supporters. Competing energy paradigms vie for support in German society, which are now reflected in national-level party politics as well as the energy industry itself.[44]

The competing paradigms are visible in recent controversies over the energy transition. One of these has to do with the distribution of costs and benefits. The renewable energy surcharge on electricity has been raised sharply in recent years, evoking socioeconomic justice issues. Some critics point to the high rates given to small producers feeding into the grid as the culprit; others point to the exemption from the surcharge offered to many industries in the interest of international competitiveness.[45]

Another controversy has to do with technological issues. The government's recent revisions to the law promote large-scale renewables projects like offshore wind farms, whose huge costs and technical challenges give an opening to the big energy firms. Such projects have proven very difficult to implement, however, and they have experienced long delays and cost overruns.[46] The revisions seek to curtail especially small-scale solar installations but also onshore wind and biomass on grounds that grid technology cannot support lots of small intermittent energy producers. These changes have run afoul of a trend toward "re-localization" of energy production, with municipal utilities attempting to play a greater role.[47] Local economies have been boosted by small-scale renewable energy generation, and locals are pushing back against the changes. Negotiating between the competing energy paradigms is one of the German government's most difficult current challenges.

Surveys show a significant learning effect when it comes to public acceptance of renewable energy technologies. Germans, especially the young, favor the expansion of renewables by a wide margin (around 90 percent) and are willing to pay more for electricity in order to support their development.[48] Recently, rifts have opened within the environmentalist community over the placement of onshore wind turbines and transmission lines, pitting nature protection advocates against some renewables producers.[49] Still, 65 percent of respondents say they would not mind a renewable energy facility near their homes, and these numbers actually increase among populations living near such facilities.[50] Support for renewables is firmly anchored in German society.

CONCLUSION

Germany's energy transition is an unprecedented national project entailing large risks. It is clear that explanations focusing on the traditional German model cannot adequately explain the emergence of renewables on the national agenda. Grassroots protest paved the way for innovation from below and has become an important component of German policy making. Although there may be little outward change in the institutional configuration, both party politics and bureaucratic planning have become more responsive to citizen participation and to the vision of an alternative energy future pushed by grassroots activists.[51] The protest served two purposes: it produced costly delays and planning uncertainty, which forced industry and the state to take the activists seriously, and it created a societal context favorable to bottom-up technological innovation.

The latter point is especially important. As the controversies stretched over years, they heightened public awareness of the full range of issues at stake, including quality of life, climate change, and citizen participation in policy making. They helped create a new renewable energy paradigm more compatible with green and alternative cultural frames. This opened the opportunity for development of an advocacy coalition of local renewable energy entrepreneurs, green and alternative lifestyle advocates, scientists, and some politicians. The landmark legislation came only after the Greens and elites in particular ministries and think tanks brought the issues to the national stage. As Rüdiger Mautz explains, government support for renewables may be "as much the *result* of the political, economic and societal 'institutionalization of environmental protection' as it is a driving force for this process."[52]

Like other contributions to the volume, this chapter has described the ways in which the German system has changed while retaining important elements of its past. In the case of renewable energy politics, grassroots activism has become part of normal policy making. Renewable energy advocates in the government keep the development of renewables on the national agenda, while the continuing potential for protest mobilization amplifies their voices and helps deflect attempts to roll back the law. The centralized expertise, power, and nontransparency of the classic corporatist model enjoy less legitimacy than before, but the networks connecting political and economic elites remain. New actors outside these networks have built networks of their own, supported by a significant portion of the citizenry. This new German model is more conflictual and bottom-up than the traditional model. It depicts a system in which collaboration and conflict both have a place.

Carol Hager is Professor of Political Science on the Clowes Professorship in Science and Public Policy at Bryn Mawr College. She received her BA from the University of Nevada, Las Vegas (German) and her MA and PhD from the University of California, San Diego (comparative politics). Her research focuses on citizen participation in issue areas with high technical content. She is coeditor of *NIMBY Is Beautiful: Cases of Local Activism and Environmental Innovation around the World* (New York, 2015, with Mary Alice Haddad) and *Germany's Energy Transition: A Comparative Perspective* (New York, 2016, with Christoph Stefes).

NOTES

1. Christopher S Allen, "The Making of the Modern German State," in *European Politics in Transition,* 5th ed., ed. Mark Kesselman and Joel Krieger (Boston, 2006), 322.
2. Peter Hall and David Soskice, *Varieties of Capitalism* (Oxford, 2001), classify Germany as a "coordinated market economy." See also Steven Casper, Mark Lehrer, and David Soskice, "Can High-Technology Industries Prosper in Germany? Institutional Frameworks and the Evolution of the German Software and Biotechnology Industries," in *Debating Varieties of Capitalism,* ed. Bob Hancké (Oxford, 2009), 203.
3. Claus Offe, "The Attribution of Public Status to Interest Groups: Observations on the West German Case," in *Organizing Interests in Western Europe,* ed. Suzanne Berger (Cambridge, 1981), 123–58.
4. Rüdiger Mautz, "The Expansion of Renewable Energies in Germany between Niche Dynamics and System Integration–Opportunities and Restraints," *Science, Technology and Innovation Studies* 3, no. 2 (2007): 114. Mautz notes that just two of the four remaining suppliers were responsible for 70 percent of supply in 2007. A description of the traditional structure of the energy sector appears in David Toke and Volkmar Lauber, "Anglo-Saxon and German Approaches to Neoliberalism and Environmental Policy: The Case of Financing Renewable Energy," *Geoforum* 38, no. 4 (2007): 683.
5. David Toke, "Ecological Modernisation, Social Movements and Renewable Energy," *Environmental Politics* 20, no. 1 (2011).
6. Mautz, "The Expansion of Renewable Energies," 115.
7. Carol Hager, "From NIMBY to Networks: Protest and Innovation in German Energy Politics," in *NIMBY Is Beautiful: Cases of Local Activism and Environmental Innovation around the World,* ed. Carol Hager and Mary Alice Haddad (New York, 2015): 33–59.
8. See Jürgen Habermas, "The Tasks of a Critical Theory of Society," in *The Theory of Communicative Action,* vol. 2 (Boston, 1987), 374–403.

9. Burkhard Schaper, "Die Entstehungsgeschichte der AL," in *Die Alternative Liste Berlin: Entstehung, Entwicklung, Positionen,* ed. M Bühnemann, M Wendt, and J Wituschek (Berlin, 1984), 52. See also Bernd Guggenberger and Udo Kempf, eds, *Bürgerinitiativen und repräsentatives System,* rev. ed. (Opladen, 1984); Ulrich Linse, Dieter Rucht, Winfried Kretschmer, and Reinhard Falter, *Von der Bittschrift zur Platzbesetzung: Konflikte um technische Großprojekte* (Berlin, 1988).

10. See Roger Karapin, *Protest Politics in Germany: Movements on the Left and Right since the 1960s* (University Park, 2007), 120; also Carol Hager, "Three Decades of Protest in Berlin Land-Use Planning, 1975–2005," *German Studies Review* 30, no. 1 (2007): 55–74.

11. BI Oberhavel/Oberjägerweg, *Festschrift* (Berlin, undated).

12. Lutz Mez, "Von den Bürgerinitiativen zu den Grünen," in *Neue soziale Bewegungen in der Bundesrepublik Deutschland,* ed. Roland Roth and Dieter Rucht (Frankfurt am Main, 1987), 264.

13. Petra Kelly, *Fighting for Hope* (Boston, 1984), 17–18; Hubert Kleinert, *Aufstieg und Fall der Grünen: Analyse einer alternativen Partei* (Bonn, 1992), chapter 7; Andrei S Markovits and Joseph Klaver, *Thirty Years of Bundestag Presence: A Tally of the Greens' Impact on the Federal Republic of Germany's Political Life and Political Culture* (Washington, DC, 2012).

14. Werner Krauss, "The *Dingpolitik* of Wind Energy in Northern German Landscapes: An Ethnographic Case Study," *Landscape Research* 35, no. 2 (2010): 207.

15. Toke, "Ecological Modernisation," 66.

16. Staffan Jacobsson and Volkmar Lauber, "The Politics and Policy of Energy System Transformation—Explaining the German Diffusion of Renewable Energy Technology," *Energy Policy* 34, no. 3 (2006): 262.

17. Judith Lipp, "Lessons for Effective Renewable Electricity Policy from Denmark, Germany and the United Kingdom," *Energy Policy* 35, no. 11 (2007): 5488.

18. Jacobsson and Lauber, "The Politics and Policy," 263.

19. www.oeko.de/new/dok/516.php, dated 16 January 2007. Eurosolar info is from www.eurosolar.de.

20. Felix Kolb, *Protest and Opportunities: A Theory of Social Movements and Political Change* (New York, 2007), 211; also Detlef Jahn, "Nuclear Power, Energy Policy and New Politics in Sweden and Germany," *Environmental Politics* 1, no. 3 (1992): 396–97. For an account of early antinuclear protest, see Dieter Rucht, *Von Wyhl nach Gorleben: Bürger gegen Atomprogramm und nukleare Entsorgung* (Munich, 1980).

21. R Andreas Kraemer, "The Nuclear Power Endgame in Germany," *AICGS Advisor* (30 June 2011).

22. Peter Weingart, Anita Engels, and Petra Pansegrau, "Risks of Communication: Discourses on Climate Change in Science, Politics, and the Mass Media," *Public Understanding of Science* 9, no. 3 (2000): 268–69; Peter Weingart, "Science and the Media," *Research Policy* 27 (1998): 877; Volker Quaschning, *Renewable Energy and Climate Change* (Chichester, 2010), xi.

23. Jacobsson and Lauber, "The Politics and Policy," 264. Other European countries were also experimenting with legislative support for renewables. Denmark

was another early innovator (see Toke and Lauber, "Anglo-Saxon and German Approaches," 71).

24. Christoph H Stefes, "Bypassing Germany's *Reformstau*: The Remarkable Rise of Renewable Energy," *German Politics* 19, no. 2 (2010): 155–57.

25. Frank Laird and Christoph Stefes, "The Diverging Paths of German and United States Policies for Renewable Energy: Sources of Difference," *Energy Policy* 37, no. 7 (2009): 2628.

26. Jacobsson and Lauber, "The Politics and Policy," 264–65.

27. Lipp, "Lessons for Effective Renewable Electricity Policy," 5488.

28. Ion Bogdan Vasi, "Social Movements and Industry Development: The Environmental Movement's Impact on the Wind Energy Industry," *Mobilization* 14, no. 3 (2009): 328.

29. Paul Gipe, "The Aachen Solar Tariff Model," www.windworks.org, 7 April 2007.

30. Stefes, "Bypassing Germany's *Reformstau*," 158.

31. Ibid., 159.

32. Toke and Lauber, "Anglo-Saxon and German Approaches," 684.

33. The 20 20 20 targets set three objectives for EU energy policy, to be achieved by 2020: a 20 percent reduction in EU greenhouse gas emissions from 1990 levels; a 20 percent improvement in EU energy efficiency; and a rise in the share of EU energy consumption produced from renewable resources to 20 percent, ec.europa.eu/clima/policies/package/index_en.htm.

34. Interviews with political party representatives, Berlin, June/July 2009.

35. *The Economist,* various.

36. www.thelocal.de/national/20120215-40749, html; www.leben-in-stuttgart.de.

37. Corinna Fischer and Barbara Praetorius, "Carbon Capture and Storage: Settling the German Coal vs. Climate Change Dispute?," *International Journal of Environmental Technology and Management* 9, no. 2/3 (2008): 182.

38. "Wacklige Wende," *Spiegel,* 10 October 2011, 38.

39. Klaus Weber, Hayagreeva Rao, and LG Thomas, "From Streets to Suites: How the Anti-Biotech Movement Affected German Pharmaceutical Firms," *American Sociological Review* 74 (2009): 122.

40. Uwe Altrock, "Büroflächenplanung in Berlin 1981–89: Kreative nachholende Modernisierung oder Rückfall in autoritäre Muster?," in *Kommunale Entscheidungsprozesse im Wandel,* ed. J Bogumil (Opladen, 2002): 297.

41. Fischer and Praetorius, "Carbon Capture and Storage," 186.

42. www.oeko.de.

43. Interview with Federation of German Industry (BDI) representatives, Berlin, July 2009. Also Giles Parkinson, "Energy Storage: Generators to be the Biggest Losers," reneweconomy.com.au/2014/energy-storage-generators-biggest-losers-50615.

44. Mautz, "The Expansion of Renewable Energies," 126–27.

45. Kirsten Verclas, "The Reform of the German Renewable Energy Act in 2014," American Institute for Contemporary German Studies, www.aicgs.org/issue/the-reform-of-the-germany-renewable-energy-act-in-2014.

46. "Öko-Zukunftsplan bevorzugt die Konzerne," *Spiegel,* 5 May 2011; Mattias Brendel and Gerald Traufetter, "Knall auf hoher See," *Der Spiegel,* 25 August 2014, 71–72.
47. *Der Spiegel* 46 (2012): 82–84; "Stadtwerke attackieren Stromriesen," *Spiegel Online,* 22 December 2011.
48. Bundesverband der Energie- und Wasserwirtschaft e.V., www.bdew.de/internet.nsf/id/20140211-pi-bdew-umfrage-grosse-mehrheit-unterstuetzt-die-energiewende—umsetzung-wird-kritisch-be.
49. Miranda Schreurs and Dörte Ohlhorst, "NIMBY and YIMBY: Movements For and Against Renewable Energy in Germany and the United States," in *NIMBY Is Beautiful: Cases of Local Activism and Environmental Innovation around the World,* ed. Carol Hager and Mary Alice Haddad (New York, 2015): 60–86.
50. "Umfrage: Deutsche setzen zu 94 Prozent auf Erneuerbare Energien," *Umwelt-journal Online,* 7 July 2011. The survey of 1,002 people was conducted by TNS Infratest on behalf of the Agency for Renewable Energies.
51. Dieter Rucht makes this point for "left-libertarian" movements in general. See "The Changing Role of Political Protest Movements," in *Germany: Beyond the Stable State,* ed. Herbert Kitschelt and Wolfgang Streeck (Portland, OR, 2004), 166.
52. Mautz, "The Expansion of Renewable Energies," 117, emphasis added.

SELECTED BIBLIOGRAPHY

Fischer, Corinna, and Barbara Praetorius. "Carbon Capture and Storage: Settling the German Coal vs. Climate Change Dispute?" *International Journal of Environmental Technology and Management* 9, no. 2/3 (2008): 176–203.
Hager, Carol. "From NIMBY to Networks: Protest and Innovation in German Energy Politics." In *NIMBY Is Beautiful: Cases of Local Activism and Environmental Innovation around the World,* edited by Carol Hager and Mary Alice Haddad. New York, 2015: 33–59.
Jacobsson, Staffan, and Volkmar Lauber. "The Politics and Policy of Energy System Transformation—Explaining the German Diffusion of Renewable Energy Technology." *Energy Policy* 34, no. 3 (2006): 256–76.
Mautz, Rüdiger. "The Expansion of Renewable Energies in Germany between Niche Dynamics and System Integration—Opportunities and Restraints." *Science, Technology and Innovation Studies* 3, no. 2 (2007): 113–31.
Rucht, Dieter. "The Changing Role of Political Protest Movements." In *Germany: Beyond the Stable State,* edited by Herbert Kitschelt and Wolfgang Streeck. Portland, OR, 2004: 153–176.
Stefes, Christoph H. "Bypassing Germany's *Reformstau*: The Remarkable Rise of Renewable Energy." *German Politics* 19, no. 2 (2010): 148–63.
Toke, David. "Ecological Modernisation, Social Movements and Renewable Energy." *Environmental Politics* 20, no. 1 (2011): 60–77.

Toke, David, and Volkmar Lauber. "Anglo-Saxon and German Approaches to Neoliberalism and Environmental Policy: The Case of Financing Renewable Energy." *Geoforum* 38, no. 4 (2007): 677–87.

Vasi, Ion Bogdan. "Social Movements and Industry Development: The Environmental Movement's Impact on the Wind Energy Industry." *Mobilization* 14, no. 3 (2009): 315–36.

Chapter 10

Germany's Approach to the Financial Crisis
A Product of Ordo-Liberalism?

Mark K Cassell

During the past several years, Germany has been the target of widespread criticism for its approach to resolving the worst financial crisis since the Great Depression. Journalists, scholars, and policy makers characterize Germany as the "bad" economic hegemon; forcing its economic and moralistic views on the rest of Europe.[1] Brigitte Young finds German euro-politics to be overtly nationalistic, focused mostly on domestic concerns, and overtly critical of southern European countries for not modernizing their welfare systems and rationalizing their labor markets.[2] This chapter does not weigh in on the normative characterizations of German economic policy. Instead, the research seeks to better understand how ideas influenced Germany's economic policy by casting light on how Germany understood the Great Recession of 2008.

Ideas are the taken-for-granted views of policy makers and elites. Ideas operate as a lens through which policy makers make sense of the world.[3] In her work on discursive institutionalism, Vivien Schmidt[4] explains that ideas operate within the policy process at three levels: (1) as "windows of opportunity" that suddenly open up new agendas[5]; (2) as programmatic ideas for addressing public problems; and (3) as the deeper philosophical ideas or worldviews that underlie our programmatic ideas.[6] According to Schmidt, these policy ideas are shaped by (1) cognitive paradigms that establish how societies understand cause and effect relationships and (2) normative paradigms that specify a society's values and priorities.

Early in its development, the United States embraced a strong belief in the "naturalness" of markets and sought to maintain the autonomy of markets from the states. In line with the *laissez-faire* teachings of Adam Smith, David Ricardo, and later neoclassical scholars, the market was treated as a natural phenomenon: the institutional embodiment of an aggregate of individual self-interests. The ideology also included decentralized and fragmented power, and a separation of the private from the public sector. The fragmentation of power coupled with what Andrew Shonfield[7] describes as "the naturalness of private enterprise" in the United States form Schmidt's cognitive paradigm, that is, the way Americans understand how markets and government operate; and her normative paradigm, that is, something Americans value and aspire to maintain.

Germany's historic experiences with hyperinflation in the 1920s and two devastating world wars gave rise to an understanding of state-market relations that differed considerably from America's. In the postwar period, Walter Eucken and Alfred Müller-Armack, economists at the Freiburg School, established *ordo-liberalism* that conceives of an economic order based on the dynamics of a competitive market but bound by the state.[8] Eucken and Müller-Armack understood state regulation as necessary to ensure competition and prevent the debilitating cartels that had undermined the Weimar Republic. At the same time, given their experience with German authoritarianism, *ordo-liberals* favored separation and decentralization of state powers, a properly functioning price system, the establishment of independent agencies such as the Bundesbank, Germany's central bank, and regulation by a broad political and societal consensus.[9] Policies based on strong adherence to a set of rules, rather than policy-maker discretion, nurtures trust in the system as well as legitimacy toward government. Today ordo-liberalism continues to influence how policy makers understand state/markets relations (the cause and effect relationships) and policy makers' values (e.g., adherence to rules and maintenance of trust among social partners).

This chapter argues that by analyzing how American and German policy makers understood the financial crisis in the fall of 2008, one can see how cognitive and normative paradigms, rooted in place and history, produced national- or state-specific policy responses to policy problems and conditions.[10] While Germany's policy response to the financial crisis was certainly shaped by institutional factors such as the European Union's regulatory framework and by the power of political parties and interest groups, the research presented below suggests that understanding a nation's response to the financial crisis requires attention to national cognitive and normative paradigms, as developed by Vivien Schmidt and others.[11] These paradigms undergird policy ideas and produce specific national policy responses to the financial crisis. The research builds upon scholarship on how ideas influence national policy choices more generally and more recent work into the role ideas played in Germany's response to the financial crisis.[12]

GERMANY'S RESPONSE TO THE FINANCIAL CRISIS

In late 2008, at the peak of the crisis, economies in advanced industrial countries were in freefall, policy makers knew they had to do something, and the policy environment was defined by fear of what could still occur and uncertainty over how to respond. It was during the tumultuous days of October 2008 that Germany's legislature passed the German Financial Market Stabilization Act (German Stabilization Act). While subsequent laws were passed to stimulate the economy and address the long- and short-term regulatory problems, an examination of the German Stabilization Act offers a glimpse into the early days of the crisis and captures the German government's initial response.

Germany passed legislation in October 2008 in response to the sudden decline in the subprime mortgage sector of the US economy that was undermining financial institutions across the globe. In Germany, like the United States, severe downturns in financial firms deemed "too big to fail" were brought on by overleveraging toxic assets, low interest rates, and undervaluing of risk management. Initial writedowns in these firms harmed the financial system in two ways: through the direct failure of complicated financial assets that were infected by mortgage-backed securities built on residential mortgages; and second, through the spillover or contagion effect in which failing institutions undermined investor confidence in otherwise healthy institutions, thus jeopardizing the larger system.

The German government sought to avert short-term bank runs by securitizing banks' reserve capital and instilling certainty that deposits were safe. In contrast, United States' legislators targeted the balance sheets in firms that were vital to maintain the flow of capital by pulling troubled assets out of the market using taxpayer revenue.[13]

Prior to passing the Financial Market Stabilization Act on 17 October 2008, the German government dealt with firms that had exposed themselves to the international downturn on a case-by-case basis in order to prevent its spread to other insulated banks.[14] But what had originated disproportionately in the state-owned banks known as Landesbanken quickly spread to other assets throughout the private commercial and, to a lesser extent, public communal financial sectors of the domestic German economy. The Financial Market Stabilization Act set up the Financial Rescue Fund to guarantee public and private bank loans and credit lines and to inject capital into the reserves of the affected banks. Importantly, these initial responses sought to deal more with the "immediate threat" of large banks failing and causing bank runs than with the toxic assets that were forcing dramatic writedowns on banks' balance sheets.[15] That is, government policy initially sought to stabilize connections among banks and to ensure availability of short-term funds, but did not seek to relieve banks of the consequences of their faulty risk mismanagement. The Commerzbank received the first injection of capital through the Financial Market Stabilization Act to stabilize it after it had acquired the Dresdner Bank in January 2009, giving the German government a 25 percent share of the Commerzbank—enough control to constitute a blocking minority for shareholder approval.[16] In this way the German government's initial response to the 2008 financial crisis was to guard taxpayers from bearing the financial burden of bank exposure to international market fluctuation by insuring public and private banks and reasserting shareholder and managerial control over those banks that volunteered to cooperate with the Financial Rescue Fund.

Germany's initial legislative response to the crisis was thus to reduce public anxiety over the health of financial institutions by extending broad guarantees to depositors and taking a more active role in governance of the institutions. To consider the role ideas play in explaining Germany's approach, the next section looks empirically at the connection between ideas and policy.

IDEAS IN A TIME OF CRISIS

The recent financial crisis offers an unusual opportunity to study the role of ideas in the policy process. Boin et al. define a crisis as a "serious threat to the basic structures of or the fundamental values and norms of a system, which under time pressure and highly uncertain circumstances necessitates making vital decisions."[17] Under noncrisis conditions and with the luxury of time and reflection, policy makers give answers that take into account what their audiences wish to hear or what the policy maker wishes her audiences to hear. Crises, in contrast, force policy makers to reveal their true beliefs. The question is whether, in revealing their true beliefs, do we see cross-national differences as Vivian Schmidt, Collin Hay, and others who study the cross-national ideas suggest. Moreover, if there are cross-national differences, what are they? And, in examining the content of ideational differences, does one observe connections to historically based cognitive and normative paradigms?

Three Hypotheses

In his article comparing national responses to food safety crises in three countries, Martin Lodge outlines three approaches to explain how elites in different countries might respond to the financial crisis.[18] One approach suggests that given the dominance of neoliberalism globally and particularly in the area of finance, we would expect policy makers across countries to express similar views about the causes of the financial crisis. Scholars note globalization's influence in pressuring policy makers to adopt similar assumptions about states and markets that are embedded in a neoliberal ideology.[19] In short, the more freely capital and labor are able to move across borders, the more difficult it becomes for policy makers to believe in a distinct national set of ideas. The following hypothesis thus emerges:

> H1 (neoliberal dominance): Given that few industries are as global and free of borders as the financial industry, there should be little or no difference between how German and American elites understood the causes of the financial crisis.

A second approach, which Lodge labels "Pavlovian politics" also predicts policy makers across countries will react similarly to a similar crisis.[20] However, the cause of such conformity is not pressures brought on by globalization but rather the logic of crises. Lodge notes, "when under pressure, politicians—regardless of time and place—will turn to similar measures to please anxious publics."[21] In other words, the approach assumes that in times of crisis, politicians' reactions are akin to Pavlov's dog salivating in response to a bell: they (politicians and dogs) just can not help themselves. From this approach, the following hypothesis emerges:

> H2 (Pavlovian politics): One would expect little or no difference between how German and American policy makers understood the causes of the crisis: the automatic response should be the same.

Finally, a third approach builds on work by comparative political economists discussed above, which makes the case for national differences; arguing that ideas are shaped by cognitive and normative paradigms that are specific to a country and shaped by history.[22] The paradigms influence how the financial crisis is understood, constrain policy makers' options, and lead to nation-specific policy outcomes.[23] The following hypothesis emerges from the work of comparativists:

> H3 (National differences): Given the differences between German and American institutional landscapes as well as the interest group environment in each other country, one would expect policy makers to understand the causes of the financial crisis differently.

In sum, the three approaches outlined by Lodge and applied here to the financial crisis, suggest three possible outcomes: two predict little difference between American and German perceptions of the causes of the financial crisis (albeit for different reasons), and a third that predicts clear cross-national differences.

Methodology and Research Design

To test the hypotheses, I use content analysis, which Robert Philip Weber notes is appropriate to discover "international differences in communication content," describe "attitudinal and behavioral responses," identify "cultural patterns of groups, institutions, or societies," and reveal the focus of "individual, group, institutional, or societal attention."[24] Content analysis is a systematic, replicable technique for compressing words of text into content categories based on rules of coding.[25] Content analysis measures the frequency of word patterns enabling one to determine authorship of documents as well as trends and patterns in texts. In addition, by relying on coding and categorizing of the data content analysis enables one to draw inferences "from symbolic data what would be too costly or too obtrusive by the use of other techniques."[26]

Using the search words "banking crisis," "economic crisis," and "financial crisis" (in the German case *Bankenkrise, Wirtschaftskrise,* and *Finanzkrise*), a search was conducted using *Lexis-Nexis News* of two national daily newspapers, the *New York Times* and *Die Welt,* for the period six weeks prior to passage of each countries' respective stabilization act.[27] The six-week window was selected because this was when attention of elites in both countries was most focused on the financial crisis and when uncertainty about the nature and extent of the crisis was highest. The frequency of comments concerning the financial crisis was highest during this period. Thus, the perspectives voiced at this moment in time were expressed without the advantage of opinion polls or broader consensus of the nature of the problem. Elites in the United States and Germany were reacting to what they perceived this crisis was.

Although their political ideologies differ, the more liberal *New York Times* and more conservative *Die Welt* were selected for three reasons. First, each newspaper is widely viewed as among the most respected and objective news outlets in each country. Second, both newspapers take a national perspective in their coverage as opposed to regional or local focus. And third, the *New York Times* and *Die Welt* are published for a national audience with a national distribution. Thus, notwithstanding the ideological differences reflected on their editorial pages, the newspapers' journalistic reputation, national coverage, and national audience offer the clearest window into elite perspectives toward the financial crisis in Germany and the United States.

The search yielded initially 362 *New York Times* articles and 927 articles in *Die Welt*. Articles were included in the final cut if they fulfilled two criteria: (1) the article includes a reference to the views of an elite person (politician, academic, journalist, businessperson, etc.); and (2) the elite person articulates a cause of the financial crisis. Excluded were articles quoting members of the general population, letters to the editor, and articles in which elites comment on some aspect of the financial crisis (i.e., its severity or impact on a particular industry) but not on what they understand as the cause. Applying these criteria generated 99 *New York Times* articles and 136 articles from *Die Welt*. The qualitative software program Nvivo 8 was used to carry out the content analysis and code each article. Each article was coded for the following: (1) stated cause of financial crisis; (2) identity of the source; and (3) date. Table 10.1 presents the percentage breakdown of the types of sources. Sources were coded according to the following categories: (1) academics, journalists, and economists; (2) politicians from any party or

Table 10.1: Type and Percentage Frequency of Newspaper Sources.
The percentage breakdown of each source type by country.

	Germany*	United States**
Academics, Journalists, Economists	44%	32%
Politicians	33%	39%
Banking Interest Groups	19%	20%
Union/Labor Groups	1%	1.5%
Bureaucracy/Regulators	4%	8%

*   The absolute number of references collected from *Die Welt* is 226.
**   The absolute number of references collected from the *New York Times* is 253.

level; (3) banking interest groups; (4) groups representing workers such as unions; and (5) bureaucrats and regulators. There is similarity across the two publications. Approximately a third of the sources are from politicians in both cases. There is a higher percentage of academics, journalists, and economists referenced in *Die Welt* (44 percent) over the *New York Times* (32 percent). There is a slightly higher percentage of bureaucrats and regulators referenced in the *New York Times* (8 percent) over the *Die Welt* (4 percent). Notwithstanding the differences, the comparison shows comparability across the two publications with both giving voice to the views of politicians, academics, journalists, and economists.

To increase the internal validity of the coding, two individuals (myself and a graduate assistant) coded the *New York Times* articles. Because of time and resource constraints, articles in *Die Welt* were read, coded, and translated by the author.

Table 10.2: All Elites. Top nine causes of the financial crisis as expressed by all elites and ranked based on the percentage of times the cause was mentioned in the *New York Times* and *Die Welt* in the six weeks prior to passage of each country's respective bailout legislation.

Germany	United States
1. Erosion of confidence (8.7%)	1. Regulatory neglect (7.53%)
2. Speculation (4.77%)	2. Interconnectedness between banks and hedge funds (4.44%)
3. Greed and irresponsibility on Wall Street (4.65%)	3. Greed and irresponsibility on Wall Street (4.43%)
4. Naive faith in markets or neo-liberal ideology (4.29%)	4. Shaky real estate investment—hikes in mortgage rates. (4.42%)
5. Operation of the Landesbanken (3.96%)	5. Generation gap on Wall Street—inability to deal with modern complexity (4.11%)
6. Deregulation and lack of rules (3.79%)	6. Inadequate computer systems (3.93%)
7. Compensation system for financial industry (3.76%)	7. Lack of transparency (3.57%)
8. Public involvement in German banks (3.59%)	8. Erosion of confidence (3.53%)
9. Bad management (3.58%)	9. The practice of short-selling (3.39%)

Source: Author's own calculations.

The findings from the content analysis reveal differences in the way German and American elites understood the causes of the financial crisis. The analysis first examines the ten most frequent causes given for the financial crisis in the two countries by all elites (Table 10.1). Next, a secondary analysis compares statements by conservative and liberal politicians in both countries to determine whether there are similarities across political parties with similar ideologies (Tables 10.2–10.4).

Table 10.3: Conservative Politicians. Top ten causes for the financial crisis as expressed by conservative politicians and ranked based on the percentage of times the cause was mentioned or attributed to a politician in the *New York Times* and *Die Welt* in the six weeks prior to passage of each country's respective bailout legislation.

Germany*	United States*
1. Deregulation and lack of rules (9.21%)	1. Decade-old practice of borrowing (15.31%)
2. Naive faith in markets or neo-liberal ideology (7.25%)	2. Greed and irresponsibility on Wall Street (12.11%)
3. Operation of the Landesbanken (5.85%)	3. Regulatory neglect (9.14%)
4. Operation of US banks, not German banks (5.85%)	4. Risk caused by the concentrated power of politically and financially powerful institutions with huge portfolios (8.63%)
5. Regulatory neglect (4.9%)	5. Cronyism, special interest, lobbyists (7.86%)
6. Speculation (4.83%)	6. Did nothing to reign in Fannie and Freddie (6.93%)
7. Erosion of confidence (4.55%)	7. SEC trading rules (4.9%)
8. Public involvement in German banks (4.45 %)	8. Inadequate mortgage conventions (4.41%)
9. Operation of the Kreditanstalt für Wiederaufbau (KfW) (4.2%)	9. Balkanization of the fin. regulatory system, i.e., too many regulators (4.27%)
10. Lack of uniform European set of rules (4.17%)	10. Erosion of confidence (3.67%)

Source: Author's own calculations.
*   Includes German politicians from the three major conservative parties: The Christian Social Union (CSU); the Christian Democratic Union (CDU); and the Free Democratic Party (FDP).
**   Includes US politicians from the Republican Party.

Table 10.4: Liberal Politicians. Top ten causes for the financial crisis as expressed by liberal politicians and ranked based on the percentage of times the cause was mentioned or attributed to a politician in the *New York Times* and *Die Welt* in the six weeks prior to passage of each country's respective bailout legislation.

Germany*	United States**
1. Greed and irresponsibility (12.01%)	1. Regulatory neglect (16.31%)
2. Bad management (10.23%)	2. Greed and irresponsibility on Wall Street (12.05%)
3. Speculation (9.03%)	3. Hands-off policies of the Republicans (7.66%)
4. Naive faith in markets or neoliberal ideology (7.8%)	4. Cronyism, special interest, lobbyists (7.09%)
5. Deregulation and lack of rules (6.28%)	5. Did nothing to reign in Fannie and Freddie (4.71%)
6. Public involvement in banks (5.4%)	6. Risk caused by the concentrated power of politically and financially powerful institutions with huge portfolios (4.39%)
7. Regulatory neglect (5.24%)	7. New international powers are free-riding (3.85%)
8. Lack of uniform European set of rules (5.08%)	8. Shaky real estate investments and hike in mortgage rates (3.74%)
9. Domestic regulations in a global world (3.82%)	9. Interconnectedness–banks and hedge funds (3.37%)
10. Lack of expertise on the supervisory boards of Landesbanken (2.94%)	10. SEC trading rules (3.33%)

Source: Author's own calculations.
* Includes German politicians from the three major leftist parties: Social Democratic Party (SPD); the Greens; and the Party of the Left [Die Linken].
** Includes US politicians from the Democratic Party and Bernie Sanders, an Independent member of Congress from Vermont.

The comparison reveals that for German elites, the erosion of confidence in a range of institutions is the most important cause of the financial crisis, followed by speculation, greed and irresponsibility on Wall Street, a naïve faith in markets or neoliberal ideology, and the poor operation of publicly-chartered Landesbanken. In contrast, top causes of the financial crisis cited most often by American elites included: regulatory neglect, the interconnectedness between banks and hedge funds, greed and irresponsibility on Wall Street, questionable real estate investments, and a generation gap on Wall Street in which an old guard is unable to understand the modern complexities of finance. "Regulatory neglect" which topped the American list, was tenth on the German list of important causes. Alternatively, "erosion of confidence," which was the cause most often given in Germany, was only eighth on the American list.

The comparison of German and American conservative and liberal politicians also reveals a difference in understanding. German conservatives cited deregulation and a lack of rules as the primary cause of the crisis followed by a "naïve faith in markets," "the poor operation of the state Landesbanken," and the poor operation of US banks as the primary causes of the crisis. American conservatives, in contrast, cited most often the excessive public borrowing, Wall Street greed and irresponsibility, and regulatory neglect.

Among German and American liberal politicians, there were differences and similarities. Liberal politicians in Germany and the United States cited greed and irresponsibility on Wall Street coupled with a more general deregulatory philosophy as causing the crisis. German liberals cited most often "Wall Street greed and irresponsibility" as the cause of the crisis followed by "bad management," "speculation," and "naïve faith in markets" or neoliberal ideology. US liberals cited most often "regulatory neglect" as the cause of the financial crisis, followed by "Wall Street greed and irresponsibility," the "hands-off policies of Republicans" and "cronyism and the influence of special interest groups" as the main causes of the financial crisis.

Two quotes are typical of elite understandings of the financial crisis in the United States. Lawrence Summers, a Democrat and former Treasury Secretary under Bill Clinton stated,

> Today's necessary but likely very expensive action for taxpayers is the consequence of regulatory neglect and of a broader political system's reluctance to take on what should have been clearly seen as festering problems. (*New York Times*, 2008)[28]

Similarly, Senator John McCain, the Republican nominee for president, argued that the financial crisis is "an example of cronyism, special interest, lobbyists." McCain added that the companies needed "more regulation, more oversight, more transparency, more of everything, and frankly, a dramatic reduction in what they do."[29]

For Germans, the narrative around the cause of the financial crisis is slightly more complicated than just the notion that the financial crisis was caused by greed and irresponsibility. Global and domestic factors undermined the confidence and trust in public and private institutions, which in turn caused and exacerbated the financial crisis. The problem of the financial crisis in Germany just prior to the largest bailout in the countries' history was defined in terms of a loss of confidence.

Three excerpts from *Die Welt* capture the narrative around the loss of confidence. Citing Arno Gottschalk, of the Consumer Advice Center in Bremen, *Die Welt* wrote on 17 September 2008:

> Financial transactions are comparable with mountaineering: you must have confidence in the safety precautions. Otherwise you should keep your fingers off it.[30]

Citing, Manfred Weber, the former director of the influential bank lobby group Bundesverband deutscher Banken, *Die Welt* wrote on 27 September 2008, three weeks before the Stabilization Act:

> Trust is what it is all about with any financial business. "Trust is the central issue for a bank," says Manfred Weber, banking professor at the University of Mannheim. "Any bank goes down if it is no longer trusted." The recent weeks showed this clearly. It does not matter at all if it is an investment bank or a normal institution with its many individual and business clients. When the trust is gone, the bank has to close its doors.
>
> It is like a self-fulfilling prophecy. If customers think it's over, then it is over for the bank. And, in contrast to claims by critics of capitalism, this phenomenon doesn't just affect the gamblers at the investment banks. It is like a natural law of the financial industry. "Students learn in their sixth banking lecture that any bank will get into difficulties when all of a sudden lots of savers withdraw their deposits," says banking professor Weber. "Banks in trouble have been known to specifically stack a lot of bills at the teller's counter." Customers have to see that money is there. (*Die Welt,* 2008)[31]

And finally, consider the argument made in *Die Welt* by Wolfgang Sofsky, sociologist and author:

> A hole opens up in the future when habits burst, institutions crumble, and uncertainty is endemic. The predictability of the world seems to be gone. The notion that history and business would go on as before proves to be what it always has been: a hypothesis based mainly on trust.[32]

The excerpts underscore the view expressed by elites that a loss of confidence was a central cause of the financial crisis. What is striking about the finding is that the direct impact of the financial crisis on the German

economy has been modest. Housing finance in Germany remains conservative and largely unchanged, house prices have only suffered a modest drop,
and economic growth remained fairly strong relative to other advanced
industrialized countries. Indeed Bleuel notes that Germany's fragmented
banking structure was positively affected by the financial crisis.[33] Only
international players such as the big private banks, the Landesbanken, and
some special banks were victims of the first wave of financial crisis. Given
the relatively positive situation Germany found itself in relative to other
European countries and the United States, it is somewhat surprising that the
loss of public confidence is viewed as the main cause of the crisis.

CONCLUSION

Ideas influence the policy process by defining new public problems, generating programmatic ideas to address those problems, and establishing worldviews that undergird those programmatic ideas. In the earliest days of the
financial crisis, German and United States' elites understood the impending
crisis differently and consequently emphasized different public problems
that required different policy solutions. For German elites, there was widespread concern about the erosion of confidence across public and private
institutions. In response to this problem, the Financial Market Stabilization
Act set up a fund to guarantee public and private bank loans and credit lines
and inject capital into the reserves of the affected banks. The government's
policy was specifically designed to shore up public confidence in financial
institutions, stabilize connections among banks, and ensure availability of
short-term funds. At the same time, there was little appetite in Germany for
relieving banks of the portfolio of toxic assets that were due to faulty risk mismanagement. Rather than purchase poor-quality assets of specific financial
institutions with tax dollars (as was tried in the United States), Germany's
Financial Rescue Fund guaranteed public and private bank loans and credit
lines to bolster reserves and reduce the threat of bank runs.[34] In other words,
in Germany, government had a responsibility to assure confidence and trust
in the economic arena. However, the rules—no matter how painful the consequences to regional banks—were to be enforced.

   In addition, Germany's corporatist regulatory system, established in the
postwar period, places a high value on trust including trust between *social
partners* or interest groups, as well as trust between state and societal actors.
Streeck and Schmitter's characterization of Germany as a "private-interest
government" means the state plays an important role in setting the arena
in which societal actors regulate themselves.[35] Trust is the currency that

runs such a system, and it is thus not surprising that German elites are particularly sensitive to any perceived threat to trust or a loss of confidence. In short, the policy ideas that shaped Germany's response to the financial crisis are rooted in cognitive and normative paradigms that developed in response to hyperinflation of the 1920s and the two world wars.[36]

In contrast, the "regulatory neglect" expressed most often as the cause of the financial crisis by American elites is consistent with cognitive and normative paradigm characterized by limited government and, in particular, a strong mistrust between interest groups and the state. The concept of a *social partner* is absent from the American regulatory landscape. Trust and cooperation under such a system are low, and distrust of state agency is high in all areas except as far as one's own interests are concerned. As a result, oversight is a constant battle, achieved through detailed rules that attempt to cover all contingencies, constant vigilance, and of course extensive use of lawyers and the court system.[37]

The cognitive and normative paradigms embedded in each system's regulatory model is particularly evident in banking regulation. Germany's banking regulatory structure relies primarily on supervisory boards, consisting of public and private stakeholders, to hold the institutions accountable. Until fairly recently the main federal banking regulators, the Bundesbank and Federal Banking Supervisory Office, did relatively little to assess financial risks.[38] A top regulator in the Banking Supervisory Office stated in an interview:

> Historically, the Bundesbank played next to no role in the supervision of Landesbanken. The Bundesbank's role in the past was mainly collecting data from the banks, maintaining databases, and then analyzing the data in the aggregate. But in terms of actually supervising a bank: the Bundesbank played almost no role at all.[39]

Reports published by the Bundesbank in the years following the Banking Act of 1961 support this view. Germany's banking regulatory model thus relies mainly on supervisory boards with a long-term stake in the institution. The effectiveness of accountability and its impact on the broader economy is understood to depend on mutual trust and confidence. In contrast, cognitive and normative paradigms reflected in America's *laissez-faire* or anti-statist ideology are embedded in how American banks are regulated. US regulation of banks is primarily dependent upon a diverse mix of state and federal agencies who often compete with each other and whose regulatory effectiveness is typically constrained by a combination of industry lobbying power and America's strong distrust of government. It is hardly surprising that "regulatory neglect" is the idea articulated most often by American elites in the tumultuous days leading to passage of the first programmatic solution to the financial crisis.

Viewed in ordo-liberal terms, it is not surprising that German elites identify (1) an erosion of confidence; (2) speculation; and (3) greed and irresponsibility on Wall Street as the major causes of the financial crisis. Ordo-liberalism is acutely aware of the fragility of society's confidence in market structures and the potential abuse of market power by the powerful. Such concerns led to a theory of the state in which rules rather than political discretion are the basis for democracy and capitalism; it is a state that creates the space for competitive markets but intervenes to ensure competitive markets are maintained. Rieter and Schmolz write, "[Walter] Eucken repeatedly stressed the importance of a strong state, which could stand above social conflicts, for the creation and preservation of the competitive order."[40]

In more recent times Germany has become the target of significant criticism for its economic policies.[41] Paul Krugman, the Nobel Prize–winning economist, wrote that Germany and the European Central Bank are encouraging Europe to commit economic suicide by resisting policy makers' calls for expansionary policies.[42] The criticisms are well founded. Scholarship on Germany's austerity policies in the wake of the financial crisis suggests that inflationary concerns are overstated, and efforts to reduce public debt through cuts in spending slowed growth within Germany and throughout Europe.[43] However, Germany's approach to the crisis should not come as a surprise. The experience of 2008 revealed that Germany's economic policies are filtered through an ideational lens that harks back to the 1930s and 1940s, and which formed the basis for the postwar economic miracle. Therefore, in thinking about the country's response to current and future economic crises, one should not expect a country to so quickly jettison the economic ideas that are the foundation of its political economy.

Mark K Cassell is Professor of Political Science at Kent State University. His publications include *Mission Expansion in the Federal Home Loan Bank System* (New York, 2010) with Susan Hoffmann and *How Governments Privatize: The Politics of Divestment in the United States and Germany* (Washington, DC, 2003). His current research examines EU Banking Union and public banking in Germany.

NOTES

1. Paul Krugman, "An Impeccable Disaster," *The New York Times,* 11 September 2011; Hans Kundnani, "Germany as a Geo-economic Power," *The Washington Quarterly* 34, no. 3 (2011); Brigitte Young, "Economic Governance in the Eurozone: A New Dawn?" *Economic Sociology: the European Electronic Newsletter* 12, no. 2 (2011).

2. Young, "Economic Governance," 2.

3. Frank Dobbin, *Forging Industrial Policy: The United States, Britain, and France in the Railway Age* (Cambridge, 1994).

4. Vivien A Schmidt, "Analysing Ideas and Tracing Discursive Interactions in Institutional Change: From Historical Institutionalism to Discursive Institutionalism," *Harvard Center for European Studies, CES Papers,* Open Forum #3 (January 2011).

5. John W Kingdon, *Agendas, Alternatives, and Public Policies,* 2nd ed. (New York, 1995).

6. See also John L Campbell, "Ideas, Politics and Public Policy," *American Review of Sociology* 28 (2002): 21–38.

7. Andrew Shonfield, *Modern Capitalism* (Oxford, 1969), 269.

8. Christopher S Allen, "'Ordo-Liberalism' Trumps Keynesianism: Economic Policy in the Federal Republic of Germany And the EU," in *Monetary Union in Crisis: The European Union as a Neo-Liberal Construction,* ed. Bernhard H Moss (New York, 2005): 199–221.

9. Heinz Rieter and Matthias Schmolz, "The Ideas of German Ordoliberalism 1938–1945: Pointing the Way to a New Economic Order," *The European Journal of the History of Economic Thought* 1, no. 1 (1993): 87–114.

10. Campbell, "Ideas, Politics and Public Policy," 21–38; Fred L Block, *The Vampire State* (New York, 1996).

11. Colin Hay, "Narrating Crisis: The Discursive Construction of the 'Winter of Discontent,'" *Sociology* 30, no. 2 (1996): 253–177.

12. Sergio Cesaratto and Antonella Stirati, "Germany and the European and Global Crises," *International Journal of Political Economy* 39, no. 4 (2010–2011): 56–86; Frank Bohn and Eelke de Jong, "The 2010 Euro Crisis Stand-Off between France and Germany: Leadership Styles and Political Culture," *International Economics and Economic Policy* 8, no. 1 (2011): 7–14; Mark Vail, "Varieties of Liberalism: Keynesianism and Crisis in Contemporary Western Europe," unpublished paper (2010).

13. Klaus J Hopt, Christoph Kumpan, and Felix Steffek, "Preventing Bank Insolvencies in the Financial Crisis: The German Financial Market Stabilisation Acts," *European Business Organization Law Review* 10, no. 4 (2009): 515–54; Hans-H Bleul, "The German Banking System and the Global Financial Crisis: Causes, Developments and Policy Responses," *Düsseldorf Working Papers in Applied Management Economics. Forschungsberichte* 8 (2009).

14. Bleul, "The German Banking System and the Global Financial Crisis," 11.

15. Felix Hüfner, "The German Banking System: Lessons from the Financial Crisis," *OECD Economics Department Working Papers*, no. 788 (2010).
16. Bleuel, "The German Banking System and the Global Financial Crisis," 14.
17. Arjen Boin et al., *The Politics of Crisis Management: Public Leadership under Pressure* (Cambridge, 2005), 2.
18. Martin Lodge, "Risk, Regulation and Crisis: Comparing National Responses in Food Safety Regulation," *Journal of Public Policy* 31, no. 1 (2010): 25–50.
19. Wolfgang Streeck, *Re-Forming Capitalism: Institutional Change in the German Political Economy* (Oxford, 2009); Peter Hall and David Soskice, eds, *Varieties of Capitalism. The Institutional Foundations of Comparative Advantage* (Oxford, 2001); Giandomenico Majone, "From the Positive to the Regulatory State: Causes and Consequences of Changes in the Mode of Governance," *Journal of Public Policy* 17, no. 2 (1997): 139–67.
20. Lodge, "Risk, Regulation and Crisis," 29.
21. Lodge, "Risk, Regulation and Crisis," 28; see also Christopher Hood and Martin Lodge, "Pavlovian Innovation, Pet Solutions and Economizing on Rationality? Politicians and Dangerous Dogs," in *Regulatory Innovation*, ed. Julia Black, Martin Lodge, and Mark Thatcher (Cheltenham, 2005).
22. Dobbin, *Forging Industrial Policy*, 22; Schmidt, "Analysing Ideas," 7–9.
23. Hall and Soskice, eds, *Varieties of Capitalism*, 1–64; Sven Steinmo, *The Evolution of Modern States: Sweden, Japan, and the United States* (Cambridge, 2010), 1–29.
24. Robert Philip Weber, *Basic Content Analysis*, 2nd ed. (Newbury Park, 1990), 9.
25. Steve Stemler, "An Overview of Content Analysis," *Practical Assessment, Research & Evaluation* 7, no. 17 (2001); Bernard Berelson, *Content Analysis in Communication Research* (Glencoe, 1952); U.S. General Accounting Office, *Content Analysis: A Methodology for Structuring and Analyzing Written Material*, GAO/PEMD-10.3.1. (Washington, DC, 1996); Weber, *Basic Content Analysis*, 40; Klaus H Krippendorff, *Content Analysis: An Introduction to Its Methodology* (Thousand Oaks, CA, 1980).
26. Krippendorff, *Content Analysis*, 51.
27. The German Financial Stabilization Act passed 18 October 2008 and the U.S. Emergency and Economic Stabilization Act passed 3 October 2008.
28. "As Crisis Grew, A Few Options Shrank to One," *New York Times*, 8 September 2008.
29. "In Their Own Words," *New York Times*, 16 September 2008.
30. "Bundesbürger verlieren Vertrauen in das Finanzsystem," *Die Welt*, 17 September 2008.
31. "Ohne Vertrauen überlebt keine Bank," *Die Welt*, 27 September 2008.
32. "Ungedeckte Wechsel auf die Zukunft," *Die Welt*, 3 October 2008.
33. Bleuel, "The German Banking System and the Global Financial Crisis," 11.
34. Hüfner, "The German Banking System: Lessons from the Financial Crisis," 6.
35. Wolfgang Streeck and Philippe C Schmitter, *Private Interest Government: Beyond Market and State Financial Reform* (Thousand Oaks, CA, 1985); see also J Campbell and L Lindberg, "The State and the Organization of Economic Activity,"

in *Governance of the American Economy,* ed. J Rogers Hollingsworth, John L Campbell, and Leon N Lindberg (Cambridge, 1991).

36. Kenneth Dyson, ed., *The Politics of German Regulation* (Brookfield, 1991).
37. Steven Kelman, "Adversary and Cooperationist Institutions for Conflict Resolution in Public Policymaking," *Journal of Policy Analysis and Management* 11, no. 2 (1992): 178–206; Joseph A Bardaracco Jr, *Loading the Dice: A Five-Country Study of Vinyl Chloride Regulation* (Boston, MA, 1985); Michael Albert, *Capitalism vs. Capitalism* (London, 1993).
38. Hüfner, "The German Banking System: Lessons from the Financial Crisis," 16.
39. Interview conducted by author on 21 April 2014 in Berlin.
40. Rieter and Schmolz, "The Ideas of German Ordoliberalism 1938–1945," 87–114.
41. "Economic Woes at Home Are Testing Angela Merkel's Understanding of How Best to Use Her Power," *The Economist,* 18 October 2014, http://www.economist.com/news/europe/21625790-economic-woes-home-are-testing-angela-merkels-understanding-how-best-use-her.
42. Paul Krugman, "Europe's Economic Suicide," *The New York Times,* 16 April 2012.
43. Mark Blyth, *Austerity: The History of a Dangerous Idea* (Oxford, 2013); Berndt Keller, "The Continuation of Early Austerity Measures: The Special Case of Germany," *Transfer: European Review of Labour and Research* 20, no. 3 (2014): 387–402; Robert Boyer, "The Four Fallacies of Contemporary Austerity Policies: The Lost Keynesian Legacy," *Cambridge Journal of Economics* 36, no. 1 (2012): 283–312.

SELECTED BIBLIOGRAPHY

Albert, Michael. *Capitalism vs. Capitalism: How America's Obsession with Individual Achievement and Short-Term Profit Has Led It to the Brink of Collapse.* London, 1993.

Allen, Christopher S. "'Ordo-Liberalism' Trumps Keynesianism: Economic Policy in the Federal Republic of Germany and the EU." In *Monetary Union in Crisis. The European Union as a Neo-Liberal Construction,* edited by Bernhard H Moss. New York, 2005: 199–221.

Bleuel, Hans-H. "The German Banking System and the Global Financial Crisis: Causes, Developments and Policy Responses." *Düsseldorf Working Papers in Applied Management Economics. Forschungsberichte* 8 (2009).

Bohn, Frank, and Eelke de Jong. "The 2010 Euro Crisis Stand-Off between France and Germany: Leadership Styles and Political Culture." *International Economics and Economic Policy* 8, no. 1 (2011): 7–14.

Dyson, Kenneth, ed. *The Politics of German Regulation.* Brookfield, 1991.

Hall, Peter, and David Soskice, eds. *Varieties of Capitalism. The Institutional Foundations of Comparative Advantage.* Oxford, 2001.

Hüfner, Felix. "The German Banking System: Lessons from the Financial Crisis."
    OECD Economics Department Working Papers, No. 788 (2010).
Shonfield, Andrew. *Modern Capitalism.* Oxford, 1969.
Streeck, Wolfgang. *Re-Forming Capitalism: Institutional Change in the German Political
    Economy.* Oxford, 2009.

Chapter 11

Dreams of Divided Berlin

Postmigrant Perspectives on German Nationhood in *Die Schwäne vom Schlachthof*

Jeffrey Jurgens

In the opening scene of Hakan Savaş Mican's *Die Schwäne vom Schlachthof* (*The Swans of the Slaughterhouse*), a weary elderly journalist, played by the actor Hendrik Arnst, delivers a monologue from the perspective of what appears to be a young child:

> That was the morning of my last birthday. I woke up and realized that I had wet my bed again. I wanted to hide the wet sheet from my mother in the closet, but of course she found it right away. She wasn't at all angry. She gave me white tennis shoes for my birthday. They were too big for me. This way, she said, you can continue to wear them as you grow. My mother's co-workers from the slaughterhouse gave me a red ball and a toy watch. I then went to play with Çetin and Cengaver. Çetin brought me a bag of hazelnuts. From Turkey, he said. We went to the playground on the Gröbenufer, where there is a big slide. I went down it and, as I did, I lost the ball and it fell into the water. Çetin and Cengaver told me that I couldn't get my ball back. That it was much too dangerous. But it was my new ball, which I had just gotten as a present. So I tried to get it back anyway.[1]

Although the play does not explicitly alert its audience to this fact, the journalist's monologue refers to a specific historical event: the drowning of Çetin Mert, the five-year-old son of a Turkish "guest worker" family, in the Spree River on 11 May 1975. The riverbank in Kreuzberg from which Mert fell, known until recently as the Gröbenufer, belonged to West Berlin, but the river itself was part of East German territory, even though it was located outside the fortifications that constituted the Berlin Wall. As a result of this peculiar jurisdictional arrangement, East German border soldiers did not permit West Berlin police and fire personnel to search for Mert when they arrived on the scene, and East German divers only recovered his body after a two-hour delay. This incident, which marked a contentious moment in a long-running diplomatic battle over the waters between East and West Berlin, was the last of five drowning deaths among West Berlin children (all of them boys) to occur on this portion of the river: the prior victims included Andreas Senk (1966), Cengaver Katrancı (1972), Siegfried Kroboth (1973), and Giuseppe Savoca (1974).[2] As the names suggest, three of the five boys were from Turkish and Italian migrant families who had come to West Berlin as a result of the labor recruitment programs that the West German federal government had administered since the mid 1950s. Significantly, the deaths of Mert and the other boys have not figured prominently in subsequent public memories of the Berlin Wall, although the past few years have witnessed a growing if still modest awareness of Mert's death in particular.[3]

Many of the details from the journalist's narrative (the birthday, the shoes, the ball, the train of events that led to the drowning) echo the documented circumstances of Mert's final hours, and the names Çetin and Cengaver offer an additional allusion to the boys and their deaths. The opening monologue thereby highlights the degree to which the history of postwar labor migration intersects—on the site of the Gröbenufer, in the bodies of migrant children—with the history of Germany's Cold War division. This scene is consistent with the larger thrust of *Die Schwäne,* which endeavors to recast dominant narratives of the postwar German past by threading the experiences of Turkish migrants into the fabric of Berlin's division and unification. In so doing, it engages in a complex form of "multidirectional memory," a concept developed by literary scholar Michael Rothberg to "draw attention to the dynamic transfers that take place between diverse times and places during the act of remembrance."[4] Rothberg contrasts the workings of multidirectional memory with a model of recollection that he calls "competitive memory," which in his rendering presumes the existence of neatly differentiated pasts that map precisely onto clearly demarcated group identities. Such an understanding does not simply propose that specific histories and memories are the exclusive possession of one and only one national, ethnic, or other collectivity; it also posits the public sphere as a zone of zero-sum struggle, one where the articulation of one group's past tends to preclude the recognition of other histories and identities.[5] Berlin has witnessed outbursts of precisely such memory competition on numerous occasions: in the 1990s, for example, debates flared over the construction of separate government-sponsored memorials for Jews, Roma, communists, and homosexuals persecuted during the Third Reich.[6] By contrast, *Die Schwäne* questions the terms of competitive public memory in contemporary Germany by foregrounding the active presence and participation of migrants from Turkey in Berlin's past. In the process, it challenges those narratives that inscribe an ethnically uniform national body that incorporates East and West Germans while largely excluding non-German migrants and their descendants.

Yet even as the opening monologue works to pluralize prevailing representations of Berlin's history, its references to the past are both oblique and highly personalized. On the one hand, the play does not situate the journalist's words within any overt exposition of the material, social, and geopolitical circumstances of Mert's demise. Instead, the work of contextualizing the event is left to the play's program and promotional materials as well as to the press coverage that accompanied performances in 2009, 2010, and 2011. On the other hand, the opening monologue addresses dominant representations of local and national history through the details of one individual's life and death. Once again, this approach resonates with the aesthetic strategies employed in the rest of the play, which intervenes in German public discourse by presenting stylized "first-person" accounts of migrant experience that build on archival research and biographical interviews with people of Turkish backgrounds.[7] For this reason, *Die Schwäne* also represents an intriguing foray into the realm of "cultural intimacy," that sphere of social engagement where ostensibly "private" and often carefully guarded dimensions of a group's life are staged for wider public consumption. As anthropologist Michael Herzfeld notes, cultural intimacy is a sphere of ambivalent emotions, for it entails "the recognition of those aspects of cultural identity that are considered a source of external embarrassment but that nonetheless provide insiders with their assurance of common sociality."[8]

Die Schwäne thematizes a number of such sore points in Turkish migrant life, including illicit drug commerce, male sexual privilege, the emotional toll of patriarchy, and gendered violence. It does so in a fashion that may elicit "rueful self-recognition" from those spectators who can appreciate its knowing evocation of migrant existence in a divided and later unified city.[9] In staging some of the intimate dimensions of Turkish migrant life, however, the play risks affirming some reductive and derogatory representations of Germany's largest minority group. I accordingly assess the varied ways that the play's narratives both undercut and reinscribe prevailing idioms of national and ethnoracial difference. Ironically, such reinscription occurs even when *Die Schwäne* employs cross-ethnic impersonation and other estrangement techniques that aim to disrupt spectators' taken-for-granted conceptions of ethnicity, race, and gender. In the case of the opening monologue, it is telling that the child's words are delivered by a character, the journalist, who differs from the child in terms of his age and presumed ethnic background. Indeed, while the monologue positions the child as a member of a Turkish migrant family, the casting of Hendrik Arnst (in keeping with naturalistic theatrical conventions that equate the actor and the role) invites the audience to interpret the journalist as a nonimmigrant German man.[10]

This chapter begins by situating *Die Schwäne* within the work of the Ballhaus Naunynstrasse, the critically acclaimed Kreuzberg theatre that commissioned Mican's play and staged its performances in Berlin. The play readily accords with the theater's larger political project, which seeks to pluralize Germany's public cultural landscape, even as it partially departs from the venue's commitment to "documentary theater." I then turn to an analysis of the play in order to trace the ambivalent implications of its multidirectional memory work. On a number of fronts, *Die Schwäne* offers a compelling rejoinder to those narratives that frame German division and unification as matters that only concern (nonimmigrant) East and West Germans. Yet the intimacy of its portrayals also threatens to reinstate some of the very representations that support exclusionary ethnic definitions of the German nation. In the end, I argue, *Die Schwäne* illuminates both the potentials and the pitfalls of public cultural projects that seek to incorporate people of migrant backgrounds into majority German history and memory. Such efforts to "migrate into other pasts" do not inevitably result in more inclusive understandings of national belonging.[11]

PRODUCING POSTMIGRANT CULTURE

The Ballhaus Naunynstrasse is located in a former dance and meeting hall that was built on the eponymous street in Kreuzberg in 1863. The premises survived World War II with little damage, and after historical preservationists blocked the building's demolition in the early 1970s, the hall underwent a restoration, became the property of the Kreuzberg District Office, and operated in the ensuing years as a cultural center, also known as the Ballhaus Naunynstrasse, under the management of the Kreuzberg Art Office. In 2008, the Ballhaus was reconceived as a "translocal theater" that aimed to promote "artists of primarily migrant and postmigrant backgrounds."[12] The immediate intellectual and artistic impetus for the new project came from the Turkish-born theater producer Shermin Langhoff, but it received further support from KulturSPRÜNGE, a network of artists, scholars, and activists established in 2003 to encourage politically engaged cultural production among migrants and postmigrants in Germany.[13] Although the Ballhaus is part of the "free scene" outside Germany's network of official city and state theaters, it has managed to build significant ties with district-, state-, and federal-level governments in Berlin as well as with some European institutions. The theater itself is affiliated with the district of Friedrichshain-Kreuzberg, and KulturSPRÜNGE, which acts as the district government's cooperating partner, has received significant funding from Berlin's Senate Office for Cultural Affairs, the Federal Culture Foundation, the EU Culture Programme, and other sources.

Given the theater's unusual degree of governmental support, it is important to locate the Ballhaus within Berlin's larger landscape of state-sponsored cultural production. As anthropologist Kira Kosnick has noted, this landscape is defined by a sharp divide between "*Kultur* in the singular"—the realm of the "high" performing and fine arts in the Western tradition—and "*Kulturen* in the plural"—the realm of ethnic diversity associated with cultural groups from non-Western contexts.[14] Cultural institutions within these two domains are generally expected to pursue different social and political objectives, and they receive widely divergent recognition and funding from government agencies at the district/communal, state, and federal levels. Many of the institutions associated with singular German *Kultur*—including Berlin's most prominent theaters, operas, orchestras, and museums—are supposed to represent the artistic vibrancy of the city and the nation on the global stage, and many receive generous funding from state and federal agencies. On the other hand, institutions associated with plural ethnic *Kulturen*—particularly neighborhood associations, youth centers, and other local organizations in districts like Kreuzberg, Wedding, and Neukölln—are commonly expected to foster social harmony and cohesion rather than artistic achievement per se, and they must often compete fiercely for the scant funding available from district agencies. The result is a bifurcated and hierarchical terrain in which "high cultural" institutions tend to occupy a position of primacy while migrant and postmigrant producers are most often relegated to the symbolic and economic margins. Within this context, most artists of Turkish and other backgrounds only receive public recognition and state funding when their work can be framed as an expression of ethnocultural difference and multiculturalist sensibility.

The Ballhaus Naunynstrasse, located at the intersection of *Kultur* and *Kulturen,* aims to interrogate and reconfigure the terms of artistic production in Germany. This much is already implied by the name of the theater's supporting organization, KulturSPRÜNGE, which suggests an effort to "crack," to "leap" past or beyond, prevailing conceptions of "culture" in the German public sphere. Such an impulse is articulated even more forcefully in the group's online mission statement:

> Artistic creation without reflection and discursive engagement is unthinkable. And a critique of an ethnic, national, and culturally essentialist understanding of art is even more urgent. The discourses and practices of the majority society, which reduce the creation of postmigrant artists to their putative origins or attempt to explain it in sociocultural terms as an aspect of their integration, are long-standing forms of exclusion. This exclusion is to be found not just within the majority society, but in migrant contexts as well; the ascriptions of others (*Fremdzuschreibung*) and the ethnicization of the self (*Selbstethnifizierung*) go hand-in-hand. The approach adopted by KulturSPRÜNGE is to intervene in this complex realm in order to define and shape it differently.[15]

As the language of this passage indicates, the organization draws on recent academic and activist critiques to challenge commonplace presumptions of German societal homogeneity and cultural purity. These presumptions, which the group contends are as prevalent in "art" as in other domains of "majority society," position people of migrant and postmigrant backgrounds as enduringly other in a fashion that places them at the edges, if not beyond the bounds, of the German nation. At best, they constitute external elements that must be "integrated," via artistic and other means, into an already established and intact national whole. KulturSPRÜNGE also implicitly takes issue with those artists of migrant backgrounds who reinscribe dominant public conceptions by contributing, wittingly or unwittingly, to their own ethnicization.

In adopting a pointedly critical stance on essentialist notions of nation and culture, KulturSPRÜNGE and the Ballhaus Naunynstrasse are similar to another prominent Berlin institution, the House of World Cultures. However, the house emphasizes the fluidity of global cultural production through exhibitions that focus almost exclusively on artists from outside Europe and the "Western world."[16] By contrast, the Ballhaus Naunynstrasse seeks to expand prevailing notions of German culture and history by showcasing the work of migrant artists who were raised and/or educated in Germany. *Die Schwäne*'s writer and director, Hakan Savaş Mican, is a case in point. Although they were born in Germany, Mican and his siblings were raised in Turkey by a grandmother and an aunt while visiting their parents, who continued to live and work in Berlin, during their summer vacations. After finishing high school in Turkey, Mican returned to Berlin, where he completed a degree in architecture at the Technical University, worked as a journalist at Radio Multikulti, and took film coursework at the German Film and Television Academy. It was during the course of his film studies that Mican began, as a self-declared autodidact, to work in the theater.[17] His first play, *Der Besuch* (*The Visit*), debuted at the Ballhaus in 2008, and since then he has written and/or directed seven dramatic productions at the theater and contributed to several other projects.

Perhaps the Ballhaus Naunynstrasse's most pointed intervention in the German public sphere, however, is related to a term that I have employed up to now without comment: postmigrant. A variety of minority intellectuals, artists, and activists have recently embraced this concept as a novel designation for people born and raised in Germany who descend from migrant parents and grandparents. Shermin Langhoff has played a leading role in this effort by framing the Ballhaus Naunynstrasse as a "postmigrant theater." As she noted in one recent interview, she and her colleagues adopted the term in order to evoke "the histories and perspectives of those who did not migrate themselves, but who bring along their migration background as personal knowledge and collective memory."[18] In its more politicized usage, the concept constitutes a tacit assertion of belonging: postmigrants are not new arrivals, as "migrant" and "immigrant" commonly imply, but Germans whose claims to national membership—despite their "atypical" names, physiognomies, and cultural affinities—are as valid as those of "natives."[19] Indeed, "postmigrant" is frequently used to highlight the exclusionary implications not simply of terms like *Fremde* (stranger) and *Ausländer* (foreigner) that are now widely regarded as derogatory, but also of concepts like *Mitbürger* (co-citizen) and *Einwanderer* (immigrant) that are ostensibly more neutral if not progressive.[20]

Langhoff's emphasis on personal knowledge and collective memory as defining aspects of postmigrant subjectivity is reflected in the Ballhaus Naunynstrasse's production practices: many of the plays staged by the theater incorporate local archival research, interviews, and artists' personal reminiscences. By foregrounding the diversity of postmigrants' quotidian experiences and perceptions, these techniques of dramatic assemblage endow the productions with a sense of sociological authority and verisimilitude, undercut tired representations of Turkish otherness, and advance novel claims for inclusion. Yet even as *Die Schwäne* is similar to other Ballhaus plays to the degree that it draws on a range of archival and biographical materials, it differs from some of the theater's other productions in that it cannot be easily characterized as "documentary theater."[21] For rather than adopting realist conventions that locate the dramatic action in readily delineated characters and clearly defined social settings, Mican's play adopts a highly mediated, elliptical, associative mode of address that lends the dramatic action a mythic or dreamlike quality. Thus, although the play refers to the realities of migrant existence in Berlin before and after the Wall, the connections it draws with the historical context require spectators to engage in a great deal of imaginative work.

REMEMBERING MIGRATION IN THE DIVIDED CITY

Several aspects of staging, costume, and script contribute to *Die Schwäne vom Schlachthof*'s surreal character. The play is performed on a minimalist set dominated by a spare, downward-sloping white ramp flanked on the left and right sides by a series of square columns. Different social settings are evoked not by realistic stage designs and elaborate scene changes, but by suggestive shifts in lighting, onstage musical performances, and a few handheld props (e.g., a remote control, a tulip-shaped tea glass, several slices of white bread, a blue sweater, a garish wig). In some instances, the props index social settings and ethnic affiliations in conventional ways: the remote control signifies the television on which one group of migrant youth watches East German TV shows, while the tea glass identifies one character as a Turkish migrant father. In others, the props stand in for rather different material objects and social worlds: the slices of white bread represent socialist reference works sanctioned by the East German party-state, while the blue sweater and wig symbolize the headscarf and other religious practices adopted by an East German convert to Islam. In addition, the six actors—three of Turkish migrant backgrounds, three of the nonimmigrant majority—wear clothing that evokes Berlin at the end of the city's division but does not mark them as "ethnic" in any stereotypical way. Moreover, the actors do not change attire even when they adopt multiple roles and move fluidly across ethnic and gender boundaries. Finally, there is a noteworthy doubling and involution of names: two of the four central protagonists are named Çetin while the other two, one male and one female, are named Cengaver.[22] Taken together, these elements work to unsettle the biographical, ethnic, gendered, and other coordinates that spectators might use to locate particular characters within the social field of Berlin before and after unification.

The play's dreamlike dimensions are further thematized in the journalist's second monologue, which immediately follows the narrative from the child's perspective. Whereas the journalist had previously opened and closed a toy watch as he spoke, one of the other performers now takes it from him and leaves the stage. After a brief pause, the journalist proceeds to address the audience in what seems to be "his own" voice:

Are you familiar with those dreams where you don't know whether you are having them just now, whether you had them long ago, or whether you will never have them? I have a dream that I've had for a very long time, during the day as well: I dream of four children. Or rather of four swans. Or of strange animals, like in a fairy-tale film. They have the head of a child and the body of a swan. Something like a sphinx. But not a lion, rather a swan. They swim on the Spree next to the other swans.[23]

The journalist then describes how he dreams of standing on a riverbank as one of the swan children, with the face of a five- or six-year-old boy, cautiously flies out of the water to eat dry bread from his hand before sliding back into the river. Overcome by the creature's beauty, the journalist gives him a name—Jeremy—and calls after him in longing and desperation.

The fantastical narrative of the swan children marks another moment when the play simultaneously alludes to, reworks, and displaces the historical past. Popular recollections and contemporaneous photographs attest to the fact that swans used to gather beside the Gröbenufer, which offered passersby a convenient spot to feed them.[24] Once again, Mican's play does not explicitly note these circumstances, although spectators might be able to relate the journalist's narrative to personal or familial recollections. The number of swan children noted by the journalist—four—can also be interpreted as an implicit reference to the four boys who drowned near the Gröbenufer in the late 1960s and early 1970s.[25]

The strangeness of the scene is further heightened by a lack of clarity concerning the relationship of the journalist's dream to the rest of the play. In particular, the connection between the first and the second monologues is at first underdetermined: is Jeremy the child whose words are spoken by the journalist? This linkage, initially implied only by the juxtaposition of the two narratives, is confirmed later in the play, when a brief scene depicts Jeremy's parents arriving in East Berlin in order to identify their drowned son's body.[26] This scene solidifies the positioning of Jeremy and his parents as a Turkish migrant family, since the mother and father require a Turkish-German translator to engage with the East German authorities. Nevertheless, the name Jeremy does not readily mark the boy as a member of a Turkish migrant family—or, for that matter, a nonimmigrant majority family—that might have lived in Kreuzberg in the 1970s. Once again, the name partially blurs his relationship with the ethnoracial group that was (and still is) most commonly associated with the neighborhood. Thus, even as the play suggests links with historical circumstances, it also has a highly refracted quality: it is as if we are watching "a fairy-tale film" of postwar migration and division, not an ostensibly transparent documentary account.

As the play unfolds, it becomes evident that the journalist's monologues function as a framing device for the four quasi-biographical narratives at the heart of the play. All of these narratives tell intimate stories that engage with Berlin's "official history" by personalizing documented events and situating them within the protagonists' everyday lives. For example, the first of these stories, "Wall Children," depicts the life of a boy named Cengaver as he grows up in Kreuzberg in the 1970s and 1980s. Among other finely drawn details, Cengaver recalls the hours his family spent watching Turkish melodramas and Italian spaghetti westerns on videotape; his friends' amazement at the rapid demolition of old tenement buildings; and the surprising comfort he took in the Hungarian, Czech, and Soviet shows on East German television. These latter broadcasts leave him with an ironically favorable impression of the Eastern Bloc: "they have it pretty good over there, the *Ossis*," Cengaver comments. "I'd really like to go there sometime."[27] This unforeseen affinity with mass-mediated images of socialist Eastern Europe contrasts sharply with the dismay he feels at the arrival of actual East Germans in Kreuzberg after the fall of the Wall: "We stood there on the corner and stared at them as they picked up their 100 DM greeting money [*Begrüssungsgeld*], and they stared back. That was my first contact with Ossis. ... We had a piece of home [*ein Stück Heimat*] here in Kreuzberg, and it was occupied by foreigners."[28] In this moment of multidirectional remembrance, Cengaver stakes a pointed claim to belonging that appropriates and recodes prevailing conceptions of who the resident "natives" are and who the travelling "strangers" are.

Because the moments of contact between the quasi-biographical narratives and more canonical accounts of Berlin's past are spare and fleeting, spectators must make a concerted effort to situate the former within familiar geographical, temporal, and discursive frameworks. Yet, despite its novel perspective and varied displacement techniques, Cengaver's story still fits relatively easily into the conventional narrative of Kreuzberg as a classic migrant enclave, the "Little Istanbul" that draws thousands of Turkish "guest workers." By contrast, the other narratives present more serious challenges to dominant versions of Berlin history and memory. The second story, "Letters from No Man's Land," recounts the life of a young female leftist, also named Cengaver, who flees Izmir after being arrested for her role in a school boycott and seeks to live out her socialist principles in East Berlin. The third story, "The Love of the Chameleon," traces the jagged course of a romantic relationship between a postmigrant man named Çetin and an East German woman. After the woman unexpectedly becomes pregnant, she agrees to marry Çetin and becomes an ardent convert to Islam, although she later abandons both the faith and the marriage, to Çetin's

chagrin. Finally, the fourth story, "The Empire of Bananas," charts the trib-
ulations of another young man named Çetin, who grows up in the Anatolian
countryside, marries a cousin named Cengaver and, at his father's behest,
migrates to Berlin. Çetin and his wife eventually open a chain of grocery
stores and fast-food restaurants in the former East Germany, but their marriage disintegrates after the revelation of Cengaver's infidelity.

Each of the last three stories stands in an uneasy relationship with dominant accounts of postwar Berlin and the role that migrants from Turkey
have played in it. "Letters from No Man's Land" upsets the commonsense
equation of Turkish migrants and "guest workers" by pointing to alternative motivations (the desire to further one's political commitments) and des-
tinations (East Berlin, not West Germany). "The Love of the Chameleon"
disrupts the usual conflation of ethnicity and religion by portraying Islam
as a faith to which nonimmigrant Germans—not just migrants from Turkey
and other Muslim-majority countries—might devote themselves. And "The
Empire of Bananas" situates migration to Germany within a constellation
of familial relations and gendered expectations that are commonly stig-
matized—if not entirely ignored—in German public discourse. Despite the
oblique nature of its remembrance, then, *Die Schwäne* interweaves memories
of migration, division, and unification in ways that unsettle a number of
hackneyed portrayals of essentialized difference. This aspect of the play,
in keeping with the larger oeuvre of the Ballhaus, is commonly noted in
mass-media commentary: one review remarked that *Die Schwäne* "flatly
rejects the clichés held by both German Turks and German Germans,"
while another profile praised the theater's ability to "parody [the usual
stereotypes], take them to extremes, and turn them around in funny and
humane ways."[29]

Such provocative engagement is not without its risks, however, for it can
inadvertently affirm the very representations it aims to undermine. In the
case of *Die Schwäne,* this point pertains most directly to the strained relationship between the protagonist Çetin and his father Ali in "The Empire
of Bananas." The play depicts Ali as a religiously devout but emotionally
distant father who leaves Çetin in Turkey while he works in Germany; he
only returns to his home village for one week each year to "drive his Opel
Commodore from door to door and hand out presents."[30] Indeed, Ali does
not appear to take interest in his son until after arranging Çetin's marriage,
as a sixteen-year-old, to his cousin Cengaver. It is then that Ali asks Çetin
for the bed-sheet from the wedding night so that he can hang it outside the
family home and show that he, the father, "has taken a virgin for his son."
When Ali discovers that the bed-sheet is wet, he initially assumes that Çetin
must have sweat a great deal during the couple's first sexual encounter, and

he takes pride in the thought that Çetin, like his father, is "a real man."[31] Ali is then appalled to learn that the sheet is wet not because of his son's sexual prowess, but because Çetin wet the bed during the wedding night. Ali immediately returns to Germany and does not interact with Çetin and Cengaver until violence between leftists and right-wing nationalists (which wracked Turkey throughout the 1970s) prompts him to bring the young couple to Germany. It is in the years after Çetin and Cengaver's migration that they open a grocery store in Neukölln and, after the Wall falls, expand their business into the former East Germany. Çetin is enormously pleased by their success, but his father punctures his happiness with the accusation that Cengaver is sleeping with their employees. Ali offers to make arrangements for Cengaver's murder, and he chastises Çetin for being a "softie" (*Weichei*) and a "donkey" (*Esel*) when his son balks at the proposal.[32] When Çetin later confronts Cengaver, she confirms his suspicions but justifies her infidelity by pointing to her entrepreneurial skills and Çetin's own escapades with prostitutes. In an effort to restore his integrity and reputation, Çetin has Cengaver killed.

Mican has repeatedly stated, in my communication with him and in other venues, that the quasi-biographical narratives recounted in *Die Schwäne* are based in part on interviews he conducted with people of Turkish backgrounds. Thus, as I have already noted, a good deal of their imputed authority rests in their claim to true-to-life credibility. I do not wish to question the veracity of Mican's statements or, for that matter, the "accuracy" of the life-historical material on which the play is based. In fact, I suspect that a fair number of people of Turkish backgrounds in contemporary Germany could point to similarities between the story narrated in "The Empire of Bananas" and aspects of either their own lives or those of their acquaintances. Yet even as many migrants and postmigrants would acknowledge the existence of paternal distance, arranged (cousin) marriage, and gendered violence, many would also question the notion that these phenomena are somehow typical of people from Turkey and therefore embody a monolithic "Turkish culture." Indeed, for many people of Turkish backgrounds, such a claim would be as problematic if it were uttered by a fellow migrant or postmigrant as it would be if it were expressed by a nonimmigrant German.

Objections of this nature are to my mind entirely understandable and legitimate. Yet they also articulate, with remarkable precision, the mix of recognition and pained sensitivity highlighted by the concept of cultural intimacy. In this case, "The Empire of Bananas" readily recalls the heated debates over patriarchal authority, coerced marriage, and "honor killing" among migrants from Turkey that have unfolded in Germany over the past fifteen years, especially in the wake of the 2005 murder of Hatun Sürücü.

As anthropologist Katherine Pratt Ewing observes, a considerable portion of both the German- and the Turkish-language press coverage surrounding Sürücü's death was inclined to portray this and other purported honor killings as the enactment of a traditional Turkish Muslim culture that is entirely incompatible with liberal political commitments to gender equality and individual self-determination.[33] Compared with such sensationalist and generalizing accounts, *Die Schwäne* is noteworthy for its attention to the emotional burdens of patriarchy not simply for women like Cengaver, but for men like Çetin as well. One could even read the play as a critical commentary on the familial pressures that might impel men to commit lethal acts of violence against female kin. Nevertheless, this portion of *Die Schwäne* threatens to reinforce many of the stereotypical representations that have underwritten the stigmatization of migrants from Turkey and their descendants. In this regard, it is revealing that virtually every review of *Die Schwäne* that I have read has studiously avoided reference to this aspect of the play.

THE PARADOX OF "AUTHENTICITY"

This chapter has sought to highlight the ways that *Die Schwäne vom Schlachthof* reorients prevailing histories of postwar Berlin by dramatizing migrant and postmigrant perspectives on the city's past. Further, it underscores the play's effort to recast authoritative representations of the postwar era through narratives that are simultaneously oblique, dreamlike, and highly personalized. As it stages the layered intersections of Cold War division and postwar labor migration, *Die Schwäne* illustrates the extent to which multidirectional memory practices can challenge and revise dominant conceptions of German nationhood. Yet my analysis also draws attention to the ambivalent cultural intimacy the play may engender: even as it seeks to pluralize Berlin's past, it can inadvertently reinstate those representations of Turkish migrants that have so often underwritten their exclusion.

The crux of these complexities may lie in the Ballhaus Naunynstrasse's recourse to archival research, life history, and personal reminiscence as crucial elements of its cultural production. Such source material lends the theater's performances the aura of verisimilitude, but it also positions the depicted experiences and perspectives as "authentic" expressions of migrant and postmigrant sensibility. As one perceptive commentary noted:

> [The reliance on archival and biographical material] is both an advantage and
> a curse for the new postmigrant theater because it ties the believability of the

stories to the authenticity of the speakers. That is precisely what many actors, for example, do not want. They want to be able to perform all roles. They strive to make a label like "with migration background" (*mit Migrationshintergrund*) superfluous. But as long as so many clichés are layered over the manifold reality, the positioning as an "authentic speaker" remains necessary. A theater like the Ballhaus Naunynstrasse must live with this paradox: to respond to the demand for stories "with a migration background" while also being reduced to it.[34]

In the end, *Die Schwäne* and other Ballhaus plays remain entangled in the very national and ethnoracial categories they would like to question and transcend.

Yet even if it cannot entirely escape the processes of ethnicization that KulturSPRÜNGE decries, the theater nevertheless offers an important response to a narrowly ethnic definition of the German nation, one that remains entrenched in many public accounts of the country's division, unification, and present state of affairs. For this reason, it would be highly uncharitable to discount *Die Schwäne* and other Ballhaus plays as failed aesthetic-political projects or mere historical revisionism. Precisely because they braid divergent pasts together in arresting ways, they also envision novel possible futures for people of Turkish backgrounds and, ultimately, for all participants in German life.

Jeffrey Jurgens teaches at Bard College, where he is Fellow for Anthropology and Social Theory at the Bard Prison Initiative and Academic Co-director of the Consortium for the Liberal Arts in Prison. He specializes in topics related to migration, citizenship, public memory, urban space, and secularism among migrants and postmigrants from Turkey in Berlin. Jurgens has received grants from the National Science Foundation, the IIE Fulbright program, and the Berlin Program for Advanced German and European Studies. His publications have appeared in *Transit, Türkisch-deutsche Studien Jahrbuch,* and *Walls, Borders, Boundaries,* among other journals and edited volumes.

NOTES

1. Hakan Savaş Mican, *Die Schwäne vom Schlachthof,* Ballhaus Naunynstrasse, Berlin, 2. I quote from the script of the March 2010 restaging of the play. The initial version, first performed in 2009, begins somewhat differently. All translations from German are my own. I would like to thank Irit Dekel, Bernhard Forchtner, and the other participants in the Civil Society, Memory, and Diversity Colloquium at the Humboldt University Berlin for their stimulating

responses to my initial presentation of this material. I would also like to extend my appreciation to Megan Callaghan, who read the first version of this chapter with her usual care and thoughtfulness.

2. Hans-Hermann Hertle and Maria Nooke, *Die Todesopfer an der Berliner Mauer 1961–1989: Ein biographisches Handbuch* (Berlin, 2009). See also the entries on the children at "Chronicle of the Wall" (*Chronik der Mauer,* http://www.chronik-der-mauder.de). The fact that all of the drowning victims were boys is not mere coincidence, but can instead be traced to gendered patterns of child-rearing that allow boys more license than girls to engage in adventurous and dangerous play. Such patterns cut across national and ethnic differences and cannot be attributed to any reified "culture" or "cultural background."

3. Jeffrey Jurgens, "'A Wall Victim from the West': Migration, German Division, and Multidirectional Memory in Kreuzberg," *Transit* 8, no. 2 (2013): 1–23.

4. Michael Rothberg, *Multidirectional Memory: Remembering the Holocaust in the Age of Decolonization* (Stanford, CA, 2009), 11.

5. Ibid., 1–7.

6. Brian Ladd, *The Ghosts of Berlin: Confronting German History in the Urban Landscape* (Chicago, 1997), 169.

7. In this respect, the play can be loosely compared with Feridun Zaimoğlu's novel *Kanak Sprak,* which is also reportedly based on research the author conducted with young men of Turkish backgrounds. Yet unlike Zaimoğlu's novel, which formulated a synthetic vernacular that creatively reworked the German language, *Die Schwäne* employs standardized varieties of German and Turkish. The play's inventiveness lies not in its language, but in its deliberately multidirectional recollection of Berlin's past. See Feridun Zaimoğlu, *Kanak Sprak: 24 Mißtöne vom Rande der Gesellschaft* (Hamburg, 1995); Yasemin Yıldız, *Beyond the Mother Tongue: The Postmonolingual Condition* (New York, 2012), 169–201.

8. Michael Herzfeld, *Cultural Intimacy: Social Poetics in the Nation-State* (New York, 1997), 3.

9. Ibid., 6.

10. This instance of cross-ethnic transposition locates the opening monologue in the tradition of "ethnic drag," the term Katrin Sieg has used to characterize performances of impersonation across ethnoracial lines. Many German theater artists, particularly those in leftist and feminist circles, have created intentional "misfits" between performers and characters in an effort to disrupt the seeming naturalness of essentialized ethnic, racial, and gender categories. In keeping with Brechtian notions of estrangement, these disjunctions are supposed to stimulate spectators' critical reflection and open previously self-evident categories to questioning and transformation. See Katrin Sieg, *Ethnic Drag: Performing Race, Nation, Sexuality in West Germany* (Ann Arbor, MI, 2002); Bertholt Brecht, "Alienation Effects in Chinese Acting," in *Brecht on Theatre: The Development of an Aesthetic,* ed. John Willett (New York, 1964), 91–99.

11. Andreas Huyssen, "Diaspora and Nation: Migration into Other Pasts," *New German Critique* 88 (2003): 147–64.

12. Ballhaus Naunynstrasse, www.ballhausnaunynstrasse.de/haus.

13. KulturSPRÜNGE, http://www.kulturspruenge.net/de/03/0301.html.

14. Kira Kosnick, *Migrant Media: Turkish Broadcasting and Multicultural Politics in Berlin* (Bloomington, IN, 2007), 81–103. Kosnick's singular/plural distinction aligns partially but not completely with the division drawn earlier between "official" city and state institutions and the "free scene." To be sure, almost all of Berlin's flagship cultural venues fit comfortably in the realm of *"Kultur* in the singular,"* and many of the institutions that embody *"Kulturen* in the plural" can be located in the alternative domain. Nevertheless, the House of World Cultures, which receives much of its funding from the federal government, espouses a distinctly multiculturalist ethos, while many institutions within the free scene dedicate themselves to traditionally Western genres of artistic production.

15. KulturSPRÜNGE.

16. Kosnick, *Migrant Media,* 89–92.

17. Hakan Savaş Mican, personal communication, 2011.

18. Bundeszentrale für politische Bildung, "Die Herkunft spielt keine Rolle— 'Postmigrantisches' Theater im Ballhaus Naunynstraße: Interview mit Shermin Langhoff," 10 March 2011, http://www.bpb.de/gesellschaft/kultur/ kulturelle-bildung/60135/interview-mit-shermin-langhoff.

19. Naika Foroutan, "Neue Deutsche, Postmigranten und Bildungs-Identitäten: Wer gehört zum neuen Deutschland?," *Aus Politik und Zeitgeschichte* 46–47 (2010): 9–15.

20. Fatima El-Tayeb, *European Others: Queering Ethnicity in Postnational Europe* (Minneapolis, MN, 2011); Ruth Mandel, *Cosmopolitan Anxieties: Turkish Challenges to Citizenship and Belonging in Germany* (Durham, NC, 2008), 126–27.

21. Katrin Sieg, "Class of 1989: Who Made Good and Who Dropped Out of German History? Postmigrant Documentary Theater in Berlin," in *The German Wall: Fallout in Europe,* ed. Marc Silberman (New York, 2011), 165–83.

22. The cross-gender use of Cengaver may or may not entail an inversion of normative naming practices. Cengaver is translated as "the fighter" *(der Kämpfer)* in *Die Schwäne,* and one female character comments that her father gave her that name because he was hoping for a son. On the other hand, several of my Turkish-speaking acquaintances do not regard Cengaver as a conventionally masculine name, and they note that a number of Turkish names are commonly given to both boys and girls.

23. Mican, *Die Schwäne,* 2.

24. The archives of the Bundesbeauftragte für Stasi-Unterlagen (BStU) contain several photographs of swans in the immediate vicinity of the Gröbenufer. See, for instance, MfS HA I 5861 Bild 1/50. I thank Detlef Krenz for drawing my attention to these images.

25. The fifth, Siegfried Kroboth, drowned near the Brommy Bridge, about a third of a mile northwest of the Gröbenufer.

26. Mican, *Die Schwäne,* 16–17.

27. Ibid., 4. *Ossi* is the colloquial term for (former) East Germans. Interestingly, it only gained prominence in German public discourse after the country's unification. Cengaver, however, uses the word at a moment when the Wall still divides East and West Berlin.

28. Ibid., 5. Cengaver uses *Fremdlinge* to designate the East German "foreigners," a word that recalls the more familiar *Ausländer* while also rendering that term strange by its very absence.

29. Michaela Schlagenwerth, "Die ertrunkenen Kinder," *Berliner Zeitung,* 23 November 2009; Peter Laudenbach, "Wir sind kein Migranten-Stadl," *Süddeutsche Zeitung,* 23 February 2011.

30. Mican, *Die Schwäne,* 24.

31. Ibid., 25.

32. Ibid., 28.

33. Katherine Pratt Ewing, *Stolen Honor: Stigmatizing Muslim Men in Berlin* (Stanford, CA, 2008), 151–79.

34. Katrin Bettina Müller, "Jenseits des Ghetto-Mainstreams," *die tageszeitung,* 11 January 2011.

SELECTED BIBLIOGRAPHY

Ewing, Katherine Pratt. *Stolen Honor: Stigmatizing Muslim Men in Berlin*. Stanford, CA, 2008.

Herzfeld, Michael. *Cultural Intimacy: Social Poetics in the Nation-State*. New York, 1997.

Jurgens, Jeffrey. "'A Wall Victim from the West': Migration, German Division, and Multidirectional Memory in Kreuzberg." *Transit* 8, no. 2 (2013): 1–23.

Kosnick, Kira. *Migrant Media: Turkish Broadcasting and Multicultural Politics in Berlin*. Bloomington, IN, 2007.

Rothberg, Michael. *Multidirectional Memory: Remembering the Holocaust in the Age of Decolonization*. Stanford, CA, 2009.

Sieg, Katrin. "Class of 1989: Who Made Good and Who Dropped Out of German History? Postmigrant Documentary Theater in Berlin." *The German Wall: Fallout in Europe,* edited by Marc Silberman, 165–183. New York, 2011.

———. *Ethnic Drag: Performing Race, Nation, Sexuality in West Germany*. Ann Arbor, MI, 2002.

Part IV

Global Implications

Chapter 12

Inventing the German Film as Foreign Film

The Origins of a Fraught Transatlantic Exchange

Sara F Hall

Filmmakers, cinephiles, and critics have long treated German film as coalescent with the modern German state, its politics, and the values and ideas of its people. To many, the publication of Siegfried Kracauer's *From Caligari to Hitler: A Psychological History of the German Film* in 1947 stands as the most important milestone in the development of the idea that German films are expressive of a unique national mentality. Yet the notion of a specific alignment between the German nation and its cinematic output predates World War II and the Holocaust and thus precedes certain assumptions and conclusions about the German character that emerged from those events in particular.[1] If we step back from Kracauer's study to trace the earlier origins of the category of the "German film," we see that it is World War I, not World War II, which functioned as the watershed event. A cultural discourse that preexisted Kracauer's study produced its own image of a distinctly German film—albeit one also born of a conflicted appreciation for the enduring value of German culture despite qualms about its association with a belligerent state and the purportedly complicit individuals in it. For over one hundred years, the ambivalent notion of a "German film" has been reconstructed and revised to serve multiple interrelated purposes, including the German film industry's laying claim to a piece of the US market and Hollywood's efforts to profit from ticket sales on both sides of the Atlantic.

This essay seeks to locate more precisely the emergence of that complex transatlantic exchange.

INVESTIGATING KRACAUER'S PREMISE

Kracauer argues in *From Caligari to Hitler* that because movies are the product of a collective creative process, because they address an anonymous multitude, and because they are capable of scanning an entire visible world, "The films of a nation reflect its mentality in a more direct way than other artistic media" and "reflect ... psychological dispositions—those deep layers of collective mentality which extend more or less below the dimension of consciousness."[2] His line of reasoning downplays a focus on the statistical popularity of individual films in favor of attention to the prevalence of certain pictorial and narrative motifs across not only popular, but also unpopular and B-grade, movies. He attributes the omnipresence of specific motifs to their capacity to express the inner urges of the German people, an attribution that in 1947 bore condemnation adherent to the events of World War II and the Holocaust. What Kracauer's analysis leaves out is the fact that the producers of the unpopular and B-grade movies were participating in the same commercial system as the producers of films that were more successful—and that systems of production and reception were international in scope.[3]

Writing from exile in New York and working with the limited source material available to him, Kracauer was attuned to international reception, but not necessarily to the key role that it might have played in decisions made on the production end. He begins his book by invoking the revelatory power of foreign press notices, granting them the authority to judge what German viewers might themselves be too close to recognize. The opening lines of his introduction recall how international reviews of *The Cabinet of Dr Caligari,* one of the first films to break the Allies' boycott against German films, conveyed a combination of admiration and extreme distaste, the latter coming from critics who saw in the film an expression of the macabre, sinister, and morbid sides of the German soul.[4] Kracauer goes on to cite both positive and negative American reviews intermittently, but rarely comments on what the reviews might say about the relationship between German films and American audiences in particular. He attributes the seemingly unlikely positive reception of Ernst Lubitsch's costume dramas toward the end of 1920 to a specifically Wilsonian American urge to see history represented as the work of "unscrupulous wire-pullers."[5] He also invokes the views of American reviewers to reinforce the significance of specific motifs in their historical context. All of these citations skirt around the possibility that the prospect of positive reception in the United States might have influenced the business and creative choices made by German producers. Readers are left to wonder whether and at what point the promise of American reception would have begun to factor into production decisions, and what the significance of those decisions would have been.

It is clear to historians now that films imported to Germany from the United States and elsewhere would have colored the tastes and expectations of domestic audiences, thus impacting domestic production practices.[6] But that fact is obscured by Kracauer. Just a little farther into the introduction, Kracauer asserts that the allegedly "Americanized" German films produced after 1924, "were in fact true expressions of contemporaneous German life" and that they, too, "are fully understandable only in relation to the actual psychological pattern of this nation."[7] Such an argument does not explain why the high-budget studio productions of the mid 1920s were esteemed as the right product for their audiences or why an internationally respected critic such as Paul Rotha, writing in England in 1930 and cited by Kracauer in the passage under discussion, would have dismissed the films influenced by American production practices and aesthetics as not sufficiently representative of German cinema of the era. Nor does it recognize the possibility that the prospect of cultivating a US audience might have been at play before or during the production of German films.[8] It is my goal in this chapter to locate the earlier origins of a commercial and cultural practice that defined the idea of a German film relative to the policies and engagements of the German state, a premise on which much of the subsequent study of a German national cinema is founded. In what follows, I trace the institutional origins of a rhetoric of alternating condemnation and redemption in the reception of German films in the United States prior to Kracauer's influential articulation of the trajectory *From Caligari to Hitler.*

Most discussions of German cinema as a site for overcoming a negative national history and for creating international understanding center on the second half of the twentieth century and explore the possibility of a critical aesthetics that is legible and meaningful across national borders. This chapter contributes to that discussion without assuming that the dialectical relationship between the quality German film and the condemnable German nation began with World War II and the Holocaust. The pages that follow excavate the preconditions for the American reception of German films after World War I. Looking back on German film history from a vantage point quite different than Kracauer's, it appears significant that it was early international producers, distributors, and exhibitors who set the initial parameters for what would come to characterize German film most broadly. During World War I, state regulators intervened, leaving the postwar movie industry to earn its profits in a divided market. The audience's wartime animosities also played a role, although not without being influenced by the imperatives of state agencies and commercial institutions. These conditions cannot be excluded from an analysis of the corpus of films that emerged over the first twenty years of cinema history. Kracauer cites that reception history for the purpose of demonstrating that films made by a suspect culture will or should be held in suspect light, but that same reception history has the potential to yield new meaning when separated from Kracauer's tautological argumentation.

TRANSATLANTIC BEGINNINGS

In order to understand how cinema became a site of transatlantic antagonism and tenuous reconciliation, it is necessary to trace the parallel emergence of the idea of a national cinema in Germany and the United States before World War I. The tendency to assess the value of a German film relative to Germany's domestic and foreign politics resulted from the imbrication of commercial affairs and affairs of the state. The modern nation-state is the arbiter of the trade agreements, import quotas, censorship policies, and distribution regulations that influence which works reach which audiences. Distributors and exhibitors in the market-based economy of early cinema were motivated to measure and respond to the tastes of audiences, which in turn put them in the position to shape and guide those tastes. So the question of which films became popular and/or rated as aesthetically valuable—and by whose measure—easily became a national one. The tendency to assess from whom it was politically correct to import films arose early in the history of film in both Germany and the United States, although exchange between the two countries was uneven. World War I radically changed the terms of that assessment and set new conditions for the negotiation of a reconciled transatlantic cultural exchange.

Initially German producers, exhibitors, and audiences did not have strong connections to countries outside of Europe, especially when compared with the French. While the Lumière Brothers and their recordings of life around the world featured as some of the most exciting elements in variety show programs in London, Paris, Vienna, Berlin, and New York in 1896, their German counterparts could not boast of the same. Max and Emil Skladanowsky measured the success (or lack thereof) of their own Bioskop projector in comparison to the phenomenal reception of the Lumières' recording and projection device, the Cinématographe.[9] Nonetheless, the dominance of non-German technology in Europe did not preclude the activity and success of German exhibitors close to home. According to Joseph Garncarz, between 1897 and 1909, German travelling cinemas appeared in Austria-Hungary, Switzerland, Italy, France, Luxemburg, Belgium, and the Netherlands, while foreign entertainment companies also traversed Germany. On German soil, both domestic and foreign entertainment companies took their programs from rural fairground to rural fairground, and international distributors brought diverse fare to variety halls and eventually to storefront cinemas in a range of small to large cities.[10] The German chocolate manufacturer Ludwig Stollwerck was able to claim his stake in the Central European marketplace by importing the inventions and films of both the Lumières and Thomas Edison and by investigating opportunities to circulate the technology and prints of British inventors (and Edison emulators/imitators) such as Brit Acres and RW Paul.[11] Estimates vary, but most would agree that between 1905 and 1910, around 30 percent of the films shown in Germany were French, with German, American, and Scandinavian producers dividing the rest of the market share.[12]

Early motion picture content was international in scope and orientation. Although national concerns, characteristics, and meanings might be discernible in the images and scenarios they depicted, it was clearly the goal of a financially ambitious producer to appeal to a broad range of international cultural consumers. Just the same, the national origin of a film, a nationalist sense of ownership adhered to it, and the appearance of a recognizable image of a nation did not always coincide.[13] Indeed, a lack of linguistic specificity in the early days of silent moving image recording forged what Charles Musser describes as a "sense of a shared, fluid world ... that could transcend national identity but also a world where performers and viewers could play with, and enjoy cultural particularity."[14] And while regional audiences responded in differing ways to distinct films, genres, or styles, they did not necessarily prefer films of a specific national or geographic origin or even to the films of the nation dominating programs in their locale.[15] They were not consuming films along national categories, per se.

Nonetheless, the modern nation-state played a role in the production, distribution, and reception of early cinema. Early films seem to have crossed borders easily, most often along pathways already paved by economic, political, and social exchanges between dominant nation-states.[16] It was imported films, especially those made and circulated by the French company Pathé, that stimulated the expansion of US movie culture by providing enough fare for ever more vaudeville houses and nickelodeons and new storefront theaters.[17] American film reception was characterized by complex interplay between tastes for the national and the international.

Many of the diverse moving images produced and circulated in the United States and across Europe emphasized family, state, and nation in ways that engendered a sense of national difference and belonging, and therefore a sense of rivalry between producers and the cultures they represented. Some films went further than others in generating nationalist sentiments, with Edison's *Monroe Doctrine* as an example of an overt appeal to the patriotism of American audiences as early as 1896.[18] In terms of exhibition, a distinction emerged between the production companies that offered foreign views rather than domestic views. The separation between nations became a concept around which motion picture programs could be built; these programs then themselves generated new ways of understanding of the world outside the exhibition site.[19]

In the 1900s, the medium's capacity for educating and influencing immigrants inspired civic organizations, municipal authorities, churches, and other institutions to employ film as a tool for transforming newcomers into patriotic, socially adjusted, healthy, uplifted American citizens.[20] As the number of new arrivals swelled around 1907, the cinema appealed especially powerfully to those from eastern and southern Europe who were concentrated in East Coast urban centers; the attention of reformers, regulators, and racist commentators turned increasingly to imported films as a source of menace. Critics began to privilege the purported lucidity, authenticity, pleasing drama, and captivating action of US films over the subjects and styles of imports. It was in this context that the Western emerged as a key genre, typifying American values and interests. The creation of Edison's Motion Picture Patents Company and its later collaboration with American Mutoscope and Biograph in the formation of a single licensing agency severely limited European access to the American market.[21] In turn, companies such as Pathé attempted to distinguish their products as artistic films of quality that would broaden the experiences of US cinema-goers. As Richard Abel has argued, "the Americanization process acted as a significant framing, even determining discourse" in cinema history.[22]

EARLY GERMAN CINEMA

Germans also used film to create a sense of national belonging and to improve the mental and physical state of the nation. Kaiser Wilhelm II ascended to the throne during the medium's infancy, and the royal family quickly became what Martin Loiperdinger has dubbed the first film stars of the German cinema. Visual reports on the activities of the Hohenzollerns were common fare in German actuality scenes and newsreels, providing audiences (predominantly the upper class audiences of the international variety theaters) with an appealing and more relatable image of autocratic leadership.[23] Parallel to this trend, Germany's Navy League, Colonial League, and other patriotic, military, and paramilitary associations produced and exhibited films to foster industrial and state support and to generate revenue.[24] Cinema reformers such as Karl Brunner, Hermann Häfker, and Konrad Lange argued for aesthetic education as a means to moral uplift suitable to the needs and desired values of the modern, industrial German nation.[25] Criticism of film's threat to Germany's status as *Kulturnation* conveyed anti-American sentiments, associating the dangers of mass culture and modernity with the medium as it was taking shape and crossing the Atlantic.[26]

Audiences' amount of interest in films representing specific national origins or traditions did not stand in direct proportion to the energy that patriots and reformers put into nationalizing their own domestic cinema. Viewer preferences remained international or pan-national, although their viewing habits became more nationally distinct. The establishment of permanent cinemas solidified watching movies as a cultural practice in Germany, generating a context in which German audiences could differentiate themselves in the eyes of producers, distributors, and marketers. The growing numbers of movie house regulars impacted programming by repeatedly choosing to see films of a certain type, which in turn further stimulated production and, in most cases, import patterns. Where an aesthetic of brevity, sensation, and attraction was internationally embraced before 1908, by 1910 Germans started to favor illusionistic narrative dramas of one reel or more in length. In cities and larger towns, legitimate theater provided a model for feature-length film dramas, so producers and exhibitors offered long-format motion pictures that catered to a preference for German-language authors and literary styles.[27] But even as they grew over the years up through 1914, the German firms of Messter, Projektions-AG Union (PAGU), and Vitascope were unable to produce enough films to meet local demand. The French film companies, including Éclair, Eclipse, Gaumont, and various Pathé subsidiaries kept better pace, supported by their branches and distribution offices in Berlin.

Although producing fewer films than France or the United States between 1911 and 1914, Germany and Denmark released the titles that became the most popular with German audiences. Their actresses repeatedly ranked as better liked than those from America. Counter to what we might expect today, very few American films received top billing in a German program in this period; in some regions none did.[28] Historical films, adventure dramas, dramas of morals centering on women's lives, and patriotic German historical epics proved to be the most popular genres. Once German film production companies began to engage in novel distribution strategies such as monopoly booking, they were able to satisfy audiences' recent hunger for more domestic fare. The production of German films increased from approximately 1,200 films between 1908 and 1909, to 1,700 between 1910 and 1911, and to 2,100 films between 1912 and 1913. Parallel to this, the share of German productions featured in cinema programs increased from an average of 17.7 percent between 1911 and 1914 to an average of 67 percent between 1915 and 1918.[29]

Despite the emergence of nationally recognized directors such as Ernst Lubitsch, Max Mack, Joe May, and Franz Hofer and the rise of Henny Porten as an idealized homegrown German star and Asta Nielsen as an exotic and foreign star contracted to German studios, Germany remained largely a film-importing nation. It did not break substantially into the US market. When confronting the question of why German films failed internationally where other nations' films succeeded, critics at home cited technique and quality. A quintessential assessment was published by Wolf Szapel in the *Union Theater* house magazine in 1912:

> In Germany we have great factories for making cameras and projectors, and also for producing first-rate film stock. But our country makes the worst films one can find anywhere on the globe. Putting aside their lack of aesthetic sense and taste, German films are distinguished by errors in focus, overexposure, fuzziness, unintentional shadows, developing flaws and bad copies. Such are the details by which, after only a few seconds, one can tell a German production.[30]

National pride and a nationalist agenda prompted a push for the development of a German cinema of both substance and quality.

WORLD WAR I

It was the combination of wartime censorship practices and quota laws and the use of movies in the propaganda campaign that eventually aligned German cinema almost completely with the goals of the German state and thus allowed the German film industry to establish a firm hold on the domestic market.[31] In November 1914, the Verband zur Wahrung gemeinsamer Interessen der Kinematographie und verwandter Branchen zu Berlin e.V., a Berlin organization representing the mutual professional interests of those in the movie business, advised cinema owners not to show films imported or financed by investors from enemy countries. In January 1915, the Bundesrat (council of representatives of the German states within the German Empire) decreed that all branches of foreign film companies must be taken over by German administrators.[32] In order to combat threats to the nation, military commanders regulated film content more strictly, using emergency powers to censor individual movies deemed objectionable. At the outbreak of fighting, the German War Ministry banned all films that portrayed espionage and treason for fear of imitation, and by 1915, the ban extended to all foreign films regardless of content.[33] In 1916, the Chancellor's Office placed an embargo on inessential imports with the stated rationale of improving the country's balance of trade and strengthening its currency, thereby further tightening access to the German market. An exception was made for the Danish firm Nordisk, which had invested so heavily in distribution and exhibition within Germany that the finances of the two national industries were deeply enmeshed. Older prints of American films seemed also to have continued to circulate after that, but the profit-producing sector of the exhibition market was effectively lost. American industry representatives lost touch with events in the German industry during the second half of the war.[34] No longer challenged by competition from the French, German production companies expanded even more aggressively to meet domestic demand. Between 1914 and 1919, almost seven hundred new cinemas opened around the country.[35]

Recognizing the wide and diverse appeal of the medium, the German high command and imperial government joined with influential nationalist businessmen to redefine the relationship between cinema and the state in Germany, mobilizing the medium in service of nationalism and the militarization of culture. In 1916 Alfred Hugenberg, the director of Krupp industries, and shipping magnate Ludwig Klitzsche, director of the Scherl publishing conglomerate, joined forces to establish the Deutsche Lichtbild Gesellschaft (The German Film Company) with the intention to gather momentum for German heavy industries expanding eastward and to promote the fatherland at home and abroad. The Deutsche Kolonial-Filmgesellschaft (The German Colonial Film Society) was founded in 1917 to propagate support for colonial expansion. General Erich Ludendorff, who was becoming ever more aware of the effective use Germany's enemies were making of film to propagandize and undermine Germany's reputation internationally, advocated with the war ministry for the formation in 1917 of the Bild- und Filmamt (BUFA), the visual propaganda office, to organize the production of newsreels and documentaries about the war effort. BUFA also established a foreign service for the spread of German propaganda abroad and developed programs for 900 military cinemas along the Eastern and Western fronts.

Germany's military and government officials recognized that the participation of successful German directors and recognizable and popular actors would be key to creating effective propaganda for the home front.[36] They set out to establish a single, vertically organized company that could infiltrate and coordinate every aspect of the business from production to distribution and exhibition, while also spearheading both domestic and foreign film propaganda efforts. At a cost of 25 million Reichsmarks, 7 million of which came from the Reich, the founding of the Universum Film AG studio (Ufa) brought together the interests of the war ministry under Ludendorff with those of major industries and financial institutions, including the Deutsche Bank, electrical giant Bosch, and the Hamburg-Amerika line. Ufa quickly bought up the sister companies of Nordisk, Messter, and Union and acquired large shares of PAGU, becoming almost monopolistic in its operations. While Ufa had to assure the Supreme Command that the state's political interests were safeguarded, the Reichskanzler rejected total state ownership in order to maintain flexibility and to avoid the perception at home and abroad that the studio was nothing more than a propaganda machine. The government's involvement in the deal was initially hidden from a war-weary public that relied on the movies as a source of distraction and entertainment.

Meanwhile in the United States, the government had begun to work closely with Hollywood through the Committee on Public Information (also known as the Creel Committee after its chair, George Creel), which formed a Division of Films in September 1916. In mid 1917, William A Brady, president of the National Association of the Motion Picture Industry of America, and director DW Griffith stepped into their roles as president and co-chair of the War Cooperation Committee. Its charge was to facilitate work on wartime goals shared between the film industry and the Creel Committee, the various government departments, the Red Cross, and the Council of National Defense. This effort eventually led to the establishment of an American Cinema Commission tasked with distributing the films of Hollywood and the Allied countries in France, Italy, and Russia. Its members decreed that all films leaving the United States had to have a license from the War Trade Board and that each application must be endorsed by the Creel Committee. At a special meeting of those concerned with film interests, Creel himself promised to expedite film export on the condition that all shipments would contain 20 percent educational films, that no American films would be rented to an exhibitor who refused to show Creel-sponsored films, and that no American films would be rented to theaters that showed German films.[37] Film producers eager to gain access to overseas markets shaped content to match Creel Committee directives.[38]

This arrangement greatly expanded the distribution of American educational, industrial, and commercial pictures worldwide, and in some areas, such as Scandinavia, it nearly succeeded in closing German movies out of a once secure market. On the home front, Americanization became a particularly urgent matter, and government officers as high up as the Secretary of the Interior developed campaigns to encourage the film industry to strengthen national devotion—especially among immigrants—by infusing the themes, subjects, intertitles, and events with American values into commercial features in order to create one national identity across a heterogeneous population.[39] In parallel efforts, the movie industry eagerly produced feature films with anti-German themes, such as *The Kaiser, The Beast of Berlin, My Four Years in Germany,* and DW Griffith's *Hearts of the World.*[40]

The Division of Films ceased to exist in February 1919, having fulfilled its purpose of using film to propagate American wartime interests abroad. Charles S Hart, its director, boasted of one of his proudest accomplishments, that: "The elimination of the German films was made possible by the patriotic service of the motion picture producers of the United States. They furnished such elaborate programs for our use in the foreign countries that the exhibitors there clamored for them."[41] Secure in its own market dominance and eager to expand the reach of Hollywood, the American War Trade Board allowed films to be sent to Germany as of 14 July 1919. But that did not instantly open up free trade. Germany set a general import quota equal to 15 percent of the negative footage produced in a year, and as of 1919, there was no backlog of films waiting to be shipped out. Germany extended its embargo against the United States until May 1920, with some German companies having block-booked their products into theaters through 1920 and 1921 to prevent American films from flooding in immediately.

During the war, almost every currency except the dollar had depreciated as a result of an abandoned gold standard, a trade balance tipped by war demands, and the inflationary measures used to finance the fighting. Able to go back on the gold standard in 1919, the United States boasted the strongest legal tender just as Germany began to suffer from hyperinflation. The dollar's strength in relation to all other currencies, especially Germany's, effectively created a barrier to exports out of the United States; it became increasingly expensive for foreign distributors to purchase films priced in dollars. Conversely, currency depression gave a potential boost to European producers who offered films for export at prices far below those of American movies. Kristin Thompson recounts that exporters travelling in Europe in 1919 returned anxious about what they had seen in terms of emergent competition. She cites the president of the Export and Import Film Company who saw Joe May's German historical epic, *Veritas Vincit,* in Copenhagen and compared it favorably with the prewar Italian version of *Quo Vadis,* which had done well in the United States. She quotes David P Howells, who commented that the American film was losing ground in Europe, "not because of any deterioration in quality, but because of the ruinous rate of exchange and the exorbitant demands of the American producer."[42] American filmmakers did not want to lower their production standards or profits to produce and sell films that would be affordable on the European market, while the German industry seemed capable of producing quality films that might not only sweep the European market, but could capture audiences across the Atlantic.

Well before the Armistice, sagacious German industry representatives had begun planning tactics for growing business by first selling to neutral countries, strengthening the production infrastructure, and amassing a catalog of viable exports in hopes of quickly breaking into reopened Allied markets in peacetime. Once having acquired the Messter and Union studios in Berlin, the Ufa corporation bought more first-run cinemas and engaged in collateral marketing and cultural production efforts that would saturate the scene. Decla and Biscop merged in 1920 to become the second largest film studio in Germany and then joined with Ufa in 1921. The German Finance Ministry extended the wartime embargo against Allied film imports to all foreign films through 1921 in an attempt to reserve currency for critical supplies like food and other essentials, a regulation that was replaced in 1921 by a quota system. It limited film imports—including those from America this time—to 15 percent of the total number of films produced in Germany. American distributors were discouraged from establishing permanent offices in Berlin in such an unreliable market.[43] Although the Reich sold its shares to Krupp, Deutsche Bank, and IG Farben to make Ufa a private company in 1921, ambitious plans for a collaborative Film Europe accompanied by strident cultural proclamations on the dangers of Americanization successfully extended Ludendorff's project of exerting national influence on and through mass entertainment.

Germany's isolation during the war had resulted in a cultural self-sufficiency that encouraged the rapid expansion of domestic movie production. Inflation and a devalued currency allowed this trend to continue in the 1920s, boosting German exports and creating opportunities on a competitive international market and momentarily shutting Hollywood out. By building elaborate distribution and exhibition networks and expanding and diversifying, Ufa created the only serious competition for the Hollywood majors at home and abroad, contributing to the development of a European alternative to a feared American hegemony. Now operating the largest studio in interwar Europe and largest chain of domestic first-run cinemas, Ufa was able to enlist the talents of high profile and influential players, including the Decla producer Erich Pommer. He and his colleagues generated an inflation cinema budgeted on devalued currency, cheap labor, and low production costs and began investing in big historical spectacles and ambitious art films that could improve the reputation of German film abroad.

CROSSING THE ATLANTIC

With its international flair and spectacular sets and crowd scenes—not to mention the appeal of its star Pola Negri—Ernst Lubitsch's historical costume drama, *Madame Dubarry* (imported with the title *Passion*), defied postwar anti-German resentment by becoming a major hit in New York in December 1920. Before it was released, the National Board of Review had identified it as one of the four most exceptional films made in 1920, a status achieved on a budget meager by Hollywood standards. It was widely estimated that this film that cost approximately $40,000 to make in Germany would have cost about $500,000 to replicate in Hollywood.[44] Its profit margin was most impressive. David P Howells had acquired the film for distribution by First National for $35,000; based on reported US box office receipts amounting to $10,000 per day, the *New York Times* estimated the value of US distribution at a total of $500,000 over the course of its two-week run.

Next came the Lubitsch hit, *Anna Boleyn,* which ran at the Roxy in New York under the title of *Deception* in March 1921. It was imported by the Hamilton Film Corporation, whose parent company, Famous Players (Paramount), had not presented a foreign title since 1914. *Deception*'s success prompted Hamilton to then import Joe May's four-part adventure series, *Die Herrin der Welt*.[45] Another (in)famous import, Robert Wiene's highly unconventional low-budget production, *Das Cabinet des Dr Caligari,* opened on 23 April 1921 at the Capitol, one of New York's largest movie palaces, to a record first-day audience of 20,000. A reviewer in the independent trade paper *Exceptional Photoplay* lamented harshly (and in abelist language offensive to our ears) that when compared with Wiene's film, US films appeared to have been made "for a group of defective adults at the nine-year-old level." Such reactions from audiences and critics sealed the impression that innovative films with a distinctively German style could play well and make a profit in the United States.[46] An emphasis on the national particularity of German cinema might well prove a valid business strategy on an increasingly competitive international market.

Early in the decade, the artistic or stylized *Kunstfilme* or *Stilfilme* constituted a broad exportable national film category offering a marketable alternative to the Hollywood aesthetic. The style of Expressionism typified by *The Cabinet of Dr Caligari* initially provided an internationally recognizable high culture brand name, albeit one that reduced in value around the mid 1920s, when larger-scale Ufa productions saw success in Europe. This inspired additional producers and marketers to attempt to break into the American market with something new along those lines.[47] Ufa's production and export strategies were exemplary and set a model for the other ambitious studios. It organized its work around principles of product differentiation and niche marketing with the goal of creating a positive field of reception for art films abroad, while domestic genre- and star-based commercial cinema was expected to provide the financial foundation.

In this context, it was essential that nationalist or propaganda aims be toned down in exports, leaving films based on nationally meaningful themes, literatures, and legends (including *Faust* and the *Nibelungenlied*) to make a thoughtful case both at home and abroad that German cinema was artistic, auteurist, and literary in its origins.[48] Thomas Elsaesser has argued that German productions that emerged in this environment achieved their distinctive look and international reputation by way of a less rationalized and budget- and deadline-driven production ethos, one that encouraged artistic experimentation and improvisation with technical effects, camera work and movement, editing, lighting, set design, costuming, and acting.[49] Unlike American films that emphasized viewer identification with stars and a logical, linear narrative based on continuity editing, the emergent Weimar cinema indulged in visual excess, narrative circumlocution, and production design that drew as much attention as the actors. Its titles were often praised by American critics for their psychological depth and emotional interiority.

On the other hand, some critics and film industry representatives actively resisted the German import wave and offered less than positive reviews. The *New York Times* asserted on 21 May 1921 that German Expressionist films were "too gruesome for the American public," that the actresses were "not young and beautiful enough" and that the content was "gloomy."[50] *Variety* wrote in June 1921 that, "[It] is a curious fact about many German pictures. They deal with freak stories and have no romance, being entirely men."[51] Jan-Christopher Horak has documented the significant debate over the status of the German film that arose in the United States around these months.[52] Trade journalists responded with anxiety to the fact that almost fifty German films had been imported recently, mostly by First National, in hopes of flooding the market with cheap acquisitions. They decried reports that Adolph Zukor of Famous Players (Paramount) had just bought up 129 German films to feed into his enormous cinema chain. One director charged in *Variety* that if all the foreign films in Paramount's vaults actually went into circulation, 560 bookings would be at stake. Indeed, representatives of Famous Players had just returned from Berlin in February with a trove of films including *Sumrun, Carmen,* and *Anna Boleyn.* In actuality, the size of the shipment was motivated by their intention to purchase films for distribution not just in the United States, but also in England and France before the expected imposition of new import taxes.

Nonetheless, the threat that such cheap imports from the recent enemy would overwhelm the market and influence the American populace loomed. The American Legion attempted to establish a boycott against German films on patriotic grounds. Certain communities, including Venice, California, placed local taxes on German and Austrian films. Some industry representatives, such as Joseph Schenk of Lowe's Inc., rallied against these imports, arguing that they would put thousands of American directors and industry personnel out of work. The resentment directed at the German quota system can been seen in an editorial in *Motion Picture News* declaring that, "If Germany insists upon shutting out American films, as Germany practally [*sic*] does at present, then we must protect ourselves by reciprocal legislation." Others were more confident in their response, like Arthur James, who expressed in *Moving Picture World* that the US markets could certainly stand up to the competition and that domestic productions might even improve as a result. Producers Samuel Goldwyn and Myron Selznick reported after a trip to Europe that only a small percentage of the films they saw would find success in American cinema in the way that *Das Cabinet des Dr Caligari* or Paul Wegener's *Der Golem* (released in June 1921) did. Many imports lay dormant in distributors' vaults. The German invasion never materialized thanks to American economic and cultural protectionism and studios' clever strategies to contract German talent for themselves.[53]

As Anton Kaes has argued in the case of the debate surrounding *Das Cabinet des Dr Caligari,* the film industry and the trade press responded to postwar commercial and cultural conditions by drawing a significant line between the two national cinemas just as they were beginning to have significant contact with one another.[54] This tactic of demarcation was equally pervasive on both sides of the Atlantic. Industry decisions and audience reactions were colored in the early 1920s by lingering resentments and stereotypes about the German character fostered during World War I. Cultural discourse and commercial practice reinforced the idea that Germany's cinematic output expressed something alternately positive and negative about Germany and the Germans. Cinema was an ideal location for steering a new course, one that preceded the arrow Kracauer would go on to draw *From Caligari to Hitler.*

Sara F Hall is Associate Professor of Germanic Studies at the University of Illinois at Chicago, where she chairs the minor in Moving Image Arts. Her publications on film, modernity, gender, and economics have appeared in *German Quarterly, German Studies Review, The Historical Journal of Film, Radio and Television,* and *Modernism/Modernity,* as well as in a variety of scholarly anthologies.

NOTES

1. Thomas Elsaesser, "Early Cinema: A Second Life?," in *A Second Life: German Cinema's First Decades,* ed. Thomas Elsaesser (Amsterdam, 1996), 9–12; and Thomas Elsaesser, *Weimar Cinema and After: Germany's Historical Imaginary* (London, 2000), 1–7.
2. Siegfried Kracauer, *From Caligari to Hitler: A Psychological History of the New German Film* (Princeton, NJ, 1947), 4–8.
3. Heide Fehrenbach, *Cinema in Democratizing Germany* (Chapel Hill, NC, 1995), 30.
4. Kracauer, *Caligari to Hitler,* 3.
5. Ibid., 51.
6. Joseph Garncarz, "Hollywood in Germany: The Role of American Films in Germany, 1925–1990," in *Hollywood in Europe: Experiences of a Cultural Hegemony,* ed. David W Ellwood and Rob Kroes (Amsterdam, 1994), 94-135; Christian Rogowski, "Introduction: Images and Imaginaries," in *The Many Faces of Weimar Cinema: Rediscovering Germany's Filmic Legacy,* ed. Christian Rogowski (Rochester, 2010).
7. Kracauer, *Caligari to Hitler,* 5. Here Kracauer engages with Paul Rotha, *The Film Till Now* (London, 1930).
8. Observations parallel to these can and have been raised about German-American cinematic relations across the twentieth century. See especially the work of Joseph Garncarz, Peter Krämer, and Kristin Thompson.
9. Lee Grieveson and Peter Krämer, "Introduction," in *The Silent Cinema Reader,* ed. Lee Grieveson and Peter Krämer (London, 2004), 3; Charles Musser, "The Edison and Lumière Companies: Motion Picture Production, Representation and Ideology at the Edison and Lumière Companies," in *The Silent Cinema Reader,* ed. Lee Grieveson and Peter Krämer (London, 2004), 25.
10. Joseph Garncarnz, "The Origins of Film Exhibition in Germany," in *The German Cinema Book,* ed. Tim Bergfelder, Erica Carter, and Deniz Göktürk (London, 2002), 112–20; Corinne Müller, *Frühe deutsche Kinematographie: Formale, wirtschaftliche und kulturelle Entwicklungen 1907–1912* (Stuttgart, 1994), cited by Thomas Elsaesser, *A Second Life: German Cinema's First Decades,* ed. Thomas Elsaesser (Amsterdam, 1996), 14–15.

11. Martin Loiperdinger, *Film und Schokolade: Stollwerks Geschäfte mit lebenden Bildern* (Frankfurt am Main, 1999).

12. Compare the numbers cited in Elsaesser, *A Second Life*, 23 with those in Fehrenbach, *Democratizing Germany*, 24, and Joseph Garncarz, "The Emergence of Nationally Specific Film Cultures in Europe, 1911–1914," in *Early Cinema and the "National,"* ed. Richard Abel, Giorgio Bertellini, and Rob King (New Barnett, UK, 2008), 187–88.

13. Nanna Verhoeff, *The West in Early Cinema. After the Beginning* (Amsterdam, 2006), 160, cited in Frank Kessler, "Images of the 'National' in Early Non-Fiction Films," in *Early Cinema and the "National,"* ed. Richard Abel, Giorgio Bertellini, and Rob King (New Barnett, UK, 2008), 22. See also Garncarz, "Emergence of Nationally Specific Film," 188.

14. Musser, "Edison and Lumière," 25–26.

15. See the essays anthologized in Abel, Bertellini, and King, *Early Cinema*, especially Garncarz, "Emergence of Nationally Specific Film," 187–88.

16. Tom Gunning, "Early Cinema as Global Cinema: The Encyclopedic Ambition," in *Early Cinema and the "National,"* ed. Richard Abel, Giorgio Bertellini, and Rob King (New Barnett, UK, 2008), 11.

17. Richard Abel, *The Red Rooster Scare: Making Cinema American, 1900–1910* (Berkeley, CA, 1999), 179.

18. Charles Musser, "Nationalism and the Beginnings of Cinema: The Lumière Cinematographe in the US, 1896–1897," *Historical Journal of Film, Radio and Television* 19, no. 2 (1999): 149–76.

19. Musser, "Edison and Lumière," 26–27.

20. Marina Dahlquist, "Teaching Citizenship via Celluloid," in *Early Cinema and the "National,"* ed. Richard Abel, Giorgio Bertellini, and Rob King (New Barnett, UK, 2008), 118–31; Miriam Hansen, *Babel and Babylon: Spectatorship in American Silent Film* (Cambridge, MA, 1991), 76–89.

21. Kristin Thompson, *Exporting Entertainment: America in the World Film Market 1907–34* (London, 1985), 10–19.

22. Abel, *Red Rooster*, 179.

23. Joseph Garncarz, "Filmprogramm im Varieté: Die optische Berichterstattung," *Geschichte des dokumentarischen Films in Deutschland, Band 1: Kaiserreich 1895–1918* (Stuttgart, 2005), 80–100. Cited by Garncarz, "Emergence of Nationally Specific Film," 191.

24. Martin Loiperdinger, "The Kaiser's Cinema: An Archeology of Attitudes and Audiences," in *A Second Life: German Cinema's First Decades*, ed. Thomas Elsaesser (Amsterdam, 1996), 41–50.

25. Scott Curtis, "The Taste of a Nation: Training the Senses and Sensibility of Cinema Audiences in Imperial Germany," *Film History* 6, no. 4 (1994): 445–69.

26. Deniz Gökturk, "How Modern Is It? Moving Images of America in Early German Cinema," in *Hollywood in Europe: Experiences of a Cultural Hegemony*, ed. David W Ellwood and Rob Kroes (Amsterdam, 1994).

27. Garncarz, "Emergence of Nationally Specific Film," 189.
28. Joseph Garncarz and Michale Rosse, "Die Siegener Datenbank zum frühen Kino in Deutschland," *KINtop* 14/15 (2006): 151–63. Cited by Garncarz, "Emergence of Nationally Specific Film," 189.
29. Garncarz, "Emergence of Nationally Specific Film," 192–93.
30. Wolf Szapel, *Union Theater* (house magazine), 1912. Quoted by G Sadoul, *Histoire générale du cinéma,* vol. 2 (Paris, 1973), 361. Cited by Elsaesser, *A Second Life,* fn. 10.
31. Wolfgang Mühl-Benninghaus, "Newsreel Images of the Military and War, 1914–1918," in *A Second Life: German Cinema's First Decades,* ed. Thomas Elsaesser (Amsterdam, 1996), 175–84.
32. Deniz Gökturk, "How Modern Is It? Moving Images of America in Early German Cinema," in *Hollywood in Europe: Experiences of a Cultural Hegemony,* ed. David W Ellwood and Rob Kroes (Amsterdam, 1994), 50.
33. Fehrenbach, *Democratizing Germany,* 24.
34. Thompson, *Exporting Entertainment,* 84.
35. Sabine Hake, *German National Cinema* (London, 2002), 23.
36. David Welch, "A Medium for the Masses: Ufa and Imperial German Film Propaganda During the First World War," *Historical Journal of Film, Radio and Television* 6, no. 1 (1986): 85–91.
37. Fehrenbach, *Democratizing Germany,* 22–23; Thompson, *Exporting Entertainment,* 92–99; David Holbrook Culbert, *Film and Propaganda in America: World War I* (New York, 1990), xxv–xxvi.
38. Culbert, *Film and Propaganda,* xvi.
39. Dahlquist, "Teaching Citizenship via Celluloid," 122.
40. Culbert, *Film and Propaganda,* xxii.
41. Quoted in Thompson, *Exporting Entertainment,* 99.
42. Thompson, *Exporting Entertainment,* 102.
43. Ibid., 100–19, 148–54.
44. Kristin Thompson, *Herr Lubitsch Goes to Hollywood: German and American Film after World War I* (Amsterdam, 2006), 60.
45. Jan-Christopher Horak, "Die Anti-Ufa: Amerikaner gründen die UFA," in *Das Ufa Buch: Kunst und Krisen. Stars und Regisseure. Wirtschaft und Politik,* ed. Hans-Michael Bock and Michael Töteberg (Frankfurt am Main, 1992), 78–79.
46. Cited in Anton Kaes, "Cinema and Expressionism," in *A New History of German Literature,* ed. David Wellbery and Judith Ryan (Cambridge, MA, 1995), 718.
47. Elsaesser, *Historical Imaginary,* 6–7.
48. Anton Kaes, "Siegfried—A German Film Star Performing the Nation in Lang's *Nibelungen* Film," in *The German Cinema Book,* ed. Tim Bergfelder, Erica Carter, and Deniz Göktürk (London, 2002), 63–70.
49. Thomas Elsaesser, "Kunst und Krise: Die Ufa in den 20er Jahren," in *Das Ufa-Buch: Kunst und Krisen. Stars und Regisseure. Wirtschaft und Politik,* ed. Hans-Michael Bock and Michael Töteberg (Frankfurt am Main, 1992), 96–105.
50. Cited by Kaes, "Cinema and Expressionism," 719.

51. Cited by Horak, "Die Anti-Ufa," 79.
52. Horak, "Die Anti-Ufa," 79.
53. Ibid., 79; Thompson, *Exporting Entertainment,* 102–3.
54. Kaes, "Cinema and Expressionism," 718.

SELECTED BIBLIOGRAPHY

Abel, Richard. *The Red Rooster Scare: Making Cinema American, 1900–1910.* Berkeley, CA, 1999.

Abel, Richard, Giorgio Bertellini, and Rob King, eds. *Early Cinema and the "National."* New Barnett, UK, 2008.

Culbert, David Holbrook. *Film and Propaganda in America: World War I.* New York, 1990.

Ellwood, David W, and Rob Kroes, eds. *Hollywood in Europe: Experiences of a Cultural Hegemony.* Amsterdam, 1994.

Elsaesser, Thomas, ed. *A Second Life: German Cinema's First Decades.* Amsterdam, 1996.

———. *Weimar Cinema and After: Germany's Historical Imaginary.* London, 2000.

Kracauer, Siegfried. *From Caligari to Hitler: A Psychological History of the New German Film.* Princeton, NJ, 1947.

Loiperdinger, Martin. *Film und Schokolade: Stollwerks Geschäfte mit lebenden Bildern.* Frankfurt am Main, 1999.

Rogowski, Christian, ed. *The Many Faces of Weimar Cinema: Rediscovering Germany's Filmic Legacy.* Rochester, 2010.

Thompson, Kristin. *Exporting Entertainment: America in the World Film Market 1907–34.* London, 1985.

———. *Herr Lubitsch Goes to Hollywood: German and American Film After World War I.* Amsterdam, 2006.

Chapter 13

Atlantic Transfers of Critical Theory

Alexander Kluge and the United States in Fiction

Matthew D Miller

The full title of a recent book publication by the German writer and multi-medial artist Alexander Kluge—*30. August 1945: Der Tag, an dem Hitler sich erschoß und die Westbindung der Deutschen begann*[1]—both marks a watershed year with which his work has been preoccupied from the very beginning and tersely encapsulates the geopolitical orientation of (West) Germany that emerged in the wake of the Nazi dictatorship's defeat. Kluge has returned repeatedly to 1945 as a year in which catastrophe and liberation could not have been more closely entwined. His single most famous story remains "Der Luftangriff auf Halberstadt am 8. April 1945," a montage-oriented approach to the Allies' bombing of his hometown that Kluge witnessed as a young person and first published in *Neue Geschichten, Hefte 1–18: "Unheimlichkeit der Zeit"* in 1977.[2] Such interests emphatically qualify his work as postwar cultural production. The beginning of Germans' *Westbindung* (integration into the West), however, enticingly raises more questions than it establishes any clarity. Which Germans and what West does Kluge have in mind here? The uncertainty belongs to the historical process itself: while the phrase may in a straightforward way refer to West Germany's signing of the treaty establishing the European Coal and Steel Community in 1951, its increasing integration into the *Urform* of what was to become the European Union, and its joining NATO in 1955, such a narrative omits some of Kluge's closest relatives in his hometown and indeed all those East Germans whose later activities during the *Wende* (peaceful revolution) the writer memorialized in his stories, in particular those collected in *Chronik der Gefühle*'s second chapter "Verfallserscheinungen der Macht," which feature would-be revolutionaries aspiring to map out a future course for East Germany amidst the very withdrawal of history's political producibility.[3] Here and throughout, Kluge's multi-medial production—much of which has focused on 2,000 years of work on a territory later called Germany[4]—is conceived as the maximum possible questioning of that unwieldy process, even as the German question of yore appears to have been provisionally settled in the wake of normalization and in the form of the European Union.

If German history is complicated, so too is any historical geography of the West. My reference to NATO above also suggests a wider geographical framework of the West's definition than that connoted in references to the origins of the European Union. Yet the unity of the NATO countries, no longer compelled by the military power of the Soviet Union, has proven more fragile in the wake of the *Wende*. In the new century, the West's perceived enemies (sometimes loosely synonymous with NATO's) have become as multifold as its arguments on how best to respond to outbreaks of violent conflict the world over. What is more, the discourse of globalization, which emerged with great prevalence after the Cold War and still appears to denote the (re-)organization of a world economy into a single mode of neoliberal capitalist production, can no longer deny its violent flipside, which continues to express itself in ethno-nationalist and (pseudo-)religious terms that seem only to exacerbate hostilities. From the perspective of the present—the fall of 2014—it is not only the violent disintegration of Yugoslavia rather than the peaceful unification of Germany that dismally appears as a harbinger of the post-1989 world. Humanity's global track record since 1989 may also lend some retroactive credence to the Soviet Union's preferred term for the Cold War as a period of "peaceful coexistence." In all of this, it can hardly be denied that the so-called cultural turn of the humanities (one of too many in North America) follows not simply a delimitation of the concept of text (including literary text) in light of the proliferation of communication technologies, but rather the tendency, amidst the putative bankruptcy of emphatically political discourses that were still operative during the Cold War, of frontlines to be drawn and enforced by cultural concepts fantastically produced and grotesquely abused. For this very reason, the value of humanities inquiry in a neoliberal world that would rather set its own values in exclusively quantifiable terms is surely related to its ability to examine critically such fault-lines with an eye toward their historicization and transcendence.

CRITICAL THEORY'S MIGRATIONS

This chapter examines Alexander Kluge's literary treatment of one such fault-line that emerged in the transatlantic relations between Germany and the United States during the 2000s in the buildup to the US invasion of Iraq. My analysis of relevant short prose texts by Kluge simultaneously seeks to confer value on the presence of the critical theory of the Frankfurt School, of which Kluge can be considered a contemporary practitioner, in the US academy as a vehicle of both socially critical analysis and cultural self-reflection. Critical theory's standing in the United States is productively fraught and was so from the beginning of what would prove to be a long history. It began on the eve of Germany's twentieth-century plunge into its darkest modern chapter that would also constitute, in the context of World War II, the most openly hostile phase of transatlantic relations imaginable. Sensing the "calamity triumphant" that Europe and the whole earth were soon to radiate before they set on fully coming to terms with it philosophically,[5] members of the Frankfurt School, many of them of Jewish background, sought refuge in the United States where they were to enjoy or suffer their exile. They were of course far from alone. The experiences resulting from German migration at that time and the contributions to culture east and west of the North Atlantic that it brought about constitute a formidable chapter not only in transatlantic intellectual history, but also, not least if one takes Hollywood into consideration—Fritz Lang, Billy Wilder, Douglas Sirk come immediately to mind—popular culture. Some of these European émigrés, however, were either not terribly well received or soon made to feel unwelcome. Indeed, for them the role of the United States as a refuge from Nazi terror changed along with postwar geopolitics in which communists replaced Nazis as the West's enemies. And so many German exiles, some of whom had regarded Marxism as a necessary analytical apparatus with which to reckon with fascism's emergence out of capitalism, came (along with many Americans) under pressure during the McCarthy years. Many opted to return to an old—and devastated—Europe, to see what good might be made of opportunities for new influence.[6] Faced with the choice of dining at a table financed by a Marshall plan vs. taking up activity in a kitchen to the east thereof, some émigrés opted for the latter, even though utensils were being removed from this kitchen while one was trying to help prepare meals.[7]

Among those Germans not necessarily so well received in the United States, perhaps simply because they were either unknown and isolated or because they advanced a social theory that fit little into then dominant American models,[8] were a couple of former Frankfurters who first settled for a time on Morningside Heights in Manhattan. Establishing limited rapport with their Columbia University counterparts, Max Horkheimer and Theodor W Adorno of the Frankfurt Institute for Social Research relocated to California where they wrote books such as *Dialektik der Aufklärung, Minima Moralia,* and *The Eclipse of Reason.*[9] These texts would subsequently be canonized. But it took decades for critical theory to achieve a firmer status in the US academy. Horkheimer and Adorno opted to return to Frankfurt after the war, where the latter especially assumed the role of a public intellectual to exert influence (some of it unintended) on the political history of West Germany. On the North American side of the Atlantic, intellectuals and critics began a thorough appraisal of critical theory in the late 1960s, and young scholars in different disciplines followed suit in the 1970s. Dissertations and publications reimported critical theory into North America by reconstructing its intellectual genealogy, arguing for its salience as a theoretical counterforce to other trends in cultural theory (such as the older new criticism or structuralism and poststructuralism), and demonstrating how it could meet a perceived need for theorization on the American Left in the wake of the protest movements of the late 1960s.[10] This surge has had tremendous results. Although references to critical theory in the American academy may still be met with resistance (motivated by disciplinary, political, or general intellectual concerns), few students and professors in humanities departments, especially those who focus on artistic media such as literature and film, dare profess unfamiliarity with Walter Benjamin and Theodor W Adorno at the least, whereas the reception of Jürgen Habermas prevails in the social sciences.

Third-generation Frankfurters such as Albrecht Wellmer and Axel Honneth have, along with Habermas, sought to address the unity of the school and its legacy.[11] Its current diffusion, however, is not entirely surprising. One of the most striking features of the institute's work during Horkheimer and Adorno's time was its bona fide practice of interdisciplinarity, which refused the academic division of labor into the disciplines. Indeed, its conceptual anchoring in Hegelian philosophy and concomitant approach to society as a complexly mediated totality were no doubt in part cause for dissonances in the institute's US reception as addressed in Martin Jay and Thomas Wheatland's histories. Today, it is arguable whether this centripetal force of philosophizing is still intact. Whereas questions of art and aesthetics were by no means external to the institute's pursuit of a comprehensive theory of society—the extent of *Dialektik der Aufklärung*'s engagement with artworks that bespeak civilization's history is exemplary—Habermas's continuation of critical theory in particular has confirmed a commitment to social theory to the neglect of art and aesthetics.[12]

As a storyteller who versed himself in critical-theoretical texts while
studying in Frankfurt, Alexander Kluge has come to represent critical theory's still active creative wing while continuing to straddle the divide of the
school's legacy into social science and aesthetics. A contemporary of Jürgen
Habermas and Oskar Negt, Kluge has not only worked extensively with the
latter sociologist to conduct a transformative archeological excavation of
critical theory's analytical instruments in the wake of catastrophes. He has
also transported sociotheoretical tenets of the Frankfurt School back into
his ever-expanding literary, cinematic, and televisual network of production.
In light of his delivery of formally experimental social theorizing with Negt
and his tireless extensions of investigations and storytelling into various
forms of media, Kluge is not only more heir to Adorno, Benjamin, and
Horkheimer than to Habermas. His sustained attempt to generate—under
existing relations of (artistic) production—a counterpublic sphere outfitted
with conduits in which resistance and freedom could take shape for individuals and emergent collectives alike recalls Bertolt Brecht's conception of
the refunctionalization of dominant uses of given institutions and media.
Focusing on Kluge's literary work in the medium of the short prose text,
this chapter demonstrates his version of critical theory's ability to handle
interpretations of history and experience—including those relevant to international politics, whether transatlantic or inner-European—via artistic production. What is revealed thereby is the benefit the United States might
derive from engaging with a playfully critical storyteller from afar.

KLUGE'S AMERICA

In some contrast to Habermas's keen reception of American thought, the
great body of Kluge's tireless work in various branches of contemporary
media culture represents no special preoccupation with the United States
per se. On the contrary, this German writer's investment in imaginary
and realistic tales pertaining to "das russische Riesenreich" (the gigantic
empire of Russia)[13] so far outweighs his treatment of the United States
that the aforementioned *Westbindung* of his country might even appear
contingent. Kluge's early films and stories reckoned most intensively with
German history, bearing a stubbornly national orientation for some time.
Yet Kluge's increasingly expanded frame of reference, from the publication
of the massive *Chronik der Gefühle* at the millennial turn onward, has repo-
sitioned his productivity to ever more global contexts. This shift is made
most palpable by *Tür an Tür mit einem anderen Leben* (2007), which pursues
the narration of a globalization long in the making and wide-reaching in

its transformative effects. Indeed, Kluge's literary publications and most recent films (from *Nachrichten aus der ideologischen Antike* in 2008 onwards) have followed his work in televisual media to become contemporary fiction in a specific sense: creative and abstruse commentaries on the news of the day, his newly global stories recast the history of the present. Such an orientation to the narration of the present is informed not only by Kluge's acute sensitivity to crucially pivotal dates that supplant the former centrality of 1945. Kluge also registers catastrophes in order to remediate in narration the forms—often images—in which they stand out in our media-saturated memories. As a multi-medial artist, Kluge knows all too well the power of *Bilder.* In his insistence on exposing the processes of mediation involved in what they purport to represent—here too Kluge's work follows a programmatic line of Horkheimer and Adorno: "Dialektik offenbart ... jedes Bild als Schrift"[14]—the writer focuses more attention on the production and reception of catastrophes than the immediacy of the events themselves.

Accordingly, Kluge's interest in the United States concerns those events that framed the new century's first decade: the coordinated attacks on the World Trade Center and other US sites in 2001 and the financial crisis of 2008. Whereas Kluge had before included American topics and venues in his stories in the form of economic-historical or academic shorts, the violent opening of the new century elicited a more probing response. This was to evolve quickly in the addition of a multifaceted essay to *Maßverhältnisse des Politischen* in *Der unterschätzte Mensch,* a two-volume collection republication of all of Negt and Kluge's writings issued in October 2001. While *Maßverhältnisse* was first published in 1992 as a critical reflection on the conditions of political life in the wake of the *Wende,* the newly added essay "Veränderung von Maßverhältnissen an der Schwelle zum 21. Jahrhundert" included a photograph of George W Bush receiving the news of the attacks while visiting an elementary classroom as well as two juxtapositions of "Phantasie und Wirklichkeit": older images of King Kong grappling with airplanes atop Manhattan skyscrapers stand adjacent to the reproduction of a television shot of the second attack plane and an image of the ruins of the World Trade Center that were to result.[15]

Kluge's sustained response to the attacks and the wars ensuing in their aftermath is to be found in *Die Lücke, die der Teufel läßt.* A sprawling collection of short stories over 900 pages long in the unabridged German original, the book's jacket placed the ruins of the World Trade Center in Lower Manhattan on clear display. The German edition appeared in 2003 and was followed by the English translation, *The Devil's Blind Spot,* in 2004. The book contains fiction speaking to the heatedness of the transatlantic dialogue that transpired during the George W Bush administration's execution of its war on terror and the second Iraq war, which began on 20 March 2003. Indeed, Kluge underscored the North American orientation of the book's 2004 translation by introducing it with the following line: "Of the 500 stories of my book *Die Lücke, die der Teufel läßt—The Devil's Blind Spot*—I am sending 173 across the Atlantic."[16] Several tales from Kluge's volume figure as timely contributions to transatlantic debates during the years of Bush II. These stories critically reframe tensions inherent to Bush's policies as well as the European responses to them. The following comparison of Kluge's literary intervention to Jürgern Habermas's public political intervention into the transatlantic debate clarifies the tenuous standing of transatlantic relations at the time, pinpoints challenges Europe faces with regard to the elaboration of its own identity at institutional and cultural levels, and evaluates the relative potential of each critical-theoretical intervention. I begin this comparison with a look at one Kluge story about a young student's modern-day confrontation with *The Dialectic of Enlightenment* in the United States.

CRITICAL THEORY IN THE UNITED STATES, CIRCA 2003

Kluge's *Lücke* stories navigate through space and time with an acute geopolitical sensitivity. In the wake of the Cold War, Kluge suggests in the foreword, the decentralization of the blocs' power has hardly made it easier to distinguish between the good and the bad, so nebulous are power's changing contours.[17] Of the stories relevant to an exploration of the volume's contribution to transatlantic dialogue is the short, but complex "Das unverrückbare Bett des Odysseus."[18] The text thematizes the relation between adventure and narration. The main character of this compact tale is no graduate student at UC Berkeley's Rhetoric Department, however. Potentially positioned a bit closer to power, this young man is studying international relations at an institution across the bay with an interest in a diplomatic career. Stanford University is home, of course, to the Hoover Institution on War, Revolution, and Peace, and, after her tenure as National Security Advisor and US Secretary of State, Bush's friend Condoleezza Rice. While *The Dialectic of Enlightenment* may seem unlikely reading at such an institution—Kluge relates that "Anglo-Saxons" regard the book as "not very readable"[19]—the student's approach to the text reveals its (meta-)significance to international relations.

This significance comes out in the story's main conversation, which resembles an oral examination. Pitting Homer against Horkheimer and Adorno, the student insistently searches for counter-images in the dialectic of enlightenment's source text to dispel the negativity of German philosophy: "Das ist nämlich in der Spiegelwelt, in der wir leben, zwingend. Läßt sich kein Gegenpol entwickeln, bleibt der Satz trivial."[20] The oral examiner's challenges to the student's mirroring strategy of interpretation give rise to a series of opposing images and terms. Of primary interest is the student's contrast of the bed, in which Odysseus will recount his adventures to his wife, to the image of the protagonist who binds himself to the mast, which is so central to Horkheimer and Adorno. The differing interpretative approaches to Homer's text stand under the signs of hope and despair for the Stanford student and the Frankfurt exiles respectively. Kluge's narration of such interpretation outlines resistance to the popular conception of Horkheimer and Adorno's work as a dead end. Opposing its "nightmare vision," the student interprets the texts dialectically to frame future tasks in a positive, if challenging, manner.[21] In staking out these tasks, Kluge intimates that the student's mirroring strategy must negotiate no fewer international relations than *Gleichnis* and *Gegengleichnis,* the familiar and the foreign, self and other, living and dead, past and future, nature and culture, and beginning and end. The mirror structure suggests that such terms are somehow opposites in appearance only. But the antithetical character of the conceptual series prevails. In the lieu of being able to sublate such terms into a common source, the student would have to cross them with one another to guard against their one-sided deployment. The simultaneous use of multiple distinctions is a precondition for successful negotiation. It is also key to rendering the student's analytical arsenal sufficiently complex to provide a cartography appropriate to the future, in which "man solche Praktiker [as him] brauchen [wird]."[22] The complex structure emerging from such an arrangement of distinctions entails a specific kind of translational practice.

The text conveys the student's own translational practice in characteristically Klugean fashion: the protagonist's obstinate efforts appear endearing, yet naïve.[23] Kluge's stories often necessitate interpretations in which his characters serve as less than positive foils, which is to say that meaning (*Sinn*) is initiated but displaced by his characters' exploits. In the case at hand, meaning gravitates toward Odysseus's bed. Indeed, the bed is the only thing that seems to be stable[24] in this story, unlike the distinctions just mentioned, which multiply exponentially when crossed to create a sense (*Sinn*) of vertigo—and a vertigo of meaning (*Sinn*). That the bed "hewn out of the living tree is STORYTELLING itself,"[25] suggests at least the possibility of successful navigation through the "zu erwartenden Krisen bis zum Jahre 2035."[26] In the eyes of the student, the bed may even obstinately guarantee the possibility of sense against the vertiginous experience of sense's withdrawal (*Sinnentzug*). The student's characterization of this bed (in Kluge's

German "original") is of further interest in this regard. His *schönes Beispiel für Nicht-Zerrissenheit* is notably set against the torn (*zerrissene*) world. This is the condition that gave rise to the tortuous traverses across it, from Odysseus through such German exiles as Horkheimer and Adorno. *Nicht-Zerrissenheit*—rendered back into the language of the anecdote's presumed origin as *harmony*[27]—is also set against the fraught practice of translation intimated in this text, the difficulties of which have perhaps not yet fully impressed the student. This kind of translation would practice the "transference of that which is not transferable," to paraphrase Detlev Claussen's outline of Adorno's intellectual program, the responsiveness of which to the experience of migration and exile the biographer underscores.[28] Such a translational practice eschews absolute equivalence—common sources are wanting—for the sake of sensitively attending to similarities and differences across the borders at which it operates. It also dovetails with what European intellectuals such as Umberto Eco and Étienne Balibar have claimed as the continent's very own language, in some contrast, no doubt, to the use of English amongst Europeans.[29] This concept of translation is moreover as germane to the transatlantic dialogue as it to Europe's ongoing elaboration of its own identity. All involved parties must learn to practice it well.

TRANSATLANTIC DIALOGUE, 2003

Second-generation critical theorist Jürgen Habermas availed himself of a rather different genre to intervene in the transatlantic dialogue during the opening months of the second Iraq war. A differentiated practice of translation is not very present in it. To recall the context: ongoing opposition to the George W Bush administration's open if dubious plans to invade Iraq (with or without UN authorization) culminated in mass demonstrations in Europe (which saw the numerically greatest assemblies) and elsewhere on 15 February 2003. In a somewhat belated, but insistent follow-up, Habermas coordinated publications by himself and other intellectuals on the state of transatlantic relations that appeared in major European dailies on 31 May 2003.[30]

In his leading text cosigned by Jacques Derrida, Habermas notes that the then current frustrations represent Europe's failure to achieve a common foreign policy, the desirability of which his piece outlines. But his text can also be read as a contrast between little less than two models of civilization on opposite sides of the North Atlantic. Given this attested divergence, it was perhaps harder to distinguish between specific opposition to the Bush administration and a more general alleged anti-American sentiment underlying the European protests, despite vigorous domestic opposition to the Bush administration in the United States. Indeed, Habermas's piece may confirm the impression of a new distinction. This concerns Europeans' increasingly keen sense of the distinctness and superiority of their own social model vis-à-vis that of the United States, a country that had once helped the older continent rebuild. In a construal of the Europe he wishes for, Habermas asserts key differences between the American and European models, including the limits of secularization in the United States, the more violent and bellicose character of both American rhetoric and social realities, and the United States' untaming embrace of capitalism.[31] In drawing such distinctions, Habermas simultaneously exposes himself to criticism for asserting another: that of a core Europe distinguished from the satellite states it might pull along in its Franco-German locomotive trek.[32] Thus does the self-positioning of this European intellectual vis-à-vis the United States signal fault-lines indicating the difficulties of European unification long before the debt crisis that began in 2011.[33] The ostensible effort to counterbalance American hegemony in the international arena dovetails with advocacy of Europe's social-democratic model. In reference to the hitherto essentially economic significance of European union, one of Habermas's copublishers, Adolf Muschg, writes that "a Europe that has no function beyond bookkeeping loses its basis as a society of solidarity."[34] The appeal to solidarity and the wish to see it institutionalized beyond the tenuous framework of the "intergovernmental method" of the Maastricht Treaty is a common denominator to all of the salvos of 31 May, as if social democracy and neoliberalism could be construed as *the* transatlantic antagonism.[35] In the views advanced here, European unity is meant to be enhanced through a shared conception of its other.

Americans might grin or wince, if not feel something of a vicarious relief at the nonchalant ease with which European intellectuals drop phrases in the press such as "the idiocy of nationalism,"[36] the "stupid and costly"[37] policies of the Bush administration, and the like. While such polemical phrases may reflect different conditions of public discourse, they tend to confirm a not implausible "good vs. bad" mentality more than they advance transatlantic dialogue. But European self-assertion against the United States is hardly framed in terms of a triumphalism here. On the contrary, it is precisely in coming to terms with Europe's long treacherous history—in addition to the self-interested American support of West European reconstruction after World War II—that its intellectuals can enjoy any sense of civilizatory advancement to begin with: "What holds Europe together and what divides it" writes Muschg, "are at heart the same thing: common memories and habits, acquired step by step through the process of *distancing oneself from fatal habits*."[38] Yet the desirability of the unity asserted cannot enforce a memory of shared experiences, which were perhaps not so common to begin with. Muschg's line denotes a gap that the interpretation of the past must fill in order for Europe to be able to accomplish such a distancing. The disparate shadows cast by its past hot and cold wars encompass all of Europe in different ways. And Habermas's core-periphery distinction seems to intensify, rather than alleviate their contrasts. Nonetheless, by embracing the suggestiveness contained in the phrase old Europe with which then US Secretary of Defense Donald Rumsfeld sought to disparage what Habermas and his colleagues limit to Europe's core, the term can be revalued as a positive aspect of mentality, identity, and politics.

DEVIL TALES CROSS THE NORTH ATLANTIC

Mobilizing Rumsfeld's phrase for immense literary benefit, Alexander Kluge quickly picks up on tensions in the transatlantic dialogue in *Die Lücke, die der Teufel läßt*. In a volume that generally deploys the devil and his lore as unlikely allies of enlightenment, Kluge's tales may enjoy a different resonance in a "less secularized" context than Habermas's old core. Kluge's playful storytelling also relaxes some of the drama to observe the present rather than attempt to steer it.[39] To be sure, contentious aspects of the 2003 US-Europe relation remain as present in Kluge's literary takes on security conferences as in the allusions to torture buried in his retellings of the Old European Inquisition.[40] One story in particular has been upgraded in the book's transatlantic journey: "The Devil in the White House" provides the final chapter's heading in the English edition. Contrary to the asymmetric logic of the distinction between good and bad, contrary also to what liberally minded readers in the United States might expect when seeing this three-page story's title, the devil in the White House is neither Bush nor Rumsfeld nor Rice, but, amidst deficient secularization, the real thing! At least this is what a journalist discusses with that month's head of White House security, who claims the devil recently assumed the appearance of a White House staff member. Their engrossing conversation undermines the binary opposition between good and (desecularized) evil to forestall the first would-be reaction to the devil's presence: namely to banish him. Such a reaction is too quick, and in any case not quick enough. Of the many metamorphoses that occur in this diabolical tale—including that between the interlocutors themselves, whose statements are unmarked and identities and affiliations unfixed[41]—the changing valuation of the devil's significance is most intriguing. *Menschenfeind* may prove to be *Menschenfreund*. He certainly was something of the latter in all the service he provided as an explanatory, if supernatural power throughout old European storytelling. In fact, the devil's status here is upgraded to that of an "alter Fahrensmann," an ancient steersman[42] of the world, whose knowledge will not quite be unpacked by "pumping him for information" as the administration wants to do.[43] As a *Fahrensmann,* the devil is also a border crosser, a migratory figure, maybe even a kind of cosmopolitan, one who has intimate experience with power failures. This is precisely what makes him so attractive to humans probing the extent of their own. This more reflective lesson about power's limitations is not, in the end, radically dissimilar from Habermas and Muschg's lectures to the United States canvassed above. Kluge's *Fahrensmann* is such a devil as Habermas could be, but there are at least two differences worth underscoring. The first follows from the above: in contrast to the spatial fixation underlying the distinctions drawn by Habermas, whose salvo still unfolds within the logic of a linear temporality by which a stalwart European core appears as the historically most advanced unit of the globe, Kluge's devil is a mobile figure, skirting about to bring himself up to speed on the spatio-temporal complexity of power constellations the contours of which are not preestablished. From this stems the devil's second importance insofar as the border crosser operates translationally as well as transnationally. To effect his schemes, he must embody his others through metamorphosis, otherwise neither the interruption of power nor any transference of experientially based lessons can take place.[44] Although such a creative strategy is absent from Habermas's campaign, which largely serves the self-clarification of Europe, the Americanization of Kluge's devil must limit itself for the devil's critical impetus to be maintained. In what reads as an amusing addendum to Kluge's "The Devil in the White House," the journalist asks the head of White House security how he derived such knowledge about the devil's presence:

– A tip from the German Intelligence Service.
– From Germany?
– Yes, information from the "old Europe."[45]

Of course, the tip fancifully bespeaks a kind of intelligence not easily chartable on intelligence services' maps.[46] Like "Das unverrückbare Bett des Odysseus," Kluge's "Der Teufel im Weißen Haus" self-reflectively thematizes storytelling as the reservoir of a different kind of knowledge. The submerged lessons of the past are brought forth via narrative transmission and the staging of the past's interpretation[47] rather than public political assertion. Kluge's genre of choice sets on sensitively enabling both Europe

and the United States to learn from the catastrophic failures of Europe's
own history. In this way, the devil's experience of power failures and calamities are to be appropriated as the North Atlantic's own.[48] In performing
this work of temporal and spatial translation from the past to the present
and across that present, Kluge's stories practice the transference of the
nontransferable. Even the English line above—"the 'old Europe,'" a direct
citation of Rumsfeld that subverts the former secretary's dismissive valuation—seems to contain a residue of another English's overuse of the definite article, which unusually underscores source-specificity. It is precisely
Europe's age and its self-distancing from fatal habits that at least bear the
promise of an advantage over and against the United States' inability to
learn from the military hubris it compulsively pursues. While a full account
of the differences underlying Habermas and Kluge's respective contributions to the transatlantic dialogue exceeds the scope of this chapter, I sketch
the shape thereof in outgoing considerations regarding critical theory's
potential service in and to the United States today.

FROM OLD EUROPEAN LITERARY NETWORKS
TO THEORY IN THE ACADEMY

Kluge's appeal to old European storytelling in "The Devil in the White
House" is part and parcel of a larger strategy governing all of his cultural
productivity. This is the establishment of trustworthy networks (*Netzwerke*)
to counter the one we know and use.[49] This network is not the preestablished
existence of a literary canon so much as a multi-medial web of "Karten
menschlicher Erfahrung,"[50] the usefulness of which is established only
through interpretative activity and the experimental execution of actual
living. By continually deferring the usefulness of his networking to recipi-
ents' own experiences with the same, Kluge refuses the separation of artistic
creativity from life practices. He presumes no easy labor of transfer thereby.
While Kluge asserts a closer and even more positive link between art and
life than his teachers Adorno and Horkheimer cared to do, his networking
propagates challenges reminiscent of those found in their work. For Kluge
also—adhering to the institute's original impetus to deny the division of academic labor into disciplines for the sake of crafting a comprehensive theory
of society—infuses social theory into his artistic creativity and vice versa.
His networks could in no way even aspire to be very useful if they were
not outfitted to respond to the demands set by social theory's aspiration to
"understand society." Such social inquiry, moreover, may thrive precisely
when it is not subjected to disciplinary division:

The Frankfurt School placed all of the scholarly disciplines at its disposal to regain the critical and historical methodologies that lay at the heart of the Marxian tradition. Thus, social research and social philosophy were complementary aspects of investigative procedures, interpretative techniques, and theory formation. ... Cultural criticism and aesthetic theory, therefore, functioned in a supporting role for the original materialist theory of society that the entire Frankfurt School was seeking to develop.[51]

"The original materialist theory of society" has turned experimental on Kluge's watch. His vessels of imaginative theorizing and sociocritical tales serve as repositories of critical-theoretical aspiration in the twenty-first century. There is hardly a hierarchy between social theory and storytelling in Kluge, so closely have the two been interlocked in his pursuit to narrate and theorize the new age. Two challenges emerge from this.

The first concerns the aesthetic character of the social theorizing Kluge has undertaken in cooperation with the sociologist Oskar Negt in volumes such as *Geschichte und Eigensinn,* which invites criticism due to its distance from the putative rationality of empirical methods and hypothesis-building as instituted in the social sciences. (It is lamentable, but not surprising, that few Americans outside of German studies are familiar with their work. Yet this may change with the 2014 publication of *History and Obstinacy* by Zone Books.) Indeed, such a charge recalls those leveled at Adorno for the steady retreat from empiricism crowned in his late works.[52] But it must be underscored that such distance can simultaneously prove an advantage. Without it, the social sciences may risk either rehearsing descriptions of surface phenomena or entertaining scenarios of theoretical synthesis that—in the absence of sufficient recourse to social fantasy that critical theory regards as indispensable—ultimately prove affirmative. While proponents of *Negative Dialektik* can appeal to Adorno's refusal to allow reason's dominating tendencies to prevail, Negt and Kluge's *Geschichte und Eigensinn* builds theory for the sake of interpreting humanity's resilience in the face of capitalist subsumption more than it paves any paths to practice. What is more, they trace the culturally expressive and not merely economic forms of this resistance by describing it in terms of *Eigensinn.* Such resilience hardly comes preformatted to the division of academic labor: it defies both the protocols of rationalized academic disciplinarity as well as the oppositions observed in heated international debates. This state of affairs reveals the continued need for broad conceptions of interpretative studies. Cultural and social studies could still work in translational tandem to concretize the interpretative work of the humanities with regard to society and its inner-workings and refer social issues and the mechanisms of their mediation to critical interpretation. Moreover, given the ways in which cultural identifications and affiliations can impede international relations—between Europe and the United States and within Europe itself—such cooperation might even constitute a service that academic work could provide to political agents at international borders.

Second, Kluge's fusion of storytelling and social theory by no means signals a facile bridging of the gap between theory and (political) practice. With regard to differences between Kluge and Habermas's interventions in the transatlantic public sphere, one can note that Habermas at least sought to wield leverage in public political action, whereas Kluge opted to observe power, even as such observations constitute integral components of a larger cultural-political project. Both offer external perspectives on the United States that such a persistently self-referential country sorely needs and jettisons at the cost of its inability to learn. It is difficult to force such learning processes. In terms of efficacy, Kluge's playful juggling of the work of distinction-making may actually prove more capable of eroding cultural and political division than frontal polemics. Whereas Habermas's efforts are directed by the attempt to practice what his theory teaches, Kluge intermingles theory and (his protagonists') practice in a genre of meta-commentary, the lessons of which at first elude direct political action. Such a critique of power is procedurally abstentious. It is easier to see the desirability of incorporating Kluge's sensitivity to the drawing of distinctions into international relations than it is to envision its implementation. In this, Kluge's own praxis is as distant from power as Adorno's, whereas political activity is the fraught attempt to close that gap at the cost of complexity's reduction. This is worth bearing in mind, not least given critical theory's originally lofty aspiration to provide, in the years of the Weimar Republic, prior to its first of many transfers to the United States, a comprehensive theory of society that was to be conducted from the left for the sake of social and political emancipation. While this political impetus still constitutes the source of the Frankfurt School's attractiveness for many, no *Flaschenpost* can reconjure such a context, the obsolescence of which Adorno's opening line to *Negative Dialectik* appeared to enshrine.[53] Yet decades later, in the diminished forms of its incorporation into US academic departments of German studies and the social sciences, critical theory's service to contemporary scholarly efforts lives on. Its critical impulse thrives both on its continued commitment to grasping society as a complexly mediated totality, the unfolding of which demands cooperation across the disciplines, as well as on the kind of playful engagement of its would-be addressees that Kluge's work offers. In an academic landscape in which the disciplines struggle with perceived impotence or have embraced affirmation altogether, the meaning of critical theory's nominal adjective has become more important than ever, even if its now distant gaze reaches us across a divide.

Matthew D Miller is Assistant Professor of German at Colgate University in Hamilton, New York, where he works on twentieth- and twenty-first-century German literature, film, and theater; critical and aesthetic theory; and Danube studies. He has coedited *Watersheds: The Poetics and Politics of the Danube River* (Boston, 2016) and published chapters and articles on the Danube in contemporary cinema, Oskar Negt and Alexander Kluge's theoretical work, Kluge's storytelling, and Christian Petzold's films. His book *Mauer, Migration, Maps: The German Epic in the Cold War* focuses on works by Peter Weiss, Uwe Johnson, and Alexander Kluge.

NOTES

1. Alexander Kluge, *30. August 1945: Der Tag, an dem Hitler sich erschoß und die Westbindung der Deutschen begann* (Frankfurt am Main, 2014).
2. Alexander Kluge, *Neue Geschichten, Hefte 1–18: "Unheimlichkeit der Zeit"* (Frankfurt am Main, 1977), 33–106.
3. Alexander Kluge, *Chronik der Gefühle,* 2 vols. (Frankfurt am Main, 2000).
4. Oskar Negt and Alexander Kluge, *Geschichte und Eigensinn,* in *Der unterschätzte Mensch: Gemeinsame Philosophie in zwei Bänden,* vol. 2 (Frankfurt am Main, 2001), 500.
5. Max Horkheimer and Theodor W Adorno, *Dialectic of Enlightenment: Philosophical Fragments,* ed. Gunzelin Schmid Noerr, trans. Edmund Jephcott (Stanford, CA, 2002), 1.
6. US historian Thomas Wheatland cites Horkheimer's interest in the chance to "shape the future West German society" as a main motivating factor behind the Institute for Social Research's return to Frankfurt in 1949 in *The Frankfurt School in Exile* (Minneapolis, MN, 2009), 259–60.
7. I allude here to a possible interpretation of Brecht's allegorical *Zwei Städte* from the *Keuner-Geschichten.* See Bertolt Brecht, *Geschichten vom Herrn Keuner,* ed. Erdmut Wizisla (Frankfurt, 2004), 52. The difficulties in socialism's kitchen in the German Democratic Republic (GDR) resulted partially from the Soviet Union's demands for reparations exercised via removing what remained of German industry for reassembly in the Soviet Union.
8. Martin Jay, *The Dialectical Imagination: A History of the Frankfurt School and the Institute of Social Research, 1923–1950* (Berkeley, CA, 1996), 39–40.
9. The first two titles appeared only in German in limited publications—thus destined to fulfill the function of *Flaschenpost* that Horkheimer and Adorno propagated at the time. Horkheimer's *Eclipse of Reason,* along with the institute's *Studies in Prejudice* (including *The Authoritarian Personality*), enjoyed a more immediate reception in the United States.
10. For an overview of this wave of reception, see Martin Jay, "Adorno in America," *New German Critique* 31 (1984): 157–82, which emphasizes the roles of Fredric Jameson's *Marxism and Form* and the journal *Telos.*

11. For a discussion of Habermas and Wellmer's approaches, see Richard Langston, "Toward an Ethics of Fantasy: The Kantian Dialogues of Oskar Negt and Alexander Kluge," *Germanic Review* 85, no. 4 (2010): 271–93. Honneth's most relevant work is *Pathologies of Reason: On the Legacy of Critical Theory*, trans. James Ingram (New York, 2009).

12. Habermas's uneasiness with the overemphasis of art's role in Frankfurt School work was already evident in *The Philosophical Discourse of Modernity*, trans. Thomas McCarthy (Cambridge, 1990), 68–69, and the essay therein "The Entwinement of Myth and Enlightenment: Max Horkheimer and Theodor Adorno," 106–30.

13. Alexander Kluge, "Ich liebe das Lakonische," *Der Spiegel* 45 (2000), http://www.spiegel.de/spiegel/print/d-17757645.html.

14. Max Horkheimer and Theodor W Adorno, *Dialektik der Aufklärung: Philosophische Fragmente* (Frankfurt am Main, 1988), 30.

15. Oskar Negt and Alexander Kluge, *Maßverhältnisse des Politischen* in *Der unterschätzte Mensch: Gemeinsame Philosophie in zwei Bänden,* vol. 1 (Frankfurt am Main, 2001), 996–1001.

16. Alexander Kluge, *The Devil's Blind Spot: Tales from the New Century,* trans. Martin Chalmers and Michael Hulse (New York, 2004), vii.

17. Alexander Kluge, *Die Lücke, die der Teufel läßt: Im Umfeld des neuen Jahrhunderts* (Frankfurt am Main, 2003), 7, rendering both *Kraft* and *Macht* as "power."

18. As will become clear, the discursive (dis)advantage of Kluge's dense literary short prose texts often entails their defiance to quick interpretative distillation. This marks their difference from the polemical texts published as part of Habermas's campaign to invigorate the European public sphere, which I discuss in the next section.

19. While this cliché may hold for many, it by no means signals Adorno's irrelevance to such a discipline. Even at my small home institution, Adorno is well *aufgehoben* in the Peace and Conflict Studies program.

20. Kluge, *Die Lücke,* 100–1.

21. The phrase "nightmare vision" is lifted from Wheatland, *Frankfurt School,* 203. Although he dispels many mythic conceptions of the Frankfurt School's history, Wheatland, with an eye toward Adorno especially, propagates the myth of "negative totality" as the "end product of Critical Theory" (xxi), which Kluge's entire oeuvre is set on refuting.

22. Kluge, *Die Lücke,* 102.

23. The Klugean ductus noticeably relies on precisely this use of characters to mobilize irony. For a fuller treatment thereof, see Amir Eshel's "The Past Recaptured?," Günter Grass's *Mein Jahrhundert,* and Alexander Kluge, "Chronik der Gefühle," *Gegenwartsliteratur: A German Studies Yearbook* 1 (2002): 78*ff.*

24. *Unverrückbar* (immovable) is perhaps also distantly associated with a kind of mental stability. Of course, the "original" German text contains added resonances that are extrapolated translations from a Californian anecdote.

25. Kluge, *Blind Spot,* 257, capitals there.

26. Kluge, *Die Lücke,* 102.
27. The positive term for *Nicht-Zerrissenheit* with which Kluge and Negt operate in *Geschichte und Eigensinn* is *Zusammenhang* (relationality). "Harmony," however, suggests a closure of which *Zerrissenheit* does not admit.
28. Detlev Claussen, "Intellectual Transfer: Theodor W. Adorno's American Experience," *New German Critique* 33 (2006): 11.
29. See Étienne Balibar, who draws on Eco's conception in *We, the People of Europe?: Reflections on Transnational Citizenship,* trans. James Swenson (Princeton, NJ, 2004), 177–79. Detlev Claussen traces Adorno's emergent interest in the idea of a European language back to the emigration experience, which constituted Adorno's self-identification as European to begin with in *Theodor W Adorno: One Last Genuis,* trans. Rodney Livingston (Cambridge, MA, 2008), 247. Today, memories of exile, destruction, and pain appear to provide Europe with insufficient glue.
30. These *salvos,* and later responses to them, are conveniently collected in Daniel Levy, Max Pensky, and John Torpey, eds, *Old Europe, New Europe, Core Europe: Transatlantic Relations after the Iraq War* (New York, 2005). I am taking Habermas's action as an example of intervention into a debate already animated especially by French, German, and Russian opposition to the United States on the question of Iraq. For a discussion of other intellectual voices not included in the *Old Europe* collection, see the final chapter of Balibar, *We, the People,* 203–35.
31. Habermas in Levy, Pensky and Torpey, *Old Europe,* 11.
32. I paraphrase Habermas here, who writes that for "the moment, only the core European nations [France, Germany, and the Benelux countries] are ready to endow the EU with certain qualities of a state" and "taking a leading role does not mean excluding. The avant-gardist core of Europe must not wall itself off into a new 'Small Europe.' It must—as it has so often—be the locomotive" in Levy, Pensky and Torpey, *Old Europe,* 5–6.
33. The motivation for both the mass protests and the intellectuals' expression of (part of) Europe's position were at least partially triggered by preexisting European division between east and west and perceptions of the United States resulting from the differences in those experiences. See Habermas in Levy, Pensky, and Torpey, as well as the editors' introduction, *Old Europe,* 8, xiv.
34. Muschg in Levy, Pensky, and Torpey, *Old Europe,* 21.
35. Gianni Vattimo in Levy, Pensky, and Torpey, *Old Europe,* 29. Indeed, the perceived neoliberal character of the European Constitution, which was regarded as failing to support such solidarity, led to its tentative burial when it was rejected by referenda in France and then the Netherlands in May and June 2005.
36. Muschg in Levy, Pensky, and Torpey, *Old Europe,* 24.
37. Habermas in Levy, Pensky, and Torpey, *Old Europe,* 6.
38. Muschg gives the claim this efficient formulation in Levy, Pensky, and Torpey, *Old Europe,* 26 (my emphasis).
39. This is in conformity with Negt and Kluge's theory of the *Feingriff* in *Geschichte und Eigensinn,* in *Der unterschätze Mensch,* 20–26.

40. See for example Kluge, *Die Lücke,* 613*ff.* and 259*ff.*
41. In this, their interwoven dialogue not only undermines the capacity for drawing the stark distinctions characteristic of the public political salvos of 31 May, but also figures as a specific fictive instantiation of what Richard Langston has described as Negt and Kluge's "maieutic labor of relationships." See Langston, "Toward an Ethics of Fantasy," 275 and 285.
42. The English translation renders *Fahrensmann* as steersman, eliding the distinction in German between *Fahrensmann* and *Fährsmann,* words that are usually rendered as sailor and steersman (sometimes ferry man), respectively. The latter is at the helm. The distinction is important: as a *Fahrensmann,* the devil, like humans, does not sit at the helm.
43. Kluge, *Die Lücke,* 904 and *Blind Spot,* 282–83.
44. The metamorphic capacities of Kluge's devil recall Horkheimer and Adorno's theory of mimesis developed in the *Dialektik der Aufklärung*'s chapter "Elemente des Antisemitismus."
45. Kluge, *Blind Spot,* 284, quotation marks there.
46. As Horkheimer and Adorno's Bacon tells, knowledge contains "viele Dinge ... welche Könige mit all ihren Schätzen nicht kaufen können, über die ihr Befehl nicht gebietet, von denen ihre Kundschafter und Zuträger keine Nachricht bringen, zu deren Ursprungsländern ihre Seefahrer und Entdecker nicht segeln können," cited in Horkheimer and Adorno, *Dialektik der Aufklärung,* 19.
47. Kluge's stories often feature dialogues about other texts or anecdotes to make precisely this mediating labor of interpretation explicit.
48. This procedure is analogous to the young Stanford student's, who struggles to bring "European philosophy home" to himself. See Kluge, *Blind Spot,* 254. Incidentally, this aspect of appropriation would have to preponderate in all necessary translational work to undertaken in Europe, especially at its lingering east-west, north-south, or core-periphery divides.
49. The programmatic account is laid out in Kluge's speech on receiving the Büchner prize, "Das Innere des Erzählens," in Alexander Kluge, *Fontane, Kleist, Deutschland, Büchner: Zur Grammatik der Zeit* (Berlin, 2004), 73–86.
50. Kluge, "Das Innere des Erzählens," 75.
51. Wheatland, *Frankfurt School,* 159–60. While Wheatland regularly refers to the Hegelian source of this aspiration, my sense is that discussion of the principles underlying critical theory's interdisciplinary work would provide a useful means for ascertaining exactly what is meant by "interdisciplinarity" in the academy today.
52. This charge can be found in Wheatland, *Frankfurt School,* 262–63.
53. "Philosophie, die einmal überholt schien, erhält sich am Leben, weil der Augenblick ihrer Verwirklichung versäumt ward," wrote Adorno in *Negative Dialektik,* vol. 4 of *Gesammelte Schriften in zwanzig Bänden,* ed. Rolf Tiedemann (Frankfurt am Main, 1997), 13.

SELECTED BIBLIOGRAPHY

Adorno, Theodor W. *Gesammelte Schriften in zwanzig Bänden, volume 6: Negative Dialektik.* Edited by Rolf Tiedemann. Frankfurt am Main, 1997.

Balibar, Étienne. *We, the People of Europe?: Reflections on Transnational Citizenship.* Translated by James Swenson. Princeton, NJ, 2004.

Brecht, Bertolt. *Geschichten vom Herrn Keuner,* edited by Erdmut Wizisla. Frankfurt am Main, 2004.

Claussen, Detlev. "Intellectual Transfer: Theodor W. Adorno's American Experience." *New German Critique* 33 (2006): 5–14.

———. *Theodor W. Adorno: One Last Genius,* translated by Rodney Livingston. Cambridge, MA, 2008.

Eshel, Amir. "The Past Recaptured? Günter Grass's *Mein Jahrhundert* and Alexander Kluge's *Chronik der Gefühle.*" *Gegenwartsliteratur: A German Studies Yearbook* 1 (2002): 63–86.

Habermas, Jürgen. *The Philosophical Discourse of Modernity,* translated by Thomas McCarthy. Cambridge, MA, 1990.

Honneth, Axel. *Pathologies of Reason: On the Legacy of Critical Theory,* translated by James Ingram. New York, 2009.

Horkheimer, Max, and Theodor W Adorno. *Dialectic of Enlightenment: Philosophical Fragments.* Edited by Gunzelin Schmid Noerr. Translated by Edmund Jephcott. Stanford, CA, 2002.

———. *Dialektik der Aufklärung: Philosophische Fragmente.* Frankfurt am Main, 1988.

Jay, Martin. "Adorno in America." *New German Critique* 31 (1984): 157–82.

———. *The Dialectical Imagination: A History of the Frankfurt School and the Institute of Social Research, 1923–1950.* Berkeley, CA, 1996.

Kluge, Alexander. *30. August 1945: Der Tag, an dem Hitler sich erschoß und die Westbindung der Deutschen begann.* Frankfurt am Main, 2014.

———. *Chronik der Gefühle.* 2 vols. Frankfurt am Main, 2000.

———. *Fontane, Kleist, Deutschland, Büchner: Zur Grammatik der Zeit.* Berlin, 2004.

———. *Die Lücke, die der Teufel läßt: Im Umfeld des neuen Jahrhunderts.* Frankfurt am Main, 2003.

———. "Ich liebe das Lakonische." *Der Spiegel* 45 (2000), http://www.spiegel.de/spiegel/print/d-17757645.html.

———. *Neue Geschichten, Hefte 1–18: "Unheimlichkeit der Zeit."* Frankfurt am Main, 1977.

———. *The Devil's Blind Spot: Tales from the New Century,* translated by Martin Chalmers and Michael Hulse. New York, 2004.

Langston, Richard. "Toward an Ethics of Fantasy: The Kantian Dialogues of Oskar Negt and Alexander Kluge." *Germanic Review* 85, no. 4 (2010): 271–93.

Levy, Daniel, Max Pensky, and John Torpey, eds. *Old Europe, New Europe, Core Europe: Transatlantic Relations after the Iraq War.* New York, 2005.

Negt, Oskar, and Alexander Kluge. *Der unterschätzte Mensch: Gemeinsame Philosophie in zwei Bänden.* Frankfurt am Main, 2001.

Wheatland, Thomas. *The Frankfurt School in Exile.* Minneapolis, MN, 2009.

Chapter 14

Nation and Memory

Redemptive and Reflective Cosmopolitanism in Contemporary Germany

Michael Meng

Since the late 1980s, perhaps no other country in the world has made public remembrance of its past crimes more central to its democratic politics than the Federal Republic of Germany (FRG). This development has recently received positive attention. While for sure some observers see limits to Germany's engagement with its Nazi past,[1] a number of commentators, scholars, and ordinary citizens have recently expressed the more sanguine view that contemporary Germany now seems to embrace a "surprisingly self-critical historical culture."[2] According to this view, Germany represents a model of national repentance: it has built a self-critically aware and introspective society. This positive assessment of *Vergangenheitsbewältigung* (coming to terms with the past) can be seen in both popular and scholarly accounts of German collective memory. Neil Gregor, for example, concludes his book on memory in Nuremberg in this way: "Germany gives ground for hoping that, if a dictatorial regime, however violent, can be successfully supplanted by a vibrant democratic political culture, those same citizens may, with time, begin to ponder those crimes and think critically about them for themselves."[3]

Gregor suggests an important link between memory and democracy that German intellectuals, writers, academics, and politicians have commonly made since 1945. The link rests on the claim that Germany cannot be successfully democratic without a self-critical memory culture.[4] This connection between memory and democracy was theorized most thoroughly by Jürgen Habermas. Over the 1980s and 1990s, Habermas argued that remembrance of Germany's crimes in general and the Nazi genocide of European Jewry in particular should form the ethical-political substance of a postnational, cosmopolitan identity committed to the universalistic principles of liberal democracy. He believed that a self-critical memory culture would be transformative and emancipatory, thereby liberating Germany from its illiberal past and antidemocratic culture.[5] If perpetually reminded of their past crimes, Germans would commit themselves all the more firmly to democracy and guard against the resurgence of ethnocultural nationalism in their country and even outside it.[6] As Richard Weizsäcker put it in 1985, the aspirations for memory were ambitious indeed: Germans, he said, might learn from their history in order to avoid "enmity and hatred against other people, against Russians or Americans, against Jews or Turks, against alternative or conservative, against white or black."[7] Memory would teach, educate, and transform.

This hope invested in memory, as Michael Geyer has astutely noted, is predicated on the assumption that public discussions about the Holocaust will have "a cathartic effect" by "combatting radical evil with enlightened knowledge."[8] In other words, this hope rests on the presupposition that remembrance is transformative and good; it rests on a positive evaluation of remembrance that has deep roots in the European philosophical tradition going back to the ancient period and to one of the earliest thinkers of the role of education in the polis—Plato. In the *Meno, Phaedo,* and *Phaedrus,* Plato's Socrates suggests that education involves recollection; it involves the process of calling back into the present what was once known. Education liberates one from the chains of ignorance by illuminating what one already knew but hitherto had forgotten prior to embodiment.[9] Continuing this Platonic view of memory as both positive and transformative, the pedagogical aim of enlightened memory in the FRG conceives of remembrance as a liberating form of education. Remembrance promises to produce the civic knowledge necessary to bring Germany out from the darkness of its Nazi past and into the light of liberal democracy. Remembrance promises to purify Germany of its sins.[10]

Has enlightened knowledge reached these ambitious aims? Has memory engendered the self-critical and tolerant society it aspires to produce? Admittedly, these questions ask for almost impossible answers: how precisely might we judge the "success" of something as nebulous and complex as collective memory? We have no tests or metrics for it. Rather than thinking in terms of "success," I propose thinking in terms of a paradox. Since reunification, Germany has experienced a notable rise in anti-Semitism, racism, and xenophobia precisely when knowledge and memory about the

Holocaust has been greater than at any other period in post-1945 German history.[11] As Geyer writes: "It was and is the firm belief of the politics of memory that the past will not be repeated, if only people remember. But as a politics and culture of memory grew in the 1970s and 1980s, so did a politics and culture of antisemitism and racism, as well as a desperate and terrorist identity politics. These were the first indications that there was something wrong with the original argument."[12]

What might have gone wrong? Why do we have a paradoxical situation of an abundance of memory on the one hand and continued expressions of intolerance on the other? Several answers come to mind: we might note that Germans today still continue to recall narratives of victimization, resistance, and ignorance more than they remember the crimes of their past; or that the memory of the Holocaust is vapidly performed in the public sphere and, thus, has failed to change people's minds; or that ethnicized notions of belonging, community, and identity in reunited Germany reprise, *à la* Theodor W Adorno, certain elements of Nazism.[13] While these analytical threads are important to pursue, I would like to take a different tack here. I would like to explore the relationship of two different kinds of memory to the nation-state in order to illuminate the dynamics of this paradox and how, possibly, it may be mediated: a kind of memory that redeems the nation-state from its dark past and a kind of remembrance that intro-spectively reflects on that past. I argue that the relationship of memory to the nation-state is key to understanding both the ambiguities and possibil-ities of democratic remembrance. The paradox Geyer notes is not inherent in the structure of German memory, but rather dependent on the kind of relationship that exists between memory and the nation-state.

NATION AND MEMORY

Memory has historically been central to constructing and reprising group identifications.[14] Recently, however, a number of scholars have suggested that the entanglement of memory with one particularly important group in the modern era—the national community—seems to be breaking down or at least weakening amid the processes of European unification and globaliza-tion. As people, goods, and ideas traverse national borders (both physically with migration and virtually with the Internet), so too are the conventionally hermetic memories of the nation-state apparently losing their emotional appeal.[15] If this is so, one might suggest that the aura of national memory began to ebb significantly earlier in the ruins of Germany among a group of German intellectuals who pondered critically the "German question" and the possibility of constructing new narratives about the nation that would negate the national myths and traditions upon which Nazism grew. In 1945, for example, Thomas Mann delivered a searching lecture into the origins of Nazism at the Library of Congress. After recalling the provincial world of his childhood in Lübeck, Mann settled on the themes of Romanticism, inwardness, and illiberalism, on the sensuous, musical German "soul that feels very close to the chthonian, irrational, and demonic forces of life."[16] Mann offered one of the first pieces of German self-criticism in the hope that perhaps a better Germany might emerge amid the ruins of Nazism. His would hardly be the last one. In 1959, Theodor W Adorno offered his well-known critique of West German attempts to work through the past, while at the same time insisting on the importance of "a pedagogy that promotes enlightenment."[17] Like Mann, Adorno cautiously nourished the possibility that remembrance could critique past national traditions.

It was, however, Habermas who turned Adorno's circumspect affirmation of democratic remembrance into a pedagogy of enlightened knowledge. Since the 1980s, Habermas has sought to perpetuate in German society and politics a "postnational" or "cosmopolitan" memory centered on remembering the Holocaust. Habermas's cosmopolitanism does not envision the end of the nation-state and the growth of a world democratic state. Rather, his Kantian-inflected cosmopolitanism involves advancing supranational institutions such as the European Union, legal norms such as human rights, the concept of human dignity, and the expansion of cosmopolitan civic solidarities across the globe.

In perhaps his most original move, Habermas emphasizes the importance of self-critical memories to cosmopolitanism, memories that critique traditional nationalistic identities so as to strengthen universalistic commitments. Habermas invests collective memory with progressive political purpose: remembering mass violence would ideally orient Germans away from ethnocultural nationalism and toward the universalistic norms and procedures of the democratic constitutional state. Holocaust memory underpins a cosmopolitan identity or what Habermas calls "constitutional patriotism."

Holocaust memory supports cosmopolitanism in at least two ways for Habermas. First, it perpetually critiques Germany's past traditions that engendered Nazism, acting as a guard against the reappearance of illiberalism and ethnocultural nationalism. A self-critical memory culture negates or edits out past traditions that conflict with the postnational identity of constitutional patriotism. As Habermas put it, "the commemoration of Auschwitz performs a kind of monitoring function that demands that traditions be tested, because after Auschwitz national self-confidence can only be derived from the better traditions of our history which we no longer simply take for granted but appropriate in a critical fashion."[18] Second, Habermas seems to recognize that postnationalism has to compete with the passionate vocabularies, symbols, and memories of ethnocultural nationalism, if it is to take hold in a national community. In the German case at least, he envisions Holocaust memory providing this necessary emotional substance and therewith solidify German commitments to postnational identifications and solidarities.[19]

The ambition of Habermas's cosmopolitan politics is worth pondering for a moment. It attempts to address one of the most persistent paradoxes of liberal democracy since the French and American revolutions.[20] While liberal democracies rest on equal rights and a unitary concept of citizenship, the scope of democratic rights and citizenship have historically been delimited by the politics and identities of nation-states, the containers of democracy since the late eighteenth century when national independence and democracy became conjoined.[21] This paradox can be seen already in *The Declaration of the Rights of Man and of the Citizen*. The declaration's first line posits that "men are born and remain free and equal in rights." This claim would seem to assert that rights exist before the formation of a sovereign polity. Yet, at the same time, the declaration affirms the nation-state as the authority that protects and adjudicates rights.[22] The third declaration reads: "The principle of all sovereignty resides essentially in the nation. No body and no individual may exercise authority which does not emanate expressly from the nation."[23] The security of democratic principles hinges on the nation, or more precisely, on how democratically imagined the nation is. Habermas wishes to address this issue by making a self-critical, postnational orientation the content of national identity. If national communities imagine themselves self-critically around past failures of democratic universalism and remember human suffering caused by violent acts, he seems to believe that they will embrace history as a kind of "critical teacher" that points them away from what they ought not to do and toward what they ought to do.[24]

In sum, Habermas's memory politics turns on the relationship of remembrance toward the politics and histories of the nation-state. Remembrance must be self-critical and introspective for Habermas. Collective memories of the nation-state can neither be heroic nor prideful as they have conventionally been in European history. They must be critically alert to the failures and fragilities of democracy so as to secure democracy in the present-future. Memory must be hopefully future-oriented; it has to take on a pedagogical purpose of enlightenment. Remembrance must promote a reflective cosmopolitanism rather than a redemptive cosmopolitanism that ends up closing off self-critical reflection on the past in the hope of securing redemption from it.

REDEMPTIVE COSMOPOLITANISM

The Federal Republic's confrontation with its Nazi past has long been expressed in terms of redemption. The hope for salvation by acknowledging and remembering Germany's sins began immediately after the war. In *The Question of German Guilt* (1947), Karl Jaspers suggested that a "guilt consciousness" would purify the national community and secure Germany's "political liberty."[25] In 1949, John McCloy, high commissioner for the US zone of occupied Germany, suggested that an "atmosphere of tolerance" and the rebuilding of Jewish life in Germany would be "one of the real touchstones and the test of Germany's progress toward the light."[26] In the late 1940s, liberal newspapers such as the *Frankfurter Rundschau* described the Nuremberg trials as a purifying process of "cleansing the German people from National Socialism."[27]

This redemptive framing of German memory work became, however, particularly widespread in public discourse over the 1980s, reaching its rhetorical crescendo in 1985 when Richard Weizsäcker equated memory with redemption at length. In his speech to the Bundestag commemorating the fortieth anniversary of the end of World War II, he remarked:

> The Jewish nation remembers and will always remember. We seek reconciliation. Precisely for this reason we must understand that there can be no reconciliation without remembrance. The experience of millionfold death is part of the very being of every Jew in the world, not only because people cannot forget such atrocities, but also because remembrance is part of the Jewish faith.
>
> "Seeking to forget makes exile all the longer. The secret of redemption lies in remembrance." This oft-quoted Jewish adage surely expresses the idea that faith in God is faith in the work of God in history. Remembrance is experience of the work of God in history. It is the source of faith in redemption. This experience creates hope, creates faith in redemption, in reunification of the divided, in reconciliation. Whoever forgets this experience loses his faith.
>
> If we for our part sought to forget what has occurred, instead of remembering it, this would not only be inhuman. We would also impinge upon the faith of the Jews who survived and destroy the basis of reconciliation. We must erect a memorial to thoughts and feelings in our own hearts.[28]

This passage includes several important conventions of German discourses about the Nazi past. Three conventions stand out: first, that remembrance is positive; second, that remembrance does not merely dwell on the past but hopefully looks to create a better future by learning from past failures; and third, that remembrance offers the possibility of redemption from catastrophe. Several traditions come together in these rhetorical moves: the Platonic evaluation of remembrance as a form of liberation; the Jewish emphasis on the importance of memory for sustaining communal identity; and the Christian eschatological belief in salvation from sin. This last belief is perhaps the most important one for this essay. If redemption expresses the hope that past sufferings and injustices will be rectified, one must wonder: what injustice is being redeemed by Holocaust memory? And to whom is redemption being offered? The answer seems clear from Weizsäcker's speech: it is the German national community that will be potentially redeemed through remembrance for its crimes against the Jews whose suffering is imbued with meaning for the postwar German nation-state.

Since Weizsäcker's speech, the Jewish adage that the "secret of redemption lies in remembrance"—and more broadly the language of redemption—has appeared regularly in German public discourses about memory across the political spectrum. In 1985, with the Bitburg controversy swirling, Chancellor Helmut Kohl spoke at Bergen-Belsen where he justified Germany's "irrevocable" connection to the West by pointing to his country's efforts to make amends with the victims of Nazism. He celebrated Germany's "Jewish co-citizens" for their "historic contribution" to building a new Germany after 1945 before citing the Jewish adage toward the end of his speech.[29] Four years later, West Germany's Postal Service issued a stamp for the fiftieth anniversary of "*Kristallnacht*," the eruption of violence against Germany's Jewish population, that featured an image of a burning synagogue in Baden-Baden inscribed with the phrase, "the secret of redemption is memory."

This redemptive purpose invested in German memory has been reinforced through the intense recovery of the prewar Jewish past that Germany has been experiencing over the past several decades. This explosion of the Jewish past into the present has been visible in a variety of media—print, film, music, and even food—but it has been expressed perhaps most of all in the built environment. Across their country, Germans have preserved, restored, and commemorated Jewish sites. In Essen, for example, the city's towering stone synagogue was neglected until 1956 when city officials decided to turn the building into the House of Industrial Design. This exhibition lasted until the late 1970s when the synagogue underwent two transformations: it was first turned into an exhibition on the Third Reich in 1980, and then eight years later was restored to house a new exhibition on Jewish life in Essen. In 2008, the synagogue underwent another change—its fourth—that has broadened its purpose. Essen's city council approved a 7.4 million euro plan to transform the building into the House of Jewish Culture.[30]

The newly designed space was unveiled in July 2010 in time for Essen's debut as the regional hub of the 2010 "European Capital of Culture." Essen's mayor spoke of the synagogue's importance in front of a large crowd gathered in the building. He connected the restored synagogue to its original unveiling in 1913, saying that "today is once again a good day for this building and for our city."[31] Noting that "dealing with Jewish culture" has long been a "measure" of German "openness, humanity, and tolerance," the mayor framed the House of Jewish Culture as evidence of Germany's redemptive transformation into a tolerant and democratic polity. As Essen now positions itself as a "European" city, the recovery of its Jewish past provides a public symbol of cathartic change. Passing over the building's complicated history in two sentences and ignoring the complex realities of ensuring tolerance today in Germany's diversifying society (24 percent of Essen's population has a "migration background"), the mayor celebrated his city's tolerant embrace of its Jewish past.[32]

In public discourse, Jewish spaces seem to function as symbols of what we might call redemptive cosmopolitanism, a panegyrical embrace of "Jewishness" as a symbol of tolerance and cosmopolitanism that redeems Germany from its sins. The symbolic reinsertion of the Jewish past in the present asserts that the body politic has been successfully transformed. This assertion of achieved tolerance, as Wendy Brown has suggested in another context, may occlude Germans from seeing new forms of racism, anti-Semitism, and xenophobia in their society, or it may even offer new ways of articulating intolerance against "others."[33] Indeed, some German politicians, commentators, and journalists—particularly but not exclusively from the right—have recently begun to speak of Germany's "Judeo-Christian heritage" as a way to separate autochthonous Germans from migrants. While a number of Germans, mostly on the left and from various ethnocultural backgrounds, have criticized this exclusive discourse, the notion that Germany's Judeo-Christian tradition distinguishes it from the "Muslim world" has endured.

REFLECTIVE COSMOPOLITANISM

Redemptive cosmopolitanism should not be viewed as hegemonic. Memories of Nazism in Germany may also motivate self-reflexive, historically conscious thinking that disrupts rigid ways of categorizing human difference and that challenges racism in the present. This kind of memory work—a reflective cosmopolitanism—does not aspire to redeem the national collective self through the recovery of the Jewish past nor does it posit the Holocaust as the normative past to be recalled across the globe. Rather, reflective cosmopolitanism is introspective, multidimensional, and multi-temporal. It embraces the Habermasian aspiration of fostering a memory culture critical of the politics and myths of the nation-state.

Reflective cosmopolitanism can be found most often on the local level. According to the Bundeszentrale für politische Bildung, Germany has 172 civic and state-sponsored initiatives against anti-Semitism, racism, and xenophobia. To mention just three of them: (1) the Amadeu Antonio Foundation, which was founded in 1998 in response to the spate of anti-foreigner violence that erupted in the early 1990s, sponsors initiatives to combat exclusion and discrimination; (2) the Kreuzberg Initiative against Anti-Semitism, which was established in 2004, focuses on preparing educational materials and programs to combat anti-Jewish sentiments among migrant children; and (3) The Foundation for Remembrance, Responsibility, and Future, created by the German parliament in 2000, aims to think about multiple violent pasts to build awareness about anti-Semitism, racism, and exclusion in the present. This latter initiative has sponsored an especially broad range of projects—from a yearlong meeting of Jews and Muslims in Berlin to a gathering of Germans and Poles in Guben/Gubin to supporting awareness about German colonialism in Africa.

But the most substantial example of reflective cosmopolitanism is a recent project sponsored by Aktion Sühnezeichen Friedensdienste (Mission for Symbolic Atonement—Peace Service, or ASF), a Protestant group founded in 1958 that has sent hundreds of Germans to Eastern Europe, the Middle East, and North America on service and commemorative trips.[34] In 2008, ASF hosted a nine-month-long seminar with a group of migrant women from the Berlin district of Neukölln. The group reflected on their engagement with the Holocaust in a video and a lengthy pamphlet published by ASF.[35] Michael Rothberg and Yasemin Yildz have recently discussed this project as part of their broader effort to assemble an archive of migrant encounters with the Holocaust, so here I merely want to illuminate very briefly its reflective cosmopolitan potential.[36]

The project—called "Our History—Your History?"—imagines more pluralistic forms of remembrance that avoid reprising stereotypes about what migrants do or do not know about the Holocaust. It also overtly contests the assumptions of redemptive cosmopolitanism: Astrid Messerschmidt, a specialist in intercultural pedagogy who reflected on the project's significance for the ASF publication, critiqued the sense of "pride" that has surfaced in Germany about its "achieved working through of the past."[37]

This pride, she argued, has turned Holocaust memory into a kind of "disciplining instrument" against migrants whose presumed ignorance about the Holocaust must be corrected before integration can advance.[38] In this view, nonmigrant Germans appear as paternalistic teachers who know the right way to reflect upon the past.[39] Messerschmidt sees the ASF project as moving beyond this conception of Holocaust memory. It involves multiple perspectives, engenders varied encounters with the Holocaust, and engages with other violent pasts without normalizing or hierarchizing them. Each episode of violence is discussed and remembered as particular iterations of human suffering.[40] This multiperspectival engagement with multiple layers of time aims to stimulate, Messerschmidt concludes, civic engagement against discrimination and violence in contemporary Germany.[41]

Many of the project's participants appeared to share these sentiments. "We live in this country and we want to grapple with the history," one seminar participant, Havva Jürgensen, wrote. She aspired that such engagement with the past would lead to introspective questions in the present: "Today, how are minorities dealt with in Germany? With which values do we want to raise our children? How can we show solidarity among each other?"[42] Another participant, Perwin Rasoul Ahmad, said: "We can all benefit from a more tolerant co-existence."[43] For others, learning about the Holocaust triggered traumatic memories of violence in their home countries of Iraq, Sri Lanka, Kosovo, and Eritrea. These recollections stimulated discussions about the similarities and differences of these histories with the Holocaust. In short, efforts such as this one—and more like it exist across Germany—point to novel conjurings of the Nazi past in Germany's diversifying society.[44] If redemptive cosmopolitanism remains strong in national, political discourse, reflective cosmopolitanism might be engendering more diffident and democratic forms of tolerance and pluralism in contemporary Germany.

Michael Meng is Associate Professor of History at Clemson University. His first book, *Shattered Spaces: Encountering Jewish Ruins in Postwar Germany and Poland,* appeared with Harvard University Press in 2011. The book won the Hans Rosenberg Prize of the Central European History Society. A volume coedited with Erica Lehrer, *Jewish Space in Contemporary Poland,* appeared in 2015 with Indiana University Press. He has published articles in *Central European History, Contemporary European History, German History, New German Critique,* and *The Journal of Modern History.*

NOTES

1. Exceptions include the following critical accounts: Ulrike Jureit, "Opferiden-
   tifikation und Erlösungshoffnung: Beobachtungen im erinnerungspolitischen
   Rampenlicht," in *Gefühlte Opfer: Illusionen der Vergangenheitsbewältigung*, ed.
   Ulrike Jureit and Christian Schneider (Stuttgart, 2010), 19–103; A Dirk Moses,
   German Intellectuals and the Nazi Past (New York, 2007); Charles Maier, "A
   Surfeit of Memory? Reflections on History, Melancholy and Denial," *History
   & Memory* 5, no. 2 (1993): 136–52; Martin Sabrow, "Die Lust an der Vergangen-
   heit. Kommentar zu Aleida Assmann," *Zeithistorische Forschungen/Studies in
   Contemporary History* 4, no. 3 (2007). See also the work on German narratives of
   victimization, resistance, and ignorance in no. 13 below.
2. Quote from Wulf Kansteiner, "What Is the Opposite of Genocide? Philosemitic
   Television in Germany, 1963–1995," in *Philosemitism in History*, ed. Jonathan
   Karp and Adam Sutcliffe (New York, 2011), 313. Whiggish accounts of Holo-
   caust memory include Daniel Levy and Natan Sznaider, *The Holocaust and
   Memory in the Global Age*, trans. Assenka Oksiloff (Philadelphia, PA, 2006); Bill
   Niven, *Facing the Nazi Past: United Germany and the Legacy of the Third Reich*
   (New York, 2002); John Torpey, ed., *Politics and the Past: On Repairing Histori-
   cal Injustices* (Lanham, MD, 2003), 2–3; Peter Steinbach, *Nationalsozialistische
   Gewaltverbrechen. Die Diskussion in der deutschen Öffentlichkeit nach 1945* (Berlin,
   1981).
3. Neil Gregor, *Haunted City: Nuremberg and the Nazi Past* (New Haven, CT, 2008),
   378.
4. Moses, *German Intellectuals*. See also Jay Howard Geller, *Jews in Post-Holocaust
   Germany, 1945–1953* (New York, 2005); Jeffrey Herf, *Divided Memory: The Nazi
   Past in the Two Germanys* (Cambridge, MA, 1997); Anthony Kauders, *Democratization and the Jews: Munich, 1945–1965* (Lincoln, NE, 2004).
5. Habermas subscribes to a Sonderweg interpretation of German history. This
   interpretation enables the possibility of Germany's postwar redemptive return
   to the path of Western modernity.
6. Habermas views memory as an ethnocultural practice for native-born Germans.
   I have examined the tensions in this framing—what I call Habermas's postnational national memory of the Holocaust—in Michael Meng, "Silences about
   Sarrazin's Racism in Contemporary Germany," *Journal of Modern History* 87,
   no.1 (2015): 102–135. On Habermas's understanding of memory to Germany's
   democratization, see Moses, *German Intellectuals*. Moses points to these tensions
   in A Dirk Moses, "Stigma and Sacrifice in the Federal Republic of Germany,"
   History and Memory 19, no. 2 (2007): 140–42. For additional discussions of the
   ethnocultural framing of German memory, see the literature cited in no. 13
   below.
7. "Rede von Bundespräsident Richard von Weizsäcker bei der Gedenkveranstal-
   tung im Plenarsaal des Deutschen Bundestages zum 40. Jahrestag des Endes
   des Zweiten Weltkrieges in Europa," 8 May 1985 (www.bundespraesident.de);

English translation located in *Bitburg in Moral and Political Perspective,* ed. Geoffrey H Hartman (Bloomington, IN, 1986), 262–73.

8. Michael Geyer, "The Politics of Memory in Contemporary Germany," in *Radical Evil,* ed. Joan Copjec (New York, 1996), 169–70.

9. Put more precisely, Socrates suggests that the immortal soul acquired knowledge of all and everything prior to its embodiment in the human being. All immortal souls see true knowledge to a certain extent before falling down to earth and residing in the human form. The incarnation of the soul disturbs the knowledge of the whole it once had. Its vision of truth becomes less pure and complete through embodiment. The soul forgets what it once knew. The task of education is thus anamnesis, the act of calling back into the present what once was. Education is recollection of truth and knowledge. The purpose of education is to bring the human being back to the hyperouranian vision of truth that the soul had before embodiment.

10. See Karl Jaspers, *The Question of German Guilt,* trans. EB Ashton (New York, 2000).

11. *Bericht des unabhängigen Expertenkreises Antisemitismus. Antisemitismus in Deutschland–Erscheinungsformen, Bedingungen, Präventionsansätze,* Deutscher Bundestag 17. Wahlperiode, Drucksache 17/7700, 10 November 2011; Wilhelm Heitmeyer, *Deutsche Zustände,* vol. 9 (Berlin, 2010); *Die Mitte in der Krise: Rechtsextreme Einstellungen in Deutschland 2010* (Berlin, 2010); Detlef Pollack, "Wahrnehmung und Akzeptanz religiöser Vielfalt," published at www.uni-muenster.de/Religion-und-Politik; *Sozialreport: Daten und Fakten zur sozialen Lage 20 Jahre nach der Vereinigung* (Berlin, 2010).

12. Geyer, "Politics of Memory," 194–95.

13. The Adorno reference is to his "What Does Coming to Terms with the Past Mean?," in *Bitburg in Moral and Political Perspective,* ed. Geoffrey Hartman (Bloomington, IN, 1986), 114–29. On narratives of victimization, resistance, and ignorance, see Frank Biess, *Homecomings: Returning POWs and the Legacy of Defeat on Postwar Germany* (Princeton, NJ, 2006); Wulf Kansteiner, *In Pursuit of German Memory: History, Television, and Politics after Auschwitz* (Athens, OH, 2006); Harold Marcuse, *The Legacies of Dachau: The Uses and Abuses of a Concentration Camp, 1933–2001* (New York, 2001); Robert G Moeller, *War Stories: The Search for a Usable Past in the Federal Republic of Germany* (Berkeley, CA, 2001); Robert G Moeller, "Germans as Victims? Thoughts on a Post–Cold War History of World War II's Legacies," *History & Memory* 17, no. 1/2 (2005): 147–94; Olaf Jensen, *Geschichte machen: Strukturmerkmale des intergenerationellen Sprechens über die NS Vergangenheit in deutschen Familien* (Tübingen, 2004); Harald Welzer, Sabine Moller, and Karoline Tschuggnall, *"Opa war kein Nazi": Nationalsozialismus und Holocaust im Familiengedächtnis* (Frankfurt am Main, 2002). On the lack of an affective, everyday memory of Nazism, see Alf Lüdtke, "'Coming to Terms with the Past': Illusions of Remembering, Ways of Forgetting Nazism in West Germany," *Journal of Modern History* 65, no. 3 (1993): 542–72. For discussions on continuities (and discontinuities) between the Nazi and postwar

periods, see Rita Chin et al., *After the Nazi Racial State: Difference and Democracy in Germany and Europe* (Ann Arbor, MI, 2009); Heide Fehrenbach, *Race after Hitler: Black Occupation Children in Postwar Germany and America* (Princeton, NJ, 2005); Uta G Poiger, *Jazz, Rock, and Rebels: Cold War Politics and American Culture in Divided Germany* (Berkeley, CA, 2000); Katrin Sieg, *Ethnic Drag: Performing Race, Nation, Sexuality in West Germany* (Ann Arbor, MI, 2002).

14. Classic statements of this argument include Jan Assmann, *Cultural Memory and Early Civilization: Writing, Remembrance, and Political Imagination* (New York, 2011); Maurice Halbwachs, *On Collective Memory,* trans. Lewis A Coser (Chicago, 1992); Yosef Hayim Yerushalmi, *Zakhor: Jewish History and Jewish Memory* (Seattle, WA, 1982).

15. See, for example, Aleida Assmann and Sebastian Conrad, eds, *Memory in a Global Age: Discourses, Practices and Trajectories* (New York, 2010); Daniel Levy and Natan Sznaider, *The Holocaust and Memory in the Global Age,* trans. Assenka Oksiloff (Philadelphia, PA, 2006).

16. Thomas Mann, *Germany and the Germans* (Washington, DC, 1945).

17. Theodor W Adorno, "The Meaning of Working through the Past," trans. Henry W Pickford, in *Can One Live after Auschwitz? A Philosophical Reader,* ed. Rolf Tiedemann (Stanford, CA, 2003), 15.

18. Jürgen Habermas, "The Finger of Blame: The Germans and Their Memorial," in *Time of Transitions,* ed. and trans. Ciaran Cronin and Max Pensky (Malden, MA, 2006), 44.

19. Jürgen Habermas, *Between Naturalism and Religion: Philosophical Essays* (Malden, MA, 2008), 106.

20. Seyla Benhabib, *Another Cosmopolitanism* (New York/Oxford, 2008), 32–36.

21. Ali Behdad, *A Forgetful Nation: On Immigration and Cultural Identity in the United States* (Durham, NC, 2005); Alice Conklin, *A Mission to Civilize: The Republican Idea of Empire in France and West Africa, 1895–1930* (Stanford, CA, 1997); Rita Chin et al., *After the Nazi Racial State: Difference and Democracy in Germany and Europe* (Ann Arbor, MI, 2009); Michael Meng, "Democratic (In)Equalities: Immigration in Twentieth-Century Western Europe," *Contemporary European History* 22, no. 1 (2013): 139–51; Samuel Moyn, *The Last Utopia: Human Rights in History* (Cambridge, MA, 2010); Jennifer Pitts, *A Turn to Empire: The Rise of Imperial Liberalism in Britain and France* (Princeton, NJ, 2005); Joan W Scott, *Only Paradoxes to Offer: French Feminists and the Rights of Man* (Cambridge, MA, 1996); Todd Shepard, *The Invention of Decolonization: The Algerian War and the Remaking of Modern France* (Ithaca, NY, 2006); Nikhil Pal Singh, *Black Is a Country: Race and the Unfinished Struggle for Democracy* (Cambridge, MA, 2004).

22. Elizabeth F Cohen, *Semi-Citizenship in Democratic Politics* (New York, 2009).

23. "Declaration of the Rights of Man and Citizen," 26 August 1789, translated by Lynn Hunt, in *The French Revolution and Human Rights: A Brief Documentary History,* ed. Lynn Hunt (New York, 1996), 77–79.

24. Jürgen Habermas, *A Berlin Republic: Writings on Germany,* trans. Steven Rendall (Lincoln, NE, 1997), 11 and 13.

25. Jaspers, *Question of German Guilt,* 96, 115.

26. "Remarks by John W McCloy," in *Conference on the "The Future of the Jews in Germany,"* ed. Office of Adviser on Jewish Affairs (Heidelberg, 1949), 21.

27. "Erklärung vom 26. März," *Frankfurter Rundschau,* 10 October 1946. See also Thomas Pegelow, "Linguistic Violence: Language, Power and Separation in the Fate of Germans of Jewish Ancestry, 1928–1948" (PhD dissertation, University of North Carolina at Chapel Hill, 2004), 515, 533–34.

28. English translation from *Bitburg in Moral and Political Perspective,* 265–66.

29. Helmut Kohl, "Ansprache in der Gedenkstunden im ehemaligen Konzentrationslager Bergen-Belsen am 21. April 1985," in *Erinnerung, Trauer, und Versöhnung: Ansprachen und Erklärungen zum vierzigsten Jahrestag des Kriegsendes* (Bonn, 1985), 21–24.

30. "Neukonzeption Alte Synagoge Essen," *Niederschrift über die Sitzung des Rates der Stadt,* 27 February 2008.

31. Reinhard Paß, "Neueröffnung der alten Synagoge zum Haus jüdischer Kultur," 13 July 2010, www.essen.de.

32. *Bevölkerung nach Migrationsstatus regional* (Wiesbaden, 2013), 36.

33. Wendy Brown, *Regulating Aversion: Tolerance in the Age of Identity and Empire* (Princeton, NJ, 2006). See Chin et al., *After the Nazi Racial State*; David Theo Goldberg, *The Threat of Race: Reflections on Racial Neoliberalism* (Malden, MA, 2009), 154–63; Damani J Partridge, "Holocaust Mahnmal (Memorial): Monumental Memory amidst Contemporary Race," *Comparative Studies in Society and History* 52, no. 4 (2010): 820–50; Andreas Huyssen, "Diaspora and Nation: Migration into Other Pasts," *New German Critique* 88 (Winter 2003): 147–64; Moses, "Stigma and Sacrifice," 140–42.

34. Christian Staffa, "Die 'Aktion Sühnezeichen.' Eine protestantische Initiative zu einer besonderen Art der Wiedergutmachung," in *Nach der Verfolgung. Wiedergutmachung nationalsozialistischen Unrechts in Deutschland?,* ed. Hans Günter Hockerts and Christiane Kuller (Göttingen, 2003), 139–56

35. Aktion Sühnezeichen Friedensdienste, *Neuköllner Stadtteilmütter und ihrer Auseinandersetzung mit der Geschichte des Nationalsozialismus* (Berlin, 2010); the video can be viewed online at https://www.asf-ev.de/de/geschichte-interkulturell/film.html.

36. Michael Rothberg and Yasemin Yildiz, "Memory Citizenship: Migrant Archives of Holocaust Remembrance in Contemporary Germany," *Parallax* 17, no. 4 (2011): 32–48.

37. *Neuköllner Stadtteilmütter,* 26.

38. To avoid any confusion here, it is important to stress that her point is not to obscure the existence of ignorance about the Holocaust and anti-Semitism among migrants. Rather, her point is to note the stereotyping involved in claims that imply a natural, intrinsic connection between anti-Semitism and ignorance to someone's ethnic, cultural, and/or religious background.

39. *Neuköllner Stadtteilmütter,* 26.

40. Ibid., 27.

41. Ibid., 28.
42. Ibid., 54.
43. Ibid., 46.
44. Another example is the Turkish-language tours through the Nazi Documentation Center in Cologne. See Doğan Akhanli, "Meine Geschichte–'Unsere' Geschichte: Türkischsprachige Führungen im NS-Dokumentationszentrum in Köln," in *Neue Judenfeindschaft? Perspektiven für den pädagogischen Umgang mit dem globalisierten Antisemitismus,* ed. Bernd Fechler et al. (Frankfurt am Main, 2006), 310–17. Other examples most certainly exist, and they can also likely be found in earlier periods of postwar German history (West Germany most likely but perhaps also East Germany). But research on the multidimensionality of German memories is just beginning (the ambitious project by Rotherberg and Yildiz will begin to rectify these lacunae). For indeed the study of German memory–and memory in general–has long been framed by the nation-state and ethnocultural groups (e.g. Pierre Nora, Maurice Halbwachs, Jan Assmann, and Aleida Assmann). While a number of scholars have started to point out the tensions within German framings of Holocaust memory as a hermetic ethnocultural practice (see no. 13 above), most studies on German memory have focused on authochthonous Germans, excluding migrants and also Jews (main exceptions are works in the field of postwar German-Jewish history, though these are not explicitly studies on memory). On Jewish and migrant memories, see Rothberg and Yildiz, "Memory Citizenship"; Lynn Rapaport, *Jews in Germany after the Holocaust: Memory, Identity, and Jewish-German Relations* (New York, 1997). The recent surge in work on postwar German-Jewish history often includes discussion of Jewish memories of the Holocaust, but this work has largely not been integrated into broader studies devoted to German memory. For historiographic overviews, see Michael Meng, "After the Holocaust: The History of Jewish Life in West Germany," *Contemporary European History* 14, no. 3 (2005): 403–13; Peter Monteath, "The German Democratic Republic and the Jews," *German History* 22, no. 3 (2004): 448–68.

SELECTED BIBLIOGRAPHY

Appiah, Kwame Anthony. *Cosmopolitanism: Ethics in a World of Strangers.* New York, 2006.

——. *The Ethics of Identity.* Princeton, NJ, 2005.

Assmann, Aleida, and Sebastian Conrad, eds. *Memory in a Global Age: Discourses, Practices and Trajectories.* New York, 2010.

Benhabib, Seyla. *Another Cosmopolitanism.* New York/Oxford, 2008.

Biess, Frank. *Homecomings: Returning POWs and the Legacy of Defeat on Postwar Germany.* Princeton, NJ, 2006.

Brown, Wendy. *Regulating Aversion: Tolerance in the Age of Identity and Empire.* Princeton, NJ, 2006.

Cohen, Deborah, and Maura O'Connor, eds. *Comparison and History: Europe in Cross-National Perspective.* New York, 2004.

Confino, Alon. "Collective Memory and Cultural History: Problems of Method." *American Historical Review* 102, no. 5 (1997): 1386–1403.

Eley, Geoff. *The "Goldhagen Effect": History, Memory, Nazism–Facing the German Past.* Ann Arbor, MI, 2000.

Fehrenbach, Heide. *Race after Hitler: Black Occupation Children in Postwar Germany and America.* Princeton, NJ, 2005.

Geller, Jay Howard. *Jews in Post-Holocaust Germany, 1945–1953.* New York, 2005.

Geyer, Michael. "The Politics of Memory in Contemporary Germany." In *Radical Evil,* edited by Joan Copjec. New York, 1996: 169–200.

Herf, Jeffrey. *Divided Memory: The Nazi Past in the Two Germanys.* Cambridge, MA, 1997.

Herzog, Dagmar. *Sex after Fascism: Memory and Memorality in Twentieth-Century Germany.* Princeton, NJ, 2005.

Jungmann, Alexander. *Jüdisches Leben in Berlin. Der aktuelle Wandel in einer metropolitanen Diasporagemeinschaft.* Bielefeld, 2007.

Kansteiner, Wulf. *In Pursuit of German Memory: History, Television, and Politics after Auschwitz.* Athens, OH, 2006.

Levy, Daniel, and Natan Sznaider. *The Holocaust and Memory in the Global Age.* Translated by Assenka Oksiloff. Philadelphia, PA, 2006.

Mani, Venkat B. *Cosmopolitical Claims: Turkish-German Literatures from Nadolny to Pamuk.* Iowa City, IA, 2007.

Marcuse, Harold. *Legacies of Dachau: The Uses and Abuses of a Concentration Camp, 1933–2001.* New York, 2001.

Moeller, Robert G. *War Stories: The Search for a Usable Past in the Federal Republic of Germany.* Berkeley, CA, 2001.

Moses, A Dirk. *German Intellectuals and the Nazi Past.* New York, 2007.

Nora, Pierre. *Realms of Memory: Rethinking the French Past.* 3 vols., translated by Arthur Holdhammer. New York, 1996.

Peck, Jeffrey M. *Being Jewish in the New Germany.* New Brunswick, 2006.

Rotherberg, Michael. *Multidirectional Memory: Remembering the Holocaust in the Age of Decolonization.* Stanford, CA, 2009.

Scott, Joan Wallach. *The Politics of the Veil.* Princeton, NJ, 2007.

Index